Get More on Nolo.com

Go to this book's companion page at:

www.nolo.com/back-of-book/SIRS.html

Checking the companion page is a good way
to stay informed on topics related to this book.

More Resources
from Nolo.com

Legal Forms, Books, & Software
Hundreds of do-it-yourself products—all written in plain English,
approved, and updated by our in-house legal editors.

Legal Articles
Get informed with thousands of free articles on everyday legal
topics. Our articles are accurate, up to date, and reader friendly.

Find a Lawyer
Want to talk to a lawyer? Use Nolo to find a lawyer who can
help you with your case.

15th Edition

Stand Up to the IRS

Tax Attorney Frederick W. Daily
and Stephen Fishman, J.D.

FIFTEENTH EDITION	JANUARY 2024
Editor	AMY LOFTSGORDON
Cover Design	SUSAN PUTNEY
Book Design	SUSAN PUTNEY
Proofreading	JENNIFER ARTER
Index	VICTORIA BAKER
Printing	SHERIDAN

ISSN: 2329-4345 (print)
ISSN: 2329-4361 (online)
ISBN: 978-1-4133-3137-0 (pbk)
ISBN: 978-1-4133-3138-7 (ebook)

This book covers only United States law, unless it specifically states otherwise.

> **Please note**
>
> Accurate, plain-English legal information can help you solve many of your own legal problems. But this text is not a substitute for personalized advice from a knowledgeable lawyer. If you want the help of a trained professional—and we'll always point out situations in which we think that's a good idea—consult an attorney licensed to practice in your state.

MH Sub I, LLC dba Nolo, 909 N. Pacific Coast Hwy, 11th Fl, El Segundo, CA 90245

Acknowledgments

Everyone who gave me thoughtful suggestions on writing, and then improving, my first book, *Winning the IRS Game*—your comments were considered and incorporated into *Stand Up to the IRS.*

My partner in life, Brenda.

Alan Rosenthal and John Raymond of San Francisco for their assistance with the (very tricky) bankruptcy issues in this book. John maintains a law office in San Francisco where Alan works as a paralegal.

My editor and all the other nice people at Nolo.

—Attorney Frederick W. Daily

About the Authors

Frederick W. Daily spent over 50 years as a tax attorney helping individuals and small business owners make smart tax decisions and stay out of trouble with the IRS. He was featured as a tax expert on *Good Morning America* and NPR, and in publications including *Money* magazine, *U.S. News & World Report*, *Newsweek*, *The New York Times*, and the *Chicago Tribune*. Daily, who passed away in 2019, is also the author of *Tax Savvy for Small Business*.

Stephen Fishman has dedicated his career as an attorney and author to writing useful, authoritative, and recognized guides on taxes and business law for small businesses, entrepreneurs, independent contractors, and freelancers. He is the author of over 20 books and hundreds of articles, and has been quoted in *The New York Times*, *The Wall Street Journal*, the *Chicago Tribune*, and many other publications. Among his books are *Deduct It! Lower Your Small Business Taxes*, *Home Business Tax Deductions: Keep What You Earn*, *Every Landlord's Tax Deduction Guide*, *Tax Deductions for Professionals*, and *Working for Yourself: Law & Taxes for Independent Contractors, Freelancers & Gig Workers of All Types*.

Table of Contents

Introduction 1

1 Inside the IRS: What You Need to Know About IRS Operations 5
    IRS Inefficiency 11
    Communicating With the IRS 13
    Rules of the Game—Tax Laws 17
    Interpreting the Tax Code 18
    Self-Assessment of Income Taxes 19
    Winning the IRS Game 19

2 Filing Tax Returns 23
    How Long Must You Worry About Not Filing a Tax Return? 24
    Consequences of Not Filing 25
    It's Better to File Before the IRS Contacts You 30
    What Will Happen When You File Late 36
    Requesting an Extension to File 39
    Filing a Tax Return When You Can't Pay What You Owe 41
    Filing a Tax Return When You Live Out of the United States 41
    Reducing the Chance of an Audit When Filing 42
    Amending Tax Returns 44
    A Word About "Aggressive" Tax Filing 45

3 Winning Your Audit 49
    How Long Do I Have to Worry About an Audit? 52
    What to Expect at an Audit 54
    Do I Have to Learn Tax Law to Win My Audit? 55
    Audit Selection—Why Me? 56
    When the IRS Increases Your Tax Bill Without an Audit 67
    Types of IRS Audits 79
    How a Field Auditor Approaches an Examination 96
    Preparing for an Audit 100

Who Should Attend the Audit? 103

How to Act at an Audit 104

Finishing Audits 118

Serious Audit Problems 129

4 Appealing Your Audit Within the IRS 139

Pros and Cons of Appealing an Audit 141

How to Appeal an Audit 142

How the Independent Office of Appeals Works 148

Preparing for an Appeals Hearing 149

Dealing With the Appeals Officer 152

Presenting a Case to an Appeals Officer 152

Negotiating a Settlement 154

Should You Hire a Tax Professional for Your Appeal? 160

If You Don't Settle on Appeal 161

5 Going to Tax Court: No Lawyer Necessary 163

Tax Court Facts 165

Small Tax Cases—People's Court 167

Regular Tax Court Cases—Over $50,000 183

Other Federal Courts—Paying First Is Required 185

Bankruptcy Court 187

6 When You Owe the IRS: Keeping the Tax Collector at Bay 189

When You Can't Pay With Your Tax Return 195

Getting Time to Pay After the Tax Bill Comes 196

IRS Tax Billing Process 196

IRS Automated Collection System 198

Revenue Officers—Frontline Collectors of the IRS 206

Offers in Compromise (OICs) 230

Using the Bankruptcy Code to Stop the IRS 249

Protecting Your Assets From the IRS 255

Suspending Collection of Your Tax Bill 257

Collection of Tax Debts by Private Debt Collectors 258

7 IRS Enforced Collection: Liens and Levies..263

Federal Tax Liens...265

Getting a Tax Lien Withdrawn..272

Tax Levies = Seizure of Assets 273

Dealing With the IRS Levy Process 274

Assets the IRS Can't or Won't Seize 274

Avoiding a Levy 279

Getting a Tax Levy Released..283

IRS Sales of Levied Assets...286

8 The Taxpayer Advocate: A Friend at the IRS 293

Who Qualifies for Help From a Taxpayer Advocate?..................294

Contacting the Taxpayer Advocate Service................................297

Emergency Help: Taxpayer Assistance Orders 298

9 Family, Friends, Heirs, and the IRS...303

It's a Family Affair..304

Owning Property Jointly 312

Death and Taxes 313

10 Fraud and Tax Crimes: Do You Really Have to Worry?.................321

How People Commit Tax Fraud...322

If You Are Caught Cheating...322

IRS Criminal Investigations 329

If You Are Prosecuted..336

11 Small Business/Self-Employed: When IRS Trouble Comes.........341

Self-Employed—You're a Prime Audit Target 342

Employees or Independent Contractors? 343

Payroll Taxes—IRS Dynamite 348

The Dreaded Trust Fund Recovery Penalty................................350

Cash Transactions Over $10,000...359

12 **Penalties and Interest** 361

Penalties Added to Tax Bills 362

Interest on Tax Bills 367

Understanding Penalty and Interest Notices 367

Reducing or Eliminating Penalties and Interest 368

Designating Late Tax Payments 377

13 **Help Beyond the Book: Tax Professionals and Tax Information** 379

Finding and Using a Tax Professional 380

Tax Pros for Serious Problems 386

Hiring a Tax Return Preparer 388

Researching Tax Questions 389

14 **When You Owe State Income Taxes** 395

The IRS and State Taxing Authorities 396

Does Your State Have a Taxpayer Bill of Rights? 397

State Time Limits to Assess and Collect Income Taxes 397

State Tax Collection Departments 398

State Tax Bills 398

When All Else Fails, Try Your Political Connections 402

15 **The Taxpayer Bill of Rights** 403

Taxpayer Bill of Rights I 404

Taxpayer Bill of Rights II 406

Taxpayer Bill of Rights III 408

16 **The 25 Most Frequently Asked Questions** 415

G **Glossary of Tax Terms** 427

Index 437

Introduction

Chances are that you'll have trouble with the taxman at least once in your life. Nearly everyone will face an audit, receive a bill for back taxes, or have some other serious dispute with the Internal Revenue Service. If your number comes up, you need to understand how your adversary—the IRS—is organized and the rules it plays by.

Contrary to what you might think, you don't have to be a tax expert to successfully deal with the IRS. It usually isn't necessary to know anything about the tax law. However, you do have to know how the IRS works—its rules and procedures. This book gives you the tools you need to successfully deal with the IRS. Really.

It addresses all of the issues people have most frequently faced with the IRS, including:

- what to do if you are behind in filing tax returns
- how to handle an IRS audit, from start to finish
- appealing when you don't agree with an audit report or other IRS decision
- taking your tax problems to court
- negotiating with an IRS tax collector when you can't pay
- settling a tax debt through the Offer in Compromise program
- removing tax liens and levies
- self-employed and small business tax issues
- avoiding tax scams and phony tax experts, and
- invoking the Taxpayer Bill of Rights.

This book also discusses ways to lower your audit profile, legally protect your assets from IRS seizures, and reduce tax penalties, and how to deal with the IRS in the event of divorce or the death of a loved one. In addition, we'll cover the most serious of all tax issues—tax fraud, and the likelihood of your ever being charged with a tax crime.

Every action recommended here is legal. So, this book isn't for you if you're looking to learn how to cheat on your taxes, claim the income tax law is unconstitutional, or hide from the IRS.

Can you really stand up to the IRS yourself without hiring a tax expert? For over 90% of the tax problems the average person is likely to face, "The answer is a big, money-saving "yes." However, some types of IRS and tax problems might be over your head. In these cases, this book will tell you so and how to find the right kind of professional tax help.

The IRS and the Coronavirus (COVID-19) Pandemic

Like every government agency, the coronavirus (COVID-19) pandemic severely impacted the IRS. The IRS sent its employees home and didn't process postal mail for months, resulting in a substantial backlog of unprocessed paper tax returns and mail.

The IRS also enacted an unprecedented "People First Initiative"—a sweeping series of steps designed to make life easier on people facing tax issues. These included:

- suspending most field collection activities initiated by revenue officers, including liens and levies
- not filing any new automated liens and levies
- suspending new IRS audits
- allowing taxpayers with installment agreements or Offers in Compromise to suspend their payments
- suspending the filing of notice to the State Department that taxpayers are seriously delinquent so their passports can be revoked, and
- not forwarding delinquent accounts to private collection agencies.

These measures were temporary and will have almost all ended by the time you read this book. You can learn about the IRS's current operational status at www.irs.gov/newsroom/irs-operations-status-of-mission-critical-functions.

However, the COVID-19 pandemic had a lasting impact on the IRS. For example, taxpayers may now interact with the IRS through video conferencing in many instances. The IRS is also working to make all its operations, including collections, as paperless as possible.

Many self-help people who have failed in their IRS encounters did not bother to learn and follow the IRS procedures. These people are the ones who try to handle IRS issues with casual phone calls or rambling letters. This approach is a recipe for failure. What these unfortunates should have done was filed the correct IRS forms, contacted the right IRS department, or furnished some vital information to the tax agency. And, of course, they didn't read this book. This book explains the process and shows you what steps to take, what IRS forms you need to file, and the right way to fill in those forms.

Just receiving an envelope with "IRS" stamped across it can make your heart skip a beat. The IRS knows this too and tries to use this intimidation factor to gain the psychological advantage. Don't let this happen to you. This book will level the playing field by providing practical and supportive advice every step of the way. Yes, you can *Stand Up to the IRS*.

Inside the IRS: What You Need to Know About IRS Operations

IRS Inefficiency.. 11

Communicating With the IRS... 13

    Getting Your Tax Data From the IRS.. 14

Rules of the Game—Tax Laws... 17

Interpreting the Tax Code.. 18

Self-Assessment of Income Taxes.. 19

Winning the IRS Game.. 19

L et's take a look at the Internal Revenue Service (IRS). The IRS's stated mission is to "Provide America's taxpayers top quality service by helping them understand and meet their tax responsibilities and enforce the law with integrity and fairness to all."

A chart of the main IRS divisions appears below. Here is a description of the divisions and offices you're most likely to encounter.

National. The IRS is a branch of the U.S. Treasury Department, with headquarters in Washington, D.C., and is ruled by a commissioner appointed by the president. The national IRS office sets tone and policy, while procedures—especially audits and collections—are left to the regional and local offices.

The IRS is divided into four operating divisions, but only two concern most of us: the Wage and Investment Division and the Small Business/Self-Employed Division.

IRS campuses. IRS campuses (formerly called "service centers") annually process over 262 million tax filings, including over 160 million individual income tax returns. IRS campuses collect over $4.9 trillion in tax payments each year. Regional campuses are located in Austin, Kansas City, and Ogden. They mail out tax notices, collection notices, or bills; tax return problem notices; and tax forms. Contacts with the IRS campuses are usually by postal mail or fax, or occasionally by telephone.

Automated Collection System, or ACS. This program communicates with taxpayers who owe the IRS. It is a computerized collection system staffed by personnel working by phone and mail. You might talk to an ACS person, but you'll never meet one.

Local offices. Local IRS offices sit in major cities with suboffices in smaller cities. You can bet one is near you.

Each local office is divided into several departments, four of which you might encounter: examination, collection, criminal investigation, and Taxpayer Advocate Service.

Let's look at these departments in more detail:

- **Examination** personnel perform audits, or examinations in IRS-speak. The people who audit tax returns are either tax auditors if they work inside the local IRS office or revenue agents if they come to your home or business, which is called the "field." The term "auditors" in this book refers to both.

- **Collection** personnel collect tax dollars from people who haven't voluntarily and timely paid. Local IRS collectors are called "revenue officers." If your case goes to collection, you or your representative will meet with a collector face to face. The IRS campuses and Automated Collection System are also part of the collection apparatus, but they don't employ revenue officers.

- **Criminal Investigation** is the police force of the IRS, and its employees are called "special agents." If you ever meet an IRS criminal investigator, it means that you or someone you know is under investigation for a tax crime.

- **Taxpayer Advocate Service** has the IRS troubleshooters to call on when you can't get tax problems solved through normal IRS channels. These officers are found at IRS campuses and local IRS offices. Taxpayer advocates hold powers to cut through red tape and get things done quickly.

The total number of IRS permanent and seasonal employees at all levels is approximately 79,000. Auditors make up 25%, collectors 15%, and criminal investigators 3%. The other 57% make policy, run the computers, answer taxpayer inquiries, and God only knows what else. The IRS has been downsized by 22% since 2011. Increased reliance on electronic data processing enables the IRS to continue to function.

If you're confused about the structure of the IRS, don't worry—you're not alone.

The IRS Is Due to Grow

The IRS budget fell by 18.5% over the past decade, leading to a 20% decline in the agency's workforce. Staff reductions have been most significant for revenue officers who collect taxes (a 50% decline to 8,200) and revenue agents who audit complex returns (a 35% decline). Today, the IRS has fewer auditors than at any time since World War II. However, this situation might be about to change.

In 2022, Congress passed the Inflation Reduction Act, giving the IRS an additional $80 billion in funding over the next decade. This amount was reduced to about $61 billion in 2023, but it's still the biggest budget increase the IRS has ever received. This funding should be enough to enable the IRS to add thousands of new employees and significantly upgrade its operations.

Over half of the additional funding is earmarked for enforcement. The IRS plans to hire thousands of new revenue agents over the next several years to increase audits and other enforcement and collection activities. It will focus on larger businesses and high-income individuals (those making over $400,000 per year). One of the IRS's goals is to increase audits of taxpayers earning $1 million or more by tenfold. For more details on how the IRS plans to spend this windfall, see the *Internal Revenue Service Inflation Reduction Act Strategic Operating Plan FY2023-2031* at www.irs.gov/pub/irs-pdf/p3744.pdf.

The Taxpayer Roadmap

For an outstanding overview of the U.S. tax system and its complexities, check out the online Taxpayer Roadmap created by the Taxpayer Advocate. It shows step by step how taxes work from filing through appeal. This map makes the New York City Subway Map look like a child's doodle. The Taxpayer Roadmap is available at www.taxpayeradvocate.irs.gov/get-help/roadmap.

The following example shows how the various divisions work.

EXAMPLE:

1. On April 15, Arnold and Aimee Tyson file their income tax return by mail with their IRS campus.

2. The information on their return is transmitted to the National Computer Center for analysis and given a potential audit score. If the score is high enough (it is), the return is screened at the IRS campus. If the return is then deemed to have a high enough audit potential (it does), it is sent to their local office.

3. At the local office, the Tysons' return is scrutinized again and selected for examination (audit). An IRS agent calls the Tysons or sends them an examination notice.

4. The Tysons make an appointment with a tax auditor at the local IRS office. (Or alternatively, a revenue agent comes to the Tysons' business to conduct the audit.)

5. The auditor looks at the Tysons' records and suspects fraud. He refers their file to Criminal Investigation for handling by an IRS special agent. The audit is temporarily suspended. A criminal investigation is very rare.

6. The special agent concludes that the Tysons made many errors, but they were not serious enough to be criminal acts. He sends the file back to the auditor.

7. The auditor concludes the audit and sends the Tysons an examination report. The report states that they owe the IRS additional taxes, interest, and penalties. The Tysons disagree with the report.

8. The Tysons file an appeal, or protest, of their audit.

9. The appeal is heard at the nearest IRS Independent Office of Appeals. The appeals officer upholds the auditor, and the Tysons file a petition in Tax Court. Tax Court is independent of the IRS. The Tysons win a partial victory in Tax Court.

10. After their Tax Court hearing, the Tysons still owe the IRS. Taxes, interest, and penalties are formally entered, or assessed, in the Tysons' IRS computer records.

11. The Tysons receive their first series of computerized collection notices from their IRS campus. They don't pay or make only a partial payment.

12. The IRS campus eventually gives up. Next, collection notices and telephone calls come from an IRS call center.
13. The Tysons still don't pay. The IRS call center sends the file to a revenue officer at the local office.
14. They try to work out a payment plan, but the collector is unreasonable and threatens to take their wages and property. The Tysons seek help from the Taxpayer Advocate Service.
15. With the help of a taxpayer advocate, they arrange a monthly installment plan. Assuming the Tysons make the payments on time, the case will be closed.

Tax Return Processing

From January to May, regional campuses operate around the clock, processing income tax returns, extension requests, and tax payments. Many temporary workers are hired, trained on the job, and paid little more than the minimum wage. IRS officials admit that these seasonal employees sometimes make processing mistakes.

The IRS strongly encourages all taxpayers to file electronically since it makes processing much easier for the agency. 94% of all individual tax returns are filed electronically. For the 6% of returns filed on paper, machines must open tax return envelopes and remove tax returns and checks. Until recently, human transcribers had to review the paper returns and enter the key tax return data into a computer by hand. However, the IRS now has digital scanning technology to speed up the processing of paper returns.

During the COVID-19 pandemic, the IRS had a backlog of millions of paper-filed returns it was unable to process because many of its offices were closed and/or staff were working at home. (IRS employees can't take returns home.) The backlog has been greatly reduced, but not eliminated.

Tax return data is sent to computer centers in Detroit, Martinsburg (West Virginia), or Memphis, where each return is computer scored for its "audit potential." About 10% of all individual (nonbusiness) income tax returns are selected for further review. These files are sent back to the regional campuses. There, IRS classifiers (human beings) weed out most of the 10% scored for audit, based on their opinions of the most problematic tax returns. So, roughly 0.5% to 1% of all individual tax returns filed are selected for further taxpayer contact. (For more information on how returns are selected for audit, see Chapter 3.)

IRS Inefficiency

If you've never dealt with a bureaucracy, the IRS will give you a lesson in how one operates. The IRS machinery moves slowly and often breaks down. Internally, the IRS is very specialized, which can create problems right at the outset. Often, your first challenge is to locate the right department and person to talk to. Because most IRS employees don't know or care how the IRS operates outside of their own small area, IRS personnel often don't know where to direct you.

Here are the major challenges you'll encounter in dealing with the IRS.

Bureaucracy. Civil servants in the IRS bureaucracy are not usually self-starters. For many, the IRS provides an escape from the long hours and competitive pressures of the private business world. Others are gaining work experience or biding their time until a better job comes along. All this results in a paint-by-the-numbers approach which can drive any taxpayer nuts. In contrast, you are highly motivated in your IRS dealings—it's your pocketbook at stake. What's important is that you hang in there. Success with the IRS is possible, especially if you are armed with the information and strategies suggested in this book.

Computers. The IRS loves its computers and would replace all its people with machines if possible. Sometimes your file gets lost in the computer—usually through human error. Often this is good—for example, if you want to delay dealing with the IRS. In many cases, however, it's better to get your file out of the computer and into human hands. Every individual taxpayer's IRS file is electronically stored by tax year or period and is computer accessed by Social Security number (SSN), not by name. Returns filed by a business with employees are accessed by the business's employer identification number (EIN).

The ultimate computerization goal of the IRS is totally paperless tax returns—a goal it is near to reaching as 94% of all individual tax returns are now filed electronically. The IRS reasons that if all your income, deductions, exemptions, and credits were electronically reported, a paper tax return would be unnecessary. Information returns, such as W-2 and 1099 forms filed by employers, banks, and the like, on paper and electronically, already make it possible for the IRS to prepare tax returns for nonfilers. And electronic tax filing allows tax refunds to be processed quickly without a paper filing.

Complexity. Americans have the dubious honor of having the most complex income tax laws in the world. The IRS was created to see that we follow the rules. But nobody, including the IRS, understands all of them. It's no wonder—given that the tax code is full of contradictions and hopelessly unclear provisions. Blame Congress. It's far easier to pass a tax law than to administer it or to teach a taxpayer or tax professional how to apply it. Each major tax revision produces unworkable tax provisions that are revised or repealed in the next term of Congress.

IRS Organizational Chart (Short Version)

The IRS structure is far more complicated than the chart below indicates. Only the top-level divisions you are most likely to encounter are included. The IRS publishes its own chart showing the entire organizational scheme, but you'll probably be more confused than educated if you try to read it.

Chief Counsel — **Commissioner & Deputy Commissioner** — National Headquarters (Washington, D.C.)

- Wage & Investment
- Small Business/ Self-Employed
- Tax-Exempt & Government Entities
- Large Business and International

- Appeals
- Taxpayer Advocate Service
- Criminal Investigation
- Communications & Liaison

CAUTION

Filing tax returns isn't voluntary. Contrary to what the tax resister, protestor, and Constitutionalist folks might say, income tax filing is not, and has never been, voluntary. Don't get us wrong. We would love to not file or pay income taxes—but in decades of doing tax work, we haven't discovered how to do this legally. The only person who can legally skip filing is the one without much, if any, income to report. Many of the tax scamsters are in prison or are destined for that fate. Common sense tells you that government services aren't free.

Communicating With the IRS

If you need to communicate with the IRS, try the telephone first. A specific IRS number should be on the notice that's causing you concern. If not, call 800-829-1040, the IRS's toll-free number. Until recently, the IRS didn't use email to communicate with taxpayers, but this is starting to change. Taxpayers can now respond to some types of IRS notices electronically. Such notices contain a link and unique access code to use.

If calling doesn't work and emailing isn't an option, write a letter. However, be warned: Letters, which the IRS refers to as "white mail," aren't the best way to communicate with the IRS. The IRS gets millions of letters every year from earnest, well-meaning taxpayers with legitimate IRS concerns (in addition to letters from cranks). IRS employees are trained to respond to IRS forms, not letters. In addition, due to processing delays that the COVID-19 pandemic caused, the IRS has had a substantial backlog of unprocessed letters and other mailings.

TIP

Before contacting the IRS, find out if there is an IRS form for your problem. The IRS has a form for just about everything. For example, you can request a payment plan on Form 9465, *Installment Agreement Request*. The clerk who opens the mail will route the form to the proper department right away, but might leave a letter with the same request to languish in a pile. To find out if the IRS has a form for your concern, check the IRS website at www.irs.gov. Alternatively, you can call the IRS at 800-829-1040, or ask a tax adviser.

Getting Your Tax Data From the IRS

Can't find an old tax return or don't know the balance on an unpaid tax bill or whether the IRS has assessed a penalty? Here are three ways to get your tax data from the IRS:

IRS tax transcripts. You can get an IRS tax transcript online for whatever year you need by using the IRS Get Transcript Online tool (www.irs.gov/individuals/get-transcript). You must register with the IRS to use this online service. Alternatively, you may postal mail IRS Form 4506-T, *Request for Transcript of Tax Return*, or call the IRS at 800-908-9946. IRS transcripts are free and you can get them anytime. There are four types of IRS tax transcripts:

- *Tax Account Transcript:* This provides an overview of your account, including basic data such as return type, marital status, adjusted gross income, taxable income, and all payment types. It also shows changes made after you filed your original return, including penalties, assessments, IRS inquiries, and other account activity. This transcript is available for the current tax year and up to 10 prior years using Get Transcript Online or Form 4506-T.

- *Tax Return Transcript:* A Tax Return Transcript isn't a copy of your return, but it shows key parts, including income reports from sources such as banks and employers. It also shows that you filed (or didn't file) a tax return for a specific year. It doesn't show changes after you filed your return. This transcript is only available for the current tax year and returns processed during the prior three years.

- *Record of Account Transcript:* This combines the tax return and tax account transcripts into one complete transcript. It's available for the current tax year and returns processed during the prior three years using Get Transcript Online or Form 4506-T.

- *Wage and Income Transcript:* This shows data from IRS information returns such as Forms W-2 and 1099 reporting how much you were paid by employers, banks, and the like. Current tax year information might not be complete until July. This data is helpful if you're missing W-2 or 1099 forms and need to prepare a tax return. The information also lets you match your records against what others have reported to the IRS to let you check for discrepancies. Also, if you are ever audited, the auditor will have this data to compare against your tax return. This transcript is available for up to 10 prior years using Get Transcript Online or Form 4506-T.

Tax returns. If you want a complete photocopy of an old tax return instead of a transcript, use IRS Form 4506, *Request for Copy of Tax Return*, and make a payment of $43 for each year you need a copy. The form is available on the IRS website and has the mailing address where it should be filed based on your geographic area.

Access tax account online. You can register with the IRS (www.irs.gov/payments/your-online-account) and access your account balance and other payment and billing records online. To get the total amount of your tax debt, type "payoff" in the www.IRS.gov search line and select the "Your Online Account" page.

How Your Tax Information Can Become Public

The federal Privacy Act prohibits the IRS from disclosure of an individual's tax records. However, your tax information can become public in four notable ways:

Tax lien. The IRS may file a Notice of Federal Tax Lien in the public records if you owe back taxes. You see this occasionally in the news, especially when it happens to celebrities like Willie Nelson and Nicolas Cage.

Tax crimes. If you are formally charged with a tax crime, the government will break the news. Personal tax information will come to light at a public trial. Actor Wesley Snipes's tax history became an open book in his trial—and conviction.

Taxpayers and others. Nothing stops you or us from telling others about our private tax life. And, other third parties can bring some tax secrets to light. Take former Congressman Charles Rangel. A public interest group reviewing certain required financial disclosures by members of Congress found and made public some questionable tax items. The publicity around the disclosure ended up in Rangel's giving up his chairmanship of certain committees and he was reprimanded.

State tax and law enforcement agencies. The IRS shares taxpayer data with 49 states (Nevada is the exception). Also, under certain circumstances, your tax information is available to law enforcement agencies.

Access to Tax Data Under the FOIA

All federal governmental agencies are subject to the Freedom of Information Act, or FOIA. This law guarantees access to all data the IRS has in its files about you and about internal IRS operations. You aren't entitled to information about other taxpayers, which is protected from disclosure by the Privacy Act. And sensitive information, such as how the IRS conducts criminal investigations and whether you are under investigation, is exempted from the FOIA.

The FOIA gives you access to the contents of your IRS files, such as notes of IRS agents, workpapers, computations, and opinions. This information is particularly useful if you are contesting an IRS decision, including an audit or a bill.

Getting information under the FOIA involves making a simple written request. (A sample letter is in Chapter 4.) If you're lucky, the IRS will respond to your request within 30 days. Unfortunately, however, the IRS gives a very low priority to complying with FOIA requests; after all, this is not a function that brings in money. Typically, the first response you receive is a letter stating that the IRS needs more time to get the materials.

Delayed responses aren't the only problem; the IRS edits out materials it doesn't think you are legally entitled to—which might be exactly what you are looking for. Frequently, a person who doesn't understand the FOIA, such as an auditor or a collector, is given the file to decide what you will get. Often, you have no way of knowing what was left out. The form letter accompanying what is sent to you routinely states that materials were withheld under certain statutes. Occasionally, you'll get all the materials with blackouts on the pages. We have seen some documents 90% blacked out! This usually happens if you've been the subject of an IRS criminal investigation.

You can appeal, but the FOIA Appeals Office is several years behind in deciding appeals. So, many taxpayers are forced to proceed without having the IRS provide all documents as required under the FOIA.

A sure way to counter the IRS's disregard of the FOIA is to file a lawsuit against the IRS in federal court. Going to court is prohibitively expensive for most people. But 9 times out of 10, the IRS complies with your original FOIA request within days or weeks of your filing the lawsuit, without your having to get near a courtroom.

Detailed guidance on the FOIA can be found on the IRS website—search "Freedom of Information Act (FOIA) Guidelines."

Rules of the Game—Tax Laws

Congress writes the tax laws, which become part of the Internal Revenue Code, IRC, or tax code for short. The tax code is amended every year. The present tax code is over 4,000 pages long. It's hard to keep up, even for a tax adviser. Thankfully, most of the tax code isn't applicable to the average citizen taxpayer.

The Income Tax: Past and Future

Our income tax has its roots in the Civil War when Honest Abe asked Congress for money to finance the war effort. Enacted in 1862, the first tax law lasted until 1872. The Supreme Court struck the second income tax law down, which led to the passage of the 16th Amendment to the Constitution, which led to the basic law we have today.

In 1913, the tax rate was just 1% on all corporations and individuals. But few people paid income taxes, because the standard exemption was $3,000 for single people ($4,000 for married couples), and almost no one earned this much. In fact, only 1 out of every 271 Americans paid any income tax the first year. By 1919, another war had broken out, and the maximum rate soared to 77%.

Today, the highest federal income tax rate is 37%. With Social Security, Medicare, and various state income taxes added on, the total tax can be as high as 50% for individuals. That might seem high, but it's among the lowest in the developed world.

The one-size-fits-all flat tax is a constant political issue. The flat tax is simple, pure, and has a lot of appeal. Is it likely to become law? Even small changes to the tax code have widespread repercussions—to the banking, real estate, housing, manufacturing, and charitable industries—affecting just about everyone. Once special interest groups gear up to protect their niches in the tax code, it can become difficult to make major changes to existing laws.

Part of the problem is that many tax laws are passed for purposes other than raising money. For example, tax laws can have a *social* goal, such as attempting to alleviate the housing problem by giving tax breaks to those who invest in low-income housing. Or there might be an *economic* goal to stimulate manufacturing by allowing rapid tax write-offs to buyers of new business equipment. And there are purely *political* reasons for tax laws. Many special interest groups, such as oil companies, horse breeders, broadcasters, insurance companies, and even major league baseball clubs, have gotten tax laws passed designed to give them special treatment. These special provisions of the tax code outnumber the laws of general application.

Interpreting the Tax Code

Congress gave the IRS the power to interpret the tax code. This interpretation is done primarily through a series of IRS regulations and other pronouncements. The regulations are expanded versions of some tax code provisions, with illustrations of how the law is applied in different situations. The regulations are about four times the length of the tax code itself. The IRS also publishes revenue rulings, revenue procedures, and letter rulings, which provide guidance to taxpayers.

There are thousands of situations where it is not clear exactly how the tax law should be applied. In these gray areas, disputes often arise between the IRS and the taxpayer. This is where the tax professionals earn their keep—by fitting the tax code most advantageously to a client's case. Or put another way, if the tax case is analogized to the fence around Farmer Brown's cabbage patch, the perimeter has gotten so long and twisted that a self-respecting rabbit might have a decent chance of finding enough room to wiggle through or under it.

The IRS is not the final word on interpreting the tax code. The federal court system, composed of the U.S. Tax Court, federal district courts, the U.S. Court of Federal Claims, and U.S. Bankruptcy Courts, all have the power to decide, on a case-by-case basis, how Congress intended the tax laws to be applied. Any taxpayer or the IRS, unhappy with a court's tax decision interpreting the tax code, can appeal to a circuit court of appeal and, in rare cases, to the U.S. Supreme Court.

Self-Assessment of Income Taxes

The U.S. income tax system is based on a self-assessment theory. You are responsible for reporting your income and telling the government how much tax you owe. You assess your own income tax every time you file a tax return. This doesn't mean that the system is voluntary or that you have a legal choice whether to assess taxes against yourself. Despite what some tax protestor organizations contend, you must file a tax return if you earn above a specified annual minimum income amount.

The IRS's job is to determine whether you obeyed the self-assessment principle and the tax code by:

- reporting all your income
- stating the correct amount of taxes due, and
- paying the taxes due.

If the IRS suspects that you have violated your self-assessment obligation, you might be audited and billed for an additional assessment. If you don't file a tax return, the IRS is empowered to calculate and assess the tax for you.

Winning the IRS Game

If you file and pay your taxes on time and never get an IRS notice, then you're already winning the IRS game and probably don't need this book—at least not yet.

The rest of us who encounter the IRS up close and personal still have a chance to win, or at least to not lose disastrously. This means keeping your income and assets away from the IRS and staying out of jail. And this is one game where, despite your coach having told you "It's not whether you win or lose, it's how you play the game," you darn well want to win.

Great, but you won't win the IRS game unless you know the rules. This book tells you the most important rules—written and unwritten—and helps you develop a game plan.

Let's call the IRS team the Goliaths and your team the Goodguys. On paper, the Goliaths look unbeatable, but on the playing field it comes down to the strengths and weaknesses of the individual players. Here's an analysis of the teams and players.

Goliaths have experience. You're a rookie, so even the weakest IRS team member is ahead of you. But they probably can't make it a runaway—the IRS is characterized by low morale and a high rate of employee turnover. Score seven for the Goliaths in the first quarter, 7-0.

Goodguys have motivation and the advantage here every time. Coaches say that motivation is the key to winning. The Goliath player gets the same pay, win or lose, while the Goodguys are playing to keep their money. Score seven for the Goodguys in the second quarter. It's tied at the half, 7-7.

The game will be decided in the second half. You have to be prepared to go the distance. Know what you're doing and show strength and perseverance to the IRS. Keep your cool and don't beat yourself. Remember the words of Pogo, the comic strip philosopher: "We have met the enemy and he is us."

A costly victory—the wrong way to play. One way to lose is to play the IRS without bothering to learn the rules of the game, preparing, or devising a game plan. You'll lose if you ignore IRS contacts or respond incorrectly, miss deadlines, or lie to IRS employees. Charlie is a prime example.

> EXAMPLE: Charlie had been having IRS problems for eight years when he called a tax professional, Sheila. He had lost an IRS audit, an appeal, and then in Tax Court. When the tax bills came, he threw them away. Charlie believed he was right, and he was sticking to his principles.
>
> An IRS collector repeatedly warned Charlie that his business assets were going to be sold at auction to pay the tax bill. Sheila asked when the sale was to take place. "Tomorrow," Charlie replied. She agreed to try to help Charlie but made no promises—the game was just about over and he was behind by several touchdowns.
>
> Sheila called the IRS and got a postponement of the auction for 30 days to give Charlie a chance to get a home equity loan to pay the taxes. He tried, but the bank didn't approve the loan. The IRS refused another postponement and sold the business assets for $92,000.
>
> The sad part is that if Charlie had sought tax advice at the beginning of the game, he would have been able to settle with the IRS for $38,000. By stubbornly refusing to meet the problem, he lost his business. Charlie needed to know the rules and needed a plan before playing the IRS game.

RESOURCE

The Internal Revenue Service *Annual Report* provides a wealth of information about IRS organization and performance. View or download it at the IRS website at www.irs.gov.

Chapter Highlights

- The IRS is an inefficient megabureaucracy and not the all-knowing Big Brother it would like us to believe it is.
- Successfully dealing with the IRS comes from knowing basic IRS procedures and following those procedures.
- It is possible to beat the IRS at its own game by perseverance and going up the IRS ladder to solve problems.

Filing Tax Returns

How Long Must You Worry About Not Filing a Tax Return?............................24

Consequences of Not Filing..25

    IRS Hunting for Nonfilers 26

    IRS Notifying Nonfilers 26

    When the IRS Prepares Your Tax Return for You 28

    Nonfiling Might Be a Crime 29

It's Better to File Before the IRS Contacts You..30

    Suggestions for Completing Late-Filed Tax Returns...............................31

    Voluntary Filing to Minimize the Chance of a Criminal Investigation 35

What Will Happen When You File Late 36

    Civil Penalties and Interest Added to Your Tax Bill 36

    Criminal Charges Might Be Brought..38

    Refunds Might Be Denied 38

Requesting an Extension to File...39

Filing a Tax Return When You Can't Pay What You Owe 41

Filing a Tax Return When You Live Out of the United States 41

Reducing the Chance of an Audit When Filing 42

Amending Tax Returns 44

    How to Amend a Tax Return 44

    Audit Alert for Amended Tax Returns...45

A Word About "Aggressive" Tax Filing...45

O ver 50% of all people file annual federal income tax returns before April 1 of each year. Most of the rest file in the first two weeks of April, but 5% get an extension to October 15.

According to the IRS, about 10% don't file at all. It's likely that number is even higher. In any case, millions of folks are either illegally not filing tax returns or are filing beyond all extension dates. This number is so large that some nonfilers might never get caught—but don't bet on it. In this electronic age, it's increasingly difficult to stay below the IRS radar forever.

How Long Must You Worry About Not Filing a Tax Return?

The tax code sets out time limits, or statutes of limitations, for the IRS to pursue nonfilers.

Criminal. The government can only bring criminal charges against a nonfiler within six years of the date the tax return was due. For example, after April 15, 2024, you can't be prosecuted for failing to file a 2017 tax return that was due on April 15, 2018.

Civil. There is no deadline, however, for the IRS to go after nonfilers and impose civil penalties—in addition to any taxes owed. This means that while you can't be put in jail for not filing a 1998 tax return, you will forever owe the IRS a return—as long as you earned enough to have had an obligation to file. And fines—penalties and interest—on unfiled tax returns run forever.

IRS policy. Don't worry too much about that missed tax return after six years. The IRS usually doesn't pursue nonfilers after six years from the filing due date. The IRS materials on the Delinquent Return Program (*Internal Revenue Manual* 1.2.1.6.18; IRS Policy Statement 5-133) read as follows:

> *Taxpayers failing to file returns due will be requested to prepare and file (them). All delinquent returns ... will be accepted. However, if indications of willfulness or fraud exist, the special procedures for handling such returns must be followed .... Factors taken into account include, but are not limited to: prior history of noncompliance, existence of income from illegal sources, effect upon voluntary compliance and anticipated revenue in relation to*

the time and effort required to determine tax due. Consideration will also be given to any special circumstances existing in the case of a particular taxpayer, class of taxpayer or industry.

Normally, application of the above criteria will result in enforcement of delinquency procedures for not more than six years. Enforcement beyond such period will not be undertaken without prior managerial approval.

The IRS can still request a tax return for a period more than six years ago. But if you tell the IRS that you don't have enough information to prepare a return, the agency usually will drop the request. If the IRS computer shows income information on you, such as a W-2 or 1099 form, however, the IRS might calculate and assess the tax anyway.

Don't Forget Your State

Unless you live in Alaska, Florida, Nevada, New Hampshire, South Dakota, Tennessee, Texas, Washington, or Wyoming, the IRS isn't the only tax agency to worry about. All 41 other states have their own income tax reporting requirements, and a few cities do as well. In many cases, if you haven't filed a tax return, you might be contacted first by your state tax collector, not the IRS. If this happens, you can bet the IRS isn't far behind. If you had income from jobs in more than one state, you might need to file multiple state tax returns. All states except Nevada have agreements with the IRS to trade tax information about their residents. In this electronic age, the exchange occurs automatically; if one taxing authority finds you aren't filing, the computers will turn you in to the other. If you file a late IRS return, be sure to file a state return as well.

Consequences of Not Filing

It is a crime not to file a tax return if taxes are owed. By contrast, there is no criminal penalty if you file but can't pay your taxes. You'll owe interest and penalties, but you won't be sent to jail. So even if you don't have two dimes to rub together and owe a bundle of taxes, file your return.

If you ignore this advice and fail to file, you can be fined up to $25,000 per year and/or sentenced to one year in prison for each unfiled year. Our justice system, however, doesn't have enough jails to put away even 1% of the nonfilers, so going to jail is highly unlikely—even if you owe hundreds of thousands of dollars.

IRS Hunting for Nonfilers

The IRS looks for nonfilers through its computerized Information Returns Program (IRP). This tremendously effective operation matches information documents—W-2 wage statements and 1099 income reports from payers (such as your client or the bank where you earn interest on your deposit account)—against tax returns you have filed. If the computer search fails to find a return, the IRS initiates a Taxpayer Delinquency Investigation, or TDI. A TDI is an IRS search to find out why a taxpayer didn't file a tax return.

TDIs usually begin with computer-generated notices. If you don't respond to the notices, your case is eventually turned over to a taxpayer service representative for telephone contact or more letters. If the IRS is really serious, your file is assigned to a revenue officer at your local IRS office who goes out looking for you. (See Chapter 6 for more information on collection contacts with a taxpayer.)

If you're an independent contractor, earn investment or interest income, or sell real estate or stocks, the IRS receives payment information on you annually. The IRP will probably catch that you didn't file. The IRS is about 12 to 24 months behind in notifying the nonfilers it discovers. So don't think that you are home free because you haven't heard from the IRS within a year or two after the filing due date. The IRS will catch you—it's just a matter of time.

IRS Notifying Nonfilers

How the IRS contacts you is the key to how seriously the IRS views your case. There are four ways you can be notified—and they are not mutually exclusive. If the IRS tries one of the following methods and you don't respond, it will no doubt try another:

- **Written requests from the IRS over a 16-week period.** Most nonfilers are initially contacted in this relatively nonthreatening manner. Threats come later if you ignore these notices. These notices usually mean that you aren't targeted for criminal nonfiling.
- **Letter with a deadline** to get your returns filed, usually within 30 days. The officer will give you a deadline to file the missing returns directly with them, or will offer to help you prepare your return. If you still don't file, *the IRS can legally prepare a return for you, based on any information it has and guesses it makes.*
- **Visit by an IRS revenue officer.** Starting in 2020, IRS revenue officers began visiting the homes of high-income nonfilers to inform them of their tax filing and payment obligations. For these purposes "high-income" taxpayers are those who earn over $100,000 per year. Such visits are ordinarily made after multiple letters have been sent.
- **Visit by a Criminal Investigation Division agent.** This is the very worst way you can be contacted. It means that your nonfiling is the subject of a criminal investigation. This visit usually happens only if the IRS suspects you of not reporting hundreds of thousands of dollars in income over multiple years.

IRS Questioning About Unfiled Tax Returns

Someone from the IRS might ask you by phone or in person if you filed income tax returns for all years.

This questioning creates a dilemma. If you haven't filed but you answer "Yes, the IRS must have lost them," you will have lied to the IRS, a crime punishable by up to five years in prison. But if you answer "No," you might have confessed to the crime of failure to file a tax return.

The *best response* is to say you'll get back to the IRS after you check your records or speak with your tax adviser. You can't get into trouble with these magic words.

The IRS might keep pressing but just politely repeat "I'll get back to you."

Regardless of your answer, the IRS will set a deadline for you to respond or file your tax returns. Ask for 60 days to do it and talk with your tax adviser, if necessary. Then, you should start working on getting the returns prepared right away.

⚠️ **CAUTION**

The IRS has no tax amnesty program, so no penalties or interest on taxes are forgiven for those who file late. The IRS typically adds the maximum penalties and interest to the taxes found due.

When the IRS Prepares Your Tax Return for You

The IRS has the power to, in effect, prepare and file tax returns whenever you don't file. (I.R.C. § 6060.) In IRS-speak, this is called a "Substitute For Return," or SFR. Usually, it is not to your advantage to have the IRS do this. IRS preparers may give you the bare minimum—one exemption, no dependents, and the standard deduction. The IRS can guesstimate your tax liability, usually from W-2 forms and 1099 informational reports. If these are not available, the IRS can impute income to you based on tables from the Bureau of Labor Statistics showing income needed to sustain a minimal lifestyle by area of the country. This process can result in a much higher tax bill than you would have had if you had prepared your own tax return.

If the IRS prepares an SFR, it will mail a CP-2566 notice to your last known address asking you to accept the IRS's proposed assessment, and sign it and return it. Or you can file your own return. It might not be in your best interest to sign the IRS's proposed assessment, even if the figures are accurate. Instead, prepare a return yourself and send it to the IRS with a copy of the SFR letter it sent you. Request that your return be accepted in lieu of the SFR. If your return looks okay, the IRS will accept it. The IRS can audit it first, but this doesn't often happen.

If you don't respond to the CP-2566 notice form letter, the IRS sends CP-3219A, Notice of Deficiency, showing a proposed tax assessment. If you disagree, you have 90 days from the date of the notice to file a Tax Court petition (see Chapter 5). If you miss the deadline to file, you may prepare and file your own tax return and it will be reviewed by the Audit Reconsideration Unit. See IRS Publication 3598 for more details on the audit reconsideration process. This process is discretionary within the IRS and is far from a sure thing. Our advice: Never miss the 90-day deadline and take any chances with audit reconsideration.

Another reason to prepare the return yourself is because the normal statute of limitation rules for auditing a filed tax return don't apply with SFRs. If the IRS prepares an SFR, it will be able to audit it forever, unless you sign the SFR and agree to the tax liability. But, if you prepare a tax return, the IRS normally has only three years from the time you file it to audit you. An IRS-filed tax return also does not start the normal 10-year statute of limitations on collecting any taxes due. (See Chapter 6.)

A final reason for filing your own return has to do with qualifying to discharge (eliminate) your tax debt in bankruptcy.

If you don't offer your own return, the IRS finalizes the SFR 30 days after the date on the CP-2566 notice, whether or not you sign it. Any taxes due, plus penalties and interest, will then be formally assessed against you.

Nonfiling Might Be a Crime

Very few people are put in jail for not filing a tax return, but it can happen. A willful failure to file a tax return is a misdemeanor if you owe taxes. You can be sentenced for up to a year in jail and a $25,000 fine—for each year of nonfiling. (I.R.C. § 7203.) If your failure to file is deemed to be part of a scheme to evade taxes you can be charged with a felony, a more serious tax crime, which carries a maximum punishment of five years in prison and a monetary penalty of $100,000—but rarely is anyone criminally prosecuted for this felony. (I.R.C. § 7201.) The felony crime requires a deceitful act beyond the nonfiling, such as intentionally using a false Social Security number. The misdemeanor doesn't require any additional deceitful act.

If you are contacted by an IRS agent about your nonfiling, but you are not asked to file a return, start worrying. This might mean that you're on the way to the IRS Criminal Investigation Division, or CI. This does not guarantee you'll be prosecuted, but you might be. A small percentage of nonfiling cases result in criminal prosecutions. But, you still have to get your past-due returns prepared and filed. (Criminal investigations and other criminal matters are covered in Chapter 10.)

In deciding whether to recommend prosecuting a nonfiler, the CI considers many factors, including:

- the number of years you haven't filed returns
- the amounts of taxes due
- your occupation and education
- your previous history of tax delinquencies
- whether you're in a business largely done by cash, and
- how truthful you were during the investigation.

Certain types of nonfilers, such as reputed crime figures and politicians, might be prosecuted regardless of any other factors. And lawmakers are held to a higher standard to maintain taxpayer confidence in the tax administration system.

> **CAUTION**
>
> **If your nonfiling case is referred to the CI, there is little you can do to influence the IRS agent's decision regarding prosecution.** If you try to talk your way out of it, you'll only make matters worse. In short, if you suspect that the IRS is investigating you, see an attorney. If an agent calls you, don't consent to an interview—in fact, don't say anything except that you want to speak to an attorney. Then, find a tax or criminal attorney immediately and have no further direct contact with anyone at the IRS. Don't talk to your friends or associates about it either.

It's Better to File Before the IRS Contacts You

If you haven't filed a tax return for a year or more, it's never too late. The IRS has a policy of not criminally prosecuting those who file before they are contacted by the IRS. (IR-92-114.) Also, the IRS is often more gentle in collecting from voluntary filers than from the ones they catch. When you file your return on your own accord, the somewhat remote IRS campus initially handles your file. But if the IRS has sought you out, your local IRS office probably has the file and can put more pressure on you than a campus.

EXAMPLE: Uncle Jack worked in construction for 50 years. He bragged that he never filed a tax return or got an IRS notice. He changed addresses with the seasons and used many different Social Security numbers, none of which were his own. Because the IRS relies primarily on Social Security numbers to keep track of taxpayers, it never found Jack. He didn't get Social Security benefits either. If Jack were around today, his chances of outrunning the IRS computer would be slim—better than beating the house in Las Vegas, but not by much.

Suggestions for Completing Late-Filed Tax Returns

Most people have a hard enough time getting their tax returns prepared and filed every year. It's even more difficult if you're trying to do it for years long past. The most difficult tasks are getting the correct forms and finding the information that you need to fill them out.

Obtaining Lost W-2, 1099, and Other Tax Forms

Longtime nonfilers tend to lose their old W-2 and 1099 forms. Those forms show how much money was paid to you by businesses and are vital to filing an accurate tax return. If you have this problem, start by asking the business that issued the 1099 or W-2. Many businesses don't keep these old records around or won't go out of their way to furnish them to you. They met their legal obligation by sending the forms to you when due; you're out of luck.

Surprisingly, you can't get copies of W-2 and 1099 forms from the IRS. You can, however, get an IRS computer printout with the information on it. Use the IRS Get Transcript Online tool (www.irs.gov/individuals/get-transcript) to obtain by email a Tax Return Transcript for whatever tax year you need. You need to register with the IRS to use this online service. Alternatively, you may postal mail IRS Form 4506-T, *Request for Transcript of Tax Return*, or call the IRS at 800-908-9946. You may also call the IRS at 800-908-9946 and request a wage and income transcript for the missing tax years. It might take several weeks to receive a written response if you call or mail a request. A Tax Return Transcript is not a copy of your return, but it shows key parts including income reports from sources such as banks and employers. The free transcript also shows that you didn't file a tax return. Non-W-2 and 1099 income won't show up on the transcript, but it will show the minimum amount you must report on your tax return.

Another way to handle missing W-2 data when filing a tax return is by reconstructing your salary records on Form 4852, *Substitute for Form W-2*, available at the IRS website or by mail from the IRS. Attach it to the front of your tax return and file it. For missing non-1099 income data, make your best guess. There is no separate form for most 1099 payment reconstructions, except Form 1099-R for retirement plan distributions.

> **CAUTION**
> **Use the correct year's tax form.** You must use updated tax forms each year. For example, you can't use 2023 tax forms and change the year to 2022; the IRS makes major and subtle changes to its tax forms each year.

You have several options for obtaining past years' forms:
- Download the forms off the IRS's website (www.irs.gov).
- Check a tax software publisher like *TurboTax*.
- Call the IRS form department at 800-829-FORM (3676). The forms will be mailed in a week or two. The form center shouldn't pass your name along to other departments—such as the collection or criminal division.
- If you don't want to risk your name being passed along, have a friend or relative—who did file on time—call for you.
- Visit your local IRS office. You won't be asked why you want the forms. You won't even be asked your name.
- Ask a tax professional for forms, although the person might not provide them unless you agree to hire them.

If your state has an income tax, remember to get those old forms, too.

Preparing Late-Filed Tax Returns

Your local IRS office will help you prepare late tax returns. The question is whether this approach is wise. The IRS isn't interested in making sure you get every deduction, exemption, or credit to which you are entitled. If you can't afford to hire a tax preparer, see if any local tax professional or nonprofit groups donate their time to low-income or otherwise needy people or ask at your local IRS office.

Another free or inexpensive option is to use computer tax preparation software, such as *TurboTax*. (Check to see if you are eligible for the free version.) This program has helpful hints of what to do—and not do—and can take data directly from personal finance record-keeping programs, such as *Quicken* (Intuit). It even has built-in tax guides that flag questionable items and offer advice on finding deductions. The IRS has a bias in favor of computer-prepared tax returns. Computers don't make math errors and the IRS itself relies heavily on computers—although much of its reliance is undoubtedly misplaced. You'll probably have trouble locating older years' computer tax programs, although tax professionals keep programs back as far as 10 years.

Low-Income Taxpayer Clinics

The Low-Income Taxpayer Clinic (LITC) program provides free or low-cost legal representation for eligible individual taxpayers involved in tax disputes with IRS. The clinics also provide education and outreach to taxpayers who speak English as a second language (ESL).

Most LITCs are found at local legal aid organizations and are staffed with attorneys, CPAs, or enrolled agents. Each clinic determines whether prospective clients meet income guidelines and other criteria before agreeing to represent them. Generally, LITCs will represent anyone whose income does not exceed 250% of federal poverty guidelines and where the amount in dispute with the IRS is $50,000 or less. For example, currently someone (not living in Alaska or Hawaii) with a four-member household would be ineligible if their annual household income exceeded $75,000 (2023). There are currently LITCs in 47 states and the District of Columbia. See IRS Publication 4134 for a current list of LITCs.

Your best (but most costly) choice is to hire a tax preparer. Over 50% of tax filers do. A professional decreases the chances of mistakes and, consequently, that the return will be audited. Late returns are hand-screened by specially trained IRS personnel. Returns filed on time might never be reviewed by anyone except an IRS computer. (More on the computer processing and scoring of returns for audit selection in Chapter 3.) IRS personnel are presumably more likely to let a return go through without question if it bears the signature of a CPA, an enrolled agent, or a tax attorney. (See Chapter 13 for more information on tax professionals.) Also, a good tax professional can offer advice on what you can do in the future to cut your taxes or reduce your audit risk.

Getting Your Returns to the IRS

Get your late return to the IRS by the following means:

Hand filing. It's safer to hand file tax returns at a local IRS office than to mail them in, especially late returns. If you file in person, ask the IRS clerk to file-stamp a copy of the first page of the tax return. This shows irrefutably that the return was filed and the date of the filing. And it is better than a post office return receipt or card which shows only that something was sent to the IRS on that date—but not what was sent. Take along your own extra copy for the IRS to stamp; the IRS won't make a copy for you.

Mailing. Late-filed returns are more likely to get delayed in processing or lost by the IRS than current ones. If you plan to mail in your late returns, send them by certified mail, return receipt requested, to the IRS.

Private delivery services. Instead of the U.S. mail, you can use an IRS-approved private delivery service. These services include Federal Express (FedEx), United Parcel Service (UPS), and DHL Express.

Electronic filing. You can electronically file a late return. Get an electronic receipt back from the IRS and keep it for your records. Check the IRS website for instructions on how to do this. This method is by far the fastest way to get a tax refund.

Voluntary Filing to Minimize the Chance of a Criminal Investigation

The government policy is not to prosecute most citizens who haven't filed. The IRS claims that the typical nonfiler hasn't filed for three or more consecutive years and owes about $70,000.

Who does the IRS criminally prosecute? The most likely candidates are public figures, such as sports stars, politicians, entertainers, or known criminals. For example, President Biden's son Hunter was prosecuted for failing to file tax returns for two years. He pleaded guilty to a misdemeanor, paid $1.2 million in back taxes, and got two years' probation.

But more ordinary folks can get prosecuted too, especially if they have years of nonfiling and hundreds of thousands in taxes owed. Our advice to most nonfilers is to simply start filing their tax returns—without first contacting the IRS.

Tax attorneys typically handle the cases of high-profile nonfilers in one of three ways:

- The attorney writes the local IRS office and makes the voluntary disclosure for the client. The lawyer then files the tax returns.
- The attorney calls the local chief of the Criminal Investigation Division and requests a meeting. There they discuss the case without naming the client and the attorney asks if the client would be prosecuted if a voluntary disclosure was made. If the chief says no, the attorney makes the disclosure. Legally, the chief can't bind the government here, but I know of no one criminally prosecuted after making this kind of deal.
- The tax attorney does a "quiet disclosure." They prepare the returns for the last six years and file them, without contacting the IRS first. The tax attorney gets a power of attorney from the client—a form authorizing the attorney to act on behalf of the client—and uses the attorney's address, not the client's, on the tax returns. This ensures that any further contact about the late returns from the IRS comes to the tax attorney directly.

The advantage the tax attorney has is the attorney-client privilege. Under this ancient legal doctrine, neither the IRS nor any other government agency can force your attorney to disclose anything you say. There is also a tax practitioner-client privilege, but it doesn't apply to crimes—meaning the IRS can force a nonattorney tax professional to divulge client confidences.

What Will Happen When You File Late

The IRS can punish you for filing tax returns late by imposing civil penalties, criminal penalties, or both and by denying refunds due you.

> **TIP**
>
> **Ask for an extension if you are going to file late.** Electronically file or mail in the simple IRS Form 4868, *Application for Automatic Extension of Time to File U.S. Individual Income Tax Return,* if you aren't filing by April 15. You'll avoid the late filing penalty and get six more months to file. However, if you owe a balance you'll still have to pay interest and late payment penalties.

Civil Penalties and Interest Added to Your Tax Bill

If your seriously late tax return shows taxes due, you'll probably be fined 5% per late month, up to a maximum of 25% for five months past April 15. After five months, penalties and interest keep running, but at a lower monthly rate.

> EXAMPLE: Your return was due April 15 and you file on October 1 of that year. You may be charged 25% extra on the amount of any taxes you owe. If you file on August 16, you will be charged 20%—four months times 5% per month. There is no daily proration of the penalty, so one day late costs the same 5% penalty as does 29 days. After five months, the late filing penalty is reduced.

That's not all. In addition to the *late filing* penalty, the IRS can impose a *late payment* penalty of 0.5% to 1% per month. And here's a little more bad news: Interest is running all the while. Interest changes quarterly, and is compounded daily. And interest is charged on the penalties, too. (As of 2023, the interest rate was 7% per year.)

Tax bill interest is not deductible on your tax return, unless it's for a business-related tax debt. Penalties are never tax deductible.

Getting out of paying these penalties isn't easy, but can be done under certain circumstances. (See Chapter 12.)

Mandatory Reporting of Foreign Financial Accounts

Do you control or own any part of a financial account outside the United States? If so, you must report it on FinCEN Form 114 by April 15 every year. You're allowed an automatic extension until October 15 if you miss the April 15 deadline. Prior to 2014, these reports were made on Form 90-221, called an "FBAR." All Form 114 reports must be filed electronically with the U.S. Treasury Department (https://bsaefiling.fincen.treas.gov/main.html). The law applies not only to direct owners but to anyone with authority to conduct transactions for the account holder. You can't avoid this by using trusts or other types of entities, so don't try.

You must also report these foreign accounts on your income tax return under the so-called "FATCA rules." Why both filings? The FinCEN form goes to a division of the Treasury Department separate from the IRS. And Uncle Sam wants to make doubly sure you follow the law here. The only exception to the FinCEN reporting is when the total value of the foreign accounts is less than $10,000.

While the FinCEN form is not very difficult to complete, it is a good idea to go to a tax pro for help, at least the first time you file. The government can go back five years and impose civil penalties of $10,000 per missed report for nonfilers. But even worse, it can bring criminal charges as far back as six years.

Even if you owe no tax, you must pay a minimum penalty for filing your tax return over 60 days late. The penalty is adjusted for inflation each year. For returns to be filed in 2024, the penalty is $485. If the tax you owe is less than the penalty amount, you have to pay only the tax due, not the penalty. Some states also impose a penalty on late-filed state tax returns whether or not any tax is owed.

Criminal Charges Might Be Brought

As mentioned earlier, nonfiling an income tax return can be a crime. You can be sentenced up to one year in prison and be fined $25,000 for each year you didn't file, up to six years. You can't be criminally prosecuted for nonfiling a return once six years pass from its due date. However, you can be civilly fined beyond six years. (See Chapter 10.)

Refunds Might Be Denied

Statistically, late filers are more likely to be deserving of refunds than to owe tax balances. The tax law (I.R.C. § 6511(a)) prohibits the IRS from issuing a refund if your individual income tax return is filed more than three years past the due date, or two years from the time the tax was paid, whichever is later. Generally speaking, this means you have three years from the due date of your tax return to claim a refund for that year, plus any extension.

> EXAMPLE: Andy filed 10 years of back tax returns at one time. For the first five years he was due refunds, but in the later five years he owed taxes. Andy requested that the IRS offset the taxes owed with the refunds due. The IRS denied the request because all the refund years were beyond the three-year cut-off period.

If you make a payment for any tax due after the due date of your return, the refund time period is extended for two years from the payment date. This could extend the refund period beyond three years. However, if your claim is made outside of the three-year period, it will be limited to the amount you overpaid during the two years immediately preceding the date you file your claim.

There are exceptions to the two- and three-year time periods for:

- bad debts and worthless securities
- net operating losses or capital loss carrybacks
- foreign tax credits
- credit carrybacks

- self-employment tax
- income recapture in qualified plan terminations
- uniformed service retired pay, and
- situations when a taxpayer is unable to manage financial affairs due to disability.

There are strict rules as to how these exceptions apply. See Internal Revenue Code Section 6511 or ask a lawyer for advice.

Bells Won't Go Off When Nonfilers Start Filing

If you haven't filed for many years and decide to hop back in with this year's return, don't worry about the IRS automatically checking for all the other years you've missed. IRS computers aren't set up to do this, primarily because the IRS doesn't want to discourage nonfilers from starting to file again. So nothing will happen if you file anew even after a 10-year hiatus. If you later get a notice asking about tax returns for other years, chalk it up to coincidence—most likely due to income information already on file (W-2 and 1099 forms) in the IRS computer. However, you might run into problems if you file a return and can't pay the balance. The IRS might deny your request for an installment agreement if you have other unfiled tax returns.

Requesting an Extension to File

The only good reason for filing your tax return by April 15 is if you need a refund quickly. If you're getting large refunds, however, that is a sign that your wages are being overwithheld or you're sending in too much in estimated tax payments. If you look at tax refunds as a kind of forced savings plan, realize that you're making an interest-free loan to Uncle Sam. It might make more sense to adjust your withholding or quarterly estimated payments so that you break even or even owe a little to the IRS instead. In the meantime, you can invest the money and collect the interest, which, of course, is taxable.

The alternative to filing by April 15 is to apply for an extension to October 15. Each year about 5% of all taxpayers request extensions to file their tax returns. It's no big deal and won't get the IRS excited or increase your chances of being audited.

To get an extension to file, complete Form 4868, *Application for Automatic Extension of Time to File U.S. Individual Income Tax Return*, and send it to the IRS by April 15. This form changes each year. You can get a current copy from the IRS website, your local IRS office, or by calling 800-829-3676. Your extension is granted automatically until October 15, and you won't incur any late-filing penalties. Today, a majority of people file electronically, using a tax return preparer, the IRS e-file, or tax software like *TurboTax*.

If you're living (not vacationing) outside the United States on April 15, you get an automatic two-month extension to file to June 15. In the past, anyone physically outside the United States on April 15 could get the automatic extension. The law was changed to disqualify day trippers who made short April trips to Mexico and Canada just to get the extension. Even if you live outside the United States, however, you don't get extra time to pay the taxes you owe.

Some tax professionals contend that filing tax returns on extension decreases your chance of being audited. They reason that the IRS local offices fill their annual audit inventories before the returns on extension are processed. The IRS denies it works this way, but at the same time, the agency won't say that returns filed on extension have a higher audit frequency. At worst, extensions are a neutral factor; they can't hurt and just might help.

CAUTION

An extension to file does not extend your time to pay. Pay all expected tax due with your extension filing forms. Otherwise, you'll get hit with late payment penalties and interest for the underpaid amount. It is very difficult to get an extension of time to pay without incurring an underpayment penalty. Try by filing IRS Form 1127, *Application for Extension of Time for Payment of Tax Due to Undue Hardship* (available on the IRS website), by April 15. Follow the instructions on the form, but don't get your hopes up.

Filing a Tax Return When You Can't Pay What You Owe

If you owe taxes, but don't have the money to pay the full amount, file a return and send what you can. Remember—you can incur up to a 25% fine for the first five months you're late. Any partial payment will cut down on the penalty and interest owed.

> **TIP**
> **Avoid giving the IRS your bank account number.** The IRS always records your bank account number with your payment. If you ever owe the IRS and can't pay on time, the agency can easily seize this account to get the balance of the taxes owed—and cause your outstanding checks to bounce. (See Chapter 7.) Don't pay by check or have the IRS electronically debit your bank account using IRS Direct Pay. Instead, use a money order, cashier's check, or an attorney's trust fund check to make payments if you anticipate any future IRS collection problem.

Keep photocopies of the check or money order you send to the IRS. Write your last name, Social Security or employer identification number, type of tax—income or payroll—and year of tax in the lower left-hand corner of the payment instrument. If you want your payment credited quickly, pay electronically using IRS Direct Pay at the IRS website (www.irs.gov/payments/direct-pay). If you pay by mail, keep the payment slip and bar-coded envelope provided by the IRS for payment.

Filing a Tax Return When You Live Out of the United States

The long arm of the tax code doesn't stop at the U.S. border. If you live abroad and have income, you'll still have to file a tax return (by June 15) or you can file for an extension until October 15—but you must pay any tax due by April 15 or have to pay interest on the balance due. You must also have taxes withheld or pay quarterly estimated taxes if you're working abroad. But the tax bite might be substantially reduced if you qualify for a foreign earned income exclusion, the foreign housing exclusion, and the foreign housing deduction. (See IRS Publication 54, *Tax Guide for U.S. Citizens and Resident Aliens Abroad.*) You claim the foreign earned income tax exclusion on IRS Form 2555, *Foreign Earned Income*, filed with your Form 1040 tax return.

You might also owe taxes to the government of the country where you reside. Some countries give you credit for taxes you pay to Uncle Sam; others won't. Also, estate and inheritance tax laws vary widely across the globe.

Renouncing your U.S. citizenship to beat the IRS won't work, either. You remain subject to U.S. tax laws for 10 years after renunciation! Norman Dacey, author of *How to Avoid Probate*, found this out when he became an Irish citizen. He challenged this law in the U.S. federal courts—and lost.

There is one bit of good news. While you are subject to U.S. tax laws, it is very difficult for the IRS to grab your wages or assets located outside of the United States. Some countries, mostly in Europe, have treaties with the United States in which their tax agencies can cooperate with the IRS to collect from Americans, but most governments place a very low priority on working these kinds of cases.

Reducing the Chance of an Audit When Filing

No surefire way is available to audit-proof your tax return, though you can cut the odds. Nevertheless, a messy return—cross-outs, sloppy handwriting, smudges, missing forms—almost screams "audit me." This tells the IRS that you're careless and disorganized. So does the use of round numbers for deductions—$1,000 or $12,000 instead of $978 or $12,127. It's an indication that you're estimating things rather than keeping good records.

Here are some suggestions which might—or might not—work to reduce your audit risk:

- If you claim large deductions for unusual items, such as an earthquake, flood, or fire loss, attach documentary proof to the back of your tax return. Copies of repair receipts, canceled checks, insurance reports, and pictures are advisable. You can only do this if you file a paper return. This won't stop the IRS computer from flagging your return. These attachments, however, should catch the attention of the IRS classifier who next screens computer-picked returns for audit potential. If the person thinks your documentation looks reasonable, you won't get audited.

- Avoid filing an income tax return with Schedule C, *Profit or Loss From Business*, that reports a net loss from a small business venture. IRS auditors go after these returns like bees toward honey.
- Report side-job income as other income on Schedule 1, Line 8 of your tax return. This should be done only if this income is relatively small, and you are not claiming any business deductions against it. Technically, side-job income is usually reported on a Schedule C, *Profit or Loss From Business*. But filing a Schedule C undoubtedly increases your audit chances.
- Prepare your tax return by computer. A neat, computer-prepared return looks more official to IRS classifiers and avoids math errors, which catch the IRS's attention. Virtually all professional tax preparers use computers. If you prepare your own return, use widely available tax preparation software, such as Intuit's *TurboTax*.
- Don't use electronic filing for your tax return. This gets your return into the processing cycle, including the audit cycle, more quickly than a paper return. Anything that slows down the IRS machine can't be bad. On the flip side, using electronic filing usually means that any refund will come faster. The IRS says it takes less than 21 days to process refunds for 9 out of 10 electronically filed returns, but 6 to 8 weeks for returns filed by postal mail. If you expect a refund and have no reason to fear an audit, you'll have to weigh the pros and cons. Note that if you hire a tax professional to prepare your return the preparer is required by the IRS to file it electronically unless you direct otherwise.
- Live in a low-audit area. Your audit chances are radically different depending on where in the United States you live. For example, Nevada taxpayers are audited four times more than people in Wisconsin. While this is extreme, it might make sense if you travel most of the time or have addresses in several areas. If you have flexibility in choosing your tax reporting address, choose the one with the lower audit rate. If you're really interested in this, ask a tax professional.
- If you can, report less than $100,000 in total positive income from salaries, self-employment, and investments. These people have the lowest audit rate.
- Don't report less income than is shown on your W-2s, Form 1099s, and other third-party forms you receive. If one of them is incorrect, get the issuer to correct the form and reissue it.

Amending Tax Returns

You can change your tax return, or amend, in IRS-speak, after you've filed it. You can voluntarily correct a mistake, such as an overlooked deduction, to get a refund. If you fail to report income, the tax code requires you to amend. The sooner you do so, the less penalties and interest you'll be charged.

To amend your return, file IRS Form 1040-X, *Amended U.S. Individual Income Tax Return*. To get a *refund*, you must file a 1040-X within three years from the date the first return was filed or within two years from the date you paid the taxes due on that return—whichever is later. For example, if you filed your 2022 tax return on April 15, 2023, you can file a 1040-X any time up until April 14, 2026 and still get a refund. If you filed an extension, you can add the extended period on as well. One exception: If you file an amended return to claim a refund based on a worthless security or bad debt loss, you have up to seven years after you first filed. See a tax pro to see if you qualify.

How to Amend a Tax Return

File Form 1040-X, *Amended U.S. Individual Income Tax Return*, with documentation to support your changes. (If you don't feel comfortable with or understand this form, hire a tax preparer or use a software program like *TurboTax*.)

Starting with the 2020 tax year, you can file Form 1040-X electronically using tax software like *TurboTax*. Your tax preparer can also file it electronically for you. If you don't file electronically, it's best to hand deliver the 1040-X to the nearest IRS office and get a stamped copy as your filing receipt. If you use the mail, send it certified, with postal return receipt requested, to the IRS where you now file your tax returns.

The IRS has a substantial backlog of 1040-X filings, so it can take 20 or more weeks to process your 1040-X. You can check the status of your filing on the IRS website at www.irs.gov/filing/wheres-my-amended-return. Do not file a second amended return or call the IRS.

Don't forget to amend your state tax return at the same time. Get the proper forms from its tax department. If you don't feel comfortable or understand Form 1040-X (it's a little tricky), hire a tax preparer to do it.

Audit Alert for Amended Tax Returns

Filing amended returns claiming refunds slightly raises your audit likelihood —and not just for the amended items, but for the whole tax return. This is partly because 1040-X forms are scrutinized by IRS employees rather than just computer processed.

On the other hand, the IRS ordinarily has only three years to audit a return from the date it was filed. An amended return filing does not extend the time the IRS has to audit the first return. Filing an amended return near the three-year audit deadline gives the IRS very little time to audit your tax return and it might simply pass it through.

This ploy can backfire on you, however, as the IRS isn't legally obligated to accept an amended tax return. If you file an amended return near the three-year audit deadline, the IRS might be willing to accept it only on the condition that you agree to extend the time for audit beyond the three-year deadline. If you're considering this strategy, you might want to talk to a tax professional first. (See Chapter 13.)

A Word About "Aggressive" Tax Filing

A question we are often asked is, "What deductions and tax benefits can I safely take, and which ones are risky?" The best answer is that it depends on your personality. Are you very conservative? Or are you a risk-taker by nature? Most people have at least a little of each trait in their personality. In the end, go with your comfort level.

Aggressive tax filing means interpreting the gray areas of the law in your favor—and taking the chance that you will either not be audited or survive if you are. It doesn't mean making up numbers. You might want to peruse Chapter 3 first to find out what happens at an audit if you cross the line.

Tax professional litmus test. It's difficult to find two tax professionals who agree on the meaning of "aggressive." Find out how aggressive your tax adviser is by asking the person's opinion on deducting something. For instance, if you're self-employed, ask about deducting business lunch expenses, a combined business and pleasure trip, or health club dues. Or, if you have investment income, ask about financial publication expenses and trips to check out investments.

How tax advisers respond clues you in to how aggressive or timid they are. If a person repeatedly says "you can't do that," instead of offering advice on how to make that expense deductible, then they might be too government oriented. At the other extreme, if the response is always "not to worry, deduct anything you want because chances are you won't be audited," this approach could get you into trouble.

Comfort level. There can be a fine line between being aggressive and being dishonest. No reputable tax return preparer will sign a tax return that the person believes is a work of fiction. And, if the preparer is not reputable, you don't want that name and identification number on your return. The IRS tracks crooked tax preparers and might reward you with an audit for choosing one.

Finding and using a tax professional is covered in Chapter 13. Some things to look for and types of preparers to avoid are covered there. Don't take picking a tax preparer lightly.

The people most often concerned about audits are small business owners wanting to know how far they can go in taking deductions. Generally, the tax code lets you take a deduction for just about any expense that helps you produce income. On the other hand, the expense must be ordinary and necessary. For aggressive tax filers, this means that as long as there is a reasonable basis for claiming a deduction, they will take it. (For more information on business deductions, see *Tax Savvy for Small Business*, by Frederick W. Daily and Stephen Fishman (Nolo).)

> EXAMPLE: Dennis, a lawyer, buys and deducts an antique $10,000 grandfather clock for his home office. He could have bought a reproduction for $500 or a simple wall clock for $25—the $25 clock with the quartz movement probably will keep the best time. The tax question is, does the $10,000 clock help Dennis produce more income? If he is ever audited, Dennis could argue that the clock

is ordinary and necessary because it conveys the impression to his clients that he is successful. Will Dennis get this by an auditor? In similar cases, the courts have upheld the right of professionals to take this kind of deduction—but it's a close call.

Tax Shelter Investments and the IRS

Higher-income people, meaning six-figure or higher earners, are often targets for tax shelter promoters. These deals promise great tax benefits by using paper losses and deductions to lower taxable income. Don't get me wrong, this can be perfectly legitimate. For example, the depreciation write-off for a rental real estate property you own can be a great tax shelter. If the property you rent out produces a paper or tax loss, you might be able to legitimately use that loss to offset other income—however, there are complex restrictions on deducting such passive losses.

The IRS now scrutinizes these investments to make sure their underlying purpose is not to avoid paying taxes. To pass muster, the investment program "must possess a reasonable possibility of profits beyond the tax benefits." Or, as other courts have put it, "the transaction must be entered into for a business purpose other than tax avoidance."

If the deal doesn't pass scrutiny, it is termed an "abusive tax shelter" and any tax benefits will be disallowed, with penalties and interest tacked on. As with most things in life, if it sounds too good to be true .... Should you be tempted, run the deal by a CPA or tax attorney before you decide to try it.

 CAUTION

Creativity has its limits. In the example above, Dennis would have gone too far if he had:

- bought the antique clock and put it in his bedroom, or
- bought the clock for $1,000, added a zero to the receipt and claimed a $10,000 deduction.

In these examples, the deduction would no longer be gray, but black—it would be fraud. Where creativity ends and fraud begins is covered in Chapter 10.

TIP

Beware of joint filing. Never sign a joint tax return if you know your spouse is cheating the IRS. Your separate income and assets may be fair game if the IRS discovers the fraud. (See Chapter 9, "Filing Tax Returns—Joint or Separate?")

Chapter Highlights

- Not filing a tax return can be a crime if you owe taxes; most nonfilers, however, are not prosecuted if and when they are caught.
- If the IRS asks you if you filed returns and you haven't, don't lie, but don't answer. State that you want to consult a tax professional or check your records first.
- Filing before the IRS catches you is the safest policy.
- The time limit for criminally prosecuting a nonfiler is six years. The time limit for collecting from a nonfiler is 10 years, but the clock doesn't start until you actually file a tax return or the IRS prepares a Substitute For Return (SFR) (see "When the IRS Prepares Your Tax Return for You," above).
- Penalties and interest for late filing are substantial and rarely forgiven.
- Don't file a tax return while you are being audited. It gives the auditor another year to look at it.

Winning Your Audit

How Long Do I Have to Worry About an Audit?...52

What to Expect at an Audit 54

Do I Have to Learn Tax Law to Win My Audit?...55

Audit Selection—Why Me? 56

    Computers and Classifiers—What's the Difference? 56

    Unreported Income DIF Programs...57

    Local IRS Makes Final Decision...58

    The IRS Looks at Significant Items...58

    Living Beyond Your Means 60

    Market Segment Specialization Program 63

    Other Reasons for Audits...63

When the IRS Increases Your Tax Bill Without an Audit 67

    Dealing With IRS Automated Adjustment Notices 77

    Be Patient If You Don't Hear From the IRS Immediately................................78

Types of IRS Audits..79

    Correspondence Audits—Please, Mr. Postman 79

    Office Audits—Heigh-Ho, Heigh-Ho, It's Off to the IRS We Go 80

    Field Audits—Look Out, Here Comes the IRS...89

How a Field Auditor Approaches an Examination 96

Preparing for an Audit 100

    Your Audit Goals.. 102

    What Not to Bring to an Audit 103

Who Should Attend the Audit?.. 103

How to Act at an Audit 104

Mum's the Word 104

Don't Offer Any Favors to the Auditor 105

Try to Get Along With the Auditor 105

When a New Auditor Appears on the Scene 107

Standing Up to the Auditor 110

Negotiating With an Auditor 115

Ending the Audit 116

IRS Pressure on an Auditor to Finish—Extending the Audit
    Time Limit 117

Finishing Audits 118

Receiving the Examination Report 119

Understanding the Examination Report 125

Your Options After Getting the Examination Report 125

Serious Audit Problems 129

The Auditor Suspects You of Fraud 129

You're Billed for an Audit You Didn't Know About 129

Jeopardy Assessments 131

We call them audits; the IRS prefers examinations. Whatever term you use, it describes one of life's most dreaded experiences—having the IRS probing into your financial affairs.

This chapter deals with the types of IRS audits—both correspondence and face-to-face—that individuals and small business owners are most likely to face. The IRS also has a Large Business and International Division for auditing businesses with assets over $5 million, as well as a Tax-Exempt and Government Entities Division.

The IRS accepts the vast majority of individual and small business tax returns without question. Your chance of being contacted by the IRS about a discrepancy on your return in any one year is less than 1 in 200. But if you are self-employed, your audit chances are as much as five times greater than average.

As your income increases, so does your audit likelihood. And when your time does come, expect it to cost you—over 8 out of 10 people who are audited owe additional taxes. A few people get tax refunds after an audit, but don't count on it. The amount of money the IRS assesses in audits is 32 times greater than the amount given back.

IRS Audit Rates

Due to the COVID-19 pandemic and budget cutbacks, IRS audit rates declined to record lows in recent years. Today, an American's overall chances of being audited are 1 in 200.

However, the agency is planning to ramp up audit activity. Congress has given the IRS an additional $61 billion in funding to spend over the next decade, enabling it to add thousands of new employees and significantly upgrade its operations. The IRS plans to hire thousands of new revenue agents over the next several years so it can increase audits and other enforcement and collection activities. It will focus on larger businesses and high-income individuals (those making over $400,000 per year). One of the IRS's goals is to increase audits of taxpayers earning $1 million or more by tenfold.

Federal courts have long held that if the IRS determines at an audit that you owe taxes, there is a rebuttable presumption that the determination is correct. This means that you have the burden of proof when up against the IRS. Critics have said that it really means you're guilty until proven innocent. While this is the standard in audits, it is not the standard in court proceedings where the IRS has the burden of proof. If you take the IRS to court, the government must show that you were wrong on a disputed factual issue, not vice versa. (See Chapter 5.)

How Long Do I Have to Worry About an Audit?

Generally, your tax return can't be audited after three years from its original *filing* date. If you filed before the due date, April 15, the three years starts running from April 15 of the year it was due.

This general rule has a few exceptions, however:

- If you understate your income by 25% or more on your tax return, the audit deadline is extended to *six* years.
- If you file a fraudulent return, there is no time limit on an audit. Tax fraud is conduct meant to deceive the IRS, such as using a false Social Security number. A really big mistake, if done negligently, not intentionally, isn't fraud. The burden of proving fraud is always on the IRS. And the IRS seldom audits returns after three years even if fraud is suspected.
- The audit time limit period, called a "statute of limitations," starts to run *only* if and when you file a tax return. Nonfiled tax years are always open to audit. If, however, you haven't filed and haven't heard from the IRS within six years of the due date of a tax return, you have probably escaped the audit net.

TIP

Audit notices are usually mailed between 12 and 18 months after you file your return. Generally, if you haven't heard from the IRS within 18 months, you won't be audited. IRS audit notices are sent by first class mail and never by email or telephone contact.

The *Internal Revenue Manual* directs auditors to complete audits within 28 months after you file your tax return. Legally, the IRS has 36 months. The 28-month internal deadline is imposed, however, to allow 8 additional months for the IRS to process any appeal you might request. (Appeals are covered in Chapters 4 and 5.)

These internal IRS time limits usually work to your benefit. Audit cases are often delayed within the IRS for various reasons—backlogs, agent transfers, postponements, complex issues, and lost files. The older your file gets, the more anxious the IRS is to close it. Auditors can be fired for missing the 36-month deadline, known as blowing the statute, but it still happens.

The Audit Burden Is on You, Not the IRS

An audit is the process by which the IRS determines whether you properly reported all income—from earnings and investments—and took the correct deductions, exemptions, and credits. If the IRS finds that you didn't, you will be assessed additional taxes, interest, and—usually—penalties. An assessment is the formal entry of a tax liability in your records.

To do its job, Congress has given the IRS wide powers to inspect your financial records and to ask you and others about your financial affairs, to determine whether you're cheating Uncle Sam. (I.R.C. §§ 7601 and 7602.) The IRS will investigate the items listed on an audit notice checklist given to you and scrutinize any other areas deemed questionable. And the law specifically places the audit burden on you to demonstrate that the information shown on your tax return is correct—think of the IRS as the Show Me state of Missouri. If your dispute gets to court, however, the burden shifts to the IRS under certain conditions (see Chapter 5).

Proving the correctness of your tax return might not be that easy. The IRS wins over 80% of all audits, mostly because taxpayers can't properly verify the information on their tax returns. IRS auditors say that the biggest reason for adjustments is poor record keeping, not taxpayer dishonesty.

Stopping an audit once it begins. Once the IRS sends an examination notice to your last known address, the audit has begun. It's difficult to stop an audit. Even if you die, your spouse or the executor of your estate is obligated to carry on the audit.

You might be able to slow down—or even stop—an audit, however, if you ask for a transfer of your file to another IRS district. Audit transfers are discretionary with the IRS, and you need a good reason to get one—such as a location more convenient to that of your tax documents.

> EXAMPLE: Janiel, who lived in Pennsylvania but had a jewelry business in New York, received an audit notice for Pennsylvania. She requested a transfer to where her business was located. Janiel told the IRS that her records were at the business location in New York, which was true. The transfer was granted, but the New York office's audit plate was already full and the office never got around to Janiel's audit. The three-year statute of limitations expired and Janiel's worries came to an end.

What to Expect at an Audit

Will the auditor discover the money I made from playing the organ at weddings?

I lost my records in a move last year—what am I going to do?

Was I entitled to claim my mother as an exemption?

Will the IRS question my home office deductions?

Is the IRS going to put me in jail if they find out I've been cheating?

These are common taxpayer concerns. So, let's look at what really goes on when the IRS decides to audit you. We'll look at the two primary issues in every audit:

- Did you report all income?
- Were you entitled to the deductions, exemptions, and credits claimed?

IRS Publication 17, *Your Federal Income Tax*, explains the audit process—from the IRS point of view.

Do I Have to Learn Tax Law to Win My Audit?

The Internal Revenue Code, or tax code, contains 4,000-plus pages of very fine print. Add to that IRS regulations, revenue rulings, letter rulings, manuals, and official publications, all of which add another 100,000 or so pages of tax law. Finally, there are thousands of court decisions telling us how the tax laws should be applied in individual cases. The total number of tax law pages exceeds one million!

How will I ever understand the tax laws?

You won't. But that might not be as much of a disadvantage as you might think. Tax law is so voluminous and complex, most IRS auditors don't know it well either. Moreover, the training and experience level of IRS personnel is declining while the law is getting more difficult to master. This means that auditors normally stick to predictable audit issues. A taxpayer with very high income or an intricate tax issue, however, might be assigned an auditor with more training and experience. But normally, if you are well prepared, you'll come out okay—experiencing the minimum damage—most of the time.

In a few hours, you can learn the basic tax law for your particular audit issues. The information is in this book and other sources mentioned in Chapter 13. And you can—and probably should—consult with a tax professional before taking on the auditor.

The truth is that most people succeed in an audit without knowing any tax law at all. This is because many audit issues are factual, not legal. The distinction will become clear as you read this chapter. And it's as important to know IRS procedures—the rules of the game and your rights in dealing with the IRS—as tax law. This book explains the rules to follow and a psychology for dealing with the IRS as well.

 CAUTION

Getting a tax refund does not mean that your tax return won't be audited. Typically it takes 18 months after filing for the IRS to pick its audit victims. You might be audited or have to give any refund money you received back later—and then some.

Audit Selection—Why Me?

You just got an examination notice from the IRS. Are you merely unlucky, or are there more sinister forces at work?

Computers and Classifiers—What's the Difference?

The IRS computer is to blame for most audits. Each year, your tax return data is sent to the IRS National Computer Center where it is analyzed by a computer program called the "Discriminant Function." Your tax return is given a numerical DIF score—the higher the score, the more audit potential the return has.

Are You Claiming More Deductions Than the Norm?

One of the chief components of the IRS DIF scoring system is how close your tax return is to the norm of others with similar deductions. According to author and statistician Amir Aczel (*How to Beat the IRS at Its Own Game*, Four Walls Eight Windows Press), the IRS is most likely to audit you if your return shows a high ratio of deductions to income on three schedules:

- Schedule A, *Itemized Deductions*
- Schedule C, *Profit and Loss From Business*, or
- Schedule F, *Profit and Loss From Farming*.

Aczel claims that, as a rule, as your deductions approach 50% of your income, your audit likelihood rises. He lists precise ratios based on a study of 1,200 audit cases. For example, he claims that taxpayers filing a Schedule C are rarely audited if they claim expenses of less than 52% of gross business income, but are often audited when claiming expenses of more than 63%. If you include a Schedule A with your tax return, Aczel claims you're safe from an audit if your deductions are less than 44% of your gross income. While his book is interesting, don't use it as a manual to avoid a tax audit. If you're entitled to a deduction, it makes sense to take it, no matter what the chances of audit are.

The DIF program is super secret—few people even in the IRS know how it works or why a return is given a particular score. Outsiders guess that hundreds of variables on a return are weighed by the IRS computer. One known variable is called "total positive income," which means everything you took in from your services and investments, before any deductions or exemptions. If this number is over $200,000, your chances of an audit triple (roughly). The key variable is most likely the percentage of your deductions compared to the national averages for your income bracket. For example, in a recent year, the average charitable deduction for taxpayers in the $50,000 to $100,000 income range was $2,881. So, if you're in that bracket and claim $21,555, don't be surprised to hear from the IRS.

Unreported Income DIF Programs

The IRS has a second computer scoring program to catch people not reporting all of their income. This approach is slightly different from the DIF program, which relies heavily on deductions and exemptions claimed. This program is called the "Unreported Income Discriminant Information Function" (UIDIF). It scores individuals based on a high-expense/low-income ratio. In plain English, the tax man is looking for folks who look like they are living beyond their means. For instance, you and your spouse report income from your jobs of $40,000 and you claim mortgage interest and real estate taxes of $35,000. Even assuming that you didn't owe any taxes that year, it would be tough to live on $5,000—so the IRS believes. Of course, some people have down income years and simply borrow or dip into savings to get by. These explanations can always be made to an auditor, if necessary.

One in ten tax returns—those with the highest computer scores—are initially selected for further review. IRS classifiers (human beings) then pass this batch down the line.

Local IRS Makes Final Decision

The final say-so on who gets audited face-to-face is made at local IRS offices. Examination group managers supervise and assign the auditors, often according to their experience and expertise. Managers decide whether you will be audited at the IRS office or will get the more rigorous field audit.

IRS field offices have their own audit-screening selection process which takes into account income and expense levels in their communities—for instance, people are more likely to claim car expenses for business in Los Angeles than Manhattan. Group managers select less than 10% of the returns received from the IRS classifiers—the 10% of all tax returns—to be audited. The net result is that in a recent year, only 0.5% of all returns were actually audited.

The IRS Looks at Significant Items

According to the IRS Manual, only *significant items* should be examined. What is considered significant depends on the IRS's overall view of the return as well as particular items that seem questionable. Factors that are likely to figure into the audit selection process include:

- **Comparative size of an item to the rest of the return.** A $5,000 expense on a tax return reporting $25,000 in income would be significant; the same expense on a return reporting $100,000 in income wouldn't be.
- **An item on the return that is out of character for the taxpayer.** A plumber claiming expenses relating to a business airplane would cause suspicion.
- **An item that is reported at an inappropriate place on the return.** For example, $2,000 of credit card interest is reported as a business expense. The IRS might suspect that you improperly deducted personal interest as a business expense.
- **Evidence of intent to mislead on the return.** Filing a tax return with missing schedules or not providing all information asked for on the forms raises an IRS classifier's eyebrows.
- **Your gross income.** The IRS scrutinizes higher earners. If you make over $100,000 per year, your audit likelihood is greater than the likelihood for the general population.

- **Self-employment income.** The IRS is most suspicious of people in business for themselves. Depending on their income, sole proprietors are up to five times more likely to be audited than wage earners.
- **Losses from businesses and investments claimed on the tax return.** If your business and investments show losses on your tax return, the IRS might want to know how you paid your bills. Most likely to be audited are taxpayers reporting small business losses.
- **Foreign accounts.** Taxpayers who hold money or other assets in foreign bank or other financial accounts must say so on IRS Schedule B. They must also file IRS Form 8938 with their return if the total value of the assets exceeded $50,000 on the last day of the year, or $75,000 any time during the year. Filing the form increases audit chances. Not filing the form also increases audit chances because the IRS requires overseas banks to identify American asset holders.
- **Digital assets.** Digital assets such as Bitcoin (also called "cryptocurrency") are the IRS's newest bugaboo. In 2019, the IRS sent 10,000 letters to taxpayers it suspected of failing to report income from Bitcoin transactions. IRS Form 1040 now asks whether the taxpayer received, sold, exchanged, or otherwise disposed of a digital asset such as Bitcoin during the year. A "yes" answer likely increases audit chances.
- **COVID-19 pandemic tax credits.** The millions of businesses that received COVID-19–related tax credits, including the Employee Retention Credit (ERC) and COVID-19 sick and family leave credits, can expect increased scrutiny from the IRS. The normal three-year statute of limitations on IRS enforcement actions doesn't apply to the ERC. Instead, the IRS has five years from the date the credit was paid to seek repayment of erroneously claimed credits.
- **Sloppiness and round numbers.** A messy return, especially if handwritten, attracts the attention of a classifier who might think you don't take your tax-reporting responsibilities very seriously. Use of round numbers—for example, $5,000 for business advertising, $2,000 for transportation and $1,500 for insurance—is a dead giveaway that you are estimating, not reporting from records.

TIP

Why me? Although you might never know for certain why the IRS zeroed in on you, try to figure it out before the audit date. If you know what the IRS suspects, you can better prepare—or get professional help early on. An experienced tax professional can spot probable audit issues in a tax return or from discussing your situation with you.

Living Beyond Your Means

The IRS targets some people for financial status audits. These are special techniques to detect unreported income, including the UIDIF computer scoring program described above in "Computers and Classifiers—What's the Difference?" The IRS looks at whether the income on the tax return supports the financial condition of the taxpayer. The IRS is looking for "economic reality" by approximating expenses for personal assets and living expenses. You might have to explain how you eat at the Ritz on a fast-food salary.

The IRS can't randomly conduct financial status audits. Financial status audits aren't to take place unless the IRS sees a "reasonable indication" of a likelihood of unreported income—a fairly vague limitation. (I.R.C. § 7602.)

How the IRS Investigates Your Lifestyle

You can understand the IRS's focus on lifestyle audits by looking at the IRS training materials for auditors. They look at the following lifestyle-related issues.

The standard of living of a taxpayer:
- What does the taxpayer and dependent family consume?
- How much does it cost to maintain this consumption?
- Is reported net income sufficient to support this?

The accumulated wealth of a taxpayer:
- How much capital/assets has the taxpayer accumulated?
- When and how has this wealth accumulated?
- Has reported income been sufficient to pay for these items?
- If not, how did taxpayer obtain and repay credit?

The economic history of a taxpayer:

- What is the long-term pattern of profits and return on investment in the reported activity?
- Is the business expanding or contracting?
- Does the reported business history match with changes in the taxpayer's standard of living and wealth accumulation?

The business environment:

- What is typical profitability and return on investment for the taxpayer's industry and locality?
- What are the typical patterns of noncompliance in the taxpayer's industry?
- What are the competitive pressures and economic health of the industry within which the taxpayer operates?

Other nontaxable sources of funds:

- Do claims of nontaxable sources of support make economic sense?
- How creditworthy is the taxpayer—how many claimed loans?
- How did the sources of claimed fund transfers obtain those funds? For example, it is unlikely that subsidies will be obtained from countries where dollars are hard to obtain.

Goal: Do the taxpayer's books and records reflect the economic reality of the taxpayer's personal and business activities, or has the taxpayer omitted income in order to minimize tax liability?

Lifestyle Questions and Suggested Answers

The following sample questions are taken from IRS training materials. The suggested answers are strictly legal. Note that we never use the word no, but we don't give the IRS what it's fishing for, either. Unless otherwise noted, the auditor's questions should relate to the year or years you are being audited for, not the year the audit takes place.

1Q. (*If applicable*) Can you show me a copy of your tax return extension for the past year?

1A. "I don't see how that is related to the year under audit." (It's not.)

2Q. What is the educational background of you and your spouse?

2A. "I don't see how that is related to the year under audit."

3Q. What is the name of your previous employer and dates of employment?

3A. "I don't see how that is related to the year under audit."

4Q. Can I see the purchase documents on your home?

4A. Show only if you are claiming a casualty loss for your home, you sold it, or you are claiming a home office deduction.

5Q. What other real estate do you own?

5A. Show only if you are earning income from renting it or taking a depreciation deduction or another tax benefit from the ownership.

6Q. How many autos do you own, and what are the payments?

6A. If your cars are registered in the state of the audit, you might as well give in on this one as the auditor can easily check state records. Ditto with boats and planes.

7Q. Do you own any other large (over $10,000) assets?

7A. "I don't see how …."

8Q. Did you sell any assets, and if so, for how much and to whom?

8A. Answer this only if you sold an asset, such as shares of stock, on which you claimed a gain or loss; if there is a question about whether you reported enough income on your tax return to live on; or if the auditor asks the source of money deposited in your bank account. Otherwise, "I don't see how …."

9Q. Did you lend anyone money?

9A. (Unless you had interest income from the loan for that year) "I don't see how …."

10Q. How much cash do you have on hand at your home or business, in a safety deposit box, or buried in the backyard?

10A. "I don't see …." (As a rule, never answer this question.)

11Q. Did you transfer funds between different accounts?

11A. Answer only if the auditor is questioning the source of deposits into your accounts. Otherwise, "I don't see …."

12Q. Were you involved in cash transactions exceeding $10,000?

12A. This is a tricky one. If you say yes, then you might have had an obligation to file a Currency Transaction Report with the IRS. If you didn't make this filing, you just confessed to a crime. If you say no, it had better be the truth, or you just broke an even more serious law. Stay quiet or ask a tax lawyer how to answer if you are in doubt.

As the above hypothetical questions and answers indicate, try to answer economic reality questions with questions of your own, or don't answer them at all. Politely remind the auditor that the questions don't relate to the tax return, that you were merely selected for an audit, and that you shouldn't be treated like a criminal. Suggest that if the auditor wants to make an adjustment based on economic reality, you'll appeal. More likely than not, the auditor won't call your bluff.

Market Segment Specialization Program

The Market Segment Specialization Program, or MSSP, is a cornerstone of the IRS process. The MSSP focuses on specific industries or groups of taxpayers believed to be in significant noncompliance with the tax law. Accordingly, the IRS provides specialized training to its agents and issues *Audit Technique Guides* for its auditors.

- The IRS has made these guides public; if you fall into one of the targeted categories, you will know what the IRS is after. So far, over 100 guides have been issued on topics from architects to veterinarians. You can download them all from the IRS website, at www.irs.gov/businesses/small-businesses-self-employed/audit-techniques-guides-atgs (or search "Audit Technique Guide" at the IRS website).

Other Reasons for Audits

Besides getting picked by the IRS computer, other ways you can get into the audit soup are described below.

Local projects. Local IRS offices can initiate special audit projects based on their perceptions of abuses by individuals and groups in the community. Recent projects include gamblers, people who claim excessive earned income credits, ex-spouses who deduct or receive alimony, and people whose mortgage loan applications show different incomes from those reported on their tax returns.

Compliance initiative projects. Every year, the IRS national office decides that certain businesses and occupations merit audit attention. Past favorites have included airline pilots and flight attendants, physicians, and morticians. Perennial targets are operators of cash businesses, such as bars and laundromats, food servers, and owners and employees of gambling establishments.

Can You Get Audited If You Don't File a Return?

Don't think that because you didn't file a return that you'll escape the IRS audit telescope. If you're in the IRS's computer, the IRS will eventually request that you file—if the IRS can find you. If you ignore them, the IRS has the legal authority to file and, in effect, audit a tax return in your name. The *Internal Revenue Manual* directs the auditor to come up with a reasonable and substantially correct tax return—which gives the auditor a license for invention.

In addition to whatever information might be in the IRS records—typically income reports on W-2 and 1099 forms—the auditor may rely on tables from the Bureau of Labor Statistics (BLS) to estimate your income and expenses. This is often done when either the income sources on record show an impossibly small income, such as $4,000, when you live in a penthouse apartment in the Beacon Hill section of Boston, or when there is no income record at all. BLS data shows the government's estimate of the minimum amount of income necessary to live on, taking into account your geographic area, family size, and probable standard of living.

To approximate income from a business, the auditor may rely on industry standards. For example, the auditor may use averages for sales and profit margin on all U.S. auto parts retailers to estimate how much Simon's Auto Parts World made.

After the auditor's report of a nonfiled return is completed, the IRS will forward you a copy. If you agree with the figures, you can sign it. If you don't agree, you will be given an opportunity to dispute it with your own figures or to file a tax return. Or, the IRS will issue a Notice of Deficiency giving you 90 days to contest the IRS report in Tax Court. (See Chapter 5 for more on going to Tax Court.)

The IRS receives several clues to your occupation. W-2 and 1099 forms filed by others might indicate it. You are required to state it on your tax return. If you are self-employed, you must list a six-digit business identification code. Some people have tried creativity here, such as the prostitute whose return stated "public relations." She was fined by the IRS and could have been criminally prosecuted when the auditor learned the exact nature of those relations. Misstating the source of your income is illegal, even if you report all of it.

Prior and related audits. Audit lightning does strike twice. Previous IRS audits often beget new ones—if they produced tax bills of at least several thousand dollars. But this is not a sure thing. Some people who are audited and hit with an enormous tax bill never hear from the IRS again. If you are a partner, limited liability company member, or shareholder, and the business entity or any others in it are audited, you might not be far behind.

Criminal activity. Like grapes, trouble usually comes in bunches. If you are investigated for a drug crime or crime involving a lot of money, the IRS might be tipped off by the law enforcement agency and decide to audit. The tax code is morally neutral—it requires that all income, from sources legal or otherwise, be reported. The IRS doesn't care if you made the money as a Mafia hit man as long as you declare it.

If you'd prefer not to disclose the source of income, you can file a Fifth Amendment tax return on which you claim your constitutional right against self-incrimination. You enter the amount of your income on your 1040 form and write Fifth Amendment next to the lines where you list the source and where the form asks for your occupation. While this might keep you out of the Criminal Investigation Division of the IRS, it undoubtedly increases your audit potential.

CAUTION
Never file a Fifth Amendment tax return without first consulting a tax attorney.

Amended tax returns. You may file an amended tax return any time after you file an original one. The IRS has discretion to reject amended returns, but it usually accepts them. A few people file amended returns and wind up owing more in taxes, but most people amend their tax returns to get a refund. To get a refund, you must file the amended return within three years of the date you filed the original return, or within two years of the date you paid the tax. Because the IRS doesn't like to give back money, it investigates all refund claims, sometimes by auditing. And if you are audited, everything on the return—not just the items amended—are fair game.

Filing an amended tax return doesn't extend the time the IRS has to audit you—normally three years from the original filing date. So, the closer to the end of the three-year period you file the amended return, the less time the IRS has to audit you. But, the IRS has the discretion to reject amended returns and sometimes will accept them only on the condition the taxpayer agrees to extend the three-year audit limit.

Informants' tips. Undoubtedly, you have heard stories about disgruntled ex-spouses, business associates, and former employees turning someone in to the IRS. While an audit could result, it should put your mind at ease to know that fewer than 5% of all audits result from tattletales. IRS sources say that most tips, particularly anonymous ones, are not seriously followed up. The IRS prefers to rely on its computers for audit selection. Historically, the IRS has found that many tips are not provable and are motivated by spite.

Where you live. Everyone knows that Kansas gets tornadoes, Florida gets hurricanes, and California gets earthquakes. Similarly, some locales get more than their fair share of audits. The audit rate is 150% higher than the national average in Nevada, but 150% lower than that average in Wisconsin. Other high-audit states are Alaska, California, and Colorado. Low-audit states include Illinois, Indiana, Iowa, Maryland, Massachusetts, Michigan, New York (excluding Manhattan), Ohio, Pennsylvania, and West Virginia. The second-lowest audit rate locale is the District of Columbia.

What's more, how you come out of an audit depends on where you call home, too. Your chance of getting away without owing a nickel are more than twice as good in Las Vegas (32%) than in Manhattan (15%).

Random selection. The IRS selects some audit victims at random under its National Research Program (NRP). These Compliance Research Exams are reminiscent of the dreaded TCMP (Taxpayer Compliance Measurement Program) audits that were discontinued in the 1990s. The stated purpose of

NRP audits is to gather data to update the statistical models used to score individual tax returns. Nevertheless, these are very "real" audits—in fact, they are much more intensive than ordinary audits. You can be chosen at random for an NRP audit even if you have an impeccable history of tax compliance. And no one will reimburse you for the time and effort required to deal with the audit.

Frivolous tax return. Claiming that your income is not subject to federal taxes is a surefire way to get on the audit list.

Political selection. It is a crime for a non-IRS employee to request that the IRS conduct or terminate an audit of a taxpayer. An IRS employee must report such a request to his superiors. (I.R.C. § 7217.)

When the IRS Increases Your Tax Bill Without an Audit

The IRS increasingly relies on computer-generated tax bills that are technically not audits. This means your tax return still could be examined in the future.

The IRS is authorized to make changes to your tax account without a formal audit in some cases. (I.R.C. § 6213(g)(2).) The IRS has programs (described below) that often exceed Congressional intent of the law, which was to let the IRS correct minor taxpayer errors. Instead, the IRS effectively performs one-sided mail audits. Many poor souls pay up without question when they receive one of these:

- **Correction notices.** The IRS says there is a math error or a similar obvious problem with your tax return. For instance, you claimed four dependents but only listed the names of three on your return. The IRS corrects your return—and bills you.

- **Penalty assessment notices.** Typically, a penalty notice and bill will be sent if you didn't meet a filing or payment deadline. The IRS might be wrong for any number of reasons, or it might be right but you might have a reason to have the penalty abated, or canceled. Chapter 12 has information on dealing with a penalty notice.

- **Interest assessment notices.** If you did not pay a tax bill on time, you will always be charged interest. Sometimes, the IRS computation of interest is incorrect; occasionally, you can get it waived even if it is correct. Again, see Chapter 12.

- **Underreporter program notices.** The IRS initiates an underreporter case when its computer finds a discrepancy between two data sources. Usually, the two sources are your tax return and information reported to the IRS on a 1099 or W-2 form. You'll get either a CP-2501 notice— a letter asking you to explain (CP means computer paragraph)—or a CP-2000 notice proposing additional tax, penalties, and interest. In either case, you'll be given 30 days to respond. According to the IRS, the most common underreporter issues are:
  - IRA distributions rolled over but not properly reported (Form 1099-R)
  - income reported on the return that does not match IRS data on a Form 1099 or Form K-1
  - mortgage interest deductions that don't match the financial institution's report to the IRS (Form 1098), and
  - wages and/or tax withholding that doesn't match W-2 forms.

Underreporting notices are the most common of the four programs.

Beware IRS Scam Phone Calls and Emails

Recently, taxpayers have been receiving false email notices, texts, and telephone calls claiming they are from the IRS. The fake email, text, and phone call scams demand payment for a phony tax bill. The IRS never initiates contact with taxpayers via email or text, and will never call someone who does not owe a legitimate tax bill. Before you hear from the IRS by phone, you will have already received a bill in writing. If you get a scam call, text, or email, hang up on the caller or delete the email or text notice.

Sample CP-2000 Notice—Page 1

Department of the Treasury
Internal Revenue Service
PO Box 16335
Philadelphia, PA 19114-0439

Notice	CP2000
Tax Year	2010
Notice date	January 23, 2017
Social Security number	999-99-9999
AUR control number	99999-9999
To contact us	Phone 1-800-829-8310
	Fax 1-215-516-2335

s018999546711s

JAMES & KAREN Q. HINDS
22 BOULDER STREET
HANSON, CT 00000-7253

AUR Bar Code

Proposed changes to your 2010 Form 1040

Amount due: $2,349.00

The information you provided in your December 10, 2016 request for removal or reduction of penalties associated with your 2010 Form 1040 did not meet our guidelines. As a result, we are not removing or reducing any penalties, and the total amount you owe for tax due, including penalties and interest, is $2,349.00.

Billing Summary

Tax you owe	$2,519.00
Payments and credits	-410.00
Negligence penalty	60.00
Interest charges	180.00
Amount due by February 22, 2017	**$2,349.00**

What you need to do immediately

Review this notice, and compare our changes to the information on your 2010 tax return.

If you agree with the changes we made

- Complete, sign and date the Response form on Page 5, and mail it to us along with your payment of $2,349.00 so we receive it by February 22, 2017.
- If you can't pay the amount due, pay as much as you can now, and make payment arrangements that allow you to pay off the rest over time. If you want to apply for an installment plan, send in your Response form AND a completed Installment Agreement Request (Form 9465). Download Form 9465 from www.irs.gov, or call 1-800-829-3676 to request a copy. You can also save time and money by applying online if you qualify. Visit www.irs.gov. and search for keyword: "tax payment options" for more information about:
  - Installment and payment agreements
  - Payroll deductions
  - Credit card payments
  Or, call us at 1-800-829-8310 to discuss your options.

If you don't agree with the changes

- Complete the Response form on Page 5, and send it to us along with a signed statement and any documentation that supports your claim so we receive it by February 22, 2017.

If we don't hear from you

If we don't receive your response by February 22, 2017, we will send you a Statutory Notice of Deficiency followed by a final bill for the proposed amount due. During this time, interest will increase and penalties may apply.

Sample CP-2000 Notice—Page 2

Notice	CP2000
Tax Year	2010
Notice date	January 23, 2017
Social Security number	999-99-9999

Changes to your 2010 tax return

Your income and deductions	Shown on return	As corrected by IRS	Difference
Wages	$18,000	$30,075	$12,075
Other income	0	592	592
Nonemployee compensation	0	1,875	1,875
Income net difference			**$14,542**
Miscellaneous deductions	12,000	11,709	291
Self-employment tax deduction	0	-132	-132
Deduction net difference			**159**
Change to taxable income			**$14,701**

Your tax computations	Shown on return	As corrected by IRS	Difference
Taxable income, line 43	$32,000	$46,701	$14,701
Tax, line 44	4,000	6,254	2,254
Self-employment tax, line 58	0	265	265
Total tax, line 63	**$4,000**	**$6,519**	**$2,519**

Your payments and credits	Shown on return	As corrected by IRS	Difference
Income tax withheld, line 64	$8,745	$9,155	-$410
Total payments and credits			**-$410**

Explanation of changes to your 2010 Form 1040

This section tells you specifically what income information the IRS received about you from others (including your employers, banks, mortgage holders, etc.). This information doesn't match the information you reported on your tax return.

Use the table to compare the data the IRS received from others to the information you reported on your tax return to understand where the difference(s) occurred. To assist you in reviewing your income amounts, the table may include both reported and unreported amounts.

Tax withheld

Received from	Address	Account information	Shown on return	Reported to IRS by others	Difference
Employer A	20 Clinton Street Hanson, CT 99999	SSN 999-99-9999 Form W-2	$8,745	$9,155	$410

Wages

Received from	Address	Account information	Shown on return	Reported to IRS by others	Difference
Employer A	20 Clinton Street Hanson, CT 99999	SSN 999-99-9999 Form W-2	$18,000	$30,075	$12,075

Nonemployee compensation

Received from	Address	Account information	Shown on return	Reported to IRS by others	Difference
Payer & Partners	80 Fleming Hill Chambers, CT 00000	SSN 999-99-9999 Form 1099-MISC	$0	$1,875	$1,875

Sample CP-2000 Notice—Page 3

Notice	CP2000
Tax Year	2010
Notice date	January 23, 2017
Social Security number	999-99-9999

Explanation of changes to your 2010 Form
1040—**continued**

Other income

Received from	Address	Account information	Shown on return	Reported to IRS by others	Difference
Payer Casino	25 Lubbock Hill, Suite 25A Chambers, CT 00000	SSN 999-99-9999 Form W-2G	$0	$592	$592

Misidentified income

If any of the income shown on this notice is not yours, send us the name, address, and social security number of the person who received the income. Please notify the payers to correct their records to show the name and social security number of the person who actually received the income, so that future reports to us are accurate.

Form W-2 or 1099 not received

The law requires you to report your income correctly. If your payers did not send you a yearly income statement (Form W-2, Form 1099, etc.), you must use the information you have (pay stubs, monthly income statements, deposit slips, etc.) to estimate the total amount of income you received during the year.

Schedule A miscellaneous deductions percentage limitation

Miscellaneous deductions are reduced by 2% of your adjusted gross income (Form 1040, line 37). Since we refigured your adjusted gross income, we also refigured your miscellaneous deduction.

Self-employment tax on self-employment (SE) income

Self-Employment (SE) generally includes nonemployee compensation and other income from part-time or full-time work and is subject to Self-Employment Tax. We figured the Self-Employment Tax on the net SE income reported on your return and/or on the underreported SE income. Self-Employment Tax consists of Social Security Tax of 12.4% and Medicare Tax of 2.9%. (Even if you have paid the maximum amount of Social Security Tax, you are still liable for additional Medicare Tax.) The deduction for one-half of the Self-Employment Tax is based on the change we made to your Self-Employment Tax. If you were an employee, you will be liable for income tax and the employee's share of Social Security (6.2%) and Medicare taxes (1.45%). Your social security account will be credited with the amount of Self-Employment income shown on this notice.

Overclaimed withholding

Our records indicate you are entitled to a lesser amount of withholding than the amount claimed on your tax return. Please send us a copy of Form(s) W-2, 1099, and/or over withholding documentation from the payer(s) to verify the additional withholding claimed on your tax return.

Sample CP-2000 Notice—Page 4

Notice	CP2000
Tax Year	2010
Notice date	January 23, 2017
Social Security number	999-99-9999

Next steps

- You don't need to file an amended tax return for 2010. We will make the correction when we receive your response. However, if you choose to file an amended tax return Form 1040X, write "CP2000" on the top of your amended federal tax return Form 1040X and attach it behind your completed Response form. Go to www.irs.gov to download Form 1040X or call 1-800-TAX-FORM (1-800-829-3676).
- Please file an amended tax return Form 1040X for any other tax years in which the same error occurred.
- We send information about these changes to state and local tax agencies, so if the changes we made apply, file an amended state or local tax return as soon as possible.

Penalties

We are required by law to charge any applicable penalties. We assess a 1/2% monthly penalty for not paying the tax you owe by the due date. We base the monthly penalty for paying late on the net unpaid tax at the beginning of each penalty month following the payment due date for that tax. This penalty applies even if you filed the return on time.

We charge the penalty for each month or part of a month the payment is late; however, the penalty can't be more than 25% in total.

• The due date for payment of the tax shown on a return generally is the return due date, without regard to extensions.

• The due date for paying increases in tax is within 21 days of the date of our notice demanding payment (10 business days if the amount in the notice is $100,000 or more).

If we issue a Notice of Intent to Levy and you don't pay the balance due within 10 days of the date of the notice, the penalty for paying late increases to 1% per month.

For individuals who filed on time, the penalty decreases to 1/4% per month while an approved installment agreement with the IRS is in effect for payment of that tax.

For a detailed computation of the penalty call 1-800-829-8310.

(Internal Revenue Code Section 6651)

Negligence

Description	Amount
Total negligence	$60.00

An accuracy-related penalty is charged if there is any underpayment of tax on your return due to negligence. This penalty is 20% of the net tax increase on the portion due to negligence. (Internal Revenue Code section 6662(c))

If you think we should not charge this penalty, please explain why, send any supporting documents, and request that we waive the penalty. We will review your request and determine if there is reasonable cause to waive the penalty.

Interest charges

We are required by law to charge interest when you do not pay your liability on time. Generally, we calculate interest from the due date of

Sample CP-2000 Notice—Page 5

Notice	CP2000
Tax Year	2010
Notice date	January 23, 2017
Social Security number	999-99-9999

your return (regardless of extensions) until you pay the amount you owe in full, including accrued interest and any penalty charges. Interest on some penalties accrues from the date we notify you of the penalty until it is paid in full. Interest on other penalties, such as failure to file a tax return, starts from the due date or extended due date of the return. Interest rates are variable and may change quarterly. (Internal Revenue Code Section 6601)

Description	Amount
Total interest	$180.00

The table below shows the rates used to calculate the interest on your unpaid amount due. For a detailed calculation of your interest, call 1-800-829-8310.

Period	Interest rate
July 1, 2006–December 31, 2007	8%
January 1, 2008–March 31, 2008	7%
April 1, 2008–June 30, 2008	6%
July 1, 2008–September 30, 2008	5%
October 1, 2008–December 31, 2008	6%
Beginning January 1, 2009	5%

Additional Information

- Visit www.irs.gov/cp2000. You can also find the following online: Amended U.S. Individual Tax Return (Form 1040X).
- For tax forms, instructions, and publications, visit www.irs.gov or call 1-800-TAX-FORM (1-800-829-3676).
- Review the enclosed document Publication 3498-A, The Examination Process.
- Keep this notice for your records.

If you need assistance, please don't hesitate to contact us.

Sample CP-2000 Notice—Page 6

Department of Treasury
Internal Revenue Service
PO BOX 16335
Philadelphia, PA 19114-0439

Notice	CP2000
Tax year	2010
Notice date	January 23, 2017
Social Security number	999-99-9999
AUR control number	99999-9999

[AUR BAR CODE]

INTERNAL REVENUE SERVICE
PO BOX 105404
ATLANTA, GA 30348-5404

Fold here

Response form

Complete both sides of this form, and send it to us in the enclosed envelope so we receive it by February 22, 2017. Be sure our address shows through the window.

To request more time to respond, call us at 1-800-829-8310. Remember: Additional interest will be charged during this period if the information in this notice is correct.

Provide your contact information
If your address has changed, please make the changes below.

James & Karen Q. Hinds
22 Boulder Street
Hanson, CT 00000-7253

☐ a.m.
☐ p.m.

☐ a.m.
☐ p.m.

Primary phone   Best time to call   Secondary phone   Best time to call

1. Indicate your agreement or disagreement

☐ **I agree with all changes**
I agree with the changes to my 2010 tax return, and understand that:

- I owe $2,349.00 in additional tax, payment adjustments, and interest.
- The IRS is required by law to charge interest on taxes that weren't paid in full by April 15, 2011.
- The IRS will continue to charge interest until I've paid the tax in full. Certain penalties may also apply.
- I can challenge these changes in the U.S. Tax Court only if the IRS determines after the date I sign this form that I owe additional taxes for 2010.
- I can file for a refund at a later date.

Please sign and return this form with your payment.

_____   _____
Signature   Date

_____   _____
Spouse's signature   Date

Sample CP-2000 Notice—Page 7

Notice	CP2000
Tax year	2010
Notice date	January 23, 2017
Social Security number	999-99-9999

Indicate your agreement or disagreement--Continued

☐ **I don't agree with some or all of the changes**

Please return this form and include a statement signed by you that explains what you don't agree with. Also include copies of any documents, such as corrected W-2, 1099, or missing forms that support your statement.

Note: You can fax documentation to 1-215-516-2335.

Signature	Date
Spouse's signature	Date

2. Indicate your payment option

I am enclosing (check all that apply):
- ☐ Full payment of $2,349.00
- ☐ Partial payment of $ ....
- ☐ No payment
- ☐ A completed Installment Agreement Request (Form 9465)
  - Write your Social Security number xxx-xx-xxx, the tax year 2010, and the notice number CP2000 on your payment and any correspondence.
  - Make your check or money order payable to the United States Treasury.

3. Authorization optional

If you would like to authorize someone, in addition to you, to contact the IRS concerning this notice, please include the person's information, your signature, and the date.

The authority granted is limited as indicated by the statement above the signature line. The contact may not sign returns, enter into agreements, or otherwise represent you before the IRS. If you want to have a designee with expanded authorization, see IRS Publication 947, Practice Before the IRS and Power of Attorney.

Full name of authorized person

Address

City	State	Country	Zip code

Primary phone	Best time to call ☐ a.m. ☐ p.m.	Secondary phone	Best time to call ☐ a.m. ☐ p.m.

I authorize the person listed above to discuss and provide information to the IRS about this notice.

Signature	Date
Spouse's signature	Date

Letter to Dispute an IRS Tax Adjustment

Married couples—
use the first
spouse's number on
your tax return

Hamilton and Jill O'Brien
SSN: 123-45-6789
123 Elm St.
Ukiah, CA 90000
June 16, 20xx

IRS ADJUSTMENTS/CORRESPONDENCE
IRS Campus
Fresno, CA 93888

Choose 1, 2, or 3
below followed by
your explanation.
If none fits your
situation, explain in
your own words.

REQUEST FOR ADJUSTMENT

Re: IRS Notice Dated 6/2/xx

To Whom It May Concern:

I am responding to your notice of 6/2/xx, a copy of which
is attached.

1. Math errors

The notice is incorrect. I did not make any math errors in
my tax return. Here is how I made the calculations:
$10,432 − $3,190 = $7,242.

2. Matching error
(CP-2000 notice)

The 1099 form filed by Apex Industries was wrong and the
company has prepared a letter stating the correct amount,
which is attached to this letter.

The W-2 form filed by my former employer is incorrect in
that I made $42,815 in 20xx, not $49,815.

3. Partially corrected
errors

I responded to your notice of 5/2/xx but you did not fully
correct your error. Enclosed is a copy of my letter of 5/9/xx
with a full explanation.

In your letter to me of 5/2/xx you said that the tax bill of
$666 was corrected to $222 (copy enclosed), but I just got
a notice dated 6/2/xx for the $666 again.

Letter to Dispute an IRS Tax Adjustment (continued)

> Please abate the taxes, penalties, and interest in the amount of $ 1,612.
>
> We can be reached at 707-555-0562 anytime.
>
> Sincerely,
>
> *Hamilton O'Brien*
>
> *Jill O'Brien*
>
> Hamilton and Jill O'Brien
>
> Enclosed: Copies of IRS notices, prior correspondence

Dealing With IRS Automated Adjustment Notices

The most common automated adjustment notice is the CP-2000 (see sample above). Look at the top right-hand corner of the first page of the notice for the code. The problem with CP-2000 notices is that many are totally or partly wrong. *Money* magazine estimates that at least 25% are in error. A common IRS mistake is failing to see that the income was reported elsewhere on the form than where the computer looked. For instance, if you report earnings in a money market fund as interest instead of dividends, you might get a CP-2000 notice stating that you did not report the income.

If so many of these notices are wrong, why does the IRS keep sending them? The *Money* magazine article reported that most people who were billed for $589 or less simply paid it. The magazine estimates that the IRS collects $7 billion a year it is not entitled to.

Can you fight an automated adjustment notice? Absolutely. If you receive one of these notices, just do the following:

Step 1. Call the IRS. Call the number on the notice (or 800-829-1040) to start. Ask for a full explanation even if you suspect the IRS might be right, but you aren't sure. Ask for an abatement if you believe the IRS is, or probably is, wrong—abatement is the IRS word for canceling a bill. Tell the IRS person why the notice is wrong or that your records are different from the IRS's and promise to send the proof. You probably won't settle this during the telephone call, but you want the fact that you are disputing the notice entered into the IRS computer.

Step 2. Contest in writing. Don't rely on a telephone call to straighten out an IRS problem. The tax code provides that if you don't object to an automated adjustment notice within 60 days, it becomes final.

Mail back the CP-2000 notice after filling in and signing the response form at the end. Place your checkmark for either (a) "I agree with all changes," or (b) "I don't agree with some or all of the changes." Enclose an explanatory letter (see sample above) unless you totally agree. Make the letter brief and to the point. IRS people have short attention spans and won't struggle through long-winded explanations or unclear handwriting. Staple a copy, not the original, of the IRS notice to the front of your letter. Mail it certified, return receipt requested. Use the IRS bar-coded return envelope that was included with your notice to speed up processing.

If the notice asks you to provide documents to support your tax return entries, you can do so by mail or by fax to the fax number in the notice. When writing the IRS, always make several photocopies of whatever you send. If the IRS misplaces your correspondence, you can send it again— and again, if necessary.

Step 3. Go to Tax Court. If you fail to respond to a CP-2000 notice, or if you do respond but the IRS ignores or disagrees with your explanation, the IRS will issue a Notice of Deficiency. You'll know when it comes because these notices—also called "90-day letters"—are sent by certified mail and labeled Notice of Deficiency. If you get one, your only recourse is to file a petition in U.S. Tax Court within 90 days after the date of the letter. This is not a difficult thing to do if you're contesting less than a $50,000 bill for any one tax period. It does cost $60, however. See Chapter 5 for instructions.

Be Patient If You Don't Hear From the IRS Immediately

Don't be surprised if you keep getting bills in spite of your letters contesting an automated adjustment notice. It takes a month or more to get your response into the system to stop the computerized cycle. Simply respond to later IRS notices with a photocopy of your earlier letter. Never ignore IRS letters, and never send originals. If notices ignoring your letters keep coming after 90 days, call the Taxpayer Advocate Service at 877-777-4778. Tell the taxpayer advocate that the IRS has not answered your letters and ask for help.

Consider calling a tax professional for advice, although it is seldom cost-effective to hire one for this type of problem. Some tax professionals will talk to you on the phone free of charge. If the erroneous IRS bill is a biggie, consult with a tax professional first or have them contact the IRS on your behalf.

Even if the IRS eventually proves to be correct, by sending letters, requesting help from the taxpayer advocate, or filing a petition in Tax Court you will have greatly delayed the final tax bill. This gives you extra time to get the payment together or to figure out another way to deal with the tax bill (see Chapter 6 for alternatives in dealing with a tax debt).

Types of IRS Audits

In a recent year, the IRS performed almost one million audits. The three types of IRS audits are correspondence, office, and field.

The way the IRS goes about auditing you can produce very different results. A few years back, office audits resulted in additional tax and penalties averaging $1,965 per individual return, correspondence audits $3,817, and field audits a whopping $16,248. For those taxpayers who made more than $100,000 per year, field audits resulted in added taxes, penalties, and interest averaging $35,295!

Correspondence Audits—Please, Mr. Postman

The correspondence audit is by far the IRS's preferred method of attack. Eighty percent of all IRS audits are by mail. Like it sounds, a correspondence audit comes by first-class mail. The IRS never notifies by telephone or email of the beginning of a correspondence audit. The IRS requests that you mail information or documents instead of meeting with you. This method of auditing is used to verify such things as stock market transactions, real estate sales, and itemized deductions. Amended tax returns are often audited by mail. Correspondence audits typically are caused by an omission of income from a third-party payment report on IRS Form 1099 or W-2. For example, you overlook $232 of interest you earned on a savings account.

You should almost always cooperate with an audit by mail and be thankful that you weren't chosen for a field or an office audit. Unless the documents requested are lost or nonexistent, promptly send copies. Don't send originals—you won't get them back. It's possible to call the auditor to discuss your case. Or, write and ask the auditor to call you. A name and telephone number should be listed in the IRS notice you received. As a precaution, send document copies by certified mail, return receipt requested. Always keep photocopies of everything you send to the IRS.

If you have a problem with the correspondence auditor—for example, the auditor isn't satisfied with your supporting receipts and canceled checks—you can request that your file be transferred to your local IRS office for a face-to-face meeting. Just making this request might cause the IRS to reconsider. And sometimes, mail audits forwarded to local IRS offices are closed with no adjustments—without even contacting you. If you're given a meeting with an auditor at the local office, consider it a second chance.

See IRS Publication 3498-A, *The Examination Process (Audits by Mail)*, for more on correspondence audits (from the IRS standpoint, of course).

Office Audits—Heigh-Ho, Heigh-Ho, It's Off to the IRS We Go

The office audit is announced by an IRS letter sent to your last known address either setting a time or requesting you to call for an appointment. The letter tells you the year being audited and often specifies documents you are requested to bring with you, such as receipts and canceled checks. It might also list up to four specific areas the IRS wants to examine—such as rental property income, deducted interest expenses, deducted unreimbursed business expenses, and charitable contributions.

Thankfully, the IRS doesn't expect auditors to examine every item on a tax return. Remember—only significant items are selected by classifiers, although IRS examination group managers may modify the list before the audit appointment.

 TIP
You don't have to respond to everything immediately. If you are questioned about unlisted items and you don't want to answer, just say that you are not prepared to discuss those issues. The auditor might drop it, give you more time to mail in the items, or set a second meeting date.

Your Rights During an Audit

IRS Publication 1, *Your Rights as a Taxpayer,* should be included with your audit notice. (A copy is in Chapter 15.) It very clearly explains the Taxpayer Bill of Rights. The most important audit rights are to:

- be treated fairly by IRS personnel. If you find someone who is not professional, prompt, and courteous, you have a right to speak to a supervisor.
- have a representative handle your audit. The representative must be qualified to practice before the IRS and have your written power of attorney. With a few exceptions, the IRS can't force you to appear or even contact you if you send a representative in your place.
- sound record the audit, although this isn't recommended. Taping an audit would most likely only cause the auditor to be unfriendly and work harder.
- not have to submit to repeat audits. If you were audited within the last two years, and the IRS made few or no tax adjustments, you can't be audited for the same items again. The IRS can, however, examine different items in your return. If you believe you're being audited again for the same items, complain to the IRS appointment clerk or auditor. The no-repetitive audit policy does not apply to examinations of business-related items on an individual's return.
- have proposed adjustments explained. Audit reports are vague, so you are entitled to get a detailed explanation if you ask for it. You can do this by phone or in person. If the auditor refuses, talk to the auditor's manager.
- not be forced to incriminate yourself. You always have this constitutionally guaranteed right when dealing with the government, even the IRS. For example, if you earn your living by robbing banks, the IRS can't demand that you give details, as long as you report the income. You can't, however, lie to the IRS about the source of your income. In this case, you should state on your tax return or during an audit that you are claiming the Fifth Amendment—but see a tax or criminal attorney before doing so.
- appeal your audit. See Chapter 4.

Review the Audit Notice Carefully

By law, the IRS normally has three years to audit you after you file a tax return. So, if the year on your notice is more than three years ago, either the IRS made a mistake or the IRS suspects you of fraud or of substantially understating your income. If you believe it's a mistake, call the number on the notice and ask that the audit be canceled. If you're told it is no mistake, then head straight for a tax professional's office.

If you were audited in either of the two previous years and the IRS made a small, $100 or so, adjustment—or issued a no change report—you might be able to get the audit canceled under the no-repetitive policy rule. Explain the prior audit and the outcome to the clerk; if they seem not to know what you're talking about, ask to speak to a manager. This defense has only limited application, however, and probably won't work if you report any self-employment income.

Call the IRS to Schedule the Office Audit

After you get over the shock of reading "We have selected your federal income tax return for examination," call the IRS phone number on the letter. However, the IRS doesn't award gold stars for calling as soon as you get the notice and waiting up to 30 days won't hurt.

Even if you don't want to delay, when you call the IRS for an appointment or to reschedule a date set by the IRS, ask for the furthest date available so you have sufficient time to get your records in order. A month or two is common. If you are turned down, ask to speak to a supervisor. The Taxpayer Bill of Rights requires that you be given a say in the appointment process. However, the IRS doesn't audit at night or on weekends.

Also, some tax professionals advise getting an appointment on the last day of the week toward the end of the month, in late morning—just before the auditor's lunch break—or late afternoon. Friday afternoons are perfect, especially if a three-day weekend is coming up. Auditors don't get paid overtime and look forward to going home as much as you do.

Consequently, the auditor might race through your audit without digging too deep. Much like car dealers, IRS offices track monthly case closings. If you come in near the end of the month, an auditor who hasn't kept pace might need to finish your case or else suffer a bad performance review from their manager.

CAUTION

Don't answer an auditor's questions on the phone. The auditor might try to speak to you over the phone about the facts of your case prior to your appointment. It's better to say that you aren't prepared to talk at that time than to give off-the-cuff answers that could come back to haunt you later.

If you can't go to the IRS offices without great hardship—you are disabled or aren't capable of transporting large amounts of records—you may request that a tax auditor come to your home or business. This goes against our general advice of keeping the auditor as far away from your stomping grounds as possible.

You might turn an office audit into a mail audit. If there's a good reason as to why you can't travel—illness or disability, lack of transportation, or whatever— when you call to schedule your audit, request a correspondence audit.

Why and How to Delay an Office Audit

In general, the words to live by are, "Don't hurry, be happy," and "An audit delayed is an audit well played." The more time an audit drags on, the better the result in most cases. This is because auditors are under pressure to close files, and they want your cooperation to do it. The later it gets, the greater the pressure. The main drawback with prolonging an audit is that interest and penalties are growing— but this might be insignificant next to the damage caused by a large audit bill.

There are two ways to delay an office audit:

• Make the appointment as far into the future as possible. Then, call a day or two before and postpone the audit. You can get one, or possibly two, postponements for almost any reason. Valid excuses include having to order copies of vital documents, such as canceled checks from the bank; your accountant going out of town; and the old standby of having been ill.

• On the day of the audit, leave some records at home. Then ask for time to furnish them later. Auditors have come to expect missing records and will routinely allow taxpayers two weeks or more to get them. If you want to push it to the limit, call right before the deadline and ask for a further extension.

Meet the Office Auditor

Many office auditors are fresh out of school, and some have limited English skills. Make sure you specifically explain your deductions or exemptions. If you're a small business owner or self-employed, you might have to carefully explain how your particular enterprise functions to an auditor without business experience. The auditor you'll meet has absolutely nothing to do with picking you for the examination. So, if you ask "why me?" don't expect an answer.

Office auditors start with some easy questions to make sure you are the person under audit (you don't have to show any identification)— questions like "Are you married?" or "Where do you live?" Ordinarily, these background questions won't cause you any problem.

Before meeting an auditor on your own, review IRS Form 4700-A *Supplement* and, if you operate a business, Form 4700-B *Business Supplement*. Both forms are reproduced at the end of this chapter. These internal IRS forms are used as checklists by auditors and contain the questions you should expect. If any question might be difficult, see a tax professional before the audit or consider hiring one to attend the audit in your place.

What an IRS Office Auditor Looks For

After the background questions, the audit will start in earnest. IRS office auditors don't waste time in idle chitchat. Every question has a reason, even if it isn't obvious to you. The Internal Revenue training manual instructs office auditors to conduct the initial taxpayer interview as follows. (Comments follow in the brackets.)

> *(1) [T]he initial interview is the most important part of the audit process. The first few minutes should be spent making the taxpayer comfortable and explaining the examination process …* [Read that first sentence again; first impressions are vital.]

> *(3) sufficient information should be developed to reach informed judgments as to:*

> *(a) financial history and standard of living.* [See above for a lengthy discussion of new IRS lifestyle auditing.]

(b) nature of employment to determine relationship to other entities. [This means that the auditor might want to look at your partnership or corporation tax returns, too, and look for the possibility of any bartering.]

(c) money or property received … determined to be … not taxable … [For instance, did you get loans or inheritances or sell assets during the year?]

(d) potential for moonlighting income. [For example, are you a firefighter who does odd jobs on your days off?]

(4) if warranted … [If, in covering the above areas, the auditor gets responses or sees things on the return that cause suspicion, they should go on to find out more about these areas.]

(a) … property owned, including bank accounts, stocks and bonds, real estate, automobiles, etc., in this country and abroad [Asking these kinds of questions used to be optional; it has become common in most audits.]

(b) … purchases, sales, transfers, contributions or exchanges of … assets [Did you buy or sell anything with a value in the thousands of dollars?]

(c) the correctness of exemptions and dependents claimed. [If you claimed a large number of dependents, be prepared to explain, especially if any of the dependents are not members of your immediate family.]

(5) remember, the taxpayer is being examined and not just the return. [I can't overemphasize the importance of this one sentence—it is what an audit is really about.]

Common Audit Issues

Expect the following topics to be covered at an office audit. Not all will apply, but be prepared for the ones that do.

Income. The IRS claims that it loses infinitely more tax dollars from unreported income than from overstated deductions. Once the preliminary questions are over, the auditor will ask point blank if you reported all your income for the year or years under audit.

Auditors are taught to probe for side income—moonlighting electricians and homemakers who do child care. They are concerned with income not reported to the IRS by the person who paid you or income from which no taxes were withheld, such as tips or rent from an in-law unit in your home.

Auditors will probe further into living expenses once omitted income is suspected. For example, the auditor might want to see your insurance policies to see if you have covered expensive items like jewelry, furs, art, and other such assets. Auditors seldom go to this trouble, however.

Theft and casualty losses. Were you legally entitled to claim losses? Produce a list of items lost plus documentation that the loss occurred—copies of insurance claim forms are good ways to prove losses to the IRS.

Charitable deductions. Can you verify charitable deductions—particularly if the total exceeded $250? For example, if you dropped $40 into the collection plate every Sunday, you'll need more evidence than your own statement. Prove it by getting a letter from your church secretary attesting to your regular attendance and copies of automatic teller withdrawal slips made on Sunday mornings.

Employee business expenses. Employee business expenses are not deductible at all during 2018 through 2025, but can be deductible before and after those years. If you are a wage earner and claim such deductions before 2018 or after 2025, can you verify any unreimbursed employee business expenses claimed on your return—especially for car, travel, and home office? At a minimum, you'll need a letter from your employer describing its reimbursement policy—that it pays you back for some expenses, but not for other items or beyond certain limits. Keep receipts and a calendar. If you don't have a business diary, you can create one after the fact, but you should tell the IRS that it is a reconstruction. Note that the IRS is very picky in the employee expense area.

Itemized deductions. Can you verify large itemized deductions on your Schedule A—such as mortgage interest or medical expenses? You should have mortgage lender statements on IRS Form 1098 and medical bills or canceled checks and bank statements.

Previous audits. IRS records of previous audits are spotty. Your prior audit history might or might not be noted in the auditor's file. Thus, you will be asked if you've been audited and how it came out. Unless you came out clean, tell the auditor that you were audited, but don't recall the details. If the auditor really wants to dig out the prior report, they might do it. Don't make it easy by showing a copy—which might point out issues to probe in the new audit.

Other years' tax returns. Auditors usually ask to see copies of your tax returns for the year before and after the audit year. The reason is obvious—to see if any adjustments are appropriate in those years.

Don't Be Too Eager to Help the Auditor

Auditors frequently ask you for information not related to the year or areas listed on the audit notice. Sadly, most audit victims blindly provide whatever is asked for, often needlessly providing the rope to be hanged with.

The IRS can't require you to furnish data unless it is directly related to the year under audit. If the auditor asks for something you don't think pertains, ask for an explanation of how it specifically relates to the audit year. If you are given *written* notice that the audit has been expanded to other years, however, then you must submit information for those years.

Sometimes data on other years' tax returns—such as loss carryovers or depreciation of assets—does relate to the tax year under audit. In this case, show the auditor only the portion of the other year's tax return in question (such as a schedule of depreciation), not the whole return. Similarly, avoid letting the auditor photocopy your records unless you are certain there is nothing harmful in them. Tell the auditor that you don't see why they need copies and they will probably back down.

If you are asked if you filed all other years' tax returns and you haven't, reply that you will check your records and get back, or simply shrug your shoulders. Don't lie. If you want to avoid this question altogether, hire a tax professional to go to the audit in your place. Unless you have told your tax pro otherwise, the tax pro should answer that as far as they know, you filed all tax returns when due. An auditor who has no reason to believe otherwise almost always just moves on.

TIP
Don't bring other returns to the audit. Simply say you didn't bring them with you or couldn't find them—even if they are on the list of items to bring with you. Make a vague offer to look for them; an auditor can't force you to provide past returns.

Don't worry about making the auditor mad by not supplying other years' tax returns. Auditors know you never have to provide a copy of a tax return to the IRS once it has been filed. The only exception is if the IRS auditor says that no return is on record. Then you can give the auditor a signed copy for filing. But, in the normal audit situation when the IRS requests a copy of your return, it's not because the auditor is denying that you filed it—it's because the auditor doesn't have it in their file.

Even in this electronic age, old paper-filed tax returns are buried in warehouses across the country for 10 years and are then destroyed. Yours might be in Box 147963a-7 in the middle of Kansas. Unless you filed electronically, it will take weeks or months to find it—and there is no guarantee that it hasn't been misplaced. Usually, if you don't come up with a copy of your tax return which is on record as filed, the auditor just forgets it.

How Long Does an Office Appointment Last?

Expect to spend from one to four hours with the office auditor. In most IRS offices, two audits per day are set for taxpayers with small businesses and four audits where there is no self-employment income. Auditors must write up their findings between appointments, so they must keep moving and can't scrutinize every piece of paper. An auditor wants to zip through your audit and get you out the door every bit as much as you want to leave.

If You Didn't Bring Everything to the Audit

It's okay not to resolve all audit issues at one meeting. Auditors often ask for something you didn't bring. No problem. Just ask for a reasonable amount of time to submit it (15 to 30 days) and mail it in with a letter to jog the auditor's memory explaining how it helps your audit. To be sure the auditor got what you sent, call four or five days later and ask. If the auditor wants voluminous records or you're concerned that the auditor might not understand what you send, request another face-to-face meeting.

If you don't want the auditor to see a particular item, you can vaguely promise to send it in but conveniently forget to—the auditor might forget it, too. If not, you will probably not lose any more than you would have if you had cooperated.

Field Audits—Look Out, Here Comes the IRS

If you get a letter notifying you of an audit and asking to meet at your home or business, you have been picked for a field audit.

TIP

If you get a phone call from the IRS. Before getting notice by mail, you might get a call from someone at the IRS saying the IRS wants to audit you. Politely tell the caller you want notification in writing to make sure it really is the IRS. Refuse to discuss anything until you get a notice in the mail. Don't worry about upsetting the person; you are within your rights. Some agents like to catch you off guard, in the hope you'll say something revealing.

Field audits are the big leagues, whereas correspondence and office audits are the minors. The IRS puts its best auditors here and expects them to pay their keep. In fact, field audit tax bills are more than four times higher than those from other types of audits. In one recent year, the average field audit resulted in a $26,307 tax bill.

Local IRS audit managers make the final decision as to who gets field audited. Normally, it is the self-employed, owners of real estate rental properties, or people with high incomes or complex tax returns. Also, corporation, partnership, estate, gift, and trust tax returns are always field, not office, audited.

Revenue agents who conduct field audits must have college degrees in accounting or a minimum of 24 semester hours of college-level accounting courses. At IRS audit training, they are taught techniques similar to detectives—looking for clues to see if your tax reporting matches the home you live in, your business, and your investments. If you live in a $2 million home, drive a Tesla, and report only $20,000 of income from your dental practice, they will dig deep.

Do Auditors Have Quotas?

IRS auditors will tell you they are overworked. Because the IRS doesn't pay bonuses or overtime, there is little incentive for them to break their backs on particular cases. Job performance is judged on how many files are closed each month. The Taxpayer Bill of Rights forbids the IRS to evaluate auditors on the dollars produced from their audits. Judging auditors on the number of files closed, however, probably produces much the same result, and there is evidence that IRS managers give bonuses. Prior to 1998, auditors were evaluated by their yield—the total dollar amount of the tax adjustment on an audit, divided by the number of hours the auditor spent on the examination. For example, in the Northern California District, an auditor had to produce $1,000 in taxes for each hour the auditor devoted to a case. Hopefully, those days are gone.

A heavy caseload can work to your advantage. Auditors don't have the time to go over every tax return with a fine-tooth comb. Auditors often miss taxpayer errors that could have resulted in large adjustments in the IRS's favor.

Responding to a Field Audit Letter

The initial notice you get will probably be signed by a revenue agent. The letter will either set a date for the audit or ask you to call to arrange it. An attachment will list items the IRS wants you to produce at the meeting. However, the list should not be taken as inclusive—*everything* is fair game in a field audit. A revenue agent can probe into any area of your tax return as well as your financial or personal life. Remember that *you*, not just your tax return, are under the IRS microscope.

 TIP

Carefully consider when and where you want the audit to be held. The Taxpayer Bill of Rights (see Chapter 15) gives you the right to have a say in when an audit is to be scheduled. You should be given sufficient time to prepare and a convenient date. The IRS doesn't start before 7:30 a.m. and won't go beyond 5 p.m., weekdays only. Field audits last a minimum of four hours and might go into dozens of meetings extending over a year's time.

Agents prefer to come to wherever your records are kept. Ordinarily this is at your business, if you are self-employed. So if you work at home, the IRS will want to come there. If a representative will handle the audit for you, the agent can go to that person's office if requested.

What to Expect at a Field Audit

Be sure to read "What an IRS Office Auditor Looks For" and "Common Audit Issues," above; that information applies here as well. This section covers other issues likely to come up at a field audit.

Revenue agents' primary focus is to find unreported income and personal expenses claimed as business deductions. Field audits typically zero in on the following areas of your work and personal lives.

Unreported income. *This is the auditor's number one concern.* An agent is particularly suspicious if your small business or profession has a lot of cash transactions. This is why so many restaurant, bar, liquor store, laundromat, and grocery store owners are audited. The IRS is always looking for the skimming of cash off the gross receipts of the business.

To ferret out unreported income, the IRS uses indirect methods of detection, unless you furnish direct evidence, such as confessing to the auditor that you didn't report everything.

There are four common methods the IRS uses to probe for income. All four methods have been challenged in federal court; all four methods have survived the challenge. Each one is explained below, with possible defenses you can raise:

- **Net worth method.** Using this method, the IRS attributes any increase in your net worth during the year in question to taxable income—unless you offer a reasonable explanation. The IRS tries to establish your net worth—your total assets less your liabilities—at the beginning of the year and then again at the end. Then it compares the two figures to see if your net worth increased over the year. Assets like real estate and stock are valued at their original cost, so appreciation won't enter into the computation. Typically, the IRS asks for financial statements that might have been prepared for your business or in a loan application. Any increase in your net worth over a prior year will be compared to the income reported on your tax return. If your net worth has increased but your income has not, the IRS will assume you're not reporting all your income.

Defense. Show that the IRS's calculations are wrong or that your net worth increased due to nontaxable factors. For example, you might have inherited money or assets or have a cash hoard accumulated in prior years. The law then shifts the burden to the IRS to negate any explanation you offer before making an audit adjustment.

• **Expenditures method.** The IRS totals up all of your known and estimated expenditures for the year and compares the result with your reported income. If you spent more than you claim you earned, the IRS will attribute the difference to unreported income.

Defense. Show that the IRS didn't add and subtract correctly or that money you spent was from nontaxable sources, such as loans, gifts, inheritances, or prior accumulations.

• **Bank deposit method.** This is the IRS's favorite indirect method of proving unreported income and is always used by field auditors. The IRS simply tallies up the deposits made in all of your bank accounts and compares the total with your reported income. If you have deposited more than you claim you earned, the IRS will attribute the difference to unreported income.

Some business owners take great pains to skim receipts, but then stupidly put that money into their bank accounts. The IRS can easily obtain financial records from your bank or stock broker if you don't produce them voluntarily. Revenue agents almost always perform a bank deposit analysis early on in a field audit.

TIP

Do your own bank deposit analysis before the audit. Make notes on your bank statements that explain the source of the deposits. There can be any number of explanations when deposits exceed taxable income—loans, redeposits of bad checks, transfers between accounts, inheritances and gifts received, sales of assets, and the like.

Defense. Check the IRS's math for mistakes. And, again, the funds might have been from nontaxable sources or from cash on hand from income from prior years. Also, if you have several accounts, chances are some of the deposits reflect transfers of money between accounts. Adding up deposits leads to double counting, a common mistake.

- **Mark-up method.** If you are in a retail or wholesale goods business, the agent might look at your sales, cost of goods sold, and net profits. If these numbers are much lower than for similar businesses, the IRS will fill in the gap by asserting unreported income.

  Defense. Ask the agent for the source of statistics the IRS used. The agent might be comparing you to a completely different type of business—perhaps yours is a computer wholesale operation and the agent is relying on figures from home electronics retailing. If this isn't the case, explain why your business underperformed compared to similar businesses: It is a new business or was closed several months due to a fire, your major customer or supplier went bankrupt, or any of a thousand other reasons.

Business expense verification. Agents typically ask you to verify at least the major business expenses you claimed (for sole proprietors on Schedule C). The agent is on the lookout for disguised personal expenses—particularly auto and travel. The tax law specifically requires strict record keeping in these three areas. Bringing a business diary will help immensely. If you didn't keep one, you can create one for the audit, but you should tell the auditor it is a reconstruction.

Asset sales. Can you document your gains and losses from sales of property—particularly stocks and real estate? This can sometimes be a problem, as you might have owned the stocks or property for many years. Show the original documents from when you purchased the asset. You'll also need receipts for improvements of real estate during your ownership and annual statements showing reinvested dividends for stocks and mutual funds.

Real estate rental. Can you verify rental property expenses you claimed on Schedule E of your tax return? Can you also show that each expense was for that particular property? Auditors are on the lookout for landlords deducting items that were used at their personal residences. If you are a landlord, you should have records of all income and expenses. If not, you must reconstruct records from canceled checks, deposits, receipts, and notes. Photos of major expense items (like remodeling) are especially persuasive.

Tax Basis of an Asset

An auditor might ask you to verify your tax basis in an asset used in your business or sold by you. "Basis" is the figure from which the IRS calculates how much depreciation you get or profit or loss you've made on the sale of an asset. Essentially, tax basis starts with the amount you paid. To this figure, add the cost of improvements and tax benefits, such as rollover of gains from property exchanges, and subtract costs such as the depreciation taken on equipment or rental property. If you received a gift, the tax basis is figured from the date of the original purchase. For property you inherit, the basis is the property's value on the date of the death. A detailed explanation of tax basis is in *Tax Savvy for Small Business*, by Frederick W. Daily and Stephen Fishman (Nolo).

Independent contractors versus employees. A frequent audit issue is whether businesses have properly classified people working for them as independent contractors or employees. This issue is covered in Chapter 11.

Keeping the Auditor Away From Your Home or Business

Avoid holding an audit at your home or business, even if you have nothing to hide. Maybe you really earn only $20,000, but appear to live much better. It could be that you inherited a $1 million house from your aunt, rebuilt your Mercedes from junkyard parts, and made a few good investments. Assuming you have paperwork to prove all this, you should have no problems with the IRS, right? Well, maybe not. These are the kinds of things that can cause auditors to dig deeper until they find something to justify their efforts.

Here are some tips on how to keep the IRS auditor away from your home or business.

Taxpayer Bill of Rights. The Taxpayer Bill of Rights gives small business owners the right to refuse an audit on their business premises if an audit would virtually shut the business down. In this case, request the audit to be held at the IRS office, at your tax professional's place, or by video conferencing or telephone. If denied, complain to the agent's manager and then, if necessary, to the Taxpayer Advocate Service. (See Chapter 8.)

Tax professionals. If you give a qualified representative a signed Form 2848, *Power of Attorney and Declaration of Representative*, they can insist that the audit be at their office, not yours. (See Chapter 13.) The representative must be the audited tax return's preparer, an enrolled agent, a CPA, or an attorney, and must be in possession of your business records.

If the IRS Comes to Your Business

If the IRS holds the audit at your place, don't make it too comfortable. This doesn't mean that you should stick the agent in an unheated storeroom, but you don't have to give up your personal office, either.

Even if the audit is held at your tax professional's or an IRS office, however, agents have the right to observe your business premises. They might want to verify tax return items by spot checking your inventory or seeing that you use equipment you tax deducted. Remember—auditors are trained to be nosy and routinely want to eyeball business operations.

Before the IRS shows up, remove any items that might cause suspicion, like the picture of your Chris-Craft, private plane, or alpine ski cabin. If the agent wants to tour your business, try to schedule it at a time when employees or customers aren't present. This keeps the agent from talking to your employees and tipping them off that you're being audited. An employee's innocent remark could do a lot of harm, and a vengeful one could stab you in the back. Don't let the agent wander around on their own—stay nearby.

If the agent asks to see any records during an observation, say that they are not readily available, are at home, or are at your tax professional's office. The agent won't start opening your file cabinets to verify the truthfulness of your assertions.

An auditor doesn't have the right to enter your home to see your home office or for any other reason. If you don't let the person inside, however, they might legitimately retaliate by disallowing a home office deduction.

How a Field Auditor Approaches an Examination

The tax code gives the auditor wide latitude and authority to pry into your financial affairs. The basic tools in the auditor's kit are the interview, summons, IRS and other government files, and contacts with third parties, like your bank, who have knowledge of your finances.

> **TIP**
> **The IRS auditor's secret roadmap.** At the end of this chapter is a copy of IRS Form 4700, *Examination Workpapers*, and a *Business Supplement*. Don't look for this form on the IRS website. It is for internal use only. This is the auditor's checklist of items to be covered in every taxpayer exam. Read it before your audit. As the old saying goes: "To be forewarned is to be forearmed."

Information Document Request. Along with your audit notice might come a separate form called an "Information Document Request" (IDR). An auditor commonly issues multiple IDRs if the audit, usually a field audit, continues beyond one meeting. An IDR is a written solicitation of records or other papers either in your possession or accessible to you. Typically, bank statements and canceled checks are listed on an IDR. The IRS knows the truth of the words of a former U.S. Supreme Court justice that "a person can be defined by the checks he writes." Ordinarily, you will be given until a follow-up audit appointment or a few weeks to mail these things to the auditor. A sample IDR follows.

> **TIP**
> **Just because the IRS issues an IDR doesn't mean that you have to produce the items requested.** You may decline unless the items are really relevant to your audit. For instance, the IRS commonly uses IDRs to request copies of other years' financial records—which normally you don't have to supply. If in doubt, don't furnish the item on the IDR and see if the auditor pursues it. If the auditor does, ask how it relates to the year selected for audit. If you believe the auditor is crossing the line, just say no. An IDR is merely an informal administrative request—it doesn't carry any legal force. If what is being requested might seriously hurt or even incriminate you, see a tax attorney before responding.

Sample Information Document Request

Form **4564** (Rev. September 2006)	Department of the Treasury — Internal Revenue Service **Information Document Request**	Request Number One

To: *(Name of Taxpayer and Company Division or Branch)* Yolanda Allende 888 Rain Lane Seattle, WA 99999 *Please return Part 2 with listed documents to requester identified below*	Subject Examination-2022-Form 1040	
	SAIN number	Submitted to: Taxpayers
	Dates of Previous Requests *(mmddyyyy)* N/A	

Description of documents requested

1. All personal and business bank statements for 1/1/2022 to 12/31/2022

2. Copies of individual income tax returns Form 1040 for years 2021 and 2022

3. Credit card statements for 1/1/2022 to 12/31/2022

4. Office expenses

   a. Accounting records detailing expenses deducted

   b. Receipts, cancelled checks, electronic funds transferred statements to verify expenses deducted

5. Meals and travel

Accounting records detailing expenses deducted. The records should establish pertinent names, business relationship, and purpose of expenses deducted.

Information Due By ___4/01/2024___   At Next Appointment ☐   Mail in ☒

From:	Name and Title of Requester John Smith, Revenue Agent	Employee ID number	Date *(mmddyyyy)* 2/15/2024
	Office Location 110 44th St., Seattle, WA 88888		Telephone Number (555) 555-5555

Catalog Number 23145K	www.irs.gov	Part 1 - Taxpayer's File Copy	Form **4564** (Rev. 9-2006)

Summons. If the IRS doesn't get information from you voluntarily—through an IDR—it may issue a summons, IRS Form 2039, *Summons*. (I.R.C. §§ 7602(a) and 7604(b).) A summons is a legally enforceable order and is not to be taken lightly. It orders you to appear before the auditor to answer questions and to bring certain documents. You can raise legal objections to a summons, including:

- self-incrimination—a constitutional right not to give something to the government that would incriminate you
- the summons is vague, overbroad, or unduly burdensome—if you've been asked to produce an overwhelming amount of documents, or
- certain items are protected by a legal privilege—such as the attorney-client privilege.

CAUTION

If you get a summons, contact a tax lawyer. If you don't comply, the IRS may bring you before a federal court judge in a summons enforcement proceeding. The judge can order you to produce the documents listed in the summons or face a heavy fine or even a jail sentence. It should give you comfort to know that the IRS rarely goes to this trouble, preferring to compromise or back down.

Third-party summons. Field auditors frequently use IRS Form 2039, *Summons*, to get information from banks, employers, business associates, and anyone else. Auditors routinely summons records from these third parties when you don't cooperate, or when verification of information you have given is needed. You must be notified in writing when a third-party summons is issued and you have a right to object. Practically speaking, however, you can't stop a third-party summons.

CAUTION

Never tell another person not to comply with an IRS summons. That is illegal and could get you both into serious trouble.

If You Don't Give Auditors What They Ask For

When you don't give the auditor information that has been requested, the auditor has three choices:

- **Drop it.** You'd be surprised how many auditors back off or are forgetful. They are working on many other cases. If they have most of the information requested from you, they might let it slide.
- **Go further without your cooperation.** Auditors call, write, or issue summonses to third parties, such as your bank, for records of your transactions. Auditors can, but rarely do, summons (order) you to appear before them and provide information.
- **Issue an examination report anyway.** The auditor can issue the report based on the information in hand and estimates for the missing income or expense data. By far, this is the most likely consequence of your not cooperating with an auditor.

IRS files. Auditors can access your previous tax returns, audit reports, and tax account history. The auditor might first ask you for this information. As discussed above, you don't always have to give everything requested to an auditor. Because a lot of IRS information on you is not accessible by computer, it isn't all that easy for an auditor to get older IRS records. Recovering paper from IRS record storage facilities could take months. As a rule, auditors don't go to this trouble unless they mistrust you or feel that a large adjustment—tax bill against you—will result.

Other government and public records. Auditors have direct computer access to the Homeland Security's TECS system database, which has all kinds of data on you. TECS is not public, so you can't be sure what is in the files. The auditor can also access your Social Security Administration, passport office, and Postal Service records. Auditors can view local and state public records showing ownership of vehicles, boats, airplanes, real estate, and business entities you might be involved in. Google and private databases, such as LexisNexis and credit reporting agency files, contain a wealth of personal data and are accessible to auditors. As a rule, office auditors don't make these types of searches, but field agents, who conduct audits at homes or businesses, often do.

Third-party contacts. Auditors can send letters or call or visit businesses and people who have dealt with you, such as the secretary of a church where you claimed a charitable contribution. First, they must give you Notice 1219-B, *Notice of Potential Third Party Contact*. You can legally object to these contacts, at least in theory. If the auditor reveals personal or financial information about you to the third party, you can file a complaint with the IRS that your right to privacy has been violated by an unauthorized disclosure.

Preparing for an Audit

In preparing for an audit, begin by doing the following:

Step 1. Review the tax return being audited. If it was professionally prepared, go over it with the preparer. If you did it yourself, review it with a tax professional to see if they foresee any problems. Remember, it is always up to you to show the auditor where the data on the return came from. You might decide to hire the pro to represent you depending on your pocketbook and overall comfort level. A seasoned tax professional can offer an educated guess as to why you're being audited and you can prepare your audit defense accordingly.

> **TIP**
>
> **Mention other years' business losses to the auditor.** If you had a net operating loss for a year before or after the year being audited, point this out to the auditor. This might discourage the auditor from spending a lot of time on your audit, because any tax adjustment would be reduced by the loss you were entitled to in the subsequent year. If this might be your case, discuss it with a tax professional.

Step 2. Find all the records you used to prepare the return. Organize records logically and clearly according to the deduction category. Run adding machine tapes on totals of receipts for each classification, such as rent, travel, and utilities. If the totals don't correspond to the numbers on your tax return, be ready to explain why. We can't overemphasize the importance of well-organized records in an audit.

Not Cooperating in an Audit—
When You Have Something to Hide

If you have some "dirty laundry," it might be in your best interest not to cooperate in, or even go to, an audit appointment. Before taking this drastic step, see a tax pro (preferably a tax attorney). For example, if your bank records show deposits in great excess of your reported income or you claimed phony deductions, it might be wiser to suffer the consequences of skipping an audit appointment. Blurting something out could earn you a visit from the Criminal Investigation Division, or CI. Never say "I guess you caught me, ha, ha," or "I didn't think you would find that account." On hearing such things, auditors are instructed to stop an audit and refer the case to CI. (See Chapter 10.)

When you don't show up, the IRS will take one of three actions:

Conduct the audit without you. The IRS may also examine tax years not covered by the initial audit. The auditor may look at all open years—returns due and filed within the past three years. And if the auditor suspects serious misdeeds, the auditor may go back as far as six years. At the conclusion, the IRS will issue a report disallowing all items listed as questionable. A month or so later you'll receive a bill. Depending on the circumstances, you might want to accept the bill and move on with your life.

Contact you again. You might be contacted by the auditor and asked why you are not cooperating. Mum's the word. Eventually, the auditor will give up and issue a report, finding unreported income or disallowing most of your deductions and exemptions. A tax bill will follow.

Serve a summons and order you to appear. A summons (discussed above) is a legally enforceable order and you could be held in contempt of court—and even jailed—if you ignore it. See a tax attorney before making your next move.

Step 3. Research tax law if you are unsure whether you were entitled to a deduction or another tax benefit claimed on your tax return. For instance, did you meet all the requirements for a home office deduction? This is another point you should research or cover with a tax professional if you aren't sure.

Step 4. Look for relevant Audit Technique Guides (ATGs). The IRS has issued guides in its Market Segment Specialization Program (MSSP) telling its auditors what to look for when auditing certain businesses and occupations—real estate agents, entertainers, attorneys, fishermen, and others. Also, ATGs cover items that draw special audit attention, such as lawsuit awards, passive losses, and executive compensation. If there's a guide covering your line of work (see the IRS website at www.irs.gov; do a site search for "MSSP" or "Audit Technique Guides"), you should read it. It will tell you what the auditor will be looking for beyond the normal audit routine, and you can prepare accordingly.

Your Audit Goals

You have two goals in the audit:

- **To minimize the financial damage.** Because the odds are great that your audit will end with a tax bill, your goal should be damage control—keeping your liability as low as possible. But, don't go in with a defeatist attitude. If you owe no money, try to prove it. Just don't have unrealistic expectations. In a recent year, audits resulted in $19 billion in additional taxes and penalties, and about $600 million in refunds—a ratio of 32 to 1 against you.

- **To prevent expansion.** *Office* audits are initially limited to the items listed on the audit notice. If auditors see other problems, however, they will pursue them. This often happens when you show an auditor a document that you weren't obligated to show, or you make a slip of the tongue. As a rule, never show the auditor anything not specifically related to the tax year in the audit notice. For example, before showing your check register or business diary, edit out the portions that relate to personal matters or that overlap into other years.

  Field audits are often expanded into other tax years. An auditor may get permission from their manager to examine any "open" tax year if it is likely to be fruitful. Open years are those within three years of when a return was filed, or six years if the IRS suspects serious underreporting.

EXAMPLE: In November 2024, Noreen is audited for 2022. The auditor could expand the examination to 2021 and 2023; Noreen filed those tax returns timely. Without finding evidence of serious problems, the auditor could not expand the audit any farther back, as Noreen filed her 2020 tax return on April 15, 2021, more than three years before the audit date.

> **TIP**
> **Don't show the auditor copies of tax returns for years other than the one in the audit notice.** If the IRS expands the audit, you should demand an official written notice from the auditor. The auditor might back down.

What Not to Bring to an Audit

Don't bring anything not directly related to the year being audited. The auditor's fishing license is usually restricted to the year being audited, but the auditor can look at materials from other years—and make adjustments—if these items are presented.

Your audit letter includes a list of things to bring. Don't take anything else—*unless* it supports a deduction you missed when you filed your tax return. For example, if your checking account statements overlap two years—January's statement has checks for December—then remove the checks for the year that isn't being audited. Leave at home checks and receipts for personal expenses not claimed as deductions on your tax return. Again, don't bring tax returns for any years other than the one being audited, even if requested by the auditor.

Who Should Attend the Audit?

If you're handling the audit yourself, you can bring someone else to the meeting. The auditor may ask you to sign a form waiving your right of privacy. This person can assist, but can't represent you, unless the person is the tax return preparer or an enrolled agent, a CPA, or an attorney. Chapter 13 contains tips on selecting a tax professional. It might make sense to bring any of the following people to the audit:

- an employee—your bookkeeper, the accounts payable supervisor, or a similar employee who has knowledge of your business records and can help you explain them
- your spouse—only one spouse needs to attend an audit when a joint tax return is being audited. Both should go if they both have financial knowledge, provided different information on the return, or can substantiate that information. If only one of you is being audited, the other can attend to offer emotional support. Or,

- another family member or friend—to offer moral support, translate if your English isn't very good, wipe your eyes with a handkerchief, or do whatever would help you get through the examination.

 TIP
Even if you skip the audit, you can contest the outcome by going to Tax Court. (See Chapter 5.) The strategy is to skip the audit so as to keep the auditor from looking into your records. By going to court, you pick the items to contest and can stay away from the problem areas. Before taking this approach, however, check with a tax attorney or tax professional.

How to Act at an Audit

The *Internal Revenue Manual* tells auditors that the initial taxpayer interview is the most important phase of an audit. *You, the taxpayer—not just your tax return—are under examination.* Your actions and behavior are being observed. Does it look like you are being evasive—trying to hide something? Do you become visibly shaken when some items are being discussed?

Dress Like Yourself

Dress according to your occupation and station in life. Anything else might make you uncomfortable and an audit is uncomfortable enough already. Use your common sense. Don't wear expensive clothes and jewelry if you work at Burger King, and don't dress like a fry cook if you are a dentist. If you are a bus driver coming from work, wear your uniform. Don't try to look like someone you are not. It's simple, really. Be yourself.

Mum's the Word

IRS encounters are inherently stressful, and people under stress often talk too much. The IRS knows this principle of human behavior, so auditors are trained to listen and to create silence. They examine records without speaking, with the hope that you'll jabber away. Take this advice seriously: Don't talk. Auditors get damaging information from taxpayers who blurt out answers to questions that weren't asked. For example, one clueless soul volunteered that he always deducted clothing expenses because he had to come to work dressed. The auditor then made a disallowance of this expense in two other years.

The six best responses to a question posed by an auditor are:

- Yes.
- No.
- I don't recall.
- I'll have to check on that.
- What specific items do you want to see?
- Why do you want that?

Again, don't say more unless absolutely necessary. As a rule, you can't hurt yourself when your mouth is shut.

> **CAUTION**
>
> **Don't lie to, or mislead, an auditor.** IRS examiners are trained to ask for information they already have to test your credibility. A favorite question is to ask if you have investments when the IRS computer shows you earned interest and dividends. Or, the auditor might ask you about vehicles you own when the auditor has a printout from your state motor vehicles department.

Don't Offer Any Favors to the Auditor

Auditors are trained to watch out for, and report, all offers of favors of any kind. Some taxpayers are from countries where bribing government officials is the norm. IRS employees are closely watched and are among the cleanest of all officials anywhere. Some auditors will accept a cup of coffee, but that's as far as it goes. An offer of a favor, say tickets to a ball game, might be ignored. But any suggestion of an outright bribe will get you a visit from the Criminal Investigation Division and a very thorough audit. Don't try it.

Try to Get Along With the Auditor

When you meet an auditor, be polite and offer some chitchat about the weather, traffic, or sports to break the ice. Office auditors are under time pressures and might want to get right down to business. Field auditors, on the other hand, are encouraged to get to know you; they will chat.

It doesn't hurt to show an interest in the auditor as a person. Ask friendly questions—How long have you been with the IRS? How does someone get to be an auditor? How long have you worked in this area? Everyone likes to talk about their favorite subject—themselves. If the auditor responds, it might get them to like you, or at least it will reduce the amount of time the person spends examining your return.

In short, don't go in with an anti-IRS attitude. You're not happy to be there, but make the best of it. Remember what Grandma told you about catching more flies with honey than with vinegar.

What about turning this advice on its head and taking a defiant, aggressive attitude into an audit? One tax professional suggests that you continually ask the auditor why they want to know whenever you are asked a question. Obnoxious or peculiar behavior might work. Similarly, some taxpayers give an agent a poorly lighted, noisy, and cramped space to conduct a field audit. This is not our style, but it might work with auditors who are timid or so unused to being challenged that they will give in to get rid of you.

When the Auditor Is Unreasonable

You might run into an auditor intent on giving you a hard time. The person might be impolite, hostile, or rude. Worse, the auditor might disallow your deductions unless you produce ironclad documentation in triplicate. Perhaps you did something to upset the person, or they're having a bad day.

The important thing to understand is that you don't have to take guff from an auditor. Ask the person politely to lighten up. If that doesn't work, say you are too upset to continue and want to recess the audit to another day. If the auditor balks, tell the auditor that you want to consult a tax professional before continuing. Legally, you must be granted your request. You don't have to consult the tax professional, but the audit is finished for the day.

Threatening to leave—or demanding a recess—can have positive results. Auditors do change their tune sometimes and try to be more accommodating.

Auditors don't want to have to see people again if they can help it, as they already have a backlog of cases. Because their performance is judged by how many files they close, they won't want anything to delay them. In the end, they are looking for your agreement to close the case. If you have a second meeting, the auditor might be in a better mood. Auditors also know that a tax professional won't put up with their lack of professionalism. And it's even possible that your file will be transferred to another auditor for the next meeting. Remember, you never know what is going on in an auditor's life. If someone seems unhappy, it might not have anything to do with you. The person might be ill or in the process of quitting, getting fired, or transferring to another IRS department.

Asking for a New Auditor

If the recess didn't help and the auditor continues to abuse you, demand to see their manager. Tell the manager that you are not being treated respectfully, and that you want a different auditor. While chances are slim that you'll be granted your request, the auditor you have should start treating you more civilly.

Have You Seen This Auditor Before?

The *Internal Revenue Manual* discourages an examination by an auditor who has examined your tax return within the previous three years, if that audit was concluded and your case was closed. If you recognize the auditor from your recent past (this might happen if your local office has only a few auditors) and you don't want to deal with the same person, complain to the manager.

When a New Auditor Appears on the Scene

Field audits commonly drag on for months or even years. Your original auditor might suddenly vanish. It's usually for some perfectly understandable reason, like a job transfer, promotion, maternity leave, training, resignation, or firing. For some reason, the IRS treats this as some kind of national security secret and doesn't like to tell you what happened.

The first auditor might call you or send you an examination report prior to moving on. The motive here is to try to close your file by asking you to agree to certain adjustments. Maybe you are agreeable, but before taking the bait, read "Negotiating With an Auditor," below. For now, just realize you might have some leverage if this happens.

A second way to benefit from a change in auditors is by understanding that the new person won't want to do any more work on a half-done audit than is necessary. Few people like to clean up another person's mess. For example, no two people document their work the same way, and few people write in a way to be easily understood by others. The newcomer will probably jump at a chance to close the file as soon as possible. The following example, taken from real life, shows how a change of auditors can be a godsend.

> **EXAMPLE:** Laura had mistakenly claimed a large and improper business deduction for three years running, totaling $120,000. Auditor One raised this issue, and Laura stalled by asking for time to contact her tax professional and do further investigation and research. To her dismay, Laura found out that she was dead in the water and could only be saved by a miracle. She got one when Auditor One was replaced by Auditor Two. The new guy was either too lazy to read the file or didn't understand it, and completely missed this issue. He quickly closed the case after finding another and much smaller adjustment, and Laura cheerfully signed the examination report.

Protest if asked to produce records twice. A new auditor isn't always a positive development. The person might be determined to replow old ground. You or your representative might be asked questions you've already answered or to produce documents you showed the first auditor.

If you have produced records once during an audit, it is reasonable to object to doing so again. The longer the audit has been going on, the louder you should complain. Argue that the change of auditors isn't your fault and you shouldn't be punished. Get indignant; take control of the situation by telling the new auditor what the records show and maybe produce a few items to back up what you say. If appropriate, propose a few small adjustments and an immediate settlement.

If the new auditor persists in traveling over old terrain, demand to speak to the person's manager and renew your complaint. The manager might agree or suggest a compromise just to get rid of you. If you don't get anywhere and have a serious basis for objecting (the records are voluminous and have taken a lot of your time), ask for the head person, the examination branch chief. Even if everyone turns you down, by squeaking your wheels you have shown yourself to be someone unlikely to accept an examination report.

Documents to Bring to the Audit

The audit notice includes a list of documents you are supposed to bring to the audit. You might want to bring additional documents you need to explain or reconstruct missing records. IRS Publication 583, *Starting a Business and Keeping Records*, shows how the IRS wants you to keep your records. Don't worry if you haven't followed all the IRS suggestions. You just need to be able to show income and expenses to the auditor in some understandable manner. Listed here are specific documents to bring.

Canceled checks and receipts. Take only the checks and receipts relating to the areas listed in the audit notice. Don't let the auditor rummage through all your checks and receipts. If it appears you are spending more money than you are reporting, the auditor might become suspicious. You can bring a credit card or bank account statement instead of a canceled check. (IRS Revenue Procedure 92-71.)

Books and records, if you operated a business. You aren't required to have a formal set of books as long as the auditor believes your records reflect your true income and expenses. A check register or *Quicken* printout may take the place of a set of books, if it's backed up by canceled checks and receipts. See *Tax Savvy for Small Business* (Nolo) for more on keeping business records.

If your business has no records, you can be fined for failure to keep adequate records. The auditor can make up missing records by guesswork.

Appointment books or business diaries. If you claimed travel or meal expenses, you will need a writing showing dates and times the expenses were incurred, their business purpose, and who was visited or present at the meal. If you have no diary, you can write one up for the audit, but tell the auditor it is a reconstruction if you are asked.

Auto logs. Auto logs aren't required by law—despite what some auditors say—but they will help you prove business auto expenses. You can use a paper log or an electronic mileage app that employs GPS to track your mileage. Again, you can create one after the fact, but be up-front about it. Repair and maintenance receipts should have odometer mileage written on them, and your diary may have notations of trips and expenses.

Escrow papers. These are necessary if you claim rental property depreciation deductions to show how much of a deduction you are entitled to. They are also required if you sold the property.

Standing Up to the Auditor

As your audit progresses, the auditor will be continually making notes and filling in workpapers, seldom telling you what they are writing or thinking. Typically, the more an auditor writes, the more adjustments you can expect. To keep an auditor from running amok, we suggest that immediately after finishing with your documents for one group of items (say, business travel expenses) ask point blank, "Did you find any problems?" If the auditor says yes, don't go on to another area without having the person explain what the problem is.

This approach identifies you as someone who will not meekly take whatever the auditor dishes out without justifying the actions to your face. You are perfectly within your rights to politely ask questions during the audit. If the adjustment is because your records are missing, ask the auditor for at least 15 days to give you time to get the missing records. And if the auditor claims you don't have a legal right to a deduction—for instance, because your business is really just a nondeductible hobby—ask for the specific legal authority for that theory. Say you want to research the matter or talk to a tax professional, and ask that the adjustment not be made until you get back to the auditor.

If you continually challenge the auditor to justify any decisions, the person will likely grow weary and think longer and harder about making more waves. This isn't surprising. It's basic human nature to want to avoid conflict. This tack softens the auditor up for negotiation. I know people who have refused to leave the IRS office until the auditor gives in on at least one point! Many auditors don't like to have to justify their actions, as they would prefer to hide behind a mailed examination report rather than give you the bad news to your face.

Don't presume that standing up for yourself will get you a tougher audit—just the opposite is usually true. The more you make the auditor work, the more the auditor will want to get rid of you and go on to easier marks.

Proving Your Deductions

You must show that your tax return was prepared properly to win your audit; the IRS is not legally required to prove that you are wrong. Ideally, your proof should be in writing, but auditors have some discretion to accept oral explanations as well.

If you deducted business expenses or expenses that helped you produce income, the expenses must be reasonable and necessary as well as verifiable. This means that even if your expenses are legally allowable, if they are unreasonably large or extravagant, they won't pass muster. For example, Elmer owned a hot dog stand and claimed $20,000 in travel expenses. The auditor would disallow this amount as unreasonable, even if Elmer could substantiate it. Size or reasonableness of a deduction, however, is not usually grounds for disallowance.

TIP
Never give or mail your original documents to an IRS agent. If an auditor wants a copy, they can make it. Don't leave the auditor's office without your originals. IRS offices are black holes when it comes to misplacing things. If the IRS claims not to have received something, it's your word against the IRS's and guess who wins? Courts have said that you can't rely on "the IRS lost it" (or "the dog ate it") excuse. The burden of proof as to whatever the auditor is challenging on your tax return is always on you, and you might have to prove it more than once.

If You Don't Have Documentation

MYTH: If you can't prove a deduction in writing, it won't be allowed by an auditor because you are required to keep records.

FACT: Courts have repeatedly told the IRS that taxpayers can't be expected to keep flawless records. Tax regulations allow taxpayers, within limits, to offer oral explanations, use approximations for some expenses, claim expenses under $75 without receipts, and reconstruct records when the originals are missing.

Despite what an auditor might tell you, here are the *real* audit rules on missing records, taken from income tax regulations and court cases.

Substantial Compliance

Begin by claiming that you are in substantial compliance with the tax laws. Substantial compliance means that you have enough proof that you obeyed the tax reporting law even though your evidence is less than complete.

> EXAMPLE: The auditor agrees that Rufus is entitled to deduct a portion of his maintenance expenses as a home office expense. But the auditor finds that four months of bills that were paid in cash are missing. Rufus asserts that he is in substantial compliance and the auditor should accept the average of the other eight months of receipts to approximate the missing four and allow this much as a deduction.

This example shows the wisdom of going through your files long before the audit appointment. If you can't find bills, credit card statements, or canceled checks, order them from the companies and banks. Expect a delay in getting copies. Few businesses keep sales receipts beyond a year or two, and most do not give a priority to getting copies to you. If getting records in time looks like it will be a problem, ask the IRS for a postponement or request that your auditor allow you more time.

Oral Explanations

Tell the auditor why you are entitled to the deduction without proving it. Your spoken justification of why you can't produce a record must be given some weight by an auditor, as long as it's reasonable. If your records were lost along with your furniture and other belongings in a move from Iowa to New Mexico, your explanation should pass the believability test. But "burglars stole them when I was asleep" or "aliens with ray guns vaporized them" won't.

This is a good time to repeat the First Commandment of winning your audit: Establish and maintain credibility with the auditor. Once an auditor catches you in one lie, no matter how small, the auditor will have a hard time believing anything else you say.

Business Expenses Under $75 Each

You can claim business deductions for expenses without substantiation (such as a receipt) up to $75 per item. Lodging expenses, however, require receipts, no matter the amount.

Before you rush out to throw away all traces of these lesser expenses, keep in mind that you always need a record of some kind. This means a business calendar notation, log, or diary showing the amount, who it was paid to, the time and place of the expense, the business purpose, and relationship of the person you spent the money on.

While this regulation purports to cover only travel and meals, many auditors will allow other business deductions under $75 without receipts as well. If you have small expenses without receipts and the auditor wants to disallow them, explain that you thought you didn't need a receipt for items under $75. It might work, and the worst thing the auditor can do is say no.

Reconstruction of Records

Gaps due to missing documents may be filled by reconstruction—a process by which you rebuild lost or destroyed records. As long as the newly minted records appear to be reasonable, the auditor must consider them. This is a judgment call, however, and different auditors apply different standards. The advice that follows is necessarily general.

Courts have given some guidance on what it takes to successfully reconstruct records. If you can establish that at one time you possessed adequate records and that you no longer have them due to circumstances beyond your control, you are allowed to reconstruct them. (Internal Revenue Regulation 1.274-5(c)(5); see also *Gizzi v. Commissioner of Internal Revenue*, 65 T.C. 342 (1975).) You also must explain why they are missing. For instance, if your documents were destroyed when the town river flooded your basement, add a photo of your flooded basement or newspaper report of the flood in your area.

Documenting the expense is a little different. Let's say you spent $1,200 cash in fixing up a rented office but lost the file with the receipts for materials. You could reconstruct your expenses with a letter from your landlord attesting to the improvements or a statement from one of your clients who saw you doing the work. Typically, if you think hard enough about reconstructing paperwork to verify an expense, you can do it. Be creative.

Adjustments in Your Favor—Taking the Offensive

Auditors must make any adjustments in your favor whenever they are found during an audit. Even the most hard-nosed auditor knows that taxpayers occasionally make mistakes that hurt them, not the IRS, or overlook claiming tax benefits on their returns. This is another good reason to see a tax professional before meeting with an auditor: to find out if you missed any deductions or can find anything else in your favor to show the auditor. (In Chapter 13, we suggest some publications that might help you identify deductions you might have missed. Or, if you're self-employed, see *Tax Savvy for Small Business*, by Frederick W. Daily and Stephen Fishman (Nolo).)

If you or your preparer were overly conservative—for example, you decided not to take a certain expense as a deduction because you had no receipt—then claim it at the audit. It just might be accepted by the auditor, and nothing ventured, nothing gained.

Don't, however, bring up any favorable items until the auditor has completed the review and decided on any changes for the IRS. Then present your positive adjustments. If you show them earlier, the auditor might counter by looking harder for some offsetting adjustments. After the auditor is locked into a position, things can only get better if they accept any of your new, positive change items.

If you can't come up with any kind of paper showing an expense, create your own document. For example, you spent $700 cash on carpeting your building and Karpet King has since gone out of business. Write up your own receipt showing the name of the store, and the amount and date of purchase, or as close as you can get. But, be up front with the auditor; say you prepared the receipt as a reconstruction because it was not possible to document it in any other way.

Cohan **Rule.** An old, well-known tax case has saved many an audit victim with missing records. George M. "I'm a Yankee Doodle Dandy" Cohan was nailed for not having receipts in a 1920s IRS audit. He fought the IRS to a U.S. Court of Appeals, which held that a taxpayer may approximate expenditures for tax purposes, as long as the person can reasonably show that some amount was spent. (*Cohan v. Commissioner of Internal Revenue*, 349 F.2d 540 (2nd Cir. 1930).)

The *Cohan* Rule has its limits. First, you must make some showing of why the records are not available. They might have been lost or destroyed or be in such small amounts and from transactions in which receipts are not normally given, such as cab fares or tips. And the rule can't be applied to approximate travel and meals, as mentioned above.

In reality, the *Cohan* Rule is useful as a bargaining chip to use with the auditor. If you are told "no deduction without documentation," cry the *Cohan* Rule. Eyebrows will likely raise in surprise, and the auditor might back down, at least part of the way.

Negotiating With an Auditor

Auditors have no power to change your tax return. They can only *propose* tax changes to you. Auditors fully realize that if you don't go along with their proposals, you may appeal in most instances (Chapter 4) or go to Tax Court (Chapter 5) in all cases. In fact, the IRS's guiding principle for auditors is to close examinations with your consent to keep you from clogging up the appeals office and Tax Court. Because auditors' performance is judged on their closing ratio—how many examination reports are accepted by taxpayers—you're in a perfect position to negotiate.

Oddly, however, auditors aren't officially supposed to negotiate. They are told to discover the facts of a case and apply the tax law to those facts. In reality, if you can show an auditor that the facts are not black or white, you can reach a compromise. Let us emphasize—you can compromise based on the facts; you can't wheel and deal just because you can't afford the tax bill. For instance, never offer an auditor 50¢ on the dollar; instead ask for a 50% allowance of a questioned deduction. You can negotiate specific adjustments on particular items using this principle. Here are two examples.

Missing documentation. If your documentation is lacking, you have what the IRS calls a "substantiation" or "verification" problem. Suppose you claimed a storage rental expense of $50 per week, paid in cash, and lost your receipts. The auditor disallows the $2,600 item for lack of verification. The former manager of the storage facility writes a letter attesting to your regular payments, but the storage building has been torn down and replaced by a mall. Try proposing a compromise: Suggest a disallowance of 25% to get the audit over with. If the auditor agrees, or offers a 50% disallowance, you have just negotiated a fairly decent settlement and you've learned a lesson about keeping your records.

Questionable legal ground. You might have perfect records, but a shaky legal position. For instance, suppose you spent $5,000 to replace a deck and $5,000 for a new roof on rental property you own. On your tax return, you deducted both items as repairs. The auditor claims that these are capital improvements that must be depreciated over the 27.5-year depreciation period for residential property. Assuming the auditor is right, you would be limited to deducting only 3.636% of the cost ($318), for each of the next 28 years ($98 for the first year since the property was placed in service in June).

To propose a compromise, you can suggest that one item is an improvement, perhaps the deck, but the other is a repair—the roof, which was leaking like a sieve. You could then deduct all $5,000 for the roof and $98 for the deck. While you wanted to deduct $10,000, deducting $5,098 is much better than the IRS's initial position that you deduct only $196. You can still take depreciation deductions for the balance ($4,902) over the next 27 years.

Ending the Audit

Although it never hurts to delay the start of an audit, once it begins you might want to rush it along. For instance, if a problem lurks that the auditor has not yet found, the longer they look, the greater the chance of discovery. If the auditor hasn't yet seen your bank statements and found the mysterious $10,000 deposits, you want out of there before having to explain them. Also, having the IRS in your life is just plain stressful.

A field auditor might be maneuvered into closing a file, depending on the personality type involved.

Bored, lazy, or unexcited. As soon as the audit begins, tell the auditor that you have heard that audits usually produce adjustments. Say that you would appreciate it if it is over with quickly so you can go about your business. If the auditor gets the idea that you won't fight (at least small adjustments) the auditor might take you up on your offer. This is especially true if you point out any obvious errors in your return or records (such as 6 + 6 = 13) that will likely be found anyway. Many auditors have a personal tax adjustment level, which they know will satisfy their manager. Conversely, the more time the agent puts into your case, the more the auditor expects to find—and will.

EXAMPLE: Alison took a questionable tax position on a $2,000 deduction for her business. Nearing the end of a full day of an audit, the auditor hadn't yet reached the item. Alison volunteered that there was a $350 deduction that should not have been taken the year before. The auditor had already found $1,200 in other items to disallow, and Alison thought he might be satisfied with one more adjustment. She was right. The auditor said that another day would not be necessary. Even if she had not kept the auditor away from the $2,000 item, by volunteering the $350 item, Alison came across as reasonable. Such good deeds are often rewarded later by an auditor, such as by giving you the benefit of the doubt when documents are missing.

Overly conscientious. Some auditors (usually the younger ones straight from IRS basic training) come on strong, looking at every little thing and laying down the law like a Marine drill instructor. When this happens, drop the nice guy approach, get your back up and argue over every item that the auditor looks at, even when you know you are wrong. Let the person know two can play the game and that you won't be steamrolled. If you know serious problems are ahead due to questionable items or missing documents, demand an end to the audit for that day. Say that you want to consult a tax professional. The auditor won't like being slowed down, but knows your request must be granted.

At your next meeting, the auditor should at least be more reasonable, if not anxious to conclude the audit. If not, threaten to call in the auditor's manager. This usually causes the auditor to adjust their attitude. Often, auditors will figure they can better use their time working on other files where the taxpayer doesn't stand up to them instead of putting more time into your case.

IRS Pressure on an Auditor to Finish— Extending the Audit Time Limit

The IRS doesn't have forever to audit you. The deadline is normally three years after your return is due (usually April 15) or actually filed, whichever is later. If the IRS suspects serious fraud or underreporting of income by at least 25%, the period is extended to six years or indefinitely. But audits started beyond the normal three-year limit are rare.

The *Internal Revenue Manual* directs an auditor to issue an audit report within 28 months after the date you filed the return. If an auditor hasn't completed the work by then, you will be asked to extend the deadline by signing IRS Form 872, *Consent to Extend the Time to Assess Tax*. When asked, you have three options:

- Sign the consent form.
- Don't sign.
- Negotiate the terms of the extension.

We recommend the second or third approach in most cases.

The auditor wants you to sign an open-ended extension agreement, meaning that an audit adjustment can be made on any item, at any time in the future. Don't do it; you have the right to refuse to sign. Instead, ask that the form be limited to specific items—those on which the auditor has more work to do. Also, agree to an extension for no longer than six months. These perfectly reasonable limitations on the auditor narrow your risk of further IRS fishing into your affairs.

If you don't negotiate or sign the Form 872 extension, one of two things will happen:

- The auditor will issue the examination report and a Notice of Deficiency simultaneously. This means that you can't appeal the report within the IRS, but you can go to court. (See Chapter 5.) This is not so bad, as it isn't that difficult to take the IRS to Tax Court.
- The auditor might slip up and let the three-year audit deadline pass—meaning that no assessment can ever be made. This doesn't happen very often. The IRS gets very upset with auditors who blow the deadline. But when it does happen, it's like winning the lottery.

Finishing Audits

Toward the end of every meeting with the auditor, ask what adjustments will be made. While some auditors might not be willing to commit without running it by their managers, they might have some idea. Try to pin the person down. If you disagree, argue your case on the spot or ask for time to get more documents together. Offer to pay any balance in full, if you get a concession. It might not work, but it's always worth a try.

> ### If the IRS Loses Your Audit File
>
> Audit files sometimes get lost in the IRS bureaucratic maze for many months. When found, an unfinished audit file could be assigned to a new auditor who won't want to work on a half-done case and will look for a quick way to close out the file. Even better, the normal three-year deadline for auditing your return might expire before the file resurfaces. This means that the IRS forever loses its right to make adjustments, and you are in the clear.

Receiving the Examination Report

When the auditor completes the work, you will be handed or mailed IRS Form 4549, *Income Tax Examination Changes* in field audit cases, or Form 1902-B, *Report of Individual Income Tax Examination Changes* in office examinations. This report shows changes proposed to your tax liability for the year under audit, and for any other open years if the auditor expanded the examination. The report also provides a brief explanation for each change, such as "You did not prove the amount shown was a rental expense."

From your point of view, the examination report falls into one of three categories:

Win. Instead of a report, you will receive a "no change" or even a refund letter. These require no explanation. You've won. One in 11 audits produces no change or a refund.

Lose. The report makes changes—you owe more taxes, plus interest and maybe penalties. This means you didn't have good documentation or what you had was not accepted. Or, perhaps the auditor didn't buy your legal entitlement to the tax benefits claimed.

Mixed. Some of your documents and explanations were accepted, but others weren't. Or maybe your legal position was shaky on one or two items but strong on others.

Don't worry if it seems to take forever for the IRS to send you the final report. Three to four weeks is standard, but it can take six months. Don't take a long delay to mean that the IRS is giving your case special attention. More likely, your case has a low priority and is sitting on someone's desk for routine processing.

Sample Examination Report

Internal Revenue Service

Date: 8/10/2023

Department of the Treasury

Tax Year Ended: 2022
Person to Contact:
Contact Telephone Number:
Contact Address:

Dear Ms. McMillian:

Enclosed are two copies of our report explaining why we believe adjustments should be made in the amount of your tax. Please look this report over and let us know whether you agree with our findings.

If you accept our findings, please sign the consent to assessment and collection portion at the bottom of the report and mail one copy to this office within 30 days from the date of this letter. If additional tax is due, you may want to pay it now and limit the interest charge; otherwise, we will bill you. (See enclosed Publication 5 for payment details.)

If you do not accept our findings, you have 30 days from the date of this letter to do one of the following:

1. Mail us any additional evidence or information you would like us to consider.

2. Request a discussion of our findings with the examiner who conducted the examination. At that time, you may submit any additional evidence or information you would like us to consider. If you plan to come in for a discussion, please phone or write us in advance so that we can arrange a convenient time and place.

3. Discuss your position with the group manager or a senior examiner (designated by the group manager), if an examination has been held and you have been unable to reach an agreement with the examiner.

If you do not accept our findings and do not want to take any of the above actions, you may write us at the address shown above or call us at the telephone number shown above within 30 days from the date of this letter to request a conference with an Appeals Officer. You must provide all pertinent documentation and facts concerning disputed issues to the examiner before your case is forwarded to the Independent Office of Appeals. If your examination was conducted entirely by mail, we would appreciate your first discussing our findings with one our examiners.

(over)

Los Angeles District

Letter 915(D)

Sample Examination Report (continued)

The Appeals Office is independent of the District Director. The Appeals Officer, who has not examined your return previously, will take a fresh look at your case. Most disputes considered by Appeals are resolved informally and promptly. By going to Appeals, you may avoid court costs (such as the United States Tax Court filing fee of $60), clear up this matter sooner, and prevent interest from mounting. An Appeals Officer will promptly telephone you and, if necessary, arrange an appointment. If you decide to bypass Appeals and petition the Tax Court, your case will normally be assigned for settlement to an Appeals Office before the Tax Court hears the case.

Under Internal Revenue Code Section 6673, the Tax Court is authorized to award damages of up to $5,000 to the United States when a taxpayer unreasonably fails to pursue available administrative remedies. Damages could be awarded under this provision, for example, if the Court concludes that it was unreasonable for a taxpayer to bypass Appeals and then file a petition in the Tax Court. The Tax Court will make that determination based upon the facts and circumstances of each case. Generally, the Service will not ask the Court to award damages under this provision if you make a good faith effort to meet with Appeals and to settle your case before petitioning the Tax Court.

The enclosed Publication 5 explains your appeal rights.

If we do not hear from you within 30 days, we will have to process your case on the basis of the adjustments shown in the examination report. If you write us about your case, please write to the person whose name and address are shown in the heading of this letter and refer to the symbols in the upper right corner of the enclosed report. An envelope is enclosed for your convenience. Please include your telephone number, area code, and the most convenient time for us to call, in case we find it necessary to contact you for further information.

If you prefer, you may call the person at the telephone number shown in the heading of this letter. This person will be able to answer any questions you may have. Thank you for your cooperation.

Sincerely yours,

Mort Meyer

Los Angeles District

Letter 915(D)

Sample Examination Report (continued)

Report of Individual **Income Tax Examination Changes**				**Department of the Treasury** **Internal Revenue Service**	

Name of Taxpayer Ruth McMillian			Year 2022	Form **1040**	Filing Status Single	In Reply Refer To: OOO IRS 222

Authorized Representative	Date of Report 11/18/2023	Social Security Number 123-456-7890	Examining District 000-00

Income and Deduction Amounts Adjusted

Explanation Number (See attached)	Item Changed	Amount Shown on Return or as Previously Adjusted	Corrected Amount of Income or Deduction	Adjustment Increase (Decrease)
6102	Net Operating Loss	23226	0	23226
5605	Sch-C Rentals Loss	13757	0	13757
5605	Sch-C Acting Loss	17246	0	17246
0101	Gross Receipts Rentals	— —	— — —	— — —
0101	Gross Receipts Acting	— —	— — —	— — —
8203	S.E. Tax	— —	— — —	— — —
8138	Negligence	— —	— — —	— — —
8120	Substantial Understatement	— —	— — —	— — —

A.	Adjustment in income and deductions - increase (decrease) (See explanation of adjustments attached.)	54,229
B.	Adjusted gross or taxable income shown on return or as previously adjusted	17,660
C.	Corrected adjusted gross or taxable income	71,889
D.	Corrected tax (From: ☐ Tax Table, ☐ Tax Rate Schedules, ☐ Form 8615 or ☐ Other)	16,261
E.	Tax credits (general business, child and dependent care, foreign, etc.) (If adjusted, see explanation attached.)	———
F.	Other tax (self-employment, alternative minimum, tax from recapture of Investment credit, etc.) (If adjusted, see explanation attached.) S.E. Tax	667
G.	Total corrected tax (line D less line E plus line F)	16,928
H.	Tax shown on return or as previously adjusted	4,197
I.	Adjustments to EIC/Fuels credit - increase (decrease) (If adjusted, see explanation attached.)	
J.	Deficiency - Increase in tax or (Overassessment - Decrease in tax) (Line G adjusted by Lines H and I)	12,731
K.	Adjustments to prepayment credits - increase (decrease)	
L.	Balance due or (Overpayment) - Excluding interest and penalties (Line J adjusted by line K)	12,731
M.	Penalties (See explanation attached) (1) Negligence § 6652(a)(1)	636.55
	(2) Substantial Understatement § 6661	3,182.86
	(3)	

Consent to Assessment and Collection - I do not wish to exercise my appeal rights with the Internal Revenue Service or to contest in the United States Tax Court the findings in this report. Therefore, I give my consent to the immediate assessment and collection of any increase in tax and penalties, and accept any decrease in tax and penalties above, plus any interest as provided by law.

Although this report is subject to review, you may consider it as your notice that your case is closed if you are not notified of an exception to these findings within 45 days after a signed copy of the report or a signed waiver, Form 870, is received by the District Director.

Ruth McMillian	11/18/2023		
Your signature	Date	Spouse's signature (IF A JOINT RETURN, BOTH MUST SIGN)	Date

By		Title		Date
Cat. No. 21270C		(See notices on the back)		Form **1902-B** (Rev. 1-91)

Sample Examination Report (continued)

FORM 886-A	**EXPLANATION OF ITEMS**	SCHEDULE NO. OR EXHIBIT A
Ruth McMillian		YEAR/PERIOD ENDED 2022

6102	You did not sustain a net operating loss in the tax year within the meaning of Section 172 of the Internal Revenue Code because your loss was attributable solely to nonbusiness expenses. Therefore, there is no net operating loss carry-back or carry-over, and your deduction claimed is disallowed. Taxable income is increased accordingly.
0101	Although not adjusted, gross receipts are an open audit issue.
8203	We have adjusted your self-employment tax due to a change in your net profit from this self-employment.
5605	Since you did not establish that the business expense shown on your tax return was paid or incurred during the taxable year and that the expense was ordinary and necessary to your business, we have disallowed the amount shown.

DEPARTMENT OF THE TREASURY-INTERNAL REVENUE SERVICE   FORM **886-A**

Page _____

Sample Examination Report (continued)

FORM 886-A	EXPLANATION OF ITEMS	SCHEDULE NO. OR EXHIBIT A
Ruth McMillian		YEAR/PERIOD ENDED 2022

8138   Since all or part of the underpayment of tax you were

required to show on your return is due to negligence or

intentional disregard of rules and regulations, you are being

charged a penalty under Internal Revenue Code Section 6652(a).

For tax returns due, without regard to extensions, after

December 31, 1994, this penalty is 5% of the underpayment.

The interest on the penalty is calculated according to Internal

Revenue Code Section 6601(e)(2)(B) from the due date of the

return (including extension) until the additional tax is paid.

8120   Since there is a substantial understatement of income tax,

you are liable for a penalty of 25% of the amount of any

underpayment attributable to such understatement. This

applies to tax not assessed prior to October 21, 1992. In

addition, interest is figured on the penalty from the due date

of the return without regard to extensions. See Internal

Revenue Code Sections 6661 and 6601(e)(2).

DEPARTMENT OF THE TREASURY-INTERNAL REVENUE SERVICE

FORM 886-A

Page _____

Understanding the Examination Report

The total amount of taxes, penalties, and interest the audit added is shown on your report. Each change is listed, the tax code section cited, and a general explanation given. As stated, most explanations are vague. You are usually not specifically told how you failed to prove your case. If you don't know, call the auditor and ask. An auditor must tell you where you failed.

Your Options After Getting the Examination Report

You have four choices after you receive the Form 4549 examination report.

Agree. The IRS hopes you will sign, date, and return a copy of the report. This is referred to by the IRS as an "agreed case."

By consenting to Form 4549, you agree to the immediate assessment of the tax deficiency found, plus any penalties and interest listed on the examination report. You give up your right to appeal or go to Tax Court. Theoretically, you could pay, change your mind, and sue the IRS for a refund in court, but this seldom makes sense. Although most tax lawsuits are filed in U.S. Tax Court, a refund case must be brought in a U.S. federal District Court or the U.S. Court of Claims. (See Chapter 5.)

A report, even if signed by you, is not final until approved by the auditor's manager. Occasionally, a report you signed will be kicked back to the auditor for correction of obvious errors or to further develop issues. If this happens, the auditor might contact you once more. It might seem unfair, but you can't complain about being audited twice. The first audit was not officially concluded.

Signing doesn't mean you have to pay when you sign the report. Paying, however, might seal the deal. Auditors can offer a payment plan if you owe less than $50,000. You have up to 72 months to pay on a monthly basis. Interest and late payment penalties still accrue on the unpaid balance. Interest and penalties on late tax payments get added on. For bills over $50,000 (see Chapter 6), you might have to reveal your finances and living expenses to get a payment plan.

TIP

It's okay to tell the auditor that you'll just wait until a bill comes from the IRS campus center computer and then decide how to pay. Sometimes, the bill is less than the audit report figure because a penalty was dropped or a computation error was made or corrected. If the bill is more than the amount on the report, complain; if it's less, let your conscience be your guide. If you pay the lesser amount, no one might ever notice. Don't be surprised, however, if you are later billed for the difference.

Disagree. Examination reports aren't cast in stone until you sign off. If you want to fight the report, call the auditor. Tell the person what findings you disagree with. Ask what additional proof it would take to get the report changed. Request 30 days to get a missing document or reconstruct a record. Most auditors will hold off until you mail the proof to them. Pushing for another appointment might be better. It forces them to face you again, and shows that you are serious about contesting the report's findings. If the auditor is not cooperative, ask to speak to a manager. If you are ultimately successful, you'll be sent an amended examination report to sign.

TIP

If your new documentation doesn't help, ask for a copy of the auditor's workpapers. These are the notes the IRS requires an auditor to put in a file. Workpapers should explain and justify any changes made to a tax return. If the auditor shows you their notes, ask for a full explanation (and the conclusions) if it isn't obvious. Don't be surprised if the auditor refuses to show you the workpapers. If you are refused, say that you know you are entitled to see them under the Freedom of Information Act and you will make a formal request for them. (Chapter 4 explains how to make a Freedom of Information Act request.)

If you don't get anywhere with the auditor, ask to meet with a manager. Generally, the manager will speak with you. I call this an informal appeal. Managers don't always back their auditors. They have a strong motive to close files handled by their group with an "agreed" notation, so they might appease you.

If you talk to or meet with the manager, don't criticize the auditor. The manager might then concentrate on defending their employee instead of considering your position. Instead, talk about the adjustments you don't agree with and suggest a compromise. Even if this doesn't get you anywhere, the manager's explanations might make the IRS's position clearer to you or point out the weaknesses in your case. As a last resort, if the manager won't budge, calmly say that you are disappointed and that you don't want to appeal, but you don't know what else to do. Again, keep in mind that the IRS doesn't like appeals, and this subtle threat might get you what you want.

Team managers may delegate audit disputes to senior agents who are more experienced and might know how to smooth things over. Remember, auditors are instructed to get you to agree to the audit report, if possible. The senior agent might already be familiar with your case, especially if your auditor is fairly new at the IRS. If your auditor ever asked for time during your audit, ostensibly to make copies or check on something, the auditor might have been asking a senior auditor what to do.

If you explain your position to the senior manager and still need help, you can insist on talking to the real manager. The IRS, like most other organizations, doesn't like to be bothered by squeaking wheels—you might eventually get greased. If you want to go further up the ladder, ask to speak to a territory manager.

Do nothing. You don't have to respond to a proposed examination report at all. If you ignore it, the auditor may call, or in a month or two you'll receive something called a "30-day letter." This is your formal notice that your case is considered "unagreed" and that you have 30 days to start an appeal.

Appeal. The appeals process is covered in Chapter 4, and is also described in IRS Publication 5, *Your Appeal Rights and How to Prepare a Protest If You Disagree*. You should receive a copy of Publication 5 with your examination report.

The IRS doesn't have to grant you an administrative appeal; it's discretionary. However, the IRS must eventually send you a form, Notice of Deficiency, before the audit can become final. This letter might not arrive for months after the audit was completed. The IRS must send it by certified mail. To contest the audit results now, you must file a petition in the U.S. Tax Court within 90 days. (See Chapter 5.) If you don't, the examination report becomes final and your right to contest the audit has ended, with one exception.

Case History of an Informal Audit Appeal

Mr. Ky, a Vietnamese immigrant and San Francisco restaurant owner, was audited. When he received the examination report, Ky was so distraught he considered jumping off the Golden Gate Bridge. Ky had fallen victim to a dishonest tax return preparer who guaranteed his clients they would never have IRS problems. His clients almost always got tax refunds, and he charged a percentage of the refund received.

One day, the office of the bogus tax adviser was raided and the IRS seized his records. All of his clients got audit notices. Ky was understandably suspicious of anyone calling himself a tax expert, so he decided to handle the audit himself. He wanted to come clean knowing he would have to pay some additional taxes.

The auditor knew Ky was selected as part of a special IRS project involving the crooked tax preparer. At the meeting, things went from bad to worse. Ky spoke broken English and produced records written in his native language. The auditor became irritated and impatient. The examination report came quickly, disallowing most of Ky's business deductions and finding a great deal of unreported income. The resulting taxes, with heavy fraud penalties and interest added, came to $79,500. To pay meant Ky would have had to sell his business and lose everything he had worked for in the 10 years he had been in America.

Ky finally sought a tax professional. During their meeting, the tax professional became convinced that Ky should not owe anywhere near $79,500. The tax professional called the auditor's manager and made an appointment to meet her in two weeks. He then found a Vietnamese-American accountant to convert Ky's records and notes into a more conventional set of books. The accountant acted as an interpreter and helped the tax professional take sworn statements from Vietnamese people who had worked in the restaurant. These books and statements created a true financial picture of the business, in clear English.

When the tax professional met with the auditor's manager, he presented the statements and records. In less than an hour, they had agreed on a total tax of $13,000 and no harsh fraud penalty. After the tax bill came, Ky negotiated an installment payment agreement with the IRS Collection Division. Ky did not jump off the Golden Gate or any other bridge. His family now owns two restaurants in San Francisco.

You can also contest by paying the tax bill and filing a claim with the IRS for a refund. Refund claims are always denied. You can then file a refund suit in U.S. District Court or the U.S. Court of Claims. (See Chapter 5.)

Eventually, if you do nothing, you'll get a Notice of Tax Due. This is the beginning of the IRS collection effort. (See Chapter 6.)

Opening a Closed Audit

The procedure for reopening a closed audit, called "audit reconsideration," is initiated either by you or the IRS. Fortunately, the IRS rarely reopens closed audits. If it does, see a tax pro to find out if the IRS is acting properly, or do a little legal research yourself. (See Chapter 13; the relevant laws are Internal Revenue Code § 7605(b); IRS Regulation 601.105; Revenue Procedure 85-13; and *Internal Revenue Manual* 1.2.1.5.1, IRS Policy Statement 4-3.)

Serious Audit Problems

While everyone considers being audited a problem, a few uncommon, yet serious, audit issues merit special discussion.

The Auditor Suspects You of Fraud

Tax fraud is covered in Chapter 10.

You're Billed for an Audit You Didn't Know About

Many taxpayers receive bills from examinations they didn't know about—phantom audits. Yes, the IRS is required to notify you in writing of an audit. Theoretically, if the IRS doesn't let you know about an audit, your return can't be audited. In reality, however, the IRS is only required to mail a letter to your *last known address*. It isn't required to verify that you actually received the notice.

The Tax Court says the IRS must update its files regularly and send notices to the address on your most recent tax return or newer address that you have provided. (*Abeles v. Commissioner of Internal Revenue*, 91 U.S.T.C. 1019 (1991).) The IRS is allowed three months to update its records on a change of address after it receives notification.

If you don't answer an audit letter and it's not returned to the IRS by the post office, auditors can treat you as a "no show." Exemptions and deductions are disallowed in whatever manner the auditor wishes and an audit bill is issued. It's not a pretty picture.

> **TIP**
> **To make sure you get all IRS notices, file IRS Form 8822, *Change of Address*, whenever you move.** (A copy is available at the IRS website, www.irs.gov.) Don't just rely on a post office change of address form.

The unfairness of the IRS's charging ahead when you don't get the audit notice is underscored by what happens next. The IRS usually sends an audit report and a letter informing you of the appeal process to your old address. Or, the IRS may send a Notice of Deficiency, giving you 90 days to file in Tax Court. This notice comes by certified mail. But, again, the law doesn't require that you actually receive the letter, only that the IRS send it. The IRS doesn't seem to care if you get any of these notices. Legally, as long as the notices are sent to your address in the IRS records, the audit was legitimate. Hardly fair, but you can fight back.

There are three ways to fight a phantom audit.

Audit reconsideration. (Discussed above.) If you receive a mysterious audit tax bill, immediately write or call the IRS office that sent it. Tell them you never received notice of the audit and you are requesting an *assessment reconsideration*. Or, call the Taxpayer Advocate Service. (See Chapter 8.) Make an appointment or send the notices by fax or mail. Ask for an assessment reconsideration meeting with an auditor. See IRS Publication 3598 for details on making a request.

You don't have a right to an assessment reconsideration; it's discretionary with the IRS. Usually, however, legitimate requests are granted. The IRS also has an audit reexamination procedure. A reexamination can open up your entire file for audit—and not just the items that were charged in the phantom audit.

Petition the U.S. Tax Court. If your assessment reconsideration is denied, file a petition in Tax Court, stating that a Notice of Deficiency was not sent to your last known address as required by law. (See Chapter 5.)

Offer in Compromise. In addition to audit reconsideration and Tax Court, you can challenge a phantom audit by making an Offer in Compromise, based on a doubt as to your liability for the tax bill. (See Chapter 6.) Unlike most Offers in Compromise, which are made to settle an undisputed tax bill, with an Offer in Compromise based on doubt as to liability, you don't offer any money to the IRS. The IRS might treat your offer as it would treat an assessment reconsideration and reopen your case.

Jeopardy Assessments

The IRS has a "shoot first, ask questions later" power to make quick tax assessments without an audit. This is called the "jeopardy assessment." Normally there must be a formal assessment of taxes against you before the IRS can legally collect. The jeopardy assessment process allows the IRS to immediately grab your assets without prior notice. You have a right to a hearing, but not until after the seizure.

Thankfully, jeopardy assessments are authorized only if the IRS believes its right to collect taxes will be harmed, and that:

- You appear to be planning to hide out in or depart the United States.
- You are concealing, dissipating, or removing property from the country or transferring it to other persons.
- Your financial solvency is endangered.

Jeopardy assessments are most frequently made against foreign companies or foreigners operating businesses in the United States, or persons arrested with large amounts of cash, especially suspected drug dealers. If you are ever faced with a jeopardy assessment, see a tax lawyer right away.

Form 4700 Examination Workpapers

Form 4700. Examination Workpapers.

Examination Workpapers

Taxpayer's name, address, SSN (Use pre-addressed label or show changes)	Date		Year(s)
	Examiner		Grade
	Taxpayer(s)	Home Phone	Work Phone
	Reviewer		

A
Initial Interview
1. Examination technique: ☐ Correspondence ☐ Undeliverable mail ☐ No show ☐ Interview with:
_____
2. Receipt of Publication 1 ☐
3. Appeal rights and Privacy Act explained ☐
4. Continue on Form 4700-A, B or C

Representative - Power of Attorney ☐ Yes ☐ No
Name Phone

B
Closed No Change
Issue: ☐ Letter 590 ☐ Letter 1156 ☐ Other
Examiner

C
Examination Reminders
1. Proforma Worksheets utilized where applicable
2. Alternative minimum tax
3. Inspection of prior and subsequent year return, IRM 4215
4. Probe for unreported deductions and credits
5. Scope of Examination, IRM 4253.2
6. Automatic adjustments resulting from AGI change(s)

Case Processing Reminders
1. Claim Case - Forms 2297 and 3363
2. Information Reports (IRM 4219) - Form 5346
3. FICA, Self-Employment or Tip Income Adjustments Forms 885-E, 885-F, and 885-T
4. Inequities, Abuses, Loopholes - Form 3558
5. Inadequate Records Notice (IRM 4271)
6. Special Handling Notice 3198

D

(Items to be considered, explored, verified)	Year	Per Return	Corrected	Adjustment	Workpapers Index

E

	Year	Per Return	Corrected	Adjustment	Workpapers Index

Form 4700 (Rev. 2-90)   Department of the Treasury — Internal Revenue Service

Form 4700-A Supplement

Form 4700-A. Form 4700 Supplement.

Form 4700 Supplement

Taxpayer	Year(s)
Examiner	Date

		Yes	No	Comments
1. Preparer Information	A. Was return prepared for Compensation? (If Yes, complete remaining items)			
	B. Identification Penalties required?			
	C. Did preparer negotiate refund?			
	D. Did taxpayer receive a copy of return?			

2. Prior IRS Contacts or Prior Audits	☐ None ☐ Yes — Year(s)	Do Repetitive Audit Procedures apply? ☐ Yes ☐ No
	Issues/Reasons:	Was Amended Return(s) filed? ☐ Yes ☐ No

3. All Due Returns Filed?		Yes	No	N/A	Comments
	Individual				
	Household help				
	Employment				
	Excise				

4. Income Probe

If reported or received none, enter (√) in block. If received but not reported, enter (X) in block and comment below.

Interest (S&L) Banks, 2nd Mortgage)	Alimony	Gifts, Inheritance
	Partnerships	Scholarship, Fellowship, Grant
Dividends	Sick Pay	Loans
Sale of assets	Child support	Social Security
Other jobs	Prizes, awards, bonuses	Welfare
Investments	Gambling/Lotteries	Unemployment compensation
Tips	Insurance	VA benefits
Commission	Estate/Trusts	Military allowance
Hobbies	State/Local Tax Refund	Foreign Bank Accounts
Rent/Royalty	Employer Reimbursement	Pensions, Annuities, Profit-Sharing
Comments should indicate nature and extent of income probe		IRA/Keogh Distributions

5. Bartering	Exchange of personal services or merchandise?	Yes	No
	Belong to any bartering clubs or organizations?	Yes	No
	If Yes, explain fully		

6. Foreign Accounts and Foreign Trusts	Is the Foreign Accounts and Foreign Trusts question appearing on the tax return answered correctly? If No, explain fully.	Yes	No	☐ N/A

7. Exemptions	Name	Age	Relationship	Other Information

Form **4700-A** (Rev. 9-84) *(over please)* Department of the Treasury — Internal Revenue Service

Form 4700-A Supplement (continued)

Form 4700-A. Form 4700 Supplement. (cont'd)

Complete Remaining Items After Examination

8. Solicit Payment

- Payment solicited: Payment received — Include Interest Computation
- Payment solicited: Taxpayer desires to be billed

9. Prior/ Subsequent Year Return

Prior/subsequent year audit recommended?

- ☐ Yes — Date of AIMS Request _____ Date Information Report Submitted _____
- ☐ No — State reason:

10. Penalties Recommended For Taxpayer

Type	Asserted	Reason
Negligence	☐ Yes	Indicate issue(s) on which 50% interest is applicable.
	☐ No	
Delinquency	☐ Yes	
	☐ No	
Fraud	☐ Yes	Indicate issue(s) on which 50% interest is applicable.
	☐ No	
Other (State penalty)	☐ Yes	
	☐ No	

11. Preparer Conduct Penalties

Any indications of preparer negligence or fraud?	Yes	No

If Yes, explain:

12. Unagreed Case

Group Manager Involvement in Unagreed Case:

☐ Taxpayer Offered Conference with Group Manager. Date _____

Form **4700-A** (Rev. 9-84) GPO : 1986 0 – 161–268 Department of the Treasury — Internal Revenue Service

Form 4700-B Business Supplement

Form 4700-B. Form 4700 Business Supplement.

Form 4700 Business Supplement	Taxpayer		Year	
	Examiner		Date	

1. Brief Discription of Day-to-Day Business Operation	

2. Business History	How long in business			
	Number of employees	Full-Time		Part-Time
3. Accounting Method	☐ Cash	☐ Accrual		☐ Hybrid
	Who keeps the books?			

4. Cash on Hand		Beginning of Year	End of Year
	Home	$	$
	Business	$	$
	Elsewhere	$	$

5. Where do You Maintain Your Bank Account(s)?	Business	Account Number	Personal	Account Numb

6. Banking Practices	Were all business and personal expenses kept separately?
	Were all business receipts deposited? To which account?
	How are business expenses paid?

7. Safety Deposit Box	Location	Contents

8. Purchases	Any withdrawals of purchases for personal use?

9. Related Transactions	Any transactions between you and relative or related parties? If so, explain.

10. Gross Receipts	How were gross receipts calculated?

Workpaper Index _____

Form 4700-B Business Supplement (continued)

Form 4700-B. Form 4700 Business Supplement. (cont'd)

	Are inventories material? ☐ Yes ☐ No			
11. Inventories	a. Did beginning and ending balances agree with prior/subsequent returns?	Yes		No
	b. Were there any changes in method of valuing inventories?	Yes		No
	c. When taken:			
	How:			
	d. Include year-end purchases?	Yes		No
	e. Any write-offs or write downs?	Yes		No

12. Loans, notes, mortgages payable:	AMOUNT	Per	Bus.	PAGE, EXHIBIT, SCHEDULE

13. Capital items sold:	AMOUNT	PURCHASER	PAGE, EXHIBIT, SCHEDULE

14. Capital items purchased:		SELLER	

Form 4700-B (Rev. 8-83)   U S GOVERNMENT PRINTING OFFICE 1983 –381–541/5424   Department of the Treasury — Internal Revenue Service

Chapter Highlights

- In an audit, the IRS wants to find out if you reported all of your income and were entitled to all credits, deductions, and exemptions claimed on your tax return.
- Keep the IRS from holding the audit at your business or home. Instead, go to the IRS office or hire a tax professional to meet the IRS agent at the tax professional's office.
- Give auditors no more information than they are entitled to, and don't talk any more during the audit than is absolutely necessary.
- Don't expect to come out of the audit without owing something. The odds are against you.
- The IRS must complete an audit within three years of the time your tax return is filed, unless the IRS finds tax fraud or a significant underreporting of income (which extends the deadline).
- If the audit isn't going well, demand a recess to consult a tax professional or collect your thoughts.
- Speak to the auditor's manager if you think the auditor is treating you unfairly.
- If you are missing receipts or other documents, you are allowed to reconstruct records (in most cases).
- When you get the audit report, call the auditor if you don't understand or agree with it. Meet with the auditor's manager to see if you can reach a compromise if it looks bad.
- If you can't live with an audit result, you may appeal within the IRS or go on to Tax Court.

Appealing Your Audit Within the IRS

Pros and Cons of Appealing an Audit 141

How to Appeal an Audit 142

   Time Limit for an Appeal 142

   How to Get Your Audit to the Appeals Office 142

   IRS Form for Appeals Under $25,000 (Small Case) 143

   Protest Letter for Appeals Over $25,000 (Large Case) 143

   Requesting the Auditor's File 145

How the Independent Office of Appeals Works 148

Preparing for an Appeals Hearing 149

   Organizing and Presenting Documents 150

   Filling in the Gaps 150

   Focusing on Challenged Items 151

Dealing With the Appeals Officer 152

Presenting a Case to an Appeals Officer 152

Negotiating a Settlement 154

Should You Hire a Tax Professional for Your Appeal? 160

If You Don't Settle on Appeal 161

You tried to get the auditor to be reasonable but the person just wouldn't see things your way. In fact, you received a costly examination report. You spoke to the auditor's manager in an effort to win an informal appeal. Again, you didn't have any luck. You're not ready to give up, though. What's next?

A formal appeal, that's what. The IRS has an administrative procedure for appealing unagreed examination reports to an IRS appeals office. Officially renamed the Internal Revenue Service Independent Office of Appeals in 2019, the appeals office has nearly 2,000 employees scattered throughout the United States. Take advantage of this procedure, which is described in IRS Publication 5, *Your Appeal Rights and How To Prepare a Protest If You Disagree.*

Fewer than 1 in 10 audited taxpayers appeal. Many more taxpayers should. Appealing is neither difficult nor time-consuming, and your chance of achieving at least some tax reduction is excellent. You rarely need to hire a tax professional to file an appeal. Despite this, however, most taxpayers are either too discouraged or intimidated to appeal. That's too bad.

The official IRS position on the appeals process is this:

> *The appeals mission is to resolve tax controversies, without litigation, on a basis which is fair and impartial to both the government and the taxpayer and in a manner that will enhance voluntary compliance and public confidence in the integrity and efficiency of the [IRS]. (Internal Revenue Manual 8.1.1.1(1).)*

The Odds of Winning an Appeal

Most auditors privately refer to the appeals office as the IRS's gift shop. An IRS in-joke even says that appeals officers work on the 50% rule—they like to cut auditors' adjustments by half.

IRS statistics show that the auditors are exaggerating—but not by much. The average appeal results in a 40% decrease in taxes, penalties, and interest the auditor imposed. So, even the IRS confirms that it pays to appeal. The only mystery is why more audit victims don't.

According to the IRS, in a recent year, over 100,000 appeals were taken by taxpayers and over 80% were resolved in a manner acceptable to both sides.

Appeals of other IRS actions. In addition to audits, many other IRS decisions may be appealed, such as tax liens and levies. (See Chapters 6 and 7.)

Pros and Cons of Appealing an Audit

Three solid reasons exist for appealing an audit and there are two relatively insignificant reasons not to.

Pros

- Appealing is simple and costs nothing unless you use a tax professional, which isn't usually necessary for success.
- Appealing, in the majority of cases, results in some savings, although rarely a total victory.
- Appealing delays your audit tax bill for months, buying you time to consider payment options.

Cons

- The appeals officer can raise issues the auditor missed—but this almost never happens. Nevertheless, if you're afraid that a missed item will be discovered and you'll owe a lot more in taxes, you can skip the appeal altogether. In this case, you can go directly to Tax Court, where new issues can't be raised. (See Chapter 5.)
- Interest (and sometimes penalties) on the tax bill continue to run while you are appealing. This is typically a small item as compared with the likely tax savings resulting from most appeals.

The IRS Does Not Have to Offer an Appeal

The IRS is not legally required to let you have an administrative appeal after an audit—and sometimes it doesn't. Instead of a 30-day letter offering an appeal, you might get a so-called "90-day letter." This means the only way to challenge the audit without paying the additional tax the IRS claims you owe is to file a petition in Tax Court within 90 days. (See Chapter 5.)

Here's something odd: If you don't get an appeals hearing and do file a Tax Court petition, your case will be sent to the Independent Office of Appeals anyway. You will now probably be offered an appeal hearing, or you can request one. If you don't settle in the appeals office, your file will be sent to an IRS lawyer.

How to Appeal an Audit

After the audit, the IRS sends an examination report with proposed adjustments —additional taxes, penalties, and interest. If you don't sign and return a copy of the report within a few weeks, the IRS usually sends a letter (the 30-day letter) and IRS Publication 5, an explanation of how to appeal the report.

Time Limit for an Appeal

"Protest" is the official term for formally appealing an IRS determination. You must protest within 30 days of the date on the appeal notice letter—not the date you received it. As discussed in Chapter 3, you can also informally appeal to the auditor's manager.

> CAUTION
> **Meeting the manager does not extend the 30-day deadline to file a formal appeal.** Make sure you file a written protest, too.

Can't file your protest in time? Request an extension for another 30 to 60 days to appeal. Requests to auditors or managers are usually granted, but don't rely on an oral promise. Send a confirming letter stating the terms of the extension and the name of the person granting it.

How to Get Your Audit to the Appeals Office

There are three ways to get your audit to the IRS Independent Office of Appeals. Which one to choose depends on your preference and how much the IRS auditor says you owe:

- **If you owe less than $2,500:** You can simply ask the auditor for an appeal—technically, your oral request is sufficient. But, to make sure you are not forgotten, either write a protest letter in your own words and write at the top "Small Case Request" (following the instructions and sample below) or use IRS Form 12203, *Request for Appeals Review.*
- **If you owe between $2,500 and $25,000:** Either write a protest letter and write at the top "Small Case Request" (following the instructions and sample below) or use IRS Form 12203. We recommend using the form.

- **If you owe more than $25,000:** Write a protest letter. The IRS doesn't have a form for contesting tax debts over this amount. (See below and sample letter.)

IRS Form for Appeals Under $25,000 (Small Case)

To appeal an audit in which the IRS claims you owe $25,000 or less in extra taxes, penalties, and interest, you may use IRS Form 12203, *Request for Appeals Review.* As you'll see from the sample below, this is a simple, one-page form that lets you list the items on the IRS examination report with which you disagree and briefly explain your position. You can complete the fillable form online at the IRS website (www.irs.gov) and then print it out, or type or handwrite a printed copy of the form. If the space on the form is insufficient, add a separate page or pages. (Be sure to put your name and taxpayer identification number at the top of any extra pages.)

Where the form asks for "Taxpayer Identification Number(s)," use your Social Security number if you're an individual and your employer identification number (EIN) if you're representing a business or trust. Also, if you're appealing on behalf of your business, the line "Tax period(s) ended" can be answered with quarters of tax years—for example, 4th quarter, 2022 —rather than a whole year figure.

Send the completed form to the IRS office that issued the audit report—by certified mail, return receipt requested.

Protest Letter for Appeals Over $25,000 (Large Case)

To contest an audit debt of more than $25,000, you must file a formal protest, which is a letter, not a form (see the sample below). The letter must contain the following:
- your name (or names, if married) and Social Security number(s)
- a statement that you are appealing an examination report
- the findings in the report that you disagree with, including penalties and interest
- a brief explanation of why the report is wrong; although not required, you can attach copies of any documents supporting your explanation
- your signature(s) and date under a penalty-of-perjury clause, and
- copies of the 30-day letter and examination report.

Sample Request for Appeals Review

Form **12203** (August 2022)	Department of the Treasury - Internal Revenue Service # Request for Appeals Review

This form is to be used to request an Appeals review upon completion of an examination (audit) if you do not agree with our proposed changes from the audit. Complete the information in the spaces below, including your signature and the date.

Taxpayer name(s) Mick Rodriguez	Taxpayer Identification Number(s) 555-555-5555
Mailing address 111 Elm Street	Tax form number 1040
City Bloomington	Tax period(s) ended 2019, 2020

State Indiana	ZIP Code 47000	
Your telephone number(s) 111-111-1111		Best time to call 9:00am-5:00pm

Identify the item(s) *(for example: filing status, exemptions, interest or dividends)* you disagree with in the proposed change or assessment report you received with the enclosed letter. Tell us why you disagree. You can add more pages if this is not enough space.

Disagreed item	Reason why you disagree
Disallowance of business expense deductions of $12,999 and penalties and interest of $848	The deductions I took were legitimate expenses of my music business, and I was trying to make a profit.
Disagreed item	Reason why you disagree
Disagreed item	Reason why you disagree
Disagreed item	Reason why you disagree

Name of Taxpayer Rick Vallalobos Villalba	Signature	Date 4/14/xx
Name of Taxpayer	Signature	Date

Name and signature of authorized representative (If a representative is signing this form, please attach a copy of your completed Form 2848, Power of Attorney and Declaration of Representative.)

Name	Signature	Date
Your telephone number	Best time to call	

Catalog Number 27136N	www.irs.gov	Form **12203** (Rev. 8-2022)

Make the protest letter short and sweet. Stick to the facts and don't criticize the auditor or the IRS—whether justified or not. Blowing off steam might make you feel better, but it only detracts from an otherwise valid appeal.

Below is a sample protest letter. This sample is a skeleton type of protest letter, giving only the bare bones of why you are appealing. Some tax professionals recommend very detailed protests with copies of all documents you want to be considered. This can be difficult to do if you're not a tax expert, so go with the minimal approach. This gives you time to either send in supporting documents to the appeals officer later or bring them to the hearing.

For details, see IRS Publication 5, *Your Appeal Rights and How To Prepare a Protest If You Disagree.*

> 💡 **TIP**
>
> **Consult a tax professional if you are unsure about preparing your protest.** You can also get advice on preparing for the appeals hearing. An experienced professional can tell you what evidence—documents and statements—the appeals officer will look for. (See Chapter 13.)

Send your letter to the IRS office that issued the report—by certified mail, return receipt requested. Also send or give a copy to the auditor.

Requesting the Auditor's File

The Taxpayer First Act of 2019 requires that, starting July 1, 2020, the IRS auditor's file be made available to a qualifying taxpayer who appeals a deficiency notice to the Independent Office of Appeals. The file is supposed to be provided not less than 10 days before the scheduled date of the settlement conference with the appeals officer. You should be informed of your right to this file. Even if you're not, be sure to ask for it. It contains notes and workpapers showing how the auditor arrived at the conclusions. There might be nothing new in the file, but it could help you have the auditor's findings overturned.

Certain privileged information, notably the DIF score—the computer score that probably caused the audit in the first place—are protected from disclosure by law and will not be included in the file. This is no big deal, as the DIF number won't mean anything to you anyway. (DIF scores are covered in Chapter 3.)

Sample Protest (Appeal) Letter

August 15, 20xx

Internal Revenue Service
P.O. Box 44687 (Stop 11)
Indianapolis, IN 46244

VIA CERTIFIED MAIL—RETURN RECEIPT REQUESTED

PROTEST OF MICK RODRIGUEZ
SSN: 555-55-5555

111 Elm Street
Bloomington, IN 47000

Dear Sir/Madam:

I wish to appeal the examination report of 8/1/xx, a copy of which is attached. I request a hearing. The tax years protested are 2021 and 2022.

The adjustments that I disagree with are [*fill in something like "the disallowance of business expense deductions shown on my Schedule C of $12,999 and penalties and interest in the total amount of $848"*].

The adjustments were [*again, fill in your explanation, like "incorrect because the deductions I took were legitimate expenses of my music business, and I was trying to make a profit"*].

Under penalty of perjury, I declare that I submitted the protest and accompanying documents, and, to the best of my knowledge and belief, the information stated in the protest and accompanying documents is true, correct, and complete.

Sincerely,

Mick Rodriguez

Mick Rodriguez

Copy to Auditor

Enclosed: Copy of 30-day letter and copy of Examination Report

Sample FOIA Letter

August 15, 20xx

Internal Revenue Service
P.O. Box 44687 (Stop 11)
Indianapolis, IN 46244

VIA CERTIFIED MAIL—RETURN RECEIPT REQUESTED

PROTEST OF MICK RODRIGUEZ
SSN: 555-55-5555

111 Elm Street
Bloomington, IN 47000

Dear Sir/Madam:

Under the Privacy Act of 1974, 5 U.S.C. 552A, and the Freedom of Information Act, 5 U.S.C. 552, I request a copy of all files relevant to the audit of my tax return for years 2019 and 2020.

I agree to pay reasonable charges for copying the requested documents, up to $25. If the charges exceed this amount, please contact me for further authorization.

If you determine that any portion of these files is exempt, please identify the portion claimed exempt and the specific exemption that justifies your refusal to release it.

Sincerely,

Mick Rodriguez

Mick Rodriguez

However, this file disclosure rule applies only to taxpayers with adjusted gross incomes less than $400,000 or businesses with gross receipts less than $5 million for the tax year involved. If your income is over these amounts, you can still get a copy of the file. But, to do so, you must file a request for the file under the federal Freedom of Information Act, or FOIA. Send a separate letter to the FOIA disclosure officer at your local IRS office. (See sample above.) Specifically ask for a copy of your audit file by year audited and offer to pay for copying charges. Hand deliver your letter or send it by certified mail, return receipt requested. Enclose a photocopy of your driver's license or birth certificate with your letter.

Allow four weeks or more for a response. If you don't hear from the disclosure office, start calling. Technically, the IRS does not have to make copies for you, although it usually will. Instead, you might be told you have to come into the disclosure office to look at the file. If the date of the appeals hearing is approaching and you haven't yet received or had a chance to review your file, ask for a postponement from the appeals officer. Send a return letter confirming the postponement.

How the Independent Office of Appeals Works

The IRS Independent Office of Appeals is a separate division from the local IRS office that handled your audit. It might not even be in the same city.

Cases are viewed from a fresh perspective by appeals officers—most of the time. Some officers just rely on work done by auditors, but most review files anew. Your auditor plays no part in the process, other than the fact that their file is before the appeals officer. An auditor's file often lacks detail or notes, however, which can raise questions in the mind of the appeals officer. The appeals officer may contact the auditor to fill in the gaps and clarify the IRS's position on a particular issue. If you submit new data to the appeals officer, the officer may ask the auditor to review it, but not make the final decision on its acceptability.

Appeals Officers Are Negotiators

IRS appeals officers are senior IRS employees with accounting or legal backgrounds. Many have been promoted up from the ranks of auditors. Appeals officers have only one job—to settle cases. You might think that their work involves raising more money for the U.S. Treasury, but that's not the case.

Appeals officers are trained to be flexible and are given discretion in dealing with taxpayers that auditors don't have. Proof of this lies in IRS statistics showing 70% of appeals cases are settled. Appeals officers' job performance is judged by their success in compromising with taxpayers—not how often they uphold IRS auditors!

An appeals officer is aware of the law on recurring issues, like what kinds of documentation are legally sufficient to verify travel and entertainment or home office expenses. So, unless your case is very unusual, the appeals officer will almost surely have considered the same legal issues in the past.

Since appeals officers already know the law, they usually want to learn the facts of your situation—especially anything which might cause a judge to rule for you if you went to court. In short, appeals officers have a motivation to settle with you if, after considering the facts and applying the law, they believe you have some chance of winning in court—no matter how small.

Unlike IRS auditors, appeals officers have discretion to weigh the hazards of litigation. They often settle cases because they don't want the courts to set any precedents unfavorable to the IRS. Decisions against the IRS could be relied on by other taxpayers and cost the government much more in the long run than giving in on your case would.

Appeals officers are realists and know from IRS statistics that about 50% of all taxpayers win at least partial victories in court. Appeals officers don't have authority to settle a case based purely on its nuisance value, however. In other words, they are forbidden to settle just to avoid the expense of going to court. But, if you supply a justification for a deal, you might get one.

Besides the fear of losing in court, the appeals officer has another motivation to make deals: The IRS's resources are *not* unlimited. Most of the funding to the IRS in the last decade has gone into computerization and hiring of more collectors—not appeals officers.

No one wants your small potatoes case to use up any more of the government's time than is absolutely necessary. After all, the same court that will try your case if it isn't settled also must hear tax disputes with Google, Exxon, and GE, where the government has hundreds of millions of dollars at risk.

Preparing for an Appeals Hearing

After requesting your appeal, you will have at least 60 days to prepare for your hearing. When you will be heard depends on how backlogged your Independent Office of Appeals is. Use this time to analyze and review everything you presented to the auditor.

Get a copy of the auditor's workpapers by making your Freedom of Information Act request. Read it to see if the auditor misrepresented or just plain missed something. Check out any tax law cited by the auditor in the report to see if it really supports the auditor's position.

If you don't get a copy of the auditor's file before the appeals hearing, ask the appeals officer to show it to you.

Organizing and Presenting Documents

Audits are frequently lost because the taxpayers did not cogently present their cases to the auditors. If you provided a jumble of papers or messy files, the auditor might have refused to consider them out of frustration. So, ask yourself if there are better ways to organize and present your supporting materials to the appeals officer. For instance, you can use Excel or another spreadsheet program to create lists of payments for each category of deductions and make up schedules of these items.

Try some creativity. For example, you aren't limited to printed documents. A part-time jazz artist whose musical business was deemed a hobby by an auditor, and his deductions disallowed, brought a demo tape and player to an appeals hearing. Charts, graphs, and drawings can often more effectively make points than words can. And remember the saying about a picture being worth a thousand words. A photo of your professional-looking home office or a group picture at your business's employee picnic might win the deduction. Everyone seems to prefer looking at pictures to reading a description or listening to an explanation. Appeals officers are no different.

If neatness, typing, preparing schedules, or just plain getting paperwork together is not something you're good at, find a bookkeeper or friend to do it for you.

Filling in the Gaps

If you were missing records at the audit, try harder to find them. Make renewed attempts to get copies of checks from banks and duplicate receipts from businesses and people with whom you dealt. Recreate items when original documents can't be found. (See Chapter 3.)

Focusing on Challenged Items

Make a separate file or folder for each item the auditor challenged on your tax return with which you disagree. Write a simple statement next to each explaining why the auditor was wrong.

Collect your documents—canceled checks, receipts, and whatever else—and group them with or attach them to each statement. You can use a three-ring binder with dividers for each challenged item and make a copy of the binder. At the hearing, the appeals officer can follow along. If you lose the appeal, the binder will serve you well if you proceed to Tax Court.

Get written statements from people with knowledge about your disallowed expenses (if you didn't already do so for your audit). For example, you hired a handyperson to make repairs on your rental property who insisted on being paid in cash and has since left town. You can't find the receipts for the labor and materials. Prove the work was done through a statement from a tenant, like the following:

Sample Witness Statement

Declaration of Clara Burton

I, Clara Burton, declare that for most of 2020, I was a tenant in an apartment owned by Alexander Woolf, located at 123 Hannah Road, Appleton, Wisconsin.

Early in the spring of 2020, we had a bad storm. The rain caused plaster to fall from the ceiling in my apartment and ruin the carpet. All the damage was repaired by Joe Williams, who did a good job.

I moved out to be closer to my job in November of 2021. I now live at 456 Dover in Appleton, Wisconsin. My phone number is 555-1290.

Under penalty of perjury, I declare that the statements of fact contained in this declaration are, to the best of my knowledge and belief, true, correct, and complete.

Dated: 6/20/2022   *Clara Burton*
                        Signature

Dealing With the Appeals Officer

Unfortunately, the IRS no longer routinely offers face-to-face meetings with its appeals officers. You will be told to confer by phone or video conferencing, and to fax or mail whatever you want the appeals officer to review. If you insist, and the appeals officer thinks your case is complex enough, you could (and should) get an in-person meeting.

An appeals hearing is informal, not like going into a courtroom. You may record the conversation (with prior notice to the IRS), but this isn't usually a good idea. Your goal is to settle your case, and recording it would likely put the appeals officer on guard. Speak freely—stand up for yourself on points where you feel the auditor was wrong. At the same time, if you know that you were off base about a deduction or your documentation is weak or nonexistent, say that up front. Theoretically, your statements could be deemed admissions and used against you in a court case. But, it would be highly unusual for the IRS to call an appeals officer to testify as to what was said at an appeals hearing.

Presenting a Case to an Appeals Officer

Before the meeting, write down what you are going to say to the appeals officer—an outline of the points you want to make. List the documents and other evidence you want to present. Then try it out by explaining your case to your friends or family. Ask if they understand it clearly. Their responses might direct you to weaknesses that you can work on before the hearing.

Some appeals officers sit back and wait for you to present your case, while others run the show by asking questions. Unless the appeals officer directs otherwise, start with a brief statement outlining your case. Here's an example:

> *I believe that the auditor was incorrect in finding that I was not entitled to claim a part of my apartment as a home office deduction for my part-time sales business on my tax return in 20XX.*
>
> *I can show that my home office deduction is legitimate by my testimony and with the following documents:*

- *floor plan of my apartment showing the space used exclusively for my home office*
- *business diary showing that I spent more than 50% of my working hours in the business at my home office, and*
- *bills and canceled checks for the expenses I incurred in running my home office.*

> **TIP**
> **Point out to the appeals officer the auditor's errors but don't make it personal.** For instance, did the auditor overlook facts or documents? Did the auditor misstate something that you said? Don't bring up the auditor's lack of intelligence or mean-spiritedness; instead characterize the errors as misunderstandings or oversights. After all, the appeals officer might take offense at IRS bashing.

If you and the auditor disagreed on a legal issue—such as whether your enterprise is a legitimate business or a nondeductible hobby—then renew the argument to the appeals officer. The officer will be more knowledgeable about the intricacies of tax law than are auditors. If you did research or consulted a tax professional and came up with something favorable, show it to the appeals officer, who will probably comment on it, one way or the other. If there's no comment, ask if the officer agrees with your research. If not, ask why not.

An appeals officer who doesn't understand something in the auditor's report might call the auditor, but usually not in your presence. This doesn't mean the auditor's words will be automatically taken over yours.

You might not finish up with the appeals officer at the end of the meeting. The officer might want to research an issue before rendering a decision. And if you request it, you will usually be given time to send more documents or do further legal research. Ask for a month to get things in. Appeals officers seem to work at a more leisurely pace than the rest of the IRS, so you might get even more time.

The officer might ask you to sign a waiver extending the normal three-year limit the IRS has for assessing a tax liability. It is usually okay to sign this waiver at the appeals level, although this is contrary to our advice when you are requested by an auditor to sign the same waiver.

Negotiating a Settlement

The *Internal Revenue Manual* states that:

> *A settlement may either resolve each issue on the basis of the probable result in litigation or involve mutual concessions of issues based upon the relative strength of the opposing positions where there is substantial uncertainty of the outcome in litigation.*

In other words, the appeals officer wants to avoid the possibility of an IRS loss in court.

Your first request should be for the IRS to drop any penalties recommended by the auditor. This is the easiest item for appeals officers to give in on, as long as they believe that you or your tax preparer made an honest mistake and weren't trying to cheat the government.

Unless you believe the auditor was completely wrong on everything—be truly objective—then let the appeals officer know that you might agree to some of the adjustments. This breaks the ice, but don't get specific. Just saying this will show the officer that you can be reasoned with—unlike some of the irrational and irate taxpayers who come through the door. If the officer doesn't warm to you, the officer might at least breathe a sigh of relief. This is good psychology any way you slice it.

Speak the appeals officer's lingo. Don't talk in terms of dollars. Use the word "adjustments" or "disallowances" instead.

> EXAMPLE: An auditor disallowed 80% of Monika's business entertainment expenses because she couldn't provide complete records of the business purpose of the entertainment. Monika acknowledges to the appeals officer that her records were weak, but emphasizes that they do show that she paid the expenses and that she was in a legitimate business. Monika offered to accept a 20% disallowance of these expenses; the appeals officer responded by meeting her halfway and allowing 50% of the deduction. They finally agree on 35%—a far cry from the auditor disallowing 80%. Monika and the appeals officer never spoke in terms of dollars, only percentages.

The example demonstrates that negotiation is an art, not a science. A successful negotiation is where both sides come out with less than what they wanted but each gets something.

Case History of an Appeal

Mick was a telephone company executive by day and a rock musician on Saturday nights. For 20 years, he played in local bands. He had his dreams, but never got close to the Big Time. Mick enjoyed performing and was happy—at least until the IRS entered his life.

In recent years, raises and bonuses allowed Mick to buy new musical gear and a Ford van to haul it. He became more enthusiastic about his music, formed his own group, and hired an agent. Following his accountant's advice, Mick reported his musical income and expenses on his tax returns as a sideline business. Mick's business showed net losses in two years. These losses were used to offset Mick's income from his regular job on his tax returns, thereby lowering his total tax bill.

Sideline Business and the Tax Code

A sideline business loss can produce a tax write-off for Mick as long as the IRS believes that he is trying to make a profit. The tax code provides one test for determining if a profit motive exists—if a business does not make money in at least three of the past five years, it is presumed to be not for a profit and is considered a hobby. Hobby losses can't be deducted for tax purposes. As it turned out, Mick had made a small profit in two of the last four years he had been reporting musical activities on his tax returns.

While this three-of-five-years legal presumption isn't final, it puts the burden on Mick to show he was trying to make a profit. The issue would never arise unless Mick was audited.

Guess What?

Mick was audited. IRS audit classifiers are on the lookout for businesses that show losses. This is especially true if business losses offset income from another job—in effect creating a tax shelter. The IRS hunts tax shelters like wolves pursue sheep.

The consequence of an auditor not finding that a business was really run to make a profit is a disallowance of all expenses in excess of income. For example, if your Amway distributorship brought in $1,000 and you claimed $3,000 in expenses, the IRS could disallow your $2,000 tax loss—unless it was convinced that you were seriously trying to make a profit. (During 2018 through 2025, hobby expenses aren't deductible at all.) In this type of case, the IRS has frequently said that the real motive in this type of business was social—entertaining friends and getting home products for personal use. Dabbling in a side business is not good enough.

Case History of an Appeal (continued)

In the year audited, Mick's music income was only $300 but he claimed $12,300 in business expenses. Small wonder he was picked for audit. His largest expenses were the new van and music gear. Under the hobby loss rules, the auditor decided Mick's music expenses were primarily for his personal pleasure, and only incidentally for profit. (I.R.C. § 183.) She disallowed the $12,000 tax loss. This meant added taxes, penalties, and interest of $4,500. To make matters worse, she then said she was going to audit two more years and make the same adjustment.

Mick argued that he had worked hard to make a musical career, that he had been getting local jobs, that his band's reputation was on the rise, and that one hit record would make him millions and the IRS plenty of taxes. The auditor, apparently not a music fan, was unmoved. A meeting, an informal appeal, with her manager did not change things.

Mick got the examination report and then a 30-day letter to appeal. He decided to appeal; he had clearly been trying to make money in music, even though his efforts had been largely unsuccessful. Mick knew he had enough to show an appeals officer a justification for compromising the audit result.

The legal principle in Mick's favor is that the profit motive, not the actual result, distinguishes a business from a hobby. The intention to make a profit is sufficient under the tax law, even if the probability of financial success is small or remote. (*Dreicer v. Commissioner of Internal Revenue*, 78 U.S.T.C. 642 (1982); see also *Cornfield v. U.S.*, 797 F.2d 1049 (D.C. Cir. 1986).) At least Mick had some income.

Research for Mick's Appeal

The IRS disallowed Mick's deduction of his music equipment as a business loss. The examination report said only that the business expense was not established. Mick called the auditor to ask what tax code section she relied on to reach her decision. The answer was Internal Revenue Code Section 183.

Mick looked at the *U.S. Master Tax Guide* index under Section 183 and found the subhead "Business." It directed him to a page that defined a business as "a pursuit or occupation carried on for profit, whether or not profit actually results." The guide has an excerpt from a Tax Court case which stated that an activity may be for profit although the investment is not expected to generate

Case History of an Appeal (continued)

profits for several years under the current level of activity. This meant that Mick's musical activities are not disqualified as a business just because he lost money. Mick photocopied this page.

Next he opened J.K. Lasser's *Your Income Tax* and found more specific information. The index lists Hobby as a Sideline Business, which leads to the following: "If you show a profit in three or more years the law presumes you are in an activity for profit. The presumption does not necessarily mean that losses will be automatically allowed; the IRS may rebut the presumption." Reading further, Mick saw this as significant because it mentioned tax code Section 183 on which the auditor based her decision. Mick made another photocopy.

In two years of his tax returns since claiming his music business, Mick was still using his old equipment. And he did not claim any vehicle expense on his return. The tax result was in Year One he showed a profit of $100, and in Year Two, a $200 profit. In Year Three, however, Mick bought the van and the new equipment. These purchases caused sizable losses in Years Three and Four. The appeals hearing took place in Year Five, for which a tax return was not yet due. So Mick can't rely on the three-year presumption of profit rule. Mick had only two profitable years.

If Mick's appeal hearing was held after he filed a tax return for Year Five, it could be prepared in such a way as to show a profit—for example, by not taking some expense deductions. In this case, he could go into the hearing with the benefit of the three-year presumption of profit rule—that is, Mick made money in three of the last five years. This fact would put him in a position that could be strong enough to give him an outright win.

Mick's Appeal Hearing

After Mick filed his protest requesting an appeal, the IRS set a conference date. Several months later, Mick and an appeals officer met at the appeals office. No one else was present. Mick went directly to the most favorable facts of his case. He showed a contract from a talent booking agent who, in two years, had gotten his group one job. He also presented a flyer and an event calendar showing the group had performed in public twice during the audited year. He omitted the fact that one appearance was at a charity benefit where no performers were paid. He also gave the appeals officer a publicity photo and his diary showing band rehearsals.

Case History of an Appeal (continued)

The documents were not strong enough evidence to win his case, but they got Mick in the door. The goal was to give the officer justification for compromising, not to win outright. In a half hour, Mick finished presenting the evidence and said, "Let's settle the case. I will accept a 25% disallowance of my losses." In other words, Mick was offering to let the IRS reduce his losses from the $12,000 adjustment the auditor made to $3,000.

The appeals officer replied that he was thinking more like a 75% disallowance, from $12,000 to $9,000. Mick was in! The officer had accepted the possibility that a court might find that Mick was trying to make a profit. They took a break.

After the break, Mick commented on the photo of the Little Leaguer on the officer's desk. He had a similar picture at home, and Mick and the appeals officer talked about their kids awhile. The officer seemed relieved not to talk taxes for a bit. At 4:30, near IRS quitting time, Mick said that he'd agree to split the difference, and accept a 50% disallowance from $12,000 to $6,000 of his losses and no penalties.

He also requested the appeals officer not to recommend the other two open years for audit. The officer agreed. While this didn't guarantee those years would not be audited—appeals officers don't have this authority—their recommendations carry great weight and their reports are routinely approved. Several weeks later, Mick received a settlement letter.

Mick's case is typical of how IRS appeals are handled—and settled. If Mick hadn't appealed, he would have owed the IRS $4,500, plus he would have been audited for two other years. The potential tax disaster was over $13,000. The settlement made with the appeals officer cost Mick about $2,000.

Epilogue

Mick's appeal didn't require great knowledge of tax law. It did involve several hours of preparation as well as a basic understanding of the IRS appeals process. Evidence of Mick's profit intent was shown; a settlement was proposed and negotiated. The great majority of appeal issues—be they home office deductions, entertainment expenses, or business auto usage—can be handled successfully in this same manner.

Appeal settlements are usually reached orally and then put in writing on an IRS form. You won't be asked to prepare the settlement document—the appeals officer will. Most settlements are formalized on IRS Form 870 series or IRS Form 4549, mailed to you after the hearing. Don't expect the settlement papers right away; it might take several months, as a settlement goes through several levels of approval before leaving the IRS office.

To make sure the settlement contains no surprises or misunderstandings, make careful notes of what was agreed to at the hearing. If the settlement papers don't match up, call the officer and hash it out. If you have some questions about the terms of the settlement document, run it by a tax professional before you sign. They can check computations and explain the details to you.

> **CAUTION**
>
> **Don't sign an appeals settlement unless you are absolutely certain that you understand it.** Once you sign it, you are barred from going to Tax Court if you find an error or change your mind.

In limited situations, the appeals officer is prohibited from negotiating a settlement. For instance, if the appeals officer mentions any of the following, your only choice is to contest and take the IRS to court or deal with the tax bill:

- Your audit was part of a large group of similar taxpayers and the IRS must be sure that everyone in the group is treated equally.
- A court case or an IRS revenue ruling directly on point and supporting the IRS's position exists. As a practical matter, this is unlikely to happen, because rarely are two cases ever exactly alike or will a revenue ruling prevent you from dealing with an appeals officer.
- Your case has tax crime potential.
- You are a part of a group of investors who are claiming tax benefits from investment losses—tax shelters—that the IRS concludes were not legitimate business deals, but were solely tax dodges.

Should You Hire a Tax Professional for Your Appeal?

The pros and cons of working with tax professionals are outlined in Chapter 13. Here are a few other suggestions.

Most appeals officers respect an experienced tax representative. Appeals officers and tax professionals often know each other. Tax professionals know what appeals officers are looking for and can make their job easier by getting straight to points.

Hiring a tax professional is largely an economic decision. It might not make sense to hire one if you're contesting less than $5,000 in taxes. An attorney or CPA will charge upwards of $2,500 for an uncomplicated appeal, although an enrolled agent might do it for less. If you hire a tax professional, ask how much IRS appeals experience the person has and how the appeals came out. Listen carefully to the responses.

Bringing in a tax professional also depends on the intricacy of the case and how comfortable you are at arguing and negotiating. For example, if you lost your audit because of inadequate records and you have since located or reconstructed them, there's no need to hire a tax professional. If your case, however, turns on a point of law, such as whether or not your business's workers are employees or independent contractors, bringing in a professional could make the difference.

Types of Cases Appeals Officers Won't Hear

IRS appeals officers are prohibited from hearing certain issues under IRS policy, for example, taxpayer refusals to comply with the tax laws based on moral, political, constitutional, religious, and similar grounds. The issues are often raised by what the IRS terms tax resisters or protestors. A word to the wise: If you fit into this category, think long and hard about what you are doing. Get good professional advice before taking on the federal government.

> TIP
>
> **A preappeals consultation with a tax professional is a good idea—even if you do the appeal yourself.** An hour or two of professional time should not cost more than several hundred dollars.

If You Don't Settle on Appeal

If you and the appeals officer haven't reached a settlement by the end of your conference, ask what else you can provide to change things. Chances are it's further documentation or supporting legal precedent. Then, ask for time to get this material to them, before any decision becomes final. If in doubt how to follow through, see a tax professional.

If you don't settle, you will be mailed a letter denying your appeal. With the letter comes a Notice of Deficiency advising you of your right to go to Tax Court. If you ignore the notice, after 90 days, the taxes, penalties, and interest become final. A tax bill from the IRS will arrive several months later.

If you want to keep up the fight, see Chapter 5 on going to Tax Court.

Chapter Highlights

- You can appeal most audits to the IRS Independent Office of Appeals.
- Appeals often reduce your tax bill, but seldom are auditors totally reversed.
- Many appeal issues are simple enough for you to handle without hiring a tax professional, but a consultation with one is a good idea.
- The IRS Independent Office of Appeals is independent from the IRS audit division and wants to settle to keep you from going to court.
- Prepare for an appeals hearing by careful record organization and basic tax law research. Consult a tax professional if in doubt.
- If you don't appeal or don't win your appeal, you can always go to Tax Court.

Going to Tax Court: No Lawyer Necessary

Tax Court Facts 165

Small Tax Cases—People's Court 167

The Small Tax Case Petition and Related Forms 167

Completing the Tax Court Forms 167

Filing the Tax Court Forms 170

Meeting With IRS Appeals Officers and Attorneys Before the Trial 172

Settlement Before Trial Is Likely 173

Notices From the Court Before Your Trial 174

Preparing Your Case for Trial 175

Awaiting the Judge's Decision in a Small Case 183

The Tax Bill 183

Regular Tax Court Cases—Over $50,000 183

Bench Decisions 184

Not Contesting Amounts Over $50,000 185

Other Federal Courts—Paying First Is Required 185

Bankruptcy Court 187

Y ou lost your audit and didn't reach a settlement with the IRS on appeal. What's next? You have two choices: You can accept your fate or you can go to court.

In one recent year, more than 30,000 taxpayers filed petitions in U.S. Tax Court after losing their audits and appeals. (You can contest your tax liability in three other federal courts, but only in Tax Court can you contest without first paying.) Taking your case on to Tax Court is usually not difficult and in many cases can be done without a lawyer. And your chance of winning—at least partially reducing an audit bill—is excellent. Once you file a petition in Tax Court, the IRS knows you mean business and will often settle for less than the tax claimed due. Over 90% of Tax Court cases filed settle before trial.

While it is not necessary to have appealed within the IRS before going to Tax Court, it's a good idea. Remember—the job of the IRS Independent Office of Appeals is to settle. You can also contest an automated mail adjustment notice you receive from the IRS in Tax Court. (See Chapter 3.) And Tax Court can be used to challenge IRS decisions in several other situations—for instance, when the IRS reclassifies a worker in your business from an independent contractor to an employee (see Chapter 11) or if you are denied innocent spouse relief (see Chapter 9).

And even if the IRS doesn't settle before your trial, you have a good chance of having your tax liability reduced once you talk to a judge. More than 50% of all petitions filed in Tax Court bring some tax reduction. In cases under $50,000 (called "small cases"), 47% of all taxpayers win at least partial victories. In cases involving $50,000 or more (called "regular cases"), 60% come out ahead. Tax Court isn't a total panacea—the chance of a complete victory over the IRS is only 5%.

TIP

Filing a petition in Tax Court buys time. Just filing will delay an audit bill for at least a year. You can use this time to get your finances in order without worrying that the tax collector will seize your assets. But interest is running.

When Not to Go to Tax Court

You can be fined for filing a petition to Tax Court without legal grounds. This is not normally something to worry about, however. There is always legitimate reason for disagreeing with an audit report. Only by filing a petition that is clearly frivolous or done for the sole purpose of delay do you risk a fine.

Don't file a tax protestor type of petition; you might get coded into the IRS computer system in the same category as potentially dangerous taxpayers. In IRS computerese, these people are called "PDTs." People who use the court to protest government policy or because they don't believe the tax system is constitutional can be fined up to $25,000 for filing frivolous Tax Court petitions (I.R.C. § 6673).

So don't let the fear of a fine keep you from going to Tax Court unless you are a tax protestor or are being foolish—like the man who deducted the costs of keeping a mistress as a business expense on the theory that she made him more productive.

Tax Court Facts

There are 19 Tax Court judges headquartered in their own Tax Court building in Washington, D.C. However, Tax Court judges travel nationwide to conduct hearings and trials. In the most populous states, Tax Court hearings are held monthly throughout the year, except summer, in major cities. In smaller states, the Tax Court might meet only once a year for a week or two, usually in the state's largest city. Sessions are usually held at the local federal building.

The president appoints Tax Court judges for 15-year terms. Judges are lawyers and come from senior IRS legal staffs or from private law firms. Special temporary judges also regularly serve in small cases. Although many Tax Court judges are ex-IRS employees, they are not especially pro-IRS. Judges do not like to see the IRS cut corners in audits or mistreat taxpayers. Tax Court is completely independent from the IRS. You will get as fair and impartial a hearing in Tax Court as you would in any other federal court.

After you file your petition, it will be at least six months until you are called for trial. While most small cases (see below) are decided within one year, regular cases take much longer.

A minor drawback of Tax Court is that interest continues to run on your tax bill if the court decides you owe the IRS.

Technically, you can't pay a proposed tax bill and then go to Tax Court. You can, however, stop the interest accrual before suing in Tax Court by making a payment and labeling it a deposit or cash bond. Send a check to the IRS with the words "deposit/cash bond" written in the lower left-hand corner of the check and send a cover letter with the payment. This stops the interest accrual. But if you win, you don't get interest back from the IRS for the time the government had your money.

Strict 90-Day Limit for Filing In Tax Court

Once the IRS issues a letter called a Notice of Deficiency, you have only 90 days to file a petition in Tax Court. The deadline for filing must be stated clearly in the letter. The 90-day period begins on the date in the letter, not on the date you receive it. If you are out of the United States when the letter is sent, you have 150 days. *The law does not require that you actually receive the notice, only that the IRS mail it to your last known address.*

Don't delay. A filing on day 91 will get your case dismissed. The fastest way to get the right forms is to download them from the Tax Court website at www.ustaxcourt.gov. Or, you can call the Tax Court office and request the forms be sent to you by mail.

This 90-day deadline is strictly applied and is one good reason to let the IRS know of your new address whenever you move. Use IRS Form 8822, *Change of Address* (available on the IRS's website, www.irs.gov). If you miss the deadline, you can file in another federal court, but you will have to pay the tax first and sue the government for a refund. (See below for an explanation of this process.)

Small Tax Cases—People's Court

There is a small case division of the Tax Court for audits in which the IRS claims the taxes and penalties owed for any one tax year are $50,000 or less. For example, if you've been audited for three years and the amount the IRS claims you owe for each year is $30,000—meaning the total is $90,000—your case will still qualify as a "small case." This small claims court–type case is called an "S case."

S case election is made on the Tax Court petition form by checking a box (see the filled-in sample form below).

The filing fee is $60, and normally you'll have no further court costs.

No jury trials are allowed in Tax Court. Judges can rule on the spot, although they usually mail their decisions to you a month or so after the hearing. You can't appeal the decision in an S case but Tax Court appeals in larger cases are rarely successful anyway.

With S cases, Tax Court operates much like your local small claims court. You tell the judge your story, show your evidence, and are not expected to know legal procedures. Even if you lose, you have the satisfaction of having had your day in court.

The Small Tax Case Petition and Related Forms

You will need a petition, a *Request for Place of Trial*, and a *Statement of Taxpayer Identification Number*. The forms and instructions are available online from the U.S. Tax Court website at www.ustaxcourt.gov. Or call or write the clerk of the U.S. Tax Court, 400 Second Street, NW, Washington, D.C. 20217, 202-521-0700, and ask for a petition kit. Unlike many other government agencies, the Tax Court office is very responsive and efficient. There is no charge for these items, which will be sent promptly.

Completing the Tax Court Forms

Read *Filing a Case in the United States Tax Court*. This is the first page of the petition kit. You can fill in the forms online or print them out and fill in the hard copy.

Sample Tax Court Petition

FORM 2

United States Tax Court

Washington, DC 20217

Adam X. and Eve Y. Crumly
_____

_____
(PLEASE TYPE OR PRINT NAME OR NAMES)

Petitioner

v.

COMMISSIONER OF INTERNAL

REVENUE,

Respondent

Docket No.

PETITION
(Simplified Form)

1. Please check the appropriate box(es) to show which IRS ACTION(S) you dispute:

☑ Notice of Deficiency

☐ Notice of Determination Concerning Collection Action

☐ Notice of Final Determination for [Full/Partial] Disallowance of Interest Abatement Claim (or Failure of IRS to Make Final Determination Within 180 Days After Claim for Abatement)

☐ Notice of Determination of Worker Classification

☐ Notice of Determination Concerning Relief From Joint and Several Liability Under Section 6015 (or Failure of IRS to Make Determination Within 6 Months After Election or Request for Relief)

☐ Notice of Certification of Your Seriously Delinquent Federal Tax Debt to the Department of State

☐ Notice of Determination Under Section 7623 Concerning Whistleblower Action

   NOTE: For additional information, please see "Taxpayer Information: Starting a Case" at www.ustaxcourt.gov or in the Court's information booklet.

2. If applicable, provide the date(s) the IRS issued the NOTICE(S) checked above and the city and State of the IRS office(s) issuing the NOTICE(S): _October 27, 2023 Austin, Texas_____

3. Provide the year(s) or period(s) for which the NOTICE(S) was/were issued: _____2021, 2022_____

4. Select one of the following (unless your case is a whistleblower or a certification action):

   If you want your case conducted under small tax case procedures, check here: ☑   **(CHECK**
   If you want your case conducted under regular tax case procedures, check here: ☐   **ONE BOX)**

   NOTE: A decision in a "small tax case" cannot be appealed to a Court of Appeals by the taxpayer or the IRS. If you do not check either box, the Court will file your case as a regular tax case.

5. Explain why you disagree with the IRS action(s) in this case (please list each point separately):
   (a) For tax year 2021, we disagree with the IRS disallowance of $3,710 expenses claimed for Adam's

   royalty income on Schedule E, as they were ordinary and necessary expenses.

   For tax year 2022, (b) we disagree with the disallowance of our charitable deduction of $3,250 to the

   Church of What's Happening Now on Schedule A as this is a legitimate charitable deduction.

   (c) We disagree with the disallowance of $666 of claimed expenses on Schedule C for the business

   "Eve's Apples" as this was a business carried on with profit intent.

   FORM 2 (REV. 03/23)

Sample Tax Court Petition (continued)

6. State the facts upon which you rely (please list each point separately):

(a) The expenses were incurred on a trip to Jerusalem to research a new book "The Baloney Code."

Adam is a published author and although the book is not yet completed, it may become a best seller.

(b) The deduction for the charitable contribution should be allowed because the organization has been

granted IRC Section 501(c)(3) status as a nonprofit entity. (c) The expenses for "Eve's Apples" were

for advertising for the sales of apples from the family orchard, and the business subsequently failed to
produce any income because a tornado carried all the apples away before they could be picked.

**You may use additional pages to explain why you disagree with the IRS action(s) or to state additional facts. Please do
not submit tax forms, receipts, or other types of evidence with this petition.**

Please check the appropriate boxes to indicate that you will include the following items with this petition:

☑ A copy of any NOTICE(S) the IRS issued to you (omit or redact personal information (e.g., Social Security Numbers))

☑ Statement of Taxpayer Identification Number (Form 4) (see PRIVACY NOTICE below)

☑ Request for Place of Trial (Form 5)   ☑ The filing fee

PRIVACY NOTICE: Form 4 (Statement of Taxpayer Identification Number) will <u>not</u> be part of the Court's public files.
All other documents filed with the Court, including this petition and any IRS Notice that you enclose with this petition, will
become part of the Court's public files. To protect your privacy, omit or redact (e.g., black out or cover) from this petition, any
enclosed IRS Notice, and any other document (other than Form 4) your taxpayer identification number (e.g., your Social
Security number) and certain other confidential information as specified in the Tax Court's "Notice Regarding Privacy
and Public Access to Case Files," available at www.ustaxcourt.gov.

Adam X. Crumly	12/05/2023	(001) 000-1111
SIGNATURE OF PETITIONER	DATE	(AREA CODE) TELEPHONE NO.
848 Eden Road		Paradise, Texas 77777
MAILING ADDRESS		CITY, STATE, ZIP CODE

State of legal residence (if different from the mailing address): _____ EMAIL ADDRESS: _____

Check this box if you want to register for electronic filing and electronic service at the email address provided above. ☐
If this box is checked, then no paper service will be made to your mailing address after the Court verifies your email address.

Eve Y. Crumly	12/05/2023	(001) 000-1111
SIGNATURE OF ADDITIONAL PETITIONER (e.g., SPOUSE)	DATE	(AREA CODE) TELEPHONE NO.
848 Eden Road		Paradise, Texas 77777
MAILING ADDRESS		CITY, STATE, ZIP CODE

State of legal residence (if different from the mailing address): _____ EMAIL ADDRESS: _____

Check this box if you want to register for electronic filing and electronic service at the email address provided above. ☐
If this box is checked, then no paper service will be made to your mailing address after the Court verifies your email address.

SIGNATURE OF COUNSEL, IF RETAINED BY PETITIONER(S)	NAME OF COUNSEL	DATE
TAX COURT BAR NO.	MAILING ADDRESS, CITY, STATE, ZIP CODE	
EMAIL ADDRESS	(AREA CODE) TELEPHONE NO.	

Electronic filing is generally required for all papers filed by parties represented by counsel in open cases. See Tax Court Rule 26(b).

FORM 2 (REV. 03/23)

Look at the completed sample forms and, below, the line-by-line instructions. The *Request for Place of Trial* and *Statement of Taxpayer Identification Number* forms are self-explanatory and not reproduced here. Don't worry about typos or minor errors—the Tax Court will usually overlook them.

Fill in the petition form. Type or print your name exactly as it appears on your tax return. If a joint tax return was audited, type in your name and your spouse's name exactly as they appear on the tax return.

Check the box for "Notice of Deficiency" (for appealing an audit).

In the next blank space, type in the date of the IRS-issued notice and the city and state of the IRS office that issued the notice. Next, write the year or years for which the notice was issued. Next, check the box for either "small tax case" or "regular tax case." In the next section, explain briefly why you disagree with the IRS. Finally, state the facts on which you rely.

> TIP
> **The Tax Court doesn't expect you to sound like a tax lawyer.** Just make sure your point is clear. For example, "I disagree with the $1,200 deduction disallowed by the IRS. I incurred this expense as the rent I pay on the portion of my apartment I use for my home office."

Sign and date the petition. After completing the petition, check the box of the nearest city from the list of cities in which Tax Court trials take place. Type your name and your spouse's if a joint tax return was audited. Then sign and date the form. Again, both spouses must sign if a joint return was audited.

Filing the Tax Court Forms

You can file your petition electronically at the Tax Court's website. You must create an account with the Tax Court's electronic filing and case management system, called "DAWSON" (Docket Access Within a Secure Online Network), and then upload your petition. You can also pay the filing fee online. For detailed guidance, see "Filing a Petition" at https://ustaxcourt.gov/dawson.html. The Court must receive your electronically filed petition no later than 11:59 p.m. Eastern Time on the last date to file. Petitions received after this date may be dismissed for lack of jurisdiction.

If you don't want to file electronically, you can file a paper petition by mail. To do so, follow these steps (after making sure the filing requirements haven't changed; see the warning below):

1. Make *two* copies of your:
   - completed petition
   - *Statement of Taxpayer Identification Number*
   - completed *Request for Place of Trial,* and
   - Notice of Deficiency—90-day letter—that you received from the IRS.
2. Keep one copy of the petition, *Request for Place of Trial,* and Notice of Deficiency for your records.
3. Attach the original Notice of Deficiency to the original petition.
4. Make out a personal check or money order for $60 payable to Clerk, U.S. Tax Court.
5. Enclose these documents along with your check or money order in a large envelope. Send to Clerk, U.S. Tax Court, 400 Second Street, NW, Washington, D.C. 20217, by U.S. mail—certified and return receipt requested.

To timely and legally file your petition to the Tax Court by mail, the envelope must bear a U.S. mail postmark dated within 90 calendar days of the date on the Notice of Deficiency. Or you can use Federal Express, DHL, or Airborne Express. If it arrives after day 90, that's okay as long as there is proof it was sent within 90 days. And bear in mind that 90 days does *not* mean three calendar months. Electronic filing of all forms in Tax Court is optional, unless you are represented by counsel, in which case it becomes mandatory.

> CAUTION
>
> **Check for any changes to the filing requirements.** Call 202-521-0700 or check online at the U.S. Tax Court's website at www.ustaxcourt.gov.

If you file electronically, you'll receive an eService email from DAWSON notifying you when the Court processes your petition and serves it on the IRS. Your case will be assigned a docket number. If you ever write to or call the IRS or the Tax Court about your case, you must refer to your docket number.

If you file by mail, within seven days of receiving your petition, the Tax Court will send you a confirmation of receipt and assign you a docket number.

You don't need to file anything else, unless the IRS files a written response, called an "answer." In this highly unlikely event, you must file a legal paper called a "reply." You should consult a tax attorney before filing a reply.

A Tax Professional on the Sidelines

If you file a Tax Court case yourself, consider using a tax professional as a coach or an adviser. The tax professional can work in the background or go with you to meetings with an appeals officer or IRS attorney. The IRS will usually welcome your bringing in a tax professional if it might help reach a settlement and keep your case from going to trial. The tax professional doesn't have to be admitted to practice before the Tax Court, which is usually limited to attorneys, as long as that person doesn't actually sign papers in the case on your behalf.

Meeting With IRS Appeals Officers and Attorneys Before the Trial

After you file your Tax Court petition, your case will probably be sent from the IRS's lawyers (district counsel) to the nearest IRS Independent Office of Appeals—often in the same building. The appeals office considers or reconsiders your case.

If you did appeal, but didn't settle, your case might be reviewed again by the appeals office if the IRS lawyer thinks settlement is possible.

The IRS is in no hurry. Small cases—under $50,000—might sit in an appeals office for about six months—shorter if your trial is set for an earlier date. If you don't settle with an appeals officer, IRS lawyers prepare the case for trial.

About a month before the trial date, the IRS attorney might ask that you meet at the IRS office or talk by phone. The purpose is to discuss the documents and other evidence—both yours and the IRS's—in the case. The attorney will explain how the documents, called "exhibits," will be labeled and you both will exchange the names and addresses of any witnesses you plan to call.

The IRS attorney will also ask you to agree in writing to certain undisputed facts about your case. These are forms called "stipulations of facts" and are prepared by the IRS attorneys. Tax Court rules require both sides to agree, or stipulate, to as many facts as possible before coming to court. The purpose is to save the judge's time. Any facts not agreed to in a written stipulation must be proven in court. Judges get upset if you have refused to agree to obvious facts, like "Is this your signature?"

Written stipulations cover routine things like identifying your tax return, that receipts and various documents are yours, and that bank records are genuine and accurately reflect your deposits and withdrawals.

> ⓘ CAUTION
>
> **Read carefully before signing a stipulation of fact.** Ordinarily, you should sign a stipulation just to keep on the judge's good side. Occasionally, however, the IRS attorney might try to slip something by you. If the stipulation has items that you don't agree with, ask the IRS lawyer to revise them accordingly. Or see a tax professional for advice before you sign.

Don't over-worry about anything going wrong at this meeting. The attorney shouldn't raise new issues, make threats, or try to trap you into saying something harmful to your case. If you ask—and you should—they will tell you what witnesses are expected to say at the trial.

The IRS attorney might not say it, but the best outcome is to settle the case, not go to trial. This meeting is another chance for you to make a deal rather gamble on the outcome in court. Review Chapter 4 before going to the meeting. Present your case as you did with the auditor or appeals officer. Bring up any new documents, witnesses, or information supporting your case. You and the IRS lawyer can settle the case at any time—even after you have been in front of the judge—as long as the court has not issued a decision.

Settlement Before Trial Is Likely

Well over 90% of all cases settle without a trial. An IRS lawyer might initially turn down your settlement offer and later accept it. A review of the case might make the lawyer decide you have a better chance to win than first thought. Or a government witness might not be available or an IRS document might have been lost, so that the IRS case is weaker than first believed.

If you agree to a settlement, the IRS district counsel's office will prepare a document called a "stipulated Tax Court decision." This paper is signed by you, the IRS attorney, and the judge. Signing means you usually don't have to appear in court. This is a brief, but sometimes fairly technical, document. Ask to have it explained, or have it reviewed by a tax professional before you sign it. Once you have signed a stipulated Tax Court decision, it's nearly impossible to back out.

Notices From the Court Before Your Trial

Approximately 4 to 10 months after you file your Tax Court petition, you will receive the following items:

Notice Setting Case for Trial. This is a form letter from the Tax Court setting the place, date, and time of your trial. It also orders you to cooperate with the IRS in certain matters before the trial and warns that if you don't show up for the trial, your case will be dismissed.

Place of Trial. Trials are held in about 100 U.S. cities. You might have to travel several hundred miles to court. However, you can request to have the case heard remotely through video conferencing ("Zoomgov") by filing a motion with the court. You can find a *Motion to Proceed Remotely* to complete at https://ustaxcourt.gov/case_related_forms.html. It's up to the Tax Court judge to decide whether to grant your motion.

Standing Pretrial Order. This is a writing from the judge assigned to your case. It orders you and the IRS to discuss settlement, and if you can't settle, to prepare written stipulations. The order warns that getting a continuance, or postponement, of the trial date is not favored. At least 15 days before the trial date, you and the IRS must exchange lists of witnesses who may testify.

Trial Memorandum. You must fill out and send this form to the Tax Court at least 15 days before the trial. State the issues to be decided by the court, the names of witnesses you will have at the trial, a brief summary of what they will say, and an estimate of how long the trial will last. Most small cases can be tried in two to four hours, so you can put something in this range. Don't worry about precision when filling out this form. The judge knows you aren't an attorney.

Preparing Your Case for Trial

By now, you should have the facts of your case down cold. You might have already told your story to an auditor, a manager, the appeals officer, and the IRS lawyer. But Tax Court is a whole new ballgame. You are not limited by what went on with the IRS before you came to court. You are given a de novo, or brand new, hearing before a judge who has not seen the IRS file.

Begin preparing several months before your trial date. Make an outline of what you want to tell the judge and list your documents and witnesses backing up each point. You must convince the judge that the IRS is wrong—the IRS doesn't have to prove it's right.

Your Trial Notebook

Arrange your materials the way lawyers do, with a trial notebook. You can use a three-ring binder or a folder with a series of files or create a digital version to use with your portable computer, iPad, or similar device. Use it to practice your presentation in front of family or friends. Make sure your points are clear and your documents are understandable. Rehearsing gives you confidence in court.

Your trial notebook should contain the items listed below.

Opening statement. The first item should be an opening statement, which you will make at the beginning of the trial. This is your summary of what the case is about and an outline of what you intend to show the judge to prove that the IRS is wrong. It should be brief—5 to 10 minutes—and to the point. Tell it to the judge as if you were speaking to a friend. Here's a sample:

> *Your Honor, the IRS auditor found that I was not serious about making money in my side business of a Scamway home products distributorship in 2022. She said that the presentations I made in my home were really social gatherings, so she disallowed my $2,492 in business losses. I will show the court that I always had a profit motive and that I operated in a businesslike manner, even though my business showed a loss that year.*

Your testimony. Anytime you speak to the judge, you will be testifying. Before going to court, write down the testimony so you won't forget any points. For example, in proving that you tried to make a profit with your Scamway distribution, you might write as follows:

> *I first started selling Scamway products in 2020. In the first two years, I made small profits. In my home presentations, I strictly followed the guidelines given to me by Scamway. Although the business lost money, I did make sales at the February, May, June, and October presentations.*

Evidence. Luckily for you, formal rules of evidence don't apply in small cases. You can forget all about the TV lawyers who are forever objecting on the grounds of hearsay, relevancy, and other similar legalese. Small-case judges want to get to the bottom of the dispute and will generally consider anything you want to show them.

Arrange your papers in your trial notebook in the order you want to show them to the judge. Keep the originals and make two sets of copies, one to give the judge and one for the IRS attorney.

The most common evidence is canceled checks, bank statements, receipts, bills, photographs, tax returns, and witness statements. (A sample witness statement is in Chapter 4.) But be creative. Bring anything that helps tell your story. For example, continuing with the Scamway dealership, to show your profit motive, you might bring to Tax Court the following items:

- Schedule C, *Profit or Loss From Business*, of your 2020 and 2021 tax returns showing your profit for those years
- the Scamway home presentation guidelines
- a videotape of one of your presentations, and
- guest lists of the people attending the presentations.

Witnesses. Many small cases involve the oral testimony of only one person: you. Written witness statements—declarations or affidavits—are usually satisfactory to the judge instead of live witnesses. In some cases, however, live witnesses are more effective. If you bring people to court to testify, list them in your trial notebook and summarize what each will say.

Before the trial, review with each witness what the person plans to tell the judge. For example, to bolster your claim that you tried to make a profit in your Scamway side business, ask your neighbor Scarlet to testify. Scarlet could state that she attended Scamway parties at your home, that they were businesslike with only slight social overtones, that she bought some products and saw your Scamway inventory stored in your house.

Written Statements or Live Witnesses?

The Tax Court provides Form 18, *Unsworn Declaration Under Penalty of Perjury*, for statements of your witnesses who won't be appearing in court. It is a simple one-page form found at the Tax Court website (www.ustaxcourt.gov). In deciding whether to use live witnesses or Form 18 written statements, consider the following factors.

Persuasiveness. A person whose testimony will be extremely supportive of your position—such as a stranger who attended your Scamway presentation and thus has no motive to lie—should testify in person if possible. The testimony will be much more persuasive in person than on paper.

Convenience. Don't seriously inconvenience a witness and expect that person to be helpful in court. For instance, if someone who attended your Scamway presentation is an airline pilot who is scheduled to be 40,000 feet above ground when your case is heard, a written statement will be sufficient.

Cost. Some witnesses must be paid for their time in court. For example, suppose your trial is about work done on rental property you own, which you deducted as a repair. The IRS disallowed the deduction, saying that it was an improvement that has to be deducted pro rata over its expected useful life of five years. You would subpoena the contractor who did the work, and have the person testify that your rental property was in need of urgent repair. You must pay an expert witness fee typically by the hour. If the hourly rate is high, and there is a long wait, the fee will add up. Consider bringing a statement in declaration or affidavit form.

Harm. If you're concerned that your witness is a loose cannon—might say something harmful to your case—then just bring a written statement. Remember, the IRS attorney and judge get to ask questions in court, too.

If you're not sure a witness will show up, or the witness needs an official court paper to get off from work, you can get an order for the person's appearance—called a "subpoena." You must request a subpoena form from the Tax Court clerk in Washington, D.C. Get it at least two weeks before the trial. You can also get a subpoena at the last minute from the local Tax Court clerk if the court is sitting in your city.

The subpoena must be served on—meaning given to—the witness. Because there are strict rules of what constitutes proper service, this is best done by the U.S. Marshal's office. However, anyone over 18 and not a party to the case can legally serve the subpoena. You can't—you're a party to the case. Neither can your spouse. You must also pay a witness fee in advance, and mileage for the distance from their house to the Tax Court. Ask the clerk for the current witness fee and mileage rate when you request the subpoena.

Legal authority. If legal research is necessary to prove your case, include in your trial notebook copies of cases or other legal authority you or your tax professional found. (See Chapter 13 for information on doing legal research.) Most Tax Court cases are factual, rather than legal, disputes, so legal research isn't always necessary. If in doubt, ask a tax professional.

Closing statement. The last item for your trial notebook is your closing statement. This is the summing-up presentation you will make to the judge at the end of the trial. Like the opening statement, it should be brief and to the point. Here's a sample:

> *Your Honor, you have heard the evidence and can understand why I disagree with the IRS. I do not believe I owe the government any amount of money as a result of the audit of my tax returns for 2022.*
>
> *I explained how I have tried to make money in the music business for many years. I showed the court my receipts and canceled checks for all of my music expenses. I showed flyers I had printed to promote my appearances. I presented the declaration of my booking agent, Irving R. Clark, stating that he made valiant efforts to get me into more nightclubs.*
>
> *It should be clear to Your Honor that I always had a profit motive. I operated in a businesslike manner and not as a hobby, as the IRS contends. Therefore, my business losses should have been allowed by the auditor, and I should owe no additional taxes for 2022.*
>
> *Thank you for hearing my case.*

TIP

Show your trial notebook to the IRS attorney if you meet before trial. If it's well organized and shows that you're serious, there is a good chance the IRS attorney might be impressed and agree to a settlement.

Should You Bring a Tax Professional to Court?

If you get cold feet at the last minute, you can always bring a tax professional to court with you. The best choice is a lawyer—but you can also bring an enrolled agent or a CPA if that person is admitted to practice before the Tax Court. (See Chapter 13.) Even if your tax professional is not qualified to practice in Tax Court, they may still sit with and advise you during the trial with the permission of the judge. They can't speak to the judge, however.

Again, representatives aren't necessary in most small tax cases, although it's wise to consult with one before trial.

Your First Day in Court: Calendar Call

On the date that you're scheduled for court, show up on time. Expect to see other folks on the same trial calendar in the courtroom. The court clerk will take roll call. Don't expect your case to be heard that day.

The clerk or judge will likely assign you another date and time to come back for your trial, usually later that week or in the next one. Or you might be put on telephone notice—told to call in or expect to receive a phone message giving you the precise date and time of your hearing. If the date is impossible for you or your witnesses, ask for a change. Your request might or might not be granted, but most judges are understanding.

If you live far from the Tax Court, call the court clerk or IRS lawyer in the week prior to your scheduled court date. Ask for permission not to appear until the day your case will actually be heard. This can save you a trip if the judge allows it.

Obviously, if your trial is held remotely through Zoomgov, you'll be in a virtual courtroom instead of a real courtroom. But such remote trials are official court proceedings, and you should dress and act as you would for any other court appearance.

Your Trial Day

For your court date, don't put on fancy clothes or airs. Be yourself. Come early and watch another small case trial, if possible. You probably won't learn anything helpful to your case, but the preview should put you at ease. If your trial is being held remotely, you can link to an audio stream of the Zoomgov courtroom prior to your session. If you and your spouse were both audited, only one of you is required to attend the trial. It makes a better impression when both of you show up, however.

Tax Court meets during normal business hours—no evenings or weekends. Most court sessions are held at a local federal building. Because the Tax Court has only a few permanent locations outside Washington, D.C., the facility won't necessarily be a courtroom.

The judge will sit in the elevated area, called the "bench," or at the end of a conference table. It's hard to generalize about Tax Court judges—each is an individual. Most are patient and will give you all the time you need to present your case. Judges are assigned randomly and there is no way you can pick a particular judge, or request a different one once an assignment has been made. It's doubtful you'd ever know a Tax Court judge, anyway. They don't live in your town, as a rule. Address the judge as "Your Honor" or "judge."

Also present will be the judge's clerk, a court reporter, and the IRS lawyer. When the clerk calls your case, answer that you are present and ready for trial. If you're not ready, ask that your case be continued, or postponed. You must have a very, very good reason, such as a serious illness, death in the family, or that a crucial witness can't come to court that day. The judge came all the way from Washington, D.C., to hear your case, and might insist that it go forward.

Once the trial starts, you will be summoned forward to sit at a table in front of the judge or at a large conference table. The IRS lawyer will probably already be ensconced at another table across from you.

Bring your trial notebook and all papers with you. If you have witnesses, ask them to sit nearby.

Courtroom Tips

- Stand when you speak, unless you are sitting at a conference table with the judge close by, the judge tells you to remain seated, or you're appearing remotely.
- Avoid reading aloud to the judge; it's boring. Just speak in your own words.
- Be as brief as possible, but fully explain your case, as if you were talking to a friend.
- Be polite. Never interrupt the judge or disparage the IRS or its lawyer.
- Be well organized. Don't fumble with your papers or otherwise waste the judge's time.

Although Tax Court trials are open to the public, few spectators attend. You can bring friends and loved ones for support, but they can't sit at your table without permission from the judge. Rarely are Tax Court trials reported in the news.

The judge won't know the facts of your case before your trial begins. The judge's file contains only your petition, the IRS's answer, and any written stipulation of facts that you made with the IRS attorneys. The judge doesn't work for the IRS and won't have IRS files or anything that you submitted to the auditor or appeals officer. Your slate is clear—start from scratch in educating the judge about your case.

To begin the trial, the judge will ask if you and your witnesses swear or affirm to tell the truth. The judge will then ask you to present your case.

Ask permission to give a brief opening statement. It's rare that the judge will deny your request. The opening statement is the preview and should be the first item in your trial notebook. Don't read it word for word—that's stiff and artificial. This should not take more than five minutes.

Next, tell the judge your full story and show your evidence to back up each issue. As you present each document, give a copy to the judge and a copy to the IRS attorney. You won't get these documents back, so don't give away your originals. The judge might want to see the originals to compare them to the copies, however. So bring the originals to court. Give the judge copies of any legal authority you have found as you discuss each item. Usually this isn't really necessary, but it shows you have done your homework.

As you give your documents and legal authority to the judge, you may call witnesses to testify. Ask permission to call each witness to the witness stand. To get their story, you must ask them questions. In the example of the Scamway distributor whose losses were not allowed by the IRS, here are sample questions to ask Scarlet, the neighbor and customer:

Are you familiar with my Scamway business?

Did you come to my home for presentations?

Please describe the sales presentations.

How many other people were present?

Were you a customer in 2022?

How many times have you bought Scamway products from me?

Did other people buy products at the presentations you attended?

Have you seen where the products are stored in my house?

Do you know if I have a home office?

The Burden of Proof

In our legal system, the "burden of proof" is a rule that says that to win a civil lawsuit, you must present more credible evidence in court than the other side. But keep in mind that courtrooms aren't laboratories in which evidence can be scientifically weighed.

In 1998, Congress amended the tax code to allow courts to shift the burden of proof from the taxpayer to the IRS, but only when the taxpayer and the IRS are in court (not at an audit), and then only under certain conditions.

For example, if a taxpayer did not comply with all reasonable requests by IRS auditors for information, or did not keep good records, the court can place the burden of proof on the taxpayer. Also, a corporation, trust, or partnership with a net worth exceeding $7 million that sues the IRS in court is not entitled to the shift of the burden of proof. And the burden shifts only as to factual issues—the taxpayer still has the burden of proof in contesting legal issues. If this is too confusing, see a tax attorney for an analysis of how it might apply to your situation.

The IRS attorney may cross-examine your witnesses and call their own witnesses (such as your auditor) and present evidence (typically the auditor's work).

After you and the IRS have presented your documents, testimony, and witnesses, ask permission to sum up your case. Now is the time to present your closing statement, the last item in your trial notebook.

The typical small case trial lasts an hour or two, although you will be given more time if you need it. Try not to be nervous. The judge doesn't expect you to be a lawyer or tax law expert.

Awaiting the Judge's Decision in a Small Case

While the judge may announce a decision at the end of your trial, don't count on it. Usually, you'll get a ruling in the mail about a month or two later. Judges don't like to announce decisions in court to avoid debates with sore losers.

A judge's ruling in your small case will seldom give any explanation as to why you won or lost. Furthermore, the decision won't compute the exact amount you owe. This comes in a later bill from the IRS campus center computer.

The Tax Bill

Assuming you still owe some taxes, you'll get a bill from the IRS within about two months of the judge's decision. This bill is always higher than indicated in the decision because the court's order will state the tax and any penalties, but not any interest or late payment penalties due. By law, the IRS must charge interest from the date the tax was originally due.

If you don't pay right away, interest continues to accrue on the balance until you do. (See Chapter 6 for options in dealing with a tax bill.)

Regular Tax Court Cases—Over $50,000

If the taxes and penalties from an audit total more than $50,000 for any one audited year, your case is called a "regular" Tax Court case. This means you won't qualify for the simplified small case procedures. But unlike a small case, you may appeal a regular case decision to a higher court if you lose. Your right to appeal a Tax Court regular case is, in practice, rather meaningless. Going to a U.S. Appeals Court is a very technical process, which requires the services of a lawyer who specializes in appeals. Even then, your chances of success are around 1 in 10.

Most people hire a lawyer for cases over $50,000, but about 40% of all regular case petitions are filed by taxpayers without lawyers. Most of these cases settle before ever reaching a judge, without any legal expenses being incurred other than the court filing fee.

Like a small case, there is no jury, and one judge hears the case. Tax Court judges are not as patient with taxpayers representing themselves on a regular case as they are with small-case people. The rules are much more formal.

For a regular case, you and the IRS's attorney might be required to submit formal legal briefs within a few months after your day in court. A legal brief is a highly technical document and anything but brief. You must recite and comment on the evidence produced at trial, supporting legal theories, and tax law precedents. A tax professional—most likely an expensive tax attorney—is required for writing a decent brief.

There are no free, government-appointed attorneys in Tax Court. But you might check with a nearby law school to see if it has a free or low-cost legal clinic.

In two situations, it makes economic sense for you to handle a regular case dispute without an attorney: One is by asking for a bench decision; the other is by dropping down to the small case category.

Bench Decisions

An alternative to the complicated post-trial brief writing is to ask the judge for a bench decision at the conclusion of the trial. If the IRS agrees, the judge can dispense with legal briefs. The judge might go along if they're satisfied that the facts and law are clear-cut—either for or against you.

If your request is rejected and you don't submit an adequate legal brief, you will lose. You will have delayed the final tax bill, but you will incur extra interest. If buying time is enough of a victory for you, then congratulations.

Not Contesting Amounts Over $50,000

If your audit bill for any single year is over the $50,000 threshold, you might still be able to utilize the simplified S case procedures. The catch is that you must give up your right to contest amounts over $50,000 in taxes and penalties for any one tax year.

> **EXAMPLE:** Ronnie gets an audit report claiming he owes $62,000 for 2021 and $9,500 for 2022. Ronnie can proceed as a small case in Tax Court if he contests only $50,000 for 2021, agreeing he owes the $12,000 overage. Of course, he can contest all of the $9,500 for 2022. The total amount contested is $59,500, and this is still a small case under Tax Court rules.

Other Federal Courts—Paying First Is Required

Instead of going to Tax Court, if you pay your audit bill, you can proceed to one of two other federal courts: a U.S. District Court, located throughout the country, or the U.S. Court of Federal Claims. (If you're in bankruptcy, there's a third option, discussed below.) This is called a "refund suit." District courts follow strict rules of procedure—meaning you will need a tax lawyer from start to finish. The Court of Federal Claims is more like the Tax Court in that its judges travel throughout the country to hear cases, and its rules and hearings are less formal than in District Court.

Unlike Tax Court, where some CPAs and enrolled agents are allowed to represent taxpayers, only a lawyer can represent you in other federal courts—and the legal fees can be staggeringly high. If you win, however, you might (but probably won't) be able to persuade the judge to order that the IRS pay your attorneys' fees. (See "Can You Get the IRS to Pay Your Attorneys' Fees?" below.)

Only 5% of all tax disputes for regular cases go to a District Court or the Court of Federal Claims instead of Tax Court. Usually, these cases involve large corporations and hundreds of thousands of dollars or more. The unpopular feature of these two forums is that you must first pay the tax bill before filing your lawsuit. Technically, you are bringing a refund lawsuit against Uncle Sam for the taxes you contend were overpaid.

Can You Get the IRS to Pay Your Attorneys' Fees?

If you hire an attorney to represent you, it is possible, but difficult, to get the IRS to pay your attorneys' fees. (I.R.C. § 7430.) Not only must you win, but also you must show that the IRS's position was not "substantially justified." This means proving that the IRS knew or should have known that it was wrong on either the facts or the law, which is hard to prove.

Although there is no maximum amount of legal fees you can collect, you are limited to recovering $230 per hour for an attorney's time unless you can show the case was unusually difficult and your attorney normally charges more. The second part will be simple—most tax attorneys charge from $350 to $550 per hour.

> EXAMPLE: Thomas lost his audit after supplying documents which were ignored by the IRS. He brought the same records to his trial before a Tax Court judge and won his case. The Tax Court awarded Thomas $17,000 in legal expenses incurred in fighting the unreasonable tax assessment. (*Tinsley v. Commissioner of Internal Revenue*, T.C. Memo 1992-195 (1992).)

If you don't hire an attorney, you are not entitled to compensation for your time in fighting the case—even if you are a lawyer.

Before suing, you must file IRS Form 843, *Claim for Refund and Request for Abatement*, and either have it rejected in writing by the IRS or wait until at least six months pass without the IRS's taking any action on your refund claim.

TIP

Sometimes other federal courts are better than Tax Court. If the IRS claims you owe a lot—$50,000 or more—and you disagree and can pay first, see a tax attorney. Consider filing in a district court or the court of federal claims. You might have a better chance in these two courts than in Tax Court, depending on the tax issues involved. Don't try this without legal assistance.

The advantage of these two alternative courts lies in our sometimes inconsistent judicial system. The Tax Court, district courts, and the Court of Federal Claims, as well as some bankruptcy courts, all have the power to decide tax cases, but sometimes decide the same tax issue differently. Because their decisions are published online and in casebooks found in law libraries, it's no secret how each court has ruled in the past.

Although judges can change their minds, and the makeup of courts changes over time, courts seldom go against their own precedents. This means you can choose the court that has been most kind to your tax situation in the past. Perhaps of greater importance is that you can request a jury trial in a district court. If a jury is upset with the IRS or the tax law, it can give you a break.

There is another reason why some people sue in a court other than Tax Court. The District Court and Court of Federal Claims lawyers don't work for the IRS and are often more reasonable in settling cases than are the IRS's Tax Court lawyers. The primary disadvantages of going to these other courts are the legal expenses and the prepayment of your audit bill.

Bankruptcy Court

Bankruptcy judges also have the power to decide IRS disputes. Some very favorable tax decisions have been made in bankruptcy court adversary proceedings. Of course, you must file bankruptcy first to get your IRS dispute heard. If bankruptcy is a serious option for you, see both a bankruptcy and a tax lawyer, or one who works in both areas.

RESOURCE

For an overview of taxes and bankruptcy, see Chapter 6. Also, detailed information, including the forms and instructions for filing for bankruptcy, can be found in *How to File for Chapter 7 Bankruptcy*, by Cara O'Neill (Nolo); *Chapter 13 Bankruptcy*, by Cara O'Neill (Nolo); and *The New Bankruptcy*, by Cara O'Neill (Nolo).

RESOURCE

The Tax Court's address is U.S. Tax Court, 400 Second Street, NW, Washington, D.C., 20217, telephone number 202-521-0700. The court also has a helpful website at www.ustaxcourt.gov, where you can find forms and read Tax Court opinions and decisions.

Chapter Highlights

- The Tax Court hears disputes between taxpayers and the IRS.
- It's often easy and inexpensive to go to Tax Court without a lawyer.
- IRS lawyers settle most cases without ever going to court by reducing an individual's or a business's tax bill.

When You Owe the IRS:
Keeping the Tax Collector at Bay

When You Can't Pay With Your Tax Return...195

Getting Time to Pay After the Tax Bill Comes...196

IRS Tax Billing Process 196

    Delaying the Computerized Notice Cycle 197

    Automatic Refund, Asset, and Wage Seizures...198

IRS Automated Collection System..198

    Delaying the ACS Collector...199

    Getting an Installment Agreement (IA) From the IRS.......................................201

    Requesting That Your File Be Sent to the Local Office.....................................205

Revenue Officers—Frontline Collectors of the IRS 206

    The First Visit 206

    The Collection Interview—Meeting the Revenue Officer..............................207

    Filling in IRS Collection Forms 210

    Signing IRS Collection Forms—Proceed With Caution 218

    Protecting Yourself After Making Financial Disclosures to the IRS.............219

    What the Collector Does Next...220

    Installment Payment Plan: Individuals...220

    Installment Agreement Set-Up Fee...226

Offers in Compromise (OICs)..230

    Grounds for Making an OIC 231

    Offer in Compromise Forms 232

    Your Minimum Offer Amount 232

    OIC Payment Options...241

    Special Circumstances: Effective Tax Administration (ETA) Exception.....244

    What Happens After You Send in Your OIC Application..................................246

    If Your OIC Is Rejected 247

Using the Bankruptcy Code to Stop the IRS..249

    Types of Bankruptcy..249

    The Automatic Stay..249

    Downsides of Bankruptcy 250

    Taxes and Chapter 7 Bankruptcy 250

    Taxes and Chapter 13 Bankruptcy..253

    Taxes and Chapter 11 Bankruptcy..254

    Taxes and Chapter 12 Bankruptcy..255

Protecting Your Assets From the IRS 255

Suspending Collection of Your Tax Bill 257

Collection of Tax Debts by Private Debt Collectors 258

A ccording to the IRS, 15% of all taxpayers owe back taxes. And this figure includes only people who have actually filed tax returns. As mentioned in Chapter 2, many people required to file tax returns haven't.

There are several possible reasons you might owe the IRS back taxes:

• You didn't file a tax return; the IRS prepared a return for you and sent you a bill.

• You didn't pay your income taxes in full when you filed your tax return.

• You believed you paid your taxes in full when you filed your return, but you later received an automated adjustment notice from the IRS. This probably means you forgot to report some item of income.

• After an audit, the IRS found that you owed additional taxes; you signed the audit report in agreement.

• After an audit, the IRS found that you owed additional taxes; you didn't sign the audit report, but you neither appealed nor filed a petition in Tax Court.

• After an audit, the IRS found that you owed additional taxes; you appealed and lost and did not file a petition in Tax Court. The tax bill became final.

• After an audit, the IRS found that you owed additional taxes; you filed a petition in Tax Court and came out still owing something.

No matter which of these categories you fit into, one thing is clear—you have a problem with the IRS. Unlike other creditors, the IRS has no legal obligation to take you to court before seizing your car or paycheck. You can lose your business, your bank accounts, and even your pension. As far as the IRS is concerned, your tax obligation takes priority over all other debts. If the IRS records a notice of tax lien, your credit rating might be ruined for years.

Luckily, this doesn't have to happen to you. If you deal with the IRS—in particular, if you intelligently respond to the IRS collector—chances are good that you'll keep your property and survive the worst of what the IRS throws at you.

The IRS goal is to collect the maximum amount of taxes from you with the minimum amount of effort. The IRS starts by sending you computer-generated notices. Next, the IRS Automated Collection System, or ACS, kicks in, calling and sending you more threatening notices. If the IRS still doesn't get its money, it assigns a human being from its collection division—a revenue officer—to get up close and personal with you. Finally, if none of this works, the IRS may assign your debt to a private debt collection agency for collection.

How Long Does the IRS Have to Collect?

There is a little mercy in the tax code—it's called the "statute of limitations" on the collection of a tax debt. In general, the IRS has 10 years to collect from the date of assessment, called the "23C" date by the IRS. (I.R.C. § 6502.) After 10 years, the debt is wiped out. There are a number of ways the 10-year period can be extended:

- The 10-year period doesn't start to run until you file your return and the IRS officially assesses the tax against you. Not filing a return and hiding for 10 years accomplishes nothing.
- The IRS can extend the 10-year period by suing you in federal court. The IRS rarely does this. If it's getting close to the 10-year period and you don't owe millions, the IRS usually lets the statute of limitations run out, and you're off the hook forever.
- Certain actions on your part can extend the 10 years. For example, if you file an Offer in Compromise, are out of the United States, are in litigation with the IRS, file for bankruptcy, request a Taxpayer Assistance Order, sign a waiver form agreeing to extend, or request a Collection Due Process hearing, the 10-year period is extended until these circumstances are resolved.

These various rules are more complicated than this summary. See an experienced tax professional for more information.

Dealing With an IRS Tax Bill You Owe

You have six ways to deal with a tax bill you unquestionably owe:

- pay in full
- pay in monthly installments, by agreement with the IRS
- reduce, eliminate, or pay the debt through bankruptcy
- reduce the debt and pay it through an IRS Offer in Compromise
- have the IRS determine that you are temporarily unable to pay and suspend collection, or
- wait for the statute of limitations on collection to expire.

All of these options are covered in this chapter.

While reducing your bill through an Offer in Compromise, going into bankruptcy, or having the IRS determine you are temporarily unable to pay might be the most attractive options, they are the most difficult to get. Paying in full is the best alternative for most working people with homes and substantial assets. For many taxpayers, however, paying in installments is the only way they can do it. Recently, more than 2.6 million taxpayers were on installment plans, paying collectively in excess of $4.5 billion.

Don't jump to the conclusion that paying your IRS debt over time (or paying it at all) is your best option. Read this entire section before making your decision on how to deal with the tax collector.

First, do you really owe all the IRS says you owe?

Before you agree to pay any amount to the IRS, make sure the bill is correct. You're entitled to a full explanation of why you owe any IRS bill. Here are some suggestions for making sure your bill is correct—or for possibly reducing it:

- Review your tax returns or have a tax professional look at them to see if you might have missed any deductions, losses or carryovers, or similar items. If you find any, you can amend your tax return and reduce your bill.
- Review the bill to make sure you have been credited with all payments, including any wage or bank levies and any refunds taken. It is common for the IRS to miss or incorrectly apply payments and credits to your account.

To find out how the IRS calculated your tax bill and credited your payments, request a transcript of your account. Use the IRS Get Transcript Online tool (www.irs.gov/individuals/get-transcript) to obtain a copy by email, or call the IRS Taxpayer Assistance telephone number (800-829-1040) to get it mailed to you. It might take several weeks for the transcript to arrive.

These printouts aren't always easy to understand. You can find definitions of the transaction codes in an IRS document called *Section 8A Master File Codes*, available on the IRS website (www.irs.gov/pub/irs-pia/6209sec8a masterfilecodes.pdf). If you need an explanation, call 800-829-1040, go to your local IRS office, or ask a tax professional for help. Compare your canceled checks, prior tax notices, tax refunds withheld, and bank and wage levies with the IRS printout. If it doesn't match up—perhaps the IRS missed some credits you were due—immediately bring this to the attention of the IRS. Send copies of your proof of payment or other supporting documentation.

Almost all old tax bills include penalties and interest. It might be possible to have some or all of these unwanted additions canceled (or abated). See Chapter 12 to determine whether you qualify and how to go about asking the IRS for an abatement.

The Tax Gap

Despite its fierce image and extraordinary powers, the IRS, by its own admission, is a lousy bill collector. Recently, the amount of income taxes reported owed by almost 12 million people—but uncollected—exceeded $540 billion. The IRS collects only 85.5% of what it says it is owed by taxpayers. Add to that amount the taxes the IRS estimates are owed on unfiled returns and the total is even higher. The government calls this the "tax gap."

When You Can't Pay With Your Tax Return

If you're coming up on a tax return filing date and owe a balance you can't pay, file anyway. This avoids the hefty late filing penalty (but not the smaller late payment penalty).

If you can pay over time and owe less than $50,000, you can apply for an installment agreement online at www.irs.gov/payments/online-payment-agreement-application. If you establish your installment agreement using the Online Payment Agreement application, the user fee that you pay will be lower than it would be with Form 9465. If you want to apply by mail, complete Form 9465, *Installment Agreement Request*, attach it to the front of your tax return, and send it to the address shown in your Form 1040 instructions. Get a copy of Form 9465 at the IRS website at www.irs.gov or by calling 800-829-FORM.

Whether you apply online or by filing Form 9465, you must tell the IRS how much you can pay monthly on the balance. If you apply online and qualify, your installment agreement can be approved in as little as 30 minutes.

If you apply by filing Form 9465, the IRS should reply in 30 to 60 days to let you know if a plan has been approved, or to request more financial information from you before making the decision. During the rush of tax season (February to May), it will probably take longer for the IRS to reply. You might even receive a bill. Don't assume that the IRS lost your installment request form. Chances are the IRS simply hasn't processed it yet. Respond by sending in another copy of your completed Form 9465 along with the IRS bill.

If you owe less than $50,000 and can pay in full in 72 months or less, your request should be granted. The IRS might bump up the amount required to be paid every month. If you're turned down, or you and the IRS can't agree on an amount, you'll have to furnish financial data and negotiate over the phone, via letter, or in person.

The IRS charges interest and a late payment penalty for each month you carry a tax balance. The initial late payment penalty is 0.5% per month, which is reduced to 0.25% if you get a payment plan. The interest rate changes quarterly. Figure an additional 6%–8% average per year to the balance to get the full cost of owing the IRS. The IRS accepts payment by major credit card, but there is a hefty surcharge. Call 800-829-1040 for details or visit www.irs.gov/payments.

Getting Time to Pay After the Tax Bill Comes

If you didn't pay your taxes or apply online for an installment plan or submit Form 9465—or it was ignored or rejected—buy time by calling the IRS after you receive a tax bill. Request an extension of up to 180 days to pay a bill or a payment plan. Try this without talking to IRS personnel. Call 800-829-7650. It might work if you owe less than $50,000 (including interest and penalties), are an individual or a couple (not a business), and have no other balances due to the IRS.

You can get either an extension of up to 180 days to pay in full or a monthly payment plan. If you choose the payment plan, you'll be asked how much you want to pay each month. Be sure to think about this before you call. If you need just a little time, request a 45-day extension. If you can't pay at the end of the 45 days, you can request a payment plan or another extension.

If you don't want to interact with an IRS computer, you can mail in a request for more time or another Form 9465 or call an IRS customer service representative at 800-829-1040.

IRS Tax Billing Process

The IRS mission is to collect the tax using the least amount of human effort possible. This accounts for the reams of computer-generated tax bill notices you'll get long before ever hearing from a human being. No person is likely to even look at your account until your bill is at least six months overdue—often more like a year. And if you owe less than $1,000, no one may ever look at your account. You simply become a number in the IRS computer and get billed in the mail.

Once a balance due from a tax return has been posted to your account, a Computer Paragraph, or CP, notice is automatically mailed out. Your file is termed a "tax delinquency account," or TDA. Many automated collection notices were paused during the COVID-19 pandemic. However, the IRS began sending them out again in the summer of 2023.

The first notice is a four-page, nonthreatening CP-14, *You Have Unpaid Taxes*. These notices weren't paused during the COVID pandemic. The CP-14 includes a scannable QR code that directs to an IRS landing page for payments.

If you don't pay up within 30 days, you'll receive a series of CP notices. Individuals ordinarily receive a total of four collection notices, culminating with a Notice of Intent to Levy, while businesses get two. However, if you have other outstanding tax bills, the IRS may speed up the process. By checking below for the number or type of CP notice you've received, you can figure out how close the IRS is to taking serious action.

Individual income taxes. About five weeks after sending the friendly bill, CP-14, the IRS computer usually sends "500 series" notices, identified by the number following the date in the upper right-hand corner: CP-501, *You Have a Balance Due*; CP-504, *You Have an Amount Due—Intent to Levy*; and CP-503, *Immediate Action Is Required*. In four to eight months, you'll get CP-90, *Final Notice—Intent to Levy and Notice of Your Right to a Hearing*.

CP-90 usually means your case is going to another IRS department. So don't panic just yet, but your time might be running out.

The total cycle, from the first notice to the last computer-generated letter, averages four to six months. This is the cushion before the IRS horror stories start coming true. At some point, the IRS will also send you Publication 594, *The IRS Collection Process* (available on the IRS's website at www.irs.gov). It describes what the IRS can legally do to collect from you—which is plenty. Read it.

Payroll taxes. If you owe business or payroll taxes, collection on your account may be accelerated. The IRS often shortens the notice cycle to as few as eight weeks, depending on the size of the delinquency.

Special circumstances. If you did not file a return or owe $50,000 or more, the IRS may go straight from the CP-501, *You Have a Balance Due*, to the CP-90, *Final Notice*. Or, the IRS may stop the notices if it determines that your account is currently uncollectible, or that you are deceased, filing for bankruptcy, or incarcerated.

Delaying the Computerized Notice Cycle

If your goal is simply to buy more time, respond in writing to each IRS notice. Send a letter with the bill and a short paragraph saying that you can't pay right now. You don't need to give an excuse; just ask for 45 more days to pay. This is the maximum time period that can be entered into the IRS computer to suspend the collection notice cycle. When the next CP notice comes, try responding by requesting another 45 days. If you're able, send a small payment with each of your request letters to show that you're trying. This should buy you an unofficial short-term payment plan, which might be all you need.

Sometimes, making 45-day delay requests throws a monkey wrench into the system. Taxpayers have been known not to hear from the IRS again for as long as a year. It all depends on the efficiency of your particular IRS campus and the priority your account is given.

Automatic Refund, Asset, and Wage Seizures

Even if you ignore the first few notices, you can buy some time by responding to the CP series notices. The IRS CP-90, *Final Notice*, is really not the last notice before the IRS takes action, in spite of its ominous title. The one to pay attention to is the next one: Letter 1058 (find the number in the upper or lower right corner), *Final Notice, Notice of Intent to Levy and Notice of Your Right to a Hearing. Please Respond Immediately.* This letter explains your rights to a hearing and requests an immediate response.

If you don't respond after 30 days, the IRS computer may send levy notices to any financial institution suspected of holding funds under your Social Security number or name or to any employer or contractor who filed a W-2 or 1099 form showing they have paid you in the past. Levy notice recipients must then freeze your account or pay the IRS all or a portion of your wages or money owed to you. (Liens and levies are covered in Chapter 7.) As discussed later in this chapter, you are entitled to appeal an IRS levy. The IRS could also issue Form CP-49, *Overpaid Tax Applied to Other Taxes You Owe*, and seize tax refunds that you are owed.

IRS Automated Collection System

As mentioned above, if you don't pay during the IRS computerized CP notice series, your file will be sent to the IRS Automated Collection System, or ACS. The ACS has the authority to collect most overdue tax bills, solicit tax returns from people who haven't filed, and levy (seize) assets and wages.

The ACS is a staffed telecommunications system for collecting seriously delinquent accounts. The ACS operates by mail and phone only.

How Long Your File Stays With the ACS

Unless your case has enough "points" to be assigned to a field collector—under a secret IRS scoring system—it can stay with the ACS for as long as the IRS still has to collect (generally 10 years from the date the tax was first assessed). The chief factor is the amount you owe—most importantly, whether it's over or under $50,000. Other point factors are your past history of tax delinquencies and the number of years of taxes you owe.

As your case gets near the end of the 10-year statute of limitations for collection, even small balances may be sent to the local office for handling by a revenue officer.

The ACS computer automatically analyzes accounts that require telephone contact and dials and redials your phone number automatically if the IRS gets no answer or a busy signal. When contact is made, an IRS person will come on the line.

The ACS is the IRS's primary mail dunning and telephone harassment apparatus. We have visited ACS facilities, although they are not open to the public, and have found 150 or more clerks sitting in front of computer monitors, wearing telephone headsets. They follow scripts demanding payment from tax debtors and respond to calls or faxes requesting payment plans or more time to pay. The ACS mails collection letters and issues levies to third parties such as banks and employers.

ACS computer data is often inaccurate. For example, the ACS frequently requests tax returns from women who have filed under a new name after getting married or from deceased taxpayers.

Delaying the ACS Collector

If you want to slow down the ACS, call and ask for more time to pay. To suspend the computerized collection process, a collector must enter an appropriate freeze code into the computer. There are many freeze codes, but the precise details—such as the code designations, the exact number of codes, and when they can be used by ACS collectors—are not public information. Requesting more time to pay, filing for bankruptcy, or asking for a suspension of collection due to a hardship all have different freeze codes.

When a freeze code is entered into the computer, collection activity on your account is put on hold for the time specified for that code number—up to one year or even longer. No action will be taken on your case during that period, but you might still get tax bills. And, any tax refunds you are owed will be held by the IRS. After the time period elapses, the computer automatically pulls the case back up for further review and contact by the IRS.

Short-term hold. You can get a short-term hold—up to 45 or more days—usually by just asking for it. First, make your request over the telephone. Also, follow up with a written response to the ACS. Just photocopy the notice you were sent, write on it that you need up to 45 days to get the money to pay, and send the notice back—a separate letter isn't necessary.

Long-term hold. If you really can't afford any monthly payment amount, ask the collector to classify your account as "currently not collectible" or a "significant hardship case" and to suspend collection activities for 12 months or more. You must convince the ACS you are truly down and out—no assets, no job, or very meager income and you survive mostly through welfare or the kindness of others. If you keep giving excuses, you might come up with one that convinces the collector to seek approval to enter a long-term hold code. But, ACS collectors are on short leashes and not known for being sympathetic.

To determine whether you qualify for "currently not collectible" (CNC) status, the IRS might ask you to complete a *Collection Information Statement* form—in writing or by telephone. If you're dealing with the ACS by phone, you might be asked to complete IRS collection Form 433-F (discussed below).

The IRS will compare your monthly household income to the national and local standards for living expenses (see the IRS website for current amounts). If the IRS allowable expense table shows expenses exceeding your household income and you have minimal assets, the IRS will consider you a CNC hardship case. Expect several weeks or more for this determination.

If CNC status is approved, you'll receive an IRS CP-4624C letter stating that your case has been closed (for the time being). This doesn't mean the IRS or the balance due goes away forever. CNC status only means that you are not required to make any payments and the IRS will not take enforced collection action against you (like levy your bank accounts). The 10-year collection limitation statute continues to run, but interest and penalties also continue to run and the IRS may file a federal tax lien against you.

Should the IRS deny your request for CNC status, it will demand payment under an installment agreement (IA) or liquidation of any assets. If you don't agree, contact the IRS with any additional information that would support a CNC or request lower monthly payments. Currently Not Collectible status is subject to annual IRS review of changes in your financial situation.

Other Ways to Stop the ACS Collector

If asking for a hold doesn't delay the tax collector for long, you can try one of these tactics:

- **Question the accuracy of the tax bill.** Because tax bills are difficult to decipher, you don't need to say anything other than it doesn't look right. If you raise a doubt in an IRS collector's mind, they must exercise reasonable forbearance—that is, no further steps to collect can be taken until the bill's accuracy is verified. This could take several days or several months. If your request is refused, ask to talk to a manager. If this doesn't work, call the Taxpayer Advocate Service. (See Chapter 8.) If anyone questions your right, refer them to the *Internal Revenue Manual* 1.2.1.6.4; IRS Policy Statement 5-16.
- **Submit an Offer in Compromise.** The IRS usually suspends all collection activities while the offer is pending, often a period of several months or as long as two years.
- **File for bankruptcy.** This immediately stops all IRS collection activities.

Getting an Installment Agreement (IA) From the IRS

Do you owe less than $50,000 and can you make monthly payments within 72 months (six years)? Good news. Getting an installment agreement (IA in IRS-speak) with the IRS is fairly easy. Go to the IRS website and apply or call the taxpayer service line at 800-829-1040. You should get an IA approved as long as you don't have unfiled tax returns or a previous history of defaulted payment agreements with the IRS.

If you owe more than $50,000 (or $25,000 for businesses), you will have to negotiate with a live person and most likely have to submit a financial statement on IRS Form 433-F. See below for details.

Before talking to the IRS, have a plan of action. If the IRS calls you and you're not prepared, give a polite excuse, such as you're late for a doctor's appointment, the baby is playing with matches, or you work nights and are sleeping now, and promise to call back. Don't answer any questions, other than your name, until you're ready with your facts and figures.

Make a comprehensive list of your assets, debts, income, and—most importantly—your living expenses. The collector will be looking for information similar to that requested on IRS Form 433-A, *Collection Information Statement for Wage Earners and Self-Employed Individuals*, or Form 433-B, *Collection Information Statement for Businesses*. Use the appropriate form to organize the information, especially your expenses. Your goal is usually to convince the collector to give you time to pay your taxes. The collector's goal, however, is getting you to pay the full tax bill as soon as possible.

Once you've compiled your financial data, call the IRS. Have a notepad, pencil, and the tax bill and be ready to take notes. IRS ACS and taxpayer service telephone lines are open from the early morning to the late evening. Of course, getting through might be a different story. The best times seem to be Tuesdays, Wednesdays, and Thursdays, early morning or lunchtime. Expect to be put on hold, and be prepared for a long wait—set aside snacks, the remote control, reading material, or your knitting.

When a collector finally comes on the phone, write down the person's name and ID number. You might get only a first name or a pseudonym. The collectors often don't give their real names out of fear of retaliation. This person might be on an IRS collection team of five to seven members. Make notes of important points throughout the conversation. If you ever have to call back, you probably won't be able to talk to the same person—the system is nationwide, with thousands of employees. The IRS claims that you will get the same result no matter who you speak to, but don't believe it. If you don't like a particular collector, politely end the call and try back the next day. You will likely get a different, and hopefully more reasonable, collector.

IRS collectors sit all day long listening to every excuse in the book—and some that aren't. They hear so many lies that they become cynical and unsympathetic. Without lying, accent the negative—how hard your life is, your large expenses and low income, and the like. If the collector becomes rude or bullying, ask to speak to their supervisor. If all else fails, try begging or crying. You might be assigned another collector, or the supervisor might personally handle your case.

The telephone collector's hidden agenda is to identify assets, called "levy sources," that the IRS can seize if you don't voluntarily pay the tax bill. Don't lie—about your assets or anything else. If you're asked a question you don't want to get into with the collector, such as whether you have any sideline income, gracefully end the conversation—use a prepared excuse, such as you are running late for work. Call back later. You might not be asked the question again.

Checklist If You Contact the IRS Collector by Telephone

If you are committed to making payment arrangements with the IRS over the telephone, be prepared to provide the following information:
- alimony or child support paid or received
- employer information, including work telephone number
- investment income
- life insurance policies with cash value
- information about individuals living in your household
- out-of-pocket medical expenses
- pension and Social Security income
- profit and loss statement if self-employed
- rental income
- secured loans
- substantiation of court-ordered payments
- three months of current bank statements (all accounts)
- three months of current pay stubs
- value of retirement accounts
- value of all property and available equity
- vehicle information: year, make, value, amount owed, and monthly payments, and
- student loan payments.

The IRS telephone collector will also ask about bank balances and equity in your home or other real estate. You might be asked about your cash borrowing power, but you can't be forced to take out a loan. Remember— the goal is to get you to pay the full tax bill at once. If the collector thinks that you can pay, they'll demand payment immediately.

If the collector concludes that you can't pay now, you will be asked questions to see if you qualify for a monthly payment plan, called an "installment agreement," or IA. You will be asked about your family's size, income, and living expenses.

Then, you might be asked to send substantiating documentation, such as rent receipts or pay stubs. The collector might demand that you fill out an IRS financial statement form. Follow the instructions below for advice on completing the form, called a Collection Information Statement.

> **TIP**
> **Be prepared to negotiate a monthly payment.** State the amount you can afford. Start low, as the collector might well ask for a higher amount. The collector might insist that you cut back on some of your expenses. Be firm if the expenses are really necessary to your survival, and not luxuries.

> **EXAMPLE:** The IRS collector questioned Yung's assertion that his family's monthly grocery bill totaled $1,500, saying it was beyond IRS allowances for a family of four. Yung explained that his two children were lactose-intolerant diabetics on special costly diets.

If you verbally agree to a payment plan, the IRS will send monthly statements and payment vouchers. Start making payments on the date you and the collector agreed you would start. If you haven't yet received the IRS monthly billing, send in a payment and enclose a letter stating that you are paying "per a telephone conversation with Carol, ID# 123456, on 12/29/xx, in which I agreed to pay $350 per month beginning 1/15/xx." Send your payment to the billing address on your notice. Write your Social Security number or taxpayer identification number and tax period on the check or money order.

Interest and late payment penalties are running while you are in an installment plan.

If you're ever unable to make a monthly payment when it's due, see "Installment Payment Plan: Individuals," below.

Requesting That Your File Be Sent to the Local Office

If you can't get anywhere with the IRS by phone, or you don't want to deal with them—for example, the bill is wrong—request that your file be transferred to your local IRS office. There, your case will be handled by a revenue officer. There are several other reasons why you might want your file transferred from the ACS:

- Once ACS collectors know where you live, work, or bank, the IRS computer may garnish your wages or seize (levy) your bank accounts. (See Chapter 7.) This is less likely to happen when a person has been assigned to your case.
- Revenue officers can grant longer-term payment plans and suggest more alternatives than can collectors. You will, however, have to disclose more details of your financial life to a revenue officer than to an ACS collector.

How do you get your case out of the ACS? ACS collectors don't grant transfer requests without a good reason. Just asking probably won't do it. Reasons that might work include telling the ACS collector that you don't agree with the tax the IRS claims you owe and that you want to meet with the IRS to discuss it. Very few of us understand tax notices, so you won't be lying. ACS staff are supposed to transfer a file whenever a taxpayer questions the correctness of taxes on a notice.

If the collector refuses to send your file to your local IRS office, ask for a supervisor. Unless your complaint is clearly phony, you should get your way. Keep asking for a transfer if you don't first succeed. The more you owe, the easier it will be to get a transfer—that is, the ACS will grant transfers to people owing $50,000 more readily than to those owing $5,000.

Make the same transfer request in writing in response to the notices you receive in the mail. Write that you don't understand how the tax bill was computed and therefore don't agree with it. Ask to meet with someone from your local IRS office for an explanation and to discuss payment.

Revenue Officers—Frontline Collectors of the IRS

If you owe more than $50,000 and the IRS notices have failed to get you to pay, or if you've requested that your file be transferred to your local IRS office, your case will end up with a local IRS revenue officer. These tax collectors follow a four-step process:

1. They might make a surprise visit or telephone call to your home or work.
2. They either ask you questions on the spot or set up an interview at their office or by telephone.
3. Revenue officers may record your financial information—income, assets, liabilities, and living expenses—on detailed IRS 433 forms, which you'll be asked to verify and sign.
4. Revenue officers try to collect—in one or more of the following ways—by:
   - demanding immediate payment
   - requesting that you obtain a bank loan
   - requesting that you sell assets
   - proposing an installment payment agreement
   - suggesting an Offer in Compromise
   - beginning enforced collection—seizing your wages, bank accounts, and other assets, or
   - reporting your case as currently uncollectible.

These steps are all discussed in detail below.

The First Visit

Some revenue officers try to catch delinquent taxpayers off guard by what I call the ambush. The officer simply comes to your home or work, usually between 8 a.m. and 6 p.m. If you aren't there, the person will leave a card requesting that you call back within a few days.

If the officer finds you at home or work, or if you call back, they'll start asking financial questions or set a time for you to be interviewed at the IRS office. Don't lie, but avoid giving financial information unless you are completely prepared. Say that you have to check your records. Then you'll be asked if you've filed your tax returns. If you have, no problem. If you haven't, don't lie. Say you need to check your records or with a tax professional, but don't say yes if you haven't filed.

Assuming you clearly owe the IRS, begin your first conversation with a revenue officer by acknowledging your responsibility and stating that you have every intention of cooperating. You don't have to offer details on how you plan to pay. Don't launch into the problems of your life, complain about the unfairness of the tax law, or be generally defensive. Being positive—even if you have to grit your teeth the entire time—will send a signal that you are not unreasonable. Considering how much discretion collectors have to make your life miserable, this is a wise approach.

The revenue officer will set an in-person or telephone appointment for a collection interview. The officer might, however, want to talk to you in person or on the phone before the interview. Before giving any information, ask if you will be expected to supply financial data at the meeting.

After the officer says yes—and they'll say yes because that is the purpose of the meeting—request that you be sent a copy of the specific collection form. It will be called a *Collection Information Statement*. You will go over the form together during the interview. (For the most current form, check the IRS website at www.irs.gov.)

By requesting the IRS collection statement form (see below) before the interview, you can delay the collection process a bit. Explain that you want the form ahead of time so that you can be as accurate as possible during the interview. The officer can't argue with that. Fill in the form before you go to the meeting to shorten the meeting and calm your nerves.

The Collection Interview—Meeting the Revenue Officer

According to the *Internal Revenue Manual*, the first taxpayer interview is the most important event in the IRS's collection process. The revenue officer plays detective and is trained to first act sympathetic to gain your confidence and cooperation. But after the honey often comes the vinegar.

Legally, you can't be forced to answer any questions. But if you don't, you risk rapid "enforced collection" action—seizure of your assets and wages. What you say at the collection interview often will determine how successful you'll be in resolving your problem. Be on your best behavior.

CAUTION

Never lie to the IRS. If the IRS catches you trying to conceal assets or outright lie about them, at best it will cause the auditor to probe harder; at worst, you'll get a referral to the IRS Criminal Investigation Division. (See Chapter 10.)

The IRS purpose for the interview is to gather information for the Collection Information Statement, which details your finances.

The IRS has several versions for its financial statement:

- Form 433-A, *Collection Information Statement for Wage Earners and Self-Employed Individuals*
- Form 433-B, *Collection Information Statement for Businesses* (partnerships, corporations, and LLCs)
- Form 433-F, *Collection Information Statement*, which is a shorter version of Form 433-A, and
- Form 433-H, *Installment Agreement Request and Collection Information Statement*, used for wage earners who owe over $50,000 or who can't pay within 72 months.

To negotiate with a revenue officer, all individual and self-employed persons must undergo a personal interview. Business entities, such as corporations, or those who owe payroll taxes for their employees must submit Form 433-B.

A revenue officer will push hard to get all questions on the 433 series forms answered. All 433 series forms are divided into two main parts—assets and liabilities, and income and expenses. You will probably know the figures for your assets, debts, and income. The expense part is where problems usually arise. Most of us know exactly how much our car and house payments are, but not how much we spend on other living expenses. The IRS expects you to know these costs when it comes time to fill out the forms.

After the interview, the revenue officer will ask you to immediately sign the financial disclosure forms. Don't be coerced into signing, even if you're desperate to get out of the IRS office. If you haven't prepared your figures ahead of time, you will probably underestimate your monthly living expenses by 10% to 40%. (Precise instructions for completing this form are given below.) In turn, this gives the IRS the false impression that you have a lot of money left over after paying your monthly expenses. Then the revenue officer will demand you pay the IRS in monthly installments, all of this leftover money plus whatever amount the officer deems as "unnecessary" living expenses listed on your 433-A or 433-F.

TIP

Don't rush it. Tell the revenue officer you want to go over the forms in your home or office with your records at hand. Make this request even if you got the forms in advance and filled them out before the meeting—if nothing else, you can buy a little time. This is far less nerve-wracking than coming up with figures at the IRS office. If the officer gives you a hard time or asks what part is incorrect, say that you want to go over your records or talk with your tax adviser first. If the officer still balks, ask to discuss the matter with a supervisor. The officer probably will relent without calling in the boss.

If You Refuse to Divulge Financial Information

In general, you don't have to give the IRS financial information about yourself. While lying to a collector is a crime, refusing to give information is not. (I.R.C. § 7206.) If you don't cooperate or you only partially cooperate, the IRS has three options:

- Seize known assets and/or levy your wages and other income—the most likely outcome of your lack of cooperation. Revenue officers can check public real property and motor vehicle records, and contact financial institutions. The IRS has a hard time finding out-of-state deposit accounts and real estate, however.
- Back off and go after other tax delinquents—you should be so lucky.
- Issue a summons for you. A summons is a legal order to appear and bring records or give information. The IRS doesn't often use this power because of the paperwork and trouble. If you get a summons and aren't sure what to do, see a tax attorney. If you ignore a summons, you risk a court hearing and jail.

If it's too late—you've already signed the 433 form without the chance to review your expenses—you might still be able to revise it. Tell the revenue officer that some of your original figures were incorrect and you have further information to make them right. Then provide the correct numbers.

Defending Your Expenses to the Revenue Officer

The IRS allows only "reasonable necessary and proven living expenses for a tax debtor and his dependent family members." Be prepared to defend your expenses to a tax collector. Bring your canceled checks, rent, or mortgage receipts, apartment leases, repair bills, insurance notices, medical bills, and paid receipts to the interview. The 433-A and 433-F forms are similar so the following applies to both versions.

Filling in IRS Collection Forms

The key parts of IRS collection forms are assets and monthly expenses. Let's go over Form 433-A. The 433-F form shown below is similar but shorter so the following applies to both.

Assets

The form asks you to reveal your assets and their values. The IRS wants this information to determine your ability to pay and, if you don't pay, to possibly seize your assets or request you to sell them or borrow against them. Some assets are easy to value, like bank accounts and stocks. Other asset values can be estimated, like your home, furniture, boats, and banjos. The lower the value you place on your property, the less interested the IRS will be in seizing it or requiring you to sell or borrow on it.

TIP
Consider prepaying some expenses. Because the tax collector might pressure you to pay the IRS from any existing liquid assets revealed on a Form 433—like cash, stocks, Bitcoin, or CDs—you can beat the IRS to the punch by prepaying some of your future expenses—like your mortgage, rent, or insurance. This will reduce your cash on hand and make sure you have a roof over your head. Or, use your cash to pay past-due bills and other debts. Wouldn't you rather repay your best friend the $10,000 loan made three years ago than give that money to the IRS?

Here are some suggestions for valuing specific items in Section 4 of the form.

Vehicles (Question 18). List and value your vehicles, whether owned or leased. Start with the lowest wholesale value shown in the *Kelley Blue Book*, which the IRS follows. This book is at your local library, at car dealerships, and online at www.kbb.com. Reduce the book value accordingly if the car has a lot of miles on it or needs work. Multiply this amount by 80% and subtract any car loan amount. If the result is $3,450 or less, your car's worth is listed as zero because there currently is a $3,450 exemption for the equity in each vehicle you own.

> EXAMPLE: Marcia drives her Honda to work. It has a Blue Book value of $20,000. She enters that and multiplies the amount by 80%, leaving $16,000. She owes her credit union $10,000, which leaves $6,000 in equity. She subtracts $3,450, resulting in $2,550 in equity to be listed in column 18a.

Real estate. Call several real estate agents. They'll be happy to give you a written opinion of the fair market value of your property if they think there is any chance you might list it for sale. Check real estate websites, like Redfin, Trulia, or Zillow and ads in the paper for similar properties. Discount that value by 20% and list it on the collection form. This 20% reduction is justifiable, as you would have to pay closing costs, sales commissions, fix-up fees, and other expenses if you were forced to sell the property. Beware: Real estate agents tend to be overly optimistic in their valuations, hoping you'll list the property for sale with them. Tell them you want a price that would result in a quick sale.

Personal items. Value your appliances, furniture, and fixtures at garage sale or thrift shop prices, which are extremely low. A sofa you bought five years ago for $1,000, for instance, would probably be worth only $100 or less today. On the form, you can group items. For example, furniture—$250 total is sufficient.

The IRS rarely verifies the values you list for personal items like household goods or wearing apparel. And the IRS can't get into your home to see these items unless you invite them in—which you don't have to do.

Digital assets. You need to list the value of any digital assets you own, such as Bitcoin or another virtual currency exchange. You're required to provide the email address used to set up the digital asset. You must also provide the location of the digital asset, such as a mobile wallet, online, or external storage. You're required to list the value of the digital asset as of the day you fill out Form 433-A. You can ordinarily determine this by checking the value listed on an online exchange. Don't try to hide Bitcoin or other digital assets from the IRS. The IRS has ways of discovering them, including obtaining records from online exchanges.

Necessary Living Expenses (433-A, Page 4)

If you have trouble getting a fair installment agreement from the IRS, the problem is likely to be over what constitutes your necessary living expenses.

Most tax debtors owing more than $50,000 are put on a budget if they want an IRS payment plan. In effect, the IRS dictates how much you can spend to live. Collectors follow specific IRS national, regional, and local published guidelines on how much money they believe is necessary to sustain a family, depending on the number of children and other dependents. The IRS uses these stingy guidelines regardless of your actual living expenses.

National Standards

The *Internal Revenue Manual* establishes national standards for living expenses in six IRS-established categories:
- actual cost of health insurance plan
- out-of-pocket health care, including medical services, prescription drugs, and eyeglasses (not cosmetic surgery)

- housekeeping supplies, apparel, and services
- personal care products and services, such as haircuts and toothpaste
- food, and
- miscellaneous expenses.

Except for the miscellaneous expenses, the standards are derived from the annual Bureau of Labor Statistics Consumer Expenditure Survey. The current maximum allowances can be found on the IRS website (www.irs.gov). The allowances depend on the size of your family. It's no surprise that the IRS figures used are always a year behind and don't reflect inflation. Tax debtors must provide documentation that their actual expenses are higher than the national standards.

Local Standards

The IRS recognizes that the cost of living is higher in New York City than Platte, Nebraska. So, there are IRS local expense allowances in addition to the national standard allowances. See the IRS website and look up the "local standards" list to find out what the allowances are where you reside.

The IRS also establishes local expense allowances for:
- housing and utilities—includes mortgage or rent, property taxes, maintenance, trash pickup, utilities, and telephone expenses (and these allowances depend on the size of your family), and
- transportation—includes car payments, insurance, gasoline, registration, parking, tolls, and maintenance or public transport, such as buses or cabs.

The allowances for transportation expenses do not take into account the size of your family (unlike the national standards above). Whether you're single and childless or married with 10 kids, the IRS allows you the same amount for transportation.

Also, local housing standards don't take into account disparities in living expenses within the same locale. If you live in a better part of town, you probably spend more than the IRS local standard.

Court-ordered child support and alimony may be deducted as living expenses in addition to the above items. You must provide a signed copy of the court order and proof of payment.

Living Expense Checklist

The expense checklist below gives a far truer picture of your monthly living expenses than does Form 433-A or F. Go through this list and then transfer the information to the form. If a particular item doesn't fit on the IRS form, use a separate sheet of paper. Everyone's expenses are different; don't feel confined by this list in making yours. Remember to add up expenses that don't recur monthly (such as a doctor's visit or auto repair) and divide by 12 to get a monthly average amount.

Housing & Utilities

Rent or mortgage payment $ _____

Second mortgage payment   _____

Home equity loan payment   _____

Repairs and upkeep   _____

Electricity and gas   _____

Water and sewer   _____

Telephone/cell/cable/internet   _____

Garbage   _____

Food

Groceries   _____

Meals out   _____

School lunches   _____

Clothing

Replacement and mending   _____

Laundry and cleaning   _____

Medical

Doctors and dentists   _____

Medications   _____

Hospital bills   _____

Transportation

Public transportation   _____

Gas   _____

Registration   _____

Maintenance   _____

Parking and tolls   _____

Insurance

Homeowners' or renters' $ _____

Motor vehicle   _____

Health   _____

Life (term only)   _____

Disability or other   _____

Taxes (not deducted from wages)

Property   _____

Income—federal   _____

Income—state   _____

Other (such as back taxes)   _____

Retirement plan*
(voluntary contribution)   _____

Installment payments

Motor vehicle   _____

Credit cards*

_____   _____

_____   _____

_____   _____

_____   _____

_____   _____

Department stores*

_____   _____

_____   _____

_____   _____

* Items marked with an asterisk are not generally allowed by the IRS unless you can prove they are necessary for the health and welfare of your family or for the production of income.

Living Expense Checklist (continued)

Installment payments (continued)

Student loan $_____

Personal loan* _____

Other installment payments* _____

Family expenses _____

Child support (court ordered) _____

Alimony (court ordered) _____

Child care _____

Other (such as back taxes) _____

Private school, college* _____

Bills for professional services _____

Accountant _____

Attorney _____

Tax professional _____

Other _____

Other

Payments to help dependents
outside immediate family* $_____

Personal items _____

Charitable contributions* _____

Entertainment* _____

Recreation* _____

Subscriptions* _____

Miscellaneous* _____

Total Monthly Expenses $_____

* Items marked with an asterisk are not generally allowed by the IRS unless you can prove they are necessary for the health and welfare of your family or for the production of income.

Collection Information Statement for Individuals (Form 433-F)—Page 1

Form **433-F** (February 2019)	Department of the Treasury - Internal Revenue Service **Collection Information Statement**

Name(s) and Address	Your Social Security Number or Individual Taxpayer Identification Number
	Your Spouse's Social Security Number or Individual Taxpayer Identification Number

☐ If address provided above is different than last return filed, please check here

County of Residence

	Your telephone numbers Home: _____ Work: _____ Cell: _____	Spouse's telephone numbers Home: _____ Work: _____ Cell: _____

Enter the number of people in the household who can be claimed on this year's tax return including you and your spouse. Under 65 ____ 65 and Over ____

If you or your spouse are self employed or have self employment income, provide the following information:

Name of Business	Business EIN	Type of Business	Number of Employees *(not counting owner)*

A. ACCOUNTS / LINES OF CREDIT

PERSONAL BANK ACCOUNTS Include checking, online, mobile (e.g., PayPal), savings accounts, money market accounts. (Use additional sheets if necessary.)

Name and Address of Institution	Account Number	Type of Account	Current Balance/Value	Check if Business Account
				☐
				☐

INVESTMENTS Include Certificates of Deposit, Trusts, Individual Retirement Accounts (IRAs), Keogh Plans, Simplified Employee Pensions, 401(k) Plans, Profit Sharing Plans, Mutual Funds, Stocks, Bonds, Commodities (Silver, Gold, etc.), and other investments. If applicable, include business accounts. *(Use additional sheets if necessary.)*

Name and Address of Institution	Account Number	Type of Account	Current Balance/Value	Check if Business Account
				☐
				☐

VIRTUAL CURRENCY (CRYPTOCURRENCY) List all virtual currency you own or in which you have a financial interest (e.g., Bitcoin, Ethereum, Litecoin, Ripple, etc.). *(Use additional sheets if necessary.)*

Type of Virtual Currency	Name of Virtual Currency Wallet, Exchange or Digital Currency Exchange (DCE)	Email Address Used to Set-up With the Virtual Currency Exchange or DCE	Location(s) of Virtual Currency *(Mobile Wallet, Online, and/or External Hardware storage)*	Virtual Currency Amount and Value in US dollars as of today *(e.g., 10 Bitcoins $64,600 USD)*

B. REAL ESTATE Include home, vacation property, timeshares, vacant land and other real estate. *(Use additional sheets if necessary.)*

Description/Location/County	Monthly Payment(s)	Financing		Current Value	Balance Owed	Equity
☐ Primary Residence ☐ Other		Year Purchased	Purchase Price			
		Year Refinanced	Refinance Amount			
☐ Primary Residence ☐ Other		Year Purchased	Purchase Price			
		Year Refinanced	Refinance Amount			

C. OTHER ASSETS Include cars, boats, recreational vehicles, whole life policies, etc. Include make, model and year of vehicles and name of Life Insurance company in Description. If applicable, include business assets such as tools, equipment, inventory, etc. *(Use additional sheets if necessary.)*

Description	Monthly Payment	Year Purchased	Final Payment *(mo/yr)*	Current Value	Balance Owed	Equity
			/			
			/			

D. CREDIT CARDS *(Visa, MasterCard, American Express, Department Stores, etc.)*

Type	Credit Limit	Balance Owed	Minimum Monthly Payment

TURN PAGE TO CONTINUE

Catalog Number 62053J　　　　　www.irs.gov　　　　　Form **433-F** (Rev. 2-2019)

Collection Information Statement for Individuals (Form 433-F)—Page 2

Page 2 of 4

E. BUSINESS INFORMATION Complete E1 for Accounts Receivable owed to you or your business. *(Use additional sheets if necessary.)* Complete E2 if you or your business accepts credit card payments. Include virtual currency wallet, exchange or digital currency exchange.

E1. Accounts Receivable owed to you or your business

Name	Address	Amount Owed
	List total amount owed from additional sheets	
	Total amount of accounts receivable available to pay to IRS now	

E2. Name of individual or business on account

Credit Card *(Visa, Master Card, etc.)*	Issuing Bank Name and Address	Merchant Account Number

F. EMPLOYMENT INFORMATION If you have more than one employer, include the information on another sheet of paper. *(If attaching a copy of current pay stub, you do not need to complete this section.)*

Your current Employer *(name and address)*	Spouse's current Employer *(name and address)*

How often are you paid *(check one)*
☐ Weekly   ☐ Biweekly   ☐ Semi-monthly   ☐ Monthly
Gross per pay period
Taxes per pay period *(Fed)* _____ *(State)* _____ *(Local)* _____
How long at current employer _____

How often are you paid *(check one)*
☐ Weekly   ☐ Biweekly   ☐ Semi-monthly   ☐ Monthly
Gross per pay period
Taxes per pay period *(Fed)* _____ *(State)* _____ *(Local)* _____
How long at current employer _____

G. NON-WAGE HOUSEHOLD INCOME List monthly amounts. For Self-Employment and Rental Income, list the monthly amount received after expenses or taxes and attach a copy of your current year profit and loss statement.

Alimony Income		Net Rental Income		Interest/Dividends Income	
Child Support Income		Unemployment Income		Social Security Income	
Net Self Employment Income		Pension Income		Other:	

H. MONTHLY NECESSARY LIVING EXPENSES List monthly amounts. (For expenses paid other than monthly, see instructions.)

1. Food / Personal Care *See instructions. If you do not spend more than the standard allowable amount for your family size, fill in the Total amount only.*

	Actual Monthly Expenses	IRS Allowed
Food		
Housekeeping Supplies		
Clothing and Clothing Services		
Personal Care Products & Services		
Miscellaneous		
Total		

2. Transportation

	Actual Monthly Expenses	IRS Allowed
Gas / Insurance / Licenses / Parking / Maintenance etc.		
Public Transportation		
Total		

3. Housing & Utilities

	Actual Monthly Expenses	IRS Allowed
Rent		
Electric, Oil/Gas, Water/Trash		
Telephone/Cell/Cable/Internet		
Real Estate Taxes and Insurance *(if not included in B above)*		
Maintenance and Repairs		
Total		

4. Medical

	Actual Monthly Expenses	IRS Allowed
Health Insurance		
Out of Pocket Health Care Expenses		
Total		

5. Other

	Actual Monthly Expenses	IRS Allowed
Child / Dependent Care		
Estimated Tax Payments		
Term Life Insurance		
Retirement *(Employer Required)*		
Retirement *(Voluntary)*		
Union Dues		
Delinquent State & Local Taxes *(minimum payment)*		
Student Loans (minimum payment)		
Court Ordered Child Support		
Court Ordered Alimony		
Other Court Ordered Payments		
Other *(specify)*		
Other *(specify)*		
Other *(specify)*		
Total		

Under penalty of perjury, I declare to the best of my knowledge and belief this statement of assets, liabilities and other information is true, correct and complete.

Your signature	Spouse's signature	Date

Catalog Number 62053J   www.irs.gov   Form **433-F** (Rev. 2-2019)

Conditional Expenses

The IRS considers many types of expenses conditional, meaning they aren't absolutely necessary for your well-being. The general rules are:

- You will be allowed to claim conditional expenses only if you can pay your taxes in full within three years. Otherwise, you will be expected to pay anything spent on conditional expenses to the IRS in your payment plan.
- You have a grace period of *one year* to eliminate conditional expenses from your budget if your payment plan won't pay your tax debt in full within three years. The effect of this rule, for example, is that if you spend more than the IRS standards for housing and utilities, you'd better be moving to a cheaper place within 12 months.

In addition to expenses that exceed the national and local allowances described above, the following are examples of conditional expenses:

- charitable contributions
- educational expenses, including college costs, and
- unsecured debts, such as credit cards.

Conditional expenses are usually not allowed when you submit an Offer in Compromise or try to get your tax debt declared to be currently not collectible.

> **TIP**
>
> **IRS standards are tough but not chiseled in stone.** The *Internal Revenue Manual* lets the IRS allow greater expenses when it is convinced that the additional amounts are necessary for your family's health and welfare, or are needed to produce income. Revenue officers are reluctant to permit greater expenses, however, because they must justify their actions to their managers. You might have a fight on your hands, so be prepared with good reasons and documents.

Signing IRS Collection Forms—Proceed With Caution

If you didn't prepare an IRS collection form in advance of your IRS interview, don't let the IRS rush you into it at the meeting. Instead, take the forms home and complete them. This gives you time to remember all your expenses. Ask the revenue officer if you can phone it in, mail it back, or bring it to your next meeting.

Protecting Yourself After Making Financial Disclosures to the IRS

You went through a collection interview, telling the IRS everything. Now the IRS collectors know where you work, bank, live, and more. In short, the IRS is in great shape to seize your wages and assets. What can you do to legally protect yourself if you're worried?

Contrary to what many people think, banks do not automatically report your account information to the IRS. If you have an interest-bearing account, however, the interest is reported to the IRS annually in January after the end of each calendar year. For more privacy, you could open the account outside the area or in another state. If you don't, a local bank canvass by the IRS might find your account. In large metropolitan areas with many banks, this is not as likely to happen. Of course, this is rarely a long-term solution to your IRS debt problems.

Deposit all further income into the new account. If and when you start paying taxes, pay the IRS out of the old account or with money orders. The reason is that whenever you pay the IRS, the agency records your bank account number in its computer. Don't give the IRS your new account number by using the new account.

 TIP

Financial information must be true on the date that you give it, whether orally or on an IRS form. Do not commit to the IRS that you won't change jobs, sell assets, or switch banks the next day. In fact, switching banks is good self-defense if you fear the IRS might levy upon your account. Alternatively, reduce the known bank balances to a minimum. Take the excess funds and open a new account at a different bank. Bank account moving is only a short-term solution to dealing with IRS collectors or IRS computers, which might freeze and seize your accounts.

If the collector requests an updated Form 433-A or 433-B, you must disclose the new accounts. Updates usually aren't requested more than once a year. Then you can begin the account-moving process over again.

Revenue Officers Can Snoop

Don't expect a collector to take your word for anything. It is the collector's job to verify what you said and the information on a collection form. Revenue officers are on the lookout for transfers of your assets to other members of your family. In such a situation, a revenue officer will treat you harshly—and may try to get the property back under a law that prohibits fraudulent transfers. The revenue officer will also check public records, such as DMV files and real property recordings, and may ask for past tax returns for clues to stocks, real estate, Bitcoin or other digital assets, and businesses you previously owned. You don't have to turn these over, but the officer can retrieve some tax filing data through the IRS computer system.

What the Collector Does Next

After reviewing your financial data on one of its Series 433 collection statements, the IRS will proceed by doing one or more of the following:

- demanding immediate payment if your forms show your ability to pay right away
- requesting that you obtain a bank loan—the *Internal Revenue Manual* mentions only bank loans, so the collector should not ask you to borrow from a finance company or relative if the bank turns you down
- requesting that you sell unnecessary assets and use the proceeds to pay the IRS
- suggesting that you file an Offer in Compromise
- proposing a monthly installment payment agreement
- mentioning your bankruptcy options
- beginning enforced collection—seizing (levying) your wages, bank accounts, and other assets, and
- reporting your account as currently not collectible, subject to future review.

Installment Payment Plan: Individuals

The most widely used method for paying an old IRS debt is the monthly installment agreement, or IA. If you owe $50,000 or less in taxes, penalties, and interest, an IA is usually easy to get (but read the rest of this section before you apply). If you owe over $50,000, it's more difficult. As mentioned above, if you have money or assets available beyond the amount of the IRS calculation of your allowable expenses, the IRS isn't required to grant a payment plan, but it may do so.

There are different types of installment agreements (IAs) depending upon the amount owed, your financial ability to pay, and the number of months left on the 10-year collection statute.

- A full pay installment agreement means you will pay the bill before the 10-year collection statute expires. If your full pay IA is approved, the IRS will not file a Notice of Federal Tax Lien.

- A partial pay installment agreement, or PPIA, means you will not fully pay the balance within the collection statute. In the past, the IRS did not allow PPIAs, but the rules have changed. However, if the IRS agrees to a PPIA, it may file a Notice of Federal Tax Lien. You will have to file Form 9465, *Installment Agreement Request*, and provide detailed financial information by completing IRS Form 433-A, *Collection Information Statement for Wage Earners and Self-Employed Individuals*. Your PPIA must be approved by an IRS supervisor. You may be required to sell assets to pay off part of your tax debt before your PPIA is approved. PPIAs are only possible if you owe at least $10,000, including interest and penalties.

EXAMPLE: Full Pay IA. Tyler owes the IRS $20,000 and there are 72 months left on the 10-year collection statute. Tyler agrees to pay $500 a month. Under this payment plan, Tyler will pay the tax bill within the collection statute.

EXAMPLE: Partial Pay IA. Sandy owes the IRS $100,000 and there are only 48 months left on the collection statute. Sandy provides her financial information to the IRS and it determines that her ability to pay is $100 a month. This is a PPIA, as Sandy won't fully pay the balance within the collection statute. In 48 months, she will only pay $4,800. The IRS may send Sandy a letter in 12 to 24 months asking for updated financial information to see if she can pay more.

Direct debit payments. With an IA for over $25,000, the IRS may request you to pay via direct debit payments from a financial account. Provide your bank account information on IRS Form 433-D.

TIP

Don't assume that a payment plan is your best option. The biggest drawback is that interest and penalties continue to accrue while you pay, although the late payment penalties are reduced by half while you make your payments (from 0.5% to 0.25% per month). The interest rate is adjusted by law quarterly. Combined with late payment penalties, recently the rate has averaged between 6% and 8% per year (less than your credit card). It's possible to pay for years and still owe more than when you started because of the compounding of principal and interest.

> EXAMPLE: Rodney and Rebecca owe the IRS $50,000 in back taxes. They enter into a $300 per month payment plan at a time when interest and penalties total 8% a year, adding $4,000 to their balance. But 12 months' worth of $300 payments add up to only $3,600, and so they will owe $50,400 at the end of the year ($50,000 minus $3,600 paid plus $4,000 in interest).

Streamlined installment agreement. If you owe the IRS less than $50,000 in taxes, penalties, and interest ($25,000 for business taxpayers), you might qualify for a streamlined installment agreement. You can apply online at www.irs.gov/payments/online-payment-agreement-application, by calling the number on the IRS bill, or by filing IRS Form 9465, *Installment Agreement Request*. You must not have not owed any tax or had an installment agreement during the past five years. If you apply online, streamlined agreements are granted automatically in as little as 30 minutes without completing a financial statement. These are full pay IAs—you must agree to pay all you owe in 72 months, or within the collection statute if shorter. To figure your minimum monthly payment, divide your tax debt by 72.

Guaranteed installment agreement. If you owe less than $10,000 in taxes (not counting interest and penalties), you can obtain a guaranteed install-ment agreement. These are basically the same as streamlined IAs, but even easier to get online, or by phone or form. However, you must agree to pay your tax debt within 36 months instead of 72. To figure your minimum monthly payment, divide your tax debt by 36. If you owe less than $10,000, you can still get a streamlined IA.

CAUTION

You must be current on your tax filings. If IRS computers show that you haven't filed all past-due tax returns, you won't get an IA until you're current. Likewise, if you're self-employed, you must be making your quarterly estimated tax payments for the current year. If you are an employer, you must be current on your payroll tax deposits as well.

Stopping IRS Collectors With an Installment Agreement

In most cases, the IRS suspends collection action when you request an installment agreement (IA) and it is being considered. The IRS will note the account as "pending installment agreement" in its computer. If your IA is approved and you abide by its terms, the IRS will not take enforced collection action (levies on wages, bank accounts) while the agreement is in effect.

If your installment agreement request is rejected, you have at least 30 days before the IRS will start any collection activity. This gives you time to negotiate with the IRS or raise money to pay or file an appeal. If you appeal a rejected agreement proposal, the IRS will not take enforced collection action while the appeal is pending.

TIP

Don't use your main bank account for IRS direct payments. For protection from an IRS slip-up in the future, use a bank account other than your main account or an account at a different bank. If you do not agree to a direct debit installment agreement and owe more than $25,000, the IRS may file a Notice of Federal Tax Lien against you.

You Might Need to Extend the Statute of Limitations With an IA

The tax code gives the IRS 10 years to collect taxes. (I.R.C. § 6502.) This statute of limitations period starts on the date the tax was officially assessed, usually the date the IRS service center processed your tax return. But, it might be later, if your return was audited and additional taxes were assessed. And, if you didn't file a tax return, the 10-year period to collect never starts to run.

Sometimes, as a condition of granting an IA, the IRS will require you to sign an extension of the 10-year period using IRS Form 900. You can balk at or stall signing the form and the IRS might overlook it, but basically the IRS has you over a barrel—no extension, no payment plan. However, once an IA has been granted and not revoked, the IRS can no longer ask you to sign an extension.

If You Owe More Than $50,000

Getting an IA if you owe more than $50,000 in taxes, penalties, and interest means dealing with an IRS collector. It can be done either in person with a revenue officer, or by phone or mail. The IRS dictates this choice, not you.

Installment Plans for Payroll Taxes

Your business can apply by phone for a special Trust Fund Installment Agreement, usually without a financial statement, if:

- You owe $25,000 or less in back payroll taxes. If you owe more, you can pay down below $25,000 and qualify.
- The bill will be fully paid by installments within 24 months or prior to the collection statute expiration date (CSED), whichever is earlier.
- You enroll in a direct debit installment agreement (DDIA) if the amount you owe is between $10,000 and $25,000.
- You're up to date with all tax filing and payment requirements.

Call the IRS Business and Specialty Tax assistance line at 800-829-4933 or the number on your bill to apply for this IA.

The collector starts by taking information from you for an IRS *Collection Information Statement*, usually Form 433-F. Based on this data, the collector determines the amount you should pay monthly. If you believe the amount is greater than your ability to pay (almost always the case), then you might be able to negotiate for a lower amount.

Here are some strategies for negotiating an installment plan:

- When you hand the completed collection form to the revenue officer, immediately propose a payment plan you can live with.

- You must offer to pay at least the amount shown on the bottom of the last page of Form 433—income less necessary living expenses. This is the cash the IRS says you have left over every month after paying for the necessities of life. Don't promise to pay more than you can afford just to get your plan approved. Once an IA is approved, the IRS makes it difficult for you to renegotiate it unless your circumstances have changed dramatically.

- If your bottom line is $0 or a negative number, consider submitting an Offer in Compromise; asking for a suspension of collection activities; or filing for Chapter 7 bankruptcy.

- Give a first payment when you propose the agreement—and keep making monthly payments even if the IRS hasn't yet approved your IA. If you don't have the funds, the IRS might agree to accept a postdated check. Ask your revenue officer about this. Making voluntary payments demonstrates your good faith and creates a track record. For example, if you pay $200 a month for three months before your IA is approved, the revenue officer might be inclined to believe this is the right amount.

Your collector doesn't have sole authority to grant a payment plan for amounts over $50,000. The collector can only recommend it to their manager for approval. Most of the time approval is given, but not always.

If an IA is verbally agreed upon with the collector, it might take a few weeks for the IRS to notify you in writing that it has been formally approved.

Installment Agreement Set-Up Fee

There's no free lunch with an IRS payment plan. If you apply online, the IRS charges a user fee of $107 to set up an IA. Cut this to $31 if you agree to a direct debit arrangement with your bank to make monthly withdrawals. These fees are increased to $225 and $149 respectively if you apply by phone or mail. Or, it can be as low as $43 if your income is below the IRS poverty level (250% of the federal poverty guidelines). File IRS Form 13844 to qualify. If you miss a payment and the IA is revoked, it will cost you $45 if the IRS agrees to reinstate the payment plan.

Making Payments on the IA

When your IA is approved, you have several options as to how to make payments:

- Request a direct payroll deduction using Form 2159, *Payroll Deduction Agreement*. Your employer must agree to send payments to the IRS each month using the IRS's payment slips.
- Use a direct debit, where your bank automatically debits your checking account each month and sends a payment to the IRS. You must provide the IRS your account numbers. As long as you keep money in the account, this is the most foolproof way to make sure you don't miss a payment and risk having the IA revoked.
- Pay by debit card or credit card.
- Pay by cash at participating 7-Eleven stores and other retail stores—limited to $500 per payment (for details, see www.irs.gov/payments/pay-with-cash-at-a-retail-partner).
- Send payments by postal mailed check or money order. The IRS will send you payment vouchers and envelopes to use each month. Write your name, Social Security number, type of tax (income, payroll), and tax periods (years or quarters) covered by the IA in the lower left-hand corner of your check or money order, and make a photocopy for your records. If you don't want the IRS to know where you currently bank, use a money order or cashier's check from another financial institution.

Direct debit or payroll deductions are generally required by the IRS if you owe $25,000 to $50,000.

Denial or Revocation of United States Passport

The IRS itself may not take or revoke your passport but it must notify the State Department of taxpayers with "seriously delinquent tax debt." This means either (1) individuals owing more than $59,000 (2023), for which a Notice of Federal Tax Lien has been filed, and all appeal rights have lapsed or been exhausted, or (2) individuals against whom a levy has been issued. The State Department is the federal agency in charge of passports. It may not issue or renew your passport, or can even revoke a current passport and otherwise limit your ability to travel outside of the United States. However, you can ask the State Department to issue you a passport, or delay revoking your passport, in an emergency or for humanitarian reasons.

The IRS won't notify the State Department if you are making timely payments under an installment agreement, or have an accepted OIC, or you have timely filed a Collection Due Process hearing, or have a pending request for "innocent spouse" relief.

The IRS must send you a notice at your last known address if it determines you have a seriously delinquent tax debt. This will be a CP-508C form. You may contest this determination by filing suit in the United States Tax Court or a United States District Court. But you'd better be able to prove that the IRS is wrong. If the IRS notifies the State Department, it will hold a pending passport application for 90 days before denying it. This gives you time to try to make arrangements with the IRS, such as a payment plan or OIC.

The best way to avoid problems with your passport is to never allow the amount you owe the IRS to exceed $59,000. This includes not just back taxes, but penalties and interest, which grow annually. This ceiling amount is adjusted for inflation each year.

If the IRS Says "No" to a Payment Plan Request

Before the IRS will accept an IA, it must believe that the information on your 433 form is truthful and the IRS is getting the maximum amount you can pay monthly.

When the IRS won't grant an IA, it is for one of three reasons:

- Your living expenses are not all considered necessary under the IRS standards discussed above. For example, if you have hefty credit card payments, make any charitable contributions, or send your kids to private school, expect the IRS to balk. Although reasonable people would disagree on what is necessary and what is extravagant, the IRS is rather stingy here.

- Information you provided on a Form 433, *Collection Information Statement*, is incomplete or untruthful. The IRS might think you're hiding property or income. For example, if public records show your name on real estate or motor vehicles that you didn't list, or the IRS received W-2 or 1099 forms showing more income or sources than you listed, be prepared to explain.

- You defaulted on a prior IA. While this doesn't automatically disqualify you from a new IA, it can cause your new proposal to be met with skepticism.

TIP

If your IA proposal is first rejected, you can keep negotiating. Ask to speak to the collector's manager. Just making this request is sometimes enough. But, if you talk to the manager, don't criticize the employee or start yelling. Keep your cool and if the manager believes you're trying to be reasonable, they might take over the case or ask the collector to reconsider.

If you're still unhappy and the IRS has filed a lien or initiated a levy, your next stop is the IRS Independent Office of Appeals. (See Chapter 7 and IRS Form 12153.) If it is an emergency—the IRS collection efforts are causing a serious hardship—call the Taxpayer Advocate Service (see Chapter 8).

When the IRS Can Revoke an Installment Agreement

Once you receive written approval of your IA, you and the IRS are bound by the terms of the agreement, *unless:*

- You fail to file your future tax returns or pay taxes on time. Although IRS computers don't continue to review your finances, they do monitor you for filing future returns and making promised payments.

- You miss a payment. Under the terms of all IAs, payments not made in full, and on time, can cause the IA to be revoked. The IRS usually waits 30 to 60 days before revocation—at least on the first missed payment. You are entitled to a warning or a chance to reinstate the agreement.
- Your financial condition changes significantly—either for the better or worse. The IRS usually won't find out about this unless you tell. The IRS may review your situation periodically and require you to submit a new collection form, but this seldom happens.
- The IRS discovers that you provided inaccurate or incomplete information to the collector, for instance, not listing all of your assets or neglecting to mention your moonlighting jobs.

Before the IRS revokes your IA, you should receive CP-523, *Notice of Intent to Levy—Intent to Terminate Your Installment Agreement.* If you believe the notice was sent in error, call 800-829-8374. If this doesn't help, formally appeal the revocation by filing IRS Form 9423, *Collection Appeal Request.* (See Chapter 7 for the appeal procedure explanation.)

If You Want to Revise an Installment Agreement

Installment plans are not necessarily set in stone. If you owe less than $50,000, you can apply online at www.irs.gov/payments/online-payment-agreement-application to change your monthly plan amount or monthly due date. If your new monthly payment amount doesn't meet the requirements, the IRS computer will prompt you to revise the payment amount.

If You Can't Make an Installment Payment

If you can't make a monthly IA payment, call the taxpayer assistance number at 800-829-1040. If you negotiated with a revenue officer, call that person, too.

Explain your problem. Ask for more time to pay and that collections be suspended. You'll need a good excuse, like losing your job, becoming disabled, or a similar mishap. If you don't get anywhere and the IRS says your IA is in default—meaning the IRS can begin grabbing your property—call the Taxpayer Advocate Service. A taxpayer advocate can keep your agreement from being revoked if it would result in a significant hardship. (See Chapter 8 for information on taxpayer advocates.)

> **CAUTION**
>
> **If your IA is revoked and your appeal fails, you can start negotiations over from scratch.** The IRS may grant a reinstatement, but don't count on it. Remember, unless you owe less than $10,000, installment agreements are discretionary with the IRS. If the IRS is willing to grant a new IA, you'll need a good excuse for defaulting and likely have to furnish updated documentation of your income and living expenses. And while you are trying to get a new IA, the IRS may start seizing your bank accounts and wages.

Making an IA When You Also Owe State Taxes

Often you will owe both the IRS and your state. If you do, negotiate payment plans with both agencies at the same time. Otherwise, any deal you make with one might not leave you with anything to pacify the other. See Chapter 14 for information on negotiating installment plans with both taxing authorities.

Offers in Compromise (OICs)

Would you like to wipe your old income tax bills out for pennies on the dollar? The IRS has accepted $100 on tax bills of many thousands and called it even. For others, the IRS has turned down offers of $90,000 on a $100,000 bill. So, how does this work, and could it be the answer to your prayers?

Let's start with the proposition that no one ever has the right to have a valid income tax bill reduced. It is entirely discretionary with the IRS. You do have a legal right to make an offer that the government must consider. This right is set forth in the Internal Revenue Code Section 7122. While the IRS makes deals, there is no "tax debt fire sale" going on in Washington. Recently, 4 in 10 debtors were able to negotiate Offers in Compromise (OICs) with the IRS—the highest acceptance rate in all the years we've been in practice. Like any bargaining, this is not to say that the first offer was accepted.

Grounds for Making an OIC

Wanting to make a deal with the IRS is not enough. One of three specific grounds must exist:

- Some doubt must exist as to whether the IRS can now, or in the future, ever collect the tax bill in full. The IRS calls this "doubt as to collectibility," and it is, by far, the ground on which most OICs are granted.
- Special circumstances exist, which would make full payment cause an economic hardship or make it unfair or inequitable, even though you might have sufficient assets and income. This ground is termed "effective tax administration" and is tougher to get than it sounds.
- There is some doubt as to whether you legally owe the bill. The IRS calls this "doubt as to liability" and it is done using IRS Form 656-L. It's so rarely a ground for an OIC that we don't cover it below.

Before getting your hopes up, go to the IRS website and take the pre-qualifier online test for an OIC at https://irs.treasury.gov/oic_pre_qualifier. It's a fairly short and simple Q & A. If you fail the test, all might not be lost, as you still might qualify under the effective tax administration ground discussed below.

If you think you might qualify, you can't simply call the IRS and say: "Let's make a deal." Submitting an OIC requires disclosing a lot of personal information and providing financial documentation. To see the kind of information you'll have to disclose, look at IRS Form 656 Booklet, *Offer in Compromise.* Check the IRS website for the most current version of the Form 656 Booklet, which includes all the IRS forms and instructions you need to make an Offer in Compromise.

What follows below is a summary of what you need to do to make an OIC using Form 433-A (OIC), with some added tips for success.

Offer in Compromise Forms

Individuals must make an Offer in Compromise to the IRS using Form 433-A (OIC), *Collection Information Statement for Wage Earners and Self-Employed Individuals.* Despite its name, this form also works for those retired or not employed. Small business owners use Form 433-B, *Collection Information Statement for Businesses.* An application fee of $205 and a partial payment are required unless you meet the requirements for the low-income exception.

The IRS looks very closely at OIC applications, much more so than it does installment agreements. The OIC evaluators require proof and backup documents—pay stubs, bank records, vehicle registrations, credit card statements, deeds, and any other items bearing on your ability to pay.

Your Minimum Offer Amount

The most important question you'll have to think about when submitting your Offer in Compromise application to the IRS is: "How much should I offer?" What the IRS is interested in is what it calls your "reasonable collection potential" (RCP). This is the minimum amount the IRS will accept and is based on what it believes is the smallest amount you can pay each month over a period of up to two years based on your monthly disposable income and the assets you own.

Follow the instructions on Form 433-A (OIC) to compute and show the IRS how you arrived at your minimum offer. Basically, your offer must equal:
- the net realizable value of your assets, plus
- your excess monthly income after subtracting your monthly expenses from your monthly income.

You then multiply this amount by 12 or 24, depending on the payment period you choose for repayment (either five months or up to two years).

 TIP

Would offering more than the minimum amount increase your chances of success? No. The IRS wants you to follow the OIC form directions explicitly. Offering more than the formula on Form 433-A could actually work against you. If the IRS offer specialist decides you should pay more, they will tell you once the offer has been investigated.

Collection Information Statement (Form 433-A (OIC))—Page 1

Form **433-A (OIC)** (April 2023)	Department of the Treasury — Internal Revenue Service **Collection Information Statement for Wage Earners and Self-Employed Individuals**

Use this form if you are
- An individual who owes income tax on a Form 1040, U.S. Individual Income Tax Return
- An individual with a personal liability for Excise Tax
- An individual responsible for a Trust Fund Recovery Penalty
- An individual who is self-employed or has self-employment income. You are considered to be self-employed if you are in business for yourself, or carry on a trade or business.

- An individual who is personally responsible for a partnership liability (only if the partnership is submitting an offer)
- An individual who is submitting an offer on behalf of the estate of a deceased person

Note: Include attachments if additional space is needed to respond completely to any question. This form should only be used with the Form 656, Offer in Compromise.

Section 1 — Personal and Household Information

Last name	First name	Date of birth (mm/dd/yyyy)	Social Security Number - -

Marital status
☐ Unmarried ☐ Married
If married, date of marriage (mm/dd/yyyy)

Home physical address (street, city, state, ZIP code)

Do you
☐ Own your home ☐ Rent
☐ Other (specify e.g., share rent, live with relative, etc.)

☐ If you were married and lived in AZ, CA, ID, LA, NM, NV, TX, WA or WI within the last ten years check here

County of residence	Primary phone ( ) -	Home mailing address (if different from above or post office box number)
Secondary phone ( ) -	FAX number ( ) -	

Provide information about your spouse.

Spouse's last name	Spouse's first name	Date of birth (mm/dd/yyyy)	Social Security Number - -

Provide information for all other persons in the household or claimed as a dependent.

Name	Age	Relationship	Claimed as a dependent on your Form 1040	Contributes to household income
			☐ Yes ☐ No	☐ Yes ☐ No
			☐ Yes ☐ No	☐ Yes ☐ No
			☐ Yes ☐ No	☐ Yes ☐ No
			☐ Yes ☐ No	☐ Yes ☐ No

Section 2 — Employment Information for Wage Earners

Complete this section if you or your spouse are wage earners and receive a Form W-2. If you or your spouse have self-employment income (that is you file a Schedule C, E, F, etc.) instead of, or in addition to wage income, you must also complete Business Information in Sections 4, 5, and 6.

Your employer's name	Pay period ☐ Weekly ☐ Bi-weekly ☐ Monthly ☐ Other	Employer's address (street, city, state, ZIP code)

Do you have an ownership interest in this business
☐ Yes (also complete and submit Form 433-B) ☐ No

Your occupation	How long with this employer (years) (months)

Spouse's employer's name	Pay period ☐ Weekly ☐ Bi-weekly ☐ Monthly ☐ Other	Employer's address (street, city, state, ZIP code)

Does your spouse have an ownership interest in this business
☐ Yes (also complete and submit Form 433-B) ☐ No

Spouse's occupation	How long with this employer (years) (months)

Collection Information Statement (Form 433-A (OIC))—Page 2

Page 2

Section 3	Personal Asset Information *(Domestic and Foreign)*

Use the most current statement for each type of account, such as checking, savings, money market and online accounts, stored value cards (such as a payroll card from an employer), investment, retirement accounts (IRAs, Keogh, 401(k) plans, stocks, bonds, mutual funds, certificates of deposit) and digital assets such as virtual currency (cryptocurrency), non-fungible token (NFT), and smart contracts you own or in which you have a financial interest (e.g., Bitcoin, Ethereum, Litecoin, Ripple, etc.), life insurance policies that have a cash value, and safe deposit boxes including those located in foreign countries or jurisdictions. Asset value is subject to adjustment by IRS based on individual circumstances. Enter the total amount available for each of the following (if additional space is needed include attachments). Ensure you also include assets located in foreign countries or jurisdictions and add attachment(s) if additional space is needed to respond.

Round to the nearest dollar. Do not enter a negative number. If any line item is a negative number, enter "0".

Cash and Investments (domestic and foreign)

☐ Cash ☐ Checking ☐ Savings ☐ Money Market Account/CD ☐ Online Account ☐ Stored Value Card

Bank name and country location	Account number	
		(1a) $

☐ Checking ☐ Savings ☐ Money Market Account/CD ☐ Online Account ☐ Stored Value Card

Bank name and country location	Account number	
		(1b) $

	Total of bank accounts from attachment	(1c) $
	Add lines (1a) through (1c) minus ($1,000) =	**(1) $**

☐ Investment account ☐ Stocks ☐ Bonds ☐ Other

Name of Financial Institution and country location	Account number

Current market value   Minus loan balance

$ _____ X .8 = $ _____   – $ _____   = | (2a) $

☐ Investment account ☐ Stocks ☐ Bonds ☐ Other

Name of Financial Institution and country location	Account number

Current market value   Minus loan balance

$ _____ X .8 = $ _____   – $ _____   = | (2b) $

☐ Digital asset	Name of digital asset such as virtual currency wallet, exchange or digital currency exchange (DCE)	Email address used to set-up the digital asset such as virtual currency exchange or DCE	Location(s) of digital asset *(mobile wallet, online, and/or external hardware storage)*
Type of digital asset			

Name of individual who has access to the private key(s) and/or digital wallets	Digital asset amount and value in US dollars as of today	
	$ _____ =	(2c) $

Total investment accounts from attachment. [current market value minus loan balance(s)]	(2d) $
Add lines (2a) through (2d) =	**(2) $**

☐ Retirement account ☐ 401K ☐ IRA ☐ Other

Name of Financial Institution and country location	Account number

Current market value   Minus loan balance

$ _____ X .8 = $ _____   – $ _____   = | (3a) $

Total of retirement accounts from attachment. [current market value X .8 minus loan balance(s)]	(3b) $
Add lines (3a) through (3b) =	**(3) $**

Note: Your reduction from current market value may be greater than 20% due to potential tax consequences/withdrawal penalties.

Cash value of Life Insurance Policies

Name of Insurance Company	Policy number

Current cash value   Minus loan balance

$ _____   – $ _____   = | (4a) $

Total cash value of life insurance policies from attachment	Minus loan balance(s)

$ _____   – $ _____   = | (4b) $

Add lines (4a) through (4b) =	**(4) $**

Collection Information Statement (Form 433-A (OIC))—Page 3

Page 3

Section 3 *(Continued)*	Personal Asset Information *(Domestic and Foreign)*

Real property *(enter information about any house, condo, co-op, time share, etc. that you own or are buying including any assets owned by your spouse if you live in a community property state)*

Is your real property currently for sale or do you anticipate selling your real property to fund the offer amount

☐ Yes *(listing price)* _____ ☐ No

Property description *(indicate if personal residence, rental property, vacant, etc.)*	Purchase date *(mm/dd/yyyy)*	
Amount of mortgage payment	Date of final payment	How title is held *(joint tenancy, etc.)*
Location *(street, city, state, ZIP code, county, and country)*	Lender/Contract holder name, address *(street, city, state, ZIP code)* and phone	

Current market value   Minus loan balance *(mortgages, etc.)*

$ _____ X .8 = $ _____ – $ _____   (total value of real estate) =   **(5a)** $

Property description *(indicate if personal residence, rental property, vacant, etc.)*	Purchase date *(mm/dd/yyyy)*	
Amount of mortgage payment	Date of final payment	How title is held *(joint tenancy, etc.)*
Location *(street, city, state, ZIP code, county, and country)*	Lender/Contract holder name, address *(street, city, state, ZIP code)* and phone	

Current market value   Minus loan balance *(mortgages, etc.)*

$ _____ X .8 = $ _____ – $ _____   (total value of real estate) =   **(5b)** $

Total value of property(s) from attachment [current market value X .8 minus any loan balance(s)]	**(5c)** $
Add lines (5a) through (5c) =	**(5)** $

Vehicles *(enter information about any cars, boats, motorcycles, etc. that you own or lease).*
Include those located in foreign countries or jurisdictions. If additional space is needed, list on an attachment.

Vehicle make & model		Year	Date purchased	Mileage	License/Tag number	
☐ Lease ☐ Own	Name of creditor		Date of final payment		Monthly lease/loan amount $	

Current market value   Minus loan balance

$ _____ X .8 = $ _____ – $ _____   Total value of vehicle *(if the vehicle is leased, enter 0 as the total value)* =   **(6a)** $

Subtract $3,450 from line (6a) (If line (6a) minus $3,450 is a negative number, enter "0")	**(6b)** $

Vehicle make & model		Year	Date purchased	Mileage	License/Tag number	
☐ Lease ☐ Own	Name of creditor		Date of final payment		Monthly lease/loan amount $	

Current market value   Minus loan balance

$ _____ X .8 = $ _____ – $ _____   Total value of vehicle *(if the vehicle is leased, enter 0 as the total value)* =   **(6c)** $

If you are filing a joint offer, subtract $3,450 from line (6c) (If line (6c) minus $3,450 is a negative number, enter "0") If you are not filing a joint offer, enter the amount from line (6c)	**(6d)** $
Total value of vehicles listed from attachment [current market value X .8 minus any loan balance(s)]	**(6e)** $
Total lines (6b), (6d), and (6e) =	**(6)** $

Collection Information Statement (Form 433-A (OIC))—Page 4

Page 4

Section 3 (Continued) Personal Asset Information (Domestic and Foreign)

Other valuable items (artwork, collections, jewelry, items of value in safe deposit boxes, interest in a company or business that is not publicly traded, etc.)

Description of asset(s)

Current market value		Minus loan balance		
$ _____ X .8 = $ _____		– $ _____	=	(7a) $

Value of remaining furniture and personal effects (not listed above)

Description of asset

Current market value		Minus loan balance		
$ _____ X .8 = $ _____		– $ _____	=	(7b) $

Total value of valuable items listed from attachment [current market value X .8 minus any loan balance(s)]	(7c) $
Add lines (7a) through (7c) minus IRS deduction of $10,810 =	**(7) $**

Do not include amount on the lines with a letter beside the number. Round to the nearest whole dollar. Do not enter a negative number. If any line item is a negative, enter "0" on that line.

Add lines (1) through (7) and enter the amount in Box A =

Box A
Available Individual Equity in Assets
$

NOTE: If you or your spouse are self-employed, Sections 4, 5, and 6 must be completed before continuing with Sections 7 and 8.

Section 4 Self-Employed Information

If you or your spouse are self-employed (e.g., files Schedule(s) C, E, F, etc.), complete this section.

Is your business a sole proprietorship
☐ Yes ☐ No

Address of business (if other than personal residence)

Name of business

Business telephone number	Employer Identification Number	Business website address	Trade name or DBA
( ) -			

Description of business	Total number of employees	Frequency of tax deposits	Average gross monthly payroll $

Do you or your spouse have any other business interests? Include any interest in an LLC, LLP, corporation, partnership, etc.
☐ Yes (percentage of ownership:) Title
☐ No

Business address (street, city, state, ZIP code)

Business name	Business telephone number	Employer Identification Number
	( ) -	

Type of business (select one)
☐ Partnership ☐ LLC ☐ Corporation ☐ Other

Section 5 Business Asset Information (for Self-Employed) (Domestic and Foreign)

List business assets such as bank accounts, digital assets (cryptocurrency), tools, books, machinery, equipment, business vehicles and real property that is owned/leased/rented. If additional space is needed, attach a list of items. Do not include personal assets listed in Section 3.

Round to the nearest whole dollar. Do not enter a negative number. If any line item is a negative number, enter "0".

☐ Cash ☐ Checking ☐ Savings ☐ Money Market Account/CD ☐ Online Account ☐ Stored Value Card

Bank name and country location	Account number	
		(8a) $

☐ Cash ☐ Checking ☐ Savings ☐ Money Market Account/CD ☐ Online Account ☐ Stored Value Card

Bank name and country location	Account number	
		(8b) $

☐ Digital asset / Type of digital asset	Name of digital asset such as virtual currency wallet, exchange or digital currency exchange (DCE)	Email address used to set-up the digital asset such as virtual currency exchange or DCE	Location(s) of digital asset (mobile wallet, online, and/or external hardware storage)

Name of individual who has access to the private key(s) and/or digital wallets	Digital asset amount and value in US dollars as of today	
	$ _____ =	(8c) $

Total bank accounts from attachment	(8d) $
Add lines (8a) through (8d) =	**(8) $**

Catalog Number 55896Q www.irs.gov Form **433-A (OIC)** (Rev. 4-2023)

Collection Information Statement (Form 433-A (OIC))—Page 5

Page 5

Section 5 (Continued) Business Asset Information (for Self-Employed) (Domestic and Foreign)

Description of asset

Current market value	Minus loan balance	Total value (if leased or used in the production of income, enter 0 as the total value) =	(9a) $
$ _____ X .8 = $ _____	– $ _____		

Description of asset:

Current market value	Minus Loan Balance	Total value (if leased or used in the production of income, enter 0 as the total value) =	(9b) $
$ _____ X .8 = $ _____	– $ _____		

Total value of assets listed from attachment [current market value X .8 minus any loan balance(s)]	(9c) $
Add lines (9a) through (9c) =	(9) $
IRS allowed deduction for professional books and tools of trade for individuals and sole-proprietors –	(10) $
Enter the value of line (9) minus line (10). If less than zero enter zero. =	(11) $

Notes Receivable

Do you have notes receivable? ☐ Yes ☐ No

If yes, attach current listing that includes name(s) and amount of note(s) receivable

Accounts Receivable

Do you have accounts receivable, including e-payment, factoring companies, and any bartering or online auction accounts ☐ Yes ☐ No

If yes, provide a list of your current accounts receivable (include the age and amount)

Do not include amounts from the lines with a letter beside the number [for example: (9c)]. Round to the nearest whole dollar. Do not enter a negative number. If any line item is a negative, enter "0" on that line.
Add lines (8) and (11) and enter the amount in Box B =

Box B Available Business Equity in Assets
$

Section 6 Business Income and Expense Information (for Self-Employed)

If you provide a current profit and loss (P&L) statement for the information below, enter the total gross monthly income on line 17 and your monthly expenses on line 29 below. Do not complete lines (12) - (16) and (18) - (28). You may use the amounts claimed for income and expenses on your most recent Schedule C; however, if the amount has changed significantly within the past year, a current P&L should be submitted to substantiate the claim.

Period provided beginning _____ through _____

Round to the nearest whole dollar. Do not enter a negative number. If any line item is a negative number, enter "0".

Business Income (you may average 6-12 months income/receipts to determine your gross monthly income/receipts)

Gross receipts	(12) $
Gross rental income	(13) $
Interest income	(14) $
Dividends	(15) $
Other income	(16) $
Add lines (12) through (16) =	(17) $

Business expenses (you may average 6-12 months expenses to determine your average expenses)

Materials purchased (e.g., items directly related to the production of a product or service)	(18) $
Inventory purchased (e.g., goods bought for resale)	(19) $
Gross wages and salaries	(20) $
Rent	(21) $
Supplies (items used to conduct business and used up within one year, e.g., books, office supplies, professional equipment, etc.)	(22) $
Utilities/telephones	(23) $
Vehicle costs (gas, oil, repairs, maintenance)	(24) $
Business insurance	(25) $
Current business taxes (e.g., real estate, excise, franchise, occupational, personal property, sales and employer's portion of employment taxes)	(26) $
Secured debts (not credit cards)	(27) $
Other business expenses (include a list)	(28) $
Add lines (18) through (28) =	(29) $

Round to the nearest whole dollar. Do not enter a negative number. If any line item is a negative, enter "0" on that line.
Subtract line (29) from line (17) and enter the amount in Box C =

Box C Net Business Income
$

Collection Information Statement (Form 433-A (OIC))—Page 6

Page 6

Section 7	Monthly Household Income and Expense Information

Enter your household's average gross monthly income. Gross monthly income includes wages, social security, pension, unemployment, and other income. Examples of other income include but are not limited to: agricultural subsidies, gambling income, oil credits, rent subsidies, sharing economy income from providing on-demand work, services or goods (e.g., Uber, Lyft, AirBnB, VRBO), income through digital platforms like an app or website, etc., and recurring capital gains from the sale of securities including cryptocurrency, non-fungible tokens, etc. The information below is for yourself, your spouse, and anyone else who contributes to your household's income. The entire household includes spouse, non-liable spouse, significant other, children, and others who contribute to the household. This is necessary for the IRS to accurately evaluate your offer.

Monthly Household Income

Note: Entire household income should also include income that is considered not taxable and may not be included on your tax return.

Round to the nearest whole dollar.

Primary taxpayer

Gross wages	Social Security	Pension(s)	Other income *(e.g. unemployment)*	Total primary taxpayer income =	(30) $
$	+ $	+ $	+ $		

Spouse

Gross wages	Social Security	Pension(s)	Other Income *(e.g. unemployment)*	Total spouse income =	(31) $
$	+ $	+ $	+ $		

Additional sources of income used to support the household, e.g., non-liable spouse, or anyone else who may contribute to the household income, etc. List source(s) _____	(32) $
Interest, dividends, and royalties	(33) $
Distributions *(e.g., income from partnerships, sub-S Corporations, etc.)*	(34) $
Net rental income	(35) $
Net business income from Box C *[Deductions for non-cash expenses on Schedule C (e.g., depreciation, depletion, etc.) are not permitted as an expense for offer purposes and must be added back in to the net income figure]*	(36) $
Child support received	(37) $
Alimony received	(38) $

Round to the nearest whole dollar. Do not enter a negative number. If any line item is a negative, enter "0" on that line. **Add lines (30) through (38) and enter the amount in Box D =**	**Box D** Total Household Income $

Monthly Household Expenses

Enter your average monthly expenses.

Note: For expenses claimed in boxes (39) and (45) only, you should list the full amount of the allowable standard even if the actual amount you pay is less. For the other boxes input your actual expenses. You may find the allowable standards at http://www.irs.gov/Businesses/Small-Businesses-&-Self-Employed/Collection-Financial-Standards.

Round to the nearest whole dollar.

Food, clothing, and miscellaneous *(e.g., housekeeping supplies, personal care products, minimum payment on credit card).* A reasonable estimate of these expenses may be used	(39) $
Housing and utilities *(e.g., rent or mortgage payment and average monthly cost of property taxes, home insurance, maintenance, dues, fees and utilities including electricity, gas, other fuels, trash collection, water, cable television and internet, telephone, and cell phone)* _____ monthly rent payment	(40) $
Vehicle loan and/or lease payment(s)	(41) $
Vehicle operating costs *(e.g., average monthly cost of maintenance, repairs, insurance, fuel, registrations, licenses, inspections, parking, tolls, etc.).* A reasonable estimate of these expenses may be used	(42) $
Public transportation costs *(e.g., average monthly cost of fares for mass transit such as bus, train, ferry, etc.).* A reasonable estimate of these expenses may be used	(43) $
Health insurance premiums	(44) $
Out-of-pocket health care costs *(e.g. average monthly cost of prescription drugs, medical services, and medical supplies like eyeglasses, hearing aids, etc.)*	(45) $
Court-ordered payments *(e.g., monthly cost of any alimony, child support, etc.)*	(46) $
Child/dependent care payments *(e.g., daycare, etc.)*	(47) $
Life insurance premiums _____ Life insurance policy amount _____	(48) $
Current monthly taxes *(e.g., monthly cost of federal, state, and local tax, personal property tax, etc.)*	(49) $
Secured debts/Other *(e.g., any loan where you pledged an asset as collateral not previously listed, government guaranteed student loan, employer required retirement or dues)* List debt(s)/expense(s) _____	(50) $
Enter the amount of your monthly delinquent state and/or local tax payment(s) . Total tax owed _____	(51) $

Round to the nearest whole dollar. Do not enter a negative number. If any line item is a negative, enter "0" on that line. **Add lines (39) through (51) and enter the amount in Box E =**	**Box E** Total Household Expenses $
Round to the nearest whole dollar. Do not enter a negative number. If any line item is a negative, enter "0" on that line. **Subtract Box E from Box D and enter the amount in Box F =**	**Box F** Remaining Monthly Income $

Collection Information Statement (Form 433-A (OIC))—Page 7

Section 8   Calculate Your Minimum Offer Amount

The next steps calculate your minimum offer amount. The amount of time you take to pay your offer in full will affect your minimum offer amount. Paying over a shorter period of time will result in a smaller minimum offer amount.

Note: The multipliers below (12 and 24) and the calculated offer amount (which included the amount(s) allowed for vehicles and bank accounts) do not apply if the IRS determines you have the ability to pay your tax debt in full within the legal period to collect.

Round to the nearest whole dollar.

If you will pay your offer in 5 or fewer payments within 5 months or less, multiply "Remaining Monthly Income" (Box F) by 12 to get "Future Remaining Income" (Box G). Do not enter a number less than $0.

Enter the total from Box F	X 12 =	Box G Future Remaining Income
$		$

If you will pay your offer in 6 to 24 months, multiply "Remaining Monthly Income" (Box F) by 24 to get "Future Remaining Income" (Box H). Do not enter a number less than $0.

Enter the total from Box F	X 24 =	Box H Future Remaining Income
$		$

Determine your minimum offer amount by adding the total available assets from Box A and Box B (if applicable) to the amount in either Box G or Box H.

Enter the amount from Box A plus Box B *(if applicable)*	+	Enter the amount from either Box G or Box H	=	**Offer Amount** Your offer must be more than zero ($0). Do not leave blank. Use whole dollars only.
$		$		$

Place the offer amount shown above on the Form 656, Section 4, Payment Terms, unless you cannot pay that amount due to special circumstances. If you cannot pay that amount due to special circumstances, place the amount you can pay on the Form 656, Section 4, Payment Terms, and explain your special circumstances on the Form 656, Offer in Compromise, Section 3, Reason for Offer.

Section 9   Other Information

Additional information IRS needs to consider settlement of your tax debt. If you or your business are currently in a bankruptcy proceeding, you are not eligible to apply for an offer.

Are you a party to or involved in litigation *(if yes, answer the following)*			☐ Yes ☐ No
☐ Plaintiff ☐ Defendant	Location of filing	Represented by	Docket/Case number
Amount of dispute $	Possible completion date *(mmddyyyy)*	Subject of litigation	

Have you filed bankruptcy in the past 7 years *(if yes, answer the following)*			☐ Yes ☐ No
Date filed *(mmddyyyy)*	Date dismissed *(mmddyyyy)*	Date discharged *(mmddyyyy)*	Petition no.	Location filed

In the past 10 years, have you lived outside of the U.S. for 6 months or longer *(if yes, answer the following)*	☐ Yes ☐ No
Dates lived abroad: From *(mmddyyyy)*	To *(mmddyyyy)*

Are you or have you ever been party to any litigation involving the IRS/United States *(including any tax litigation)*	☐ Yes ☐ No

If yes and the litigation included tax debt, provide the types of tax and periods involved

Are you the beneficiary of a trust, estate, or life insurance policy, including those located in foreign countries or jurisdictions *(if yes, answer the following)*		☐ Yes ☐ No
Place where recorded		EIN
Name of the trust, estate, or policy	Anticipated amount to be received $	When will the amount be received

Are you a trustee, fiduciary, or contributor of a trust	☐ Yes ☐ No
Name of the trust	EIN

Do you have a safe deposit box *(business or personal)* including those located in foreign countries or jurisdictions *(if yes, answer the following)*		☐ Yes ☐ No
Location *(name, address and box number(s))*	Contents	Value $

Collection Information Statement (Form 433-A (OIC))—Page 8

Page 8

Section 9 *(Continued)*   Other Information

In the past 10 years, have you transferred any asset with a fair market value of more than $10,000 including real property, for less than their full value *(if yes, answer the following)*   ☐ Yes   ☐ No

List asset(s)	Value at time of transfer	Date transferred *(mmddyyyy)*	To whom or where was it transferred
	$		

Do you have any assets or own any real property outside the U.S.   ☐ Yes   ☐ No

If yes, provide description, location, and value

Do you have any funds being held in trust by a third party   ☐ Yes   ☐ No

If yes, how much $ Where

Section 10   Signatures

Under penalties of perjury, I declare that I have examined this offer, including accompanying documents, and to the best of my knowledge it is true, correct, and complete.

Signature of Taxpayer   Date *(mm/dd/yyyy)*

Signature of Spouse   Date *(mm/dd/yyyy)*

Remember to include all applicable attachments listed below.

☐ Copies of the most recent pay stub, earnings statement, etc., from each employer.

☐ Copies of the most recent statement for each investment and retirement account.

☐ Copies of the most recent statement, etc., from all other sources of income such as pensions, Social Security, rental income, interest and dividends (including any received from a related partnership, corporation, LLC, LLP, etc.), court order for child support, alimony, royalties, agricultural subsidies, gambling income, oil credits, rent subsidies, sharing economy income from providing on-demand work, services or goods (e.g., Uber, Lyft, AirBnB, VRBO), income through digital platforms like an app or website, etc., and recurring capital gains from the sale of securities including cryptocurrency, non-fungible tokens.

☐ Copies of individual complete bank statements for the three most recent months. If you operate a business, copies of the six most recent complete statements for each business bank account.

☐ Completed Form 433-B (Collection Information Statement for Businesses) if you or your spouse have an interest in a business entity other than a sole-proprietorship.

☐ Copies of the most recent statement from lender(s) on loans such as mortgages, second mortgages, vehicles, etc., showing monthly payments, loan payoffs, and balances.

☐ List of Accounts Receivable or Notes Receivable, if applicable.

☐ Verification of delinquent State/Local Tax Liability showing total delinquent state/local taxes and amount of monthly payments, if applicable.

☐ Copies of court orders for child support/alimony payments claimed in monthly expense section.

☐ Copies of Trust documents if applicable per Section 9.

☐ Documentation to support any special circumstances described in the "Explanation of Circumstances" on Form 656, if applicable.

☐ Attach a Form 2848, *Power of Attorney*, if you would like your attorney, CPA, or enrolled agent to represent you and you do not have a current form on file with the IRS. Ensure all years and forms involved in your offer are listed on Form 2848 and include the current tax year. Check the appropriate box to ensure copies of communications are sent to your representative.

☐ Completed and signed current Form 656.

OIC Payment Options

Two payment options are available when submitting an OIC.

- The lump sum option requires 20% of the offer amount to be paid with the initial offer form. If the IRS accepts your offer, you must pay the remaining 80% within five months of the date of the IRS notice of acceptance of the offer.
- The periodic payment option. Unless you qualify under the Low-Income Certification guidelines, you must make an initial payment with the offer and promise to pay the remaining balance in monthly payments within 6 to 24 months.

If you don't make the required monthly payments your offer will be voided (with no appeal rights) and the IRS will not refund any of the payments made.

> **EXAMPLE:** Kerry submits an OIC under the lump sum cash option for $5,000.00. She must pay 20% of the offer amount, equaling $1,000, with the offer. If the IRS accepts her offer, she must pay the remaining $4,000 within five months of the IRS accepting the offer.

> **EXAMPLE:** Ron submits an OIC under the periodic payment option for $12,000. He wants to pay over 24 months. He does not qualify under the Low-Income Certification Guidelines. He must submit an initial payment of $500 with the offer and then $500 every month for the next 23 months.

Net Value Calculation

To figure out the net realizable value of your assets, you must first total up the value of all of your assets including cash, bank accounts, real estate, vehicles, digital assets, life insurance cash value, and retirement plans. You list these items in Section 3 of Form 433-A (OIC). You don't have to list the value of household items and personal effects—things like clothing, furniture, and appliances. However, luxury items, such as artwork, collections, and expensive jewelry, must be included. You'll also need to list interest in any business not publicly traded and items of value held in a safe deposit box.

If you own a home, the value of that home must be figured into your OIC net value calculation. Here, taxpayers get a small break. The IRS allows OIC offerors a discount of 20% from the fair market value of their home when they calculate the property's value.

> EXAMPLE: Darlene's business failed, and she is facing a $120,000 income tax bill. She has less than $1,000 in cash and owns a home which has a fair market value of $150,000. She owes $110,000 on a mortgage and has no other assets. Here's how Darlene figures her net realizable value for her OIC forms:
>
> | | | |
> |---|---|---|
> | Fair market value of home | | $ 150,000 |
> | *Less* 20% IRS value discount | – | 30,000 |
> | *Less* mortgage | – | 110,000 |
> | | = | $10,000 |
>
> Darlene has less than $1,000 in cash and no other assets so the net realizable value of her assets is the $10,000 of equity she has in her home.

You also must include any retirement plan balances you own in the OIC asset calculation. However, you can discount these values by any income tax and early withdrawal penalties if you cashed them in already. Be sure to attach an explanation of how you arrived at the discount value.

Aside from household and personal effects mentioned above, a few other things like workers' compensation and unemployment benefits are specifically excluded from the OIC asset calculation. For a complete list of what you can exclude, see IRS Publication 594, *The IRS Collection Process* ("Property that can't be seized").

CAUTION

Make sure you consider the effect of the collection limitation statute on the OIC. When calculating a taxpayer's reasonable collection potential for an OIC, the IRS considers how many months are left on the 10-year collection statute. This could well increase the amount of an acceptable OIC. For instance, instead of multiplying your remaining monthly payments by 12 or 24, depending upon the payment option you choose, the IRS might multiply your remaining monthly payments by 60 if there are 60 months remaining on the collection statute. Consider this when filing an OIC if you have very recent tax debts.

Disposable Monthly Income and Payment Period

The second part of the RCP test requires you to calculate how much you can afford to pay the IRS on a monthly basis. This is based on your disposable income each month. You calculate this by subtracting your monthly expenses from your monthly household income. The items you must include in calculating your monthly income and expenses are on Form 433-A (OIC). Your "remaining monthly income" is the number you use to calculate your minimum offer to the IRS. You multiply this number by either 12 or 24, depending on which payment plan you choose. If you choose to pay the IRS over a 5-month period, you multiply your disposable monthly income figure by 12. If you choose the 2-year payment plan option, you multiply this monthly amount by 24.

> EXAMPLE: Darlene calculates that she has $150 per month in remaining income after deducting her monthly living expenses from her monthly income. She decides on the 5-month payment option so she multiplies $150 by 12 which is $1,800. She must add this amount to her net asset value of $10,000 (based on the equity in her home). So, her minimum offer is $11,800, which she enters in Section 8 of the form.
>
> If Darlene decides she can't pay the IRS within 5 months, she would multiply her $150 monthly available cash amount by 24 instead, which equals $3,600. She would add this to her net asset value of $10,000 for a minimum offer of $13,600. She has to pay $1,800 more under this plan but has an additional 19 months to pay the IRS than under the lump-sum method.

CAUTION

The IRS may file a tax lien notice. If it has not already done so, if the IRS accepts your offer, it may file a Notice of Federal Tax Lien. The lien will remain on the public records until every last penny of the OIC has been paid or the statute of limitations for collection has expired.

Special Circumstances: Effective Tax Administration (ETA) Exception

What if you have too many assets to qualify for an OIC under the rules above, but selling assets would cause an economic hardship for you or your dependents? For instance, it might mean selling equipment or tools you use in your trade to make a living.

IRS OIC evaluators have some leeway to accept a nonconforming offer under the effective tax administration (ETA) exception to the OIC rules. The IRS favors folks with diminished financial prospects due to advanced age, serious health problems, or similar issues. Physical and psychological infirmities, such as diabetes, HIV, and drug- and alcohol-related problems, will all be considered when evaluating an OIC under the ETA exception. The issue could even be related to another family member if it has a detrimental effect on the OIC applicant. The IRS will also likely consider the devastating economic impact of the coronavirus (COVID-19) pandemic.

Do You Need a Tax Pro to Do Your OIC?

If you carefully follow the IRS's OIC instructions in the Form 656 booklet and the advice given here, your chances of success should not be better because you hired a professional. Many, if not most, of the rejected OICs we've seen are due to not following the IRS's directions—leaving blanks on the forms, not supplying all required financial backup, undervaluing assets, and the like. If you hire a tax pro, expect to pay somewhere between $1,500 and $7,500 for representation in an OIC. A middle ground alternative would be to buy several hours of a tax pro's time during the form completion process and have the OIC packet reviewed before sending it to the IRS.

EXAMPLE: Jonas and Ashley Hill, both over 60 and in declining health, could pay off their $90,000 tax debt in full but it would mean liquidating their $150,000 401(k) retirement account. The Hills are close to retirement and this would cause an economic hardship for them. The Hills figure they could sell some of their 401(k) and come up with $35,000 and so the Hills make that offer to the IRS even though it is less than the OIC minimum offer amount. The IRS could decide to accept this offer under the ETA exception.

Get clear and comprehensive written reports from medical professionals and medical records to prove a medical issue. Add your own statement to explain how the condition affects your ability to earn money now or in the future. Don't make your tale of woe overly long, but just enough to tug the heartstrings of the OIC evaluators. The IRS doesn't grant many ETA offers, but it won't hurt to try.

If you qualify, an IRS-sanctioned Low-Income Taxpayer Clinic (LITC) might provide you with OIC assistance for free or a small fee. Call the Taxpayer Advocate Service (877-777-4778; www.irs.gov/taxpayer-advocate) to check if there is an LITC near you.

Pros and Cons of Making an Offer in Compromise

Advantages to submitting an OIC:
- You'll save money if your OIC is accepted.
- Your stress level will be reduced, at least during the time the OIC is pending, whether or not it is finally accepted.
- The IRS normally suspends all forced collection methods, such as seizing your bank accounts and wages, while the OIC is pending.
- Your credit rating will improve if the OIC is accepted, as the IRS must file a Certificate of Release of Federal Tax Lien within 30 days of full payment.

Disadvantages to submitting an OIC:
- Filing an OIC gives the IRS more time to collect if the offer is rejected. The normal 10-year statute of limitations is automatically extended for the period the OIC is under consideration, plus any appeal time, plus 30 more days.
- The OIC may be revoked if the IRS later determines you did not fully disclose all of your assets or income. It's important to be truthful with your disclosures.
- Whether the offer is accepted or rejected, you lose your right to contest in court the taxes for any years covered by the OIC.
- Unless you qualify under the Low-Income Certification guidelines (see the IRS website for information), an initial payment toward the offer plus a $205 nonrefundable application fee is required with your OIC. If rejected, anything you paid will be applied to your tax account.

Most Common Mistakes With OIC Forms

According to the IRS, the four most common errors made by people submitting OIC applications are:

- Not including essential information on the forms. Leave nothing blank, and answer "n/a" if in doubt.
- Altering an OIC form. Don't change or make deletions of any pre-printed parts of a form.
- Omitting signatures. If a husband and wife are submitting an OIC, both must sign.
- Not enclosing the application fee or required initial payment (unless the fee is waived because you're a low-income taxpayer).

While all of these mistakes are fixable, they will cause weeks or months of delays.

 CAUTION

Make sure your IRS filings are up to date before requesting an OIC. OIC Form 656 requires that you have filed all past tax returns due and made all required tax deposits, such as quarterly estimated taxes for self-employed income. If you have not filed everything, your OIC will be summarily rejected.

What Happens After You Send in Your OIC Application

There are two OIC processing centers in the United States. You can find the current application mailing address in the Form 656 booklet. When your packet arrives at one of these centers it will first get a quick review to make sure you filled in the forms correctly and submitted the payment required (or qualify for the low-income exception). If it looks okay, the IRS will formally open your case and contact you directly, or it will assign the case to an IRS office near you for investigation.

An IRS offer specialist will contact you in writing, or by phone, to request more documentation and information. Be ready to submit copies (never originals, which could get lost) of:

- your income tax returns for the past two years
- deeds and mortgage documents for all real estate you own
- titles to motor vehicles, boats, planes, and the like
- bank statements for all your accounts, business and personal, for the past three months or more
- life insurance policies if there is any cash value
- sources of nonwage income, such as unemployment, workers' comp, private disability, and retirement and pension plans
- unpaid notes, bills, and other evidence of your debts
- evidence of your major living expenses, such as rent, and
- medical bills and doctor reports.

The IRS is always impressed by paper, so lay it on.

It usually takes between 4 and 18 months for the IRS to investigate your offer and make a decision. While your offer is pending, be sure to file any tax returns that are due or make estimated tax payments for the current year. Otherwise, the IRS can reject your OIC for noncompliance with the tax law. If the IRS does not make a decision within 24 months of submission, it is automatically accepted. Don't count on this happening.

If Your OIC Is Rejected

The IRS must give a written explanation for turning down your OIC. The usual reason is that it doesn't meet what the IRS terms the "reasonable collection potential" of your case—how much the IRS could squeeze out of you. Other common reasons for rejection include failure to respond in a timely fashion to requests for information or documentation—pay stubs, bank statements, rent receipts, and the like. A few OICs are rejected for public policy reasons—if you're a notorious criminal, for instance.

You're entitled to a copy of the report that will list the factors causing the rejection. If you don't want to give up, try calling the person who signed the IRS letter and give him or her a good reason to reconsider, like upping your offer. If that doesn't work, then within 30 days of the date of the IRS notice, send a letter to the IRS stating why the IRS reason for turning down your offer is incorrect. For instance, the IRS did not compute the value of your assets correctly—and then list the reasons.

Alternatively, you can submit another OIC. It must be significantly different than your original offer to be taken seriously. The IRS frowns on offers submitted within six months of the rejection unless your circumstances have dramatically changed or you offer substantially more. Sometimes the IRS offer specialist who worked your case may help with a new offer.

You also have the option to formally appeal an IRS rejection of an OIC. This type of administrative appeal goes to the IRS Independent Office of Appeals, a division separate from the one that turned down your offer, so it will be a fresh pair of eyes that reviews the appeal.

An appeal begins with the filing of IRS Form 13711, *Request for Appeal of Offer in Compromise.* This is a fairly simple two-page form that allows you to specifically disagree with each item the IRS listed in support of the rejection. Very helpful guidance on how to complete the form is on the IRS website at www.irs.gov/appeals/appeal-your-rejected-offer-in-compromise-oic. The IRS must receive your appeal form within 30 days of the date of the rejection letter.

Your appeal won't be considered unless all of the following conditions are met:

- You furnished all data requested by the IRS during the OIC processing.
- You have filed all past tax returns.
- You are current on your tax filings and payments for the current year, including estimated taxes, and if you are an employer, payroll taxes for the current quarter and for the preceding two quarters.

Our experience with OIC appeals has been mixed. Sometimes the IRS OIC department will reconsider your OIC instead of immediately forwarding your case to the IRS Independent Office of Appeals. Or an appeals officer may ask the OIC evaluators to take another look. Or, you might win your appeal outright, but this is a long shot. If you're worried about the IRS starting up its enforced collection machinery, an appeal will further delay the process.

There are no secrets with OICs: Complete the IRS offer forms paying attention to every detail and follow the advice given above. The IRS screens out many offers on technicalities. After assisting hundreds of folks with OICs over the years, we realize how much work it can be to get an acceptable offer, but there are no shortcuts.

Using the Bankruptcy Code to Stop the IRS

[The following section was written with the assistance of two bankruptcy experts: John Raymond, J.D., and Alan Rosenthal of the law offices of John Raymond, San Francisco, California.]

Filing a petition under the bankruptcy code can often reduce or erase tax debts. Alternatively, using bankruptcy can buy time and force a repayment plan on the IRS. Bankruptcy might be just the answer to your tax debt prayers.

> **RESOURCE**
>
> **For more information on bankruptcy, including recent changes to bankruptcy law,** see Nolo's website at www.nolo.com and *The New Bankruptcy,* by Cara O'Neill (Nolo); *How to File for Chapter 7 Bankruptcy,* by Cara O'Neill (Nolo); and *Chapter 13 Bankruptcy,* by Cara O'Neill (Nolo).

Types of Bankruptcy

Bankruptcy is a legal procedure for sorting out your debt problems, including your tax debts, by filing a petition in federal bankruptcy court. There are two basic types of bankruptcies:

- **Straight bankruptcy, or Chapter 7.** This is a liquidation of your debts, which can wipe out some or all of your income taxes.
- **Repayment plans, or Chapters 11, 12, or 13.** These allow you to pay your debts, including tax bills, over an extended period of time, often at pennies on the dollar.

The Automatic Stay

One of bankruptcy's most alluring features is a legal refuge called the automatic stay. The moment you file for bankruptcy, the automatic stay stops all creditors and bill collectors—including the taxman—cold. The bankruptcy effectively removes the case from the IRS Collection Division and moves it to the IRS's Insolvency Unit, which deals with bankruptcy cases.

The only way a creditor can collect while your bankruptcy case is open is to ask the bankruptcy judge to remove, or lift, the stay. The IRS rarely applies to have a stay lifted.

Downsides of Bankruptcy

You should consider several negatives before deciding to take the plunge into bankruptcy.

Counseling Requirement

Before filing for bankruptcy, you must complete credit counseling with a government-approved agency. This doesn't stop an IRS action to collect.

Additional Time for the IRS to Collect

If you go into bankruptcy and emerge still owing the IRS—meaning that not all of your taxes were erased in bankruptcy—the IRS gains extra time to collect the balance.

The IRS normally has *10 years* to collect tax bills, penalties, and interest from you. Once your bankruptcy case is over, the IRS gets whatever time remains on the original 10 years to collect, plus the time your bankruptcy case was pending, plus another 180 days.

Your Credit Rating

A bankruptcy filing is a matter of public record and it usually remains on your credit record for up to 10 years.

Taxes and Chapter 7 Bankruptcy

Not all tax debts can be wiped out in a Chapter 7 bankruptcy. For example, you must have filed the past four years' tax returns before filing for bankruptcy. You'll need to read some mind-bending rules to determine if bankruptcy can help you with your tax debt. (See the Nolo books listed at the beginning of this section.)

Taxes That Can Be Wiped Out in Chapter 7 Bankruptcy

In Chapter 7 bankruptcy, the court can erase or discharge an individual's or a married couple's taxes in certain circumstances.

Federal tax bills can be discharged in a Chapter 7 bankruptcy only if all of the following are true.

Taxes must be income taxes. Other taxes, such as most payroll taxes, Trust Fund Recovery Penalty, or fraud penalties, can never be eliminated in bankruptcy.

No fraud or willful evasion. You must not have filed a fraudulent tax return or otherwise willfully attempted to evade paying taxes. This usually applies only if you've been assessed a fraud penalty.

Three-year rule. The taxes were due at least three years before you file for bankruptcy. This usually means three years from April 15 of the year the return was due. But, if you filed a request for an extension, it could be October 15. If the 15th fell on a Saturday or Sunday, your return wasn't due until the following Monday. That is the date you start counting from for this rule. For most people, this is the most difficult rule to meet.

State Income Taxes and Bankruptcy

The bankruptcy code only talks about taxes—not just federal income taxes. But there are three areas of special concern with state taxes and bankruptcy.

First, some states send out interim, not final, notices of tax assessments. In California, for example, the final date for bankruptcy counting is no less than 60 days after the issuance of the proposed additional tax. The result is that the waiting time to discharge California state income taxes is 300 days from assessment, not 240 days.

Second, many states require a taxpayer to file an amended return after an IRS assessment based on audit or examination. The three-year rule is measured from when the original return was due, and the two-year rule from when it was filed.

Finally, state sales taxes are usually not dischargeable in Chapter 7 or Chapter 13, so they must be paid in full. In a few states, however, including Hawaii, California, and Illinois, unpaid sales taxes can be discharged the same as income taxes if they meet the 240-day, three-year, and two-year rules. Again, see a bankruptcy attorney in your state if this might be an issue.

Two-year rule. You actually filed all tax returns at least two years before filing the bankruptcy. Having the IRS file a substitute return for you doesn't count. If you don't file a tax return, you can never discharge the taxes you owe for that year in bankruptcy. You can, however, include the taxes in a repayment plan.

240-day rule. The income taxes were assessed by the IRS at least 240 days before you file your bankruptcy petition. Normally, this applies only if you've been audited within 240 days before the petition is filed.

If any of the following apply, you will have to add time to the 3-year, 2-year, or 240-day rules for your debts to qualify for discharge in bankruptcy:

- **Prior bankruptcy.** If you filed a previous bankruptcy case, all three time periods—three years, two years, and 240 days—stopped running while you were in the prior bankruptcy case. You must add the length of your case plus 180 days to all three periods.

- **Offer in Compromise.** An Offer in Compromise delays the 240-day rule by the period starting on the date the offer is made until the IRS rejects it or you withdraw it, plus 30 days, plus any period for which an appeal is pending.

- **Tax court.** If you have a case pending before the U.S. Tax Court, the time rules are extended by 60 days after the case has been decided or dismissed.

TIP

Before filing bankruptcy for tax debts, obtain a record of your filing dates. This is called an "account transcript." You can get one online with the IRS Get Transcript Online tool (www.irs.gov/individuals/get-transcript). Alternatively, you may mail IRS Form 4506-T, *Request for Transcript of Tax Return*, or call the IRS at 800-908-9946. This free computer printout lists important tax dates—when the returns were filed, when the taxes were assessed, and the various dates of any tolling or time-extending events. Check the dates from the IRS transcript before filing bankruptcy. This is very important, so get it right.

Federal Tax Lien and Chapter 7

If your taxes qualify for discharge in a Chapter 7 bankruptcy case, you still might have a problem. This is because previously recorded tax liens are still on your record. A Chapter 7 discharge will wipe out only your personal obligation to pay the tax. *Any lien recorded before you file for bankruptcy survives the discharge to the extent your property has equity to which the lien can attach.*

After your bankruptcy is over, the IRS can seize many of the assets you owned at the time the bankruptcy was filed. (It might be possible to reduce the amount of the tax lien. See a bankruptcy attorney for more information.) Unless you owned real estate or have an IRA or a pension plan, the IRS lien probably won't harm you.

Taxes and Chapter 13 Bankruptcy

If you or your tax debts don't all qualify for Chapter 7, consider a Chapter 13 repayment plan. This can be the next-best solution to a tax bill problem and is much easier to qualify for than Chapter 7. By filing for Chapter 13, you might be able to work out a payment plan through the bankruptcy, which the IRS might have otherwise been unwilling to agree to.

RESOURCE
For more information on bankruptcy see the following resources:
- Nolo's website at www.nolo.com
- *The New Bankruptcy*, by Cara O'Neill (Nolo)
- *How to File for Chapter 7 Bankruptcy*, by Cara O'Neill (Nolo), and
- *Chapter 13 Bankruptcy*, by Cara O'Neill (Nolo).

Basics of Chapter 13

Chapter 13 is the most widely used bankruptcy option for people with tax debts. In Chapter 13, you propose a payment plan for the bankruptcy court's approval. You make monthly payments to a court-appointed trustee, who divides up the money among your creditors, including the IRS. This repayment plan runs for five years.

Taxes Paid in a Chapter 13 Plan

Secured taxes—those for which a lien was recorded and you own property whose current value is equal to the tax lien—must be paid in full in a Chapter 13 case. Once you pay off your secured taxes in Chapter 13, the tax lien is satisfied. The lien no longer attaches to property you own or might acquire in the future.

Chapter 13 can still be beneficial for many reasons, including:

- Chapter 13 forces a repayment plan on the IRS. The IRS can't get anything more than the bankruptcy judge approves. The IRS can't restart collection activities—seizures of your property or wages—as long as your Chapter 13 plan is underway. Chapter 13 is a way to get around an unreasonable revenue officer who won't agree to a fair installment agreement.

- Interest and penalties stop accruing the moment you file for Chapter 13, except on secured taxes. By contrast, with an IRS installment agreement (IA), the interest and late payment penalties continue to accrue. For example, if you owe $60,000 to the IRS and pay $1,000 a month, you'll still owe about $30,000 after five years under an IA. The same payment in a Chapter 13 plan will pay off the debt in full.

- Tax penalties may be paid at less than 100%. It is within the discretion of the bankruptcy judge.

Qualifying for Chapter 13 Bankruptcy

To file for Chapter 13 bankruptcy, much like Chapter 7, you must complete a rather imposing set of forms disclosing your assets, liabilities, income, and expenses and you must have filed all your tax returns for four years prior to filing. You must also submit a proposed payment plan to the court. See *Chapter 13 Bankruptcy*, by Cara O'Neill (Nolo), or consult a bankruptcy attorney before tackling the forms.

If you qualify under these rules, submit a Chapter 13 payment plan to the bankruptcy judge. The judge reviews your petition and appoints a trustee to oversee your case. The trustee holds a hearing in which your creditors can come and object to your plan. The IRS rarely ever contests a Chapter 13 plan—so don't worry.

The judge might make adjustments to the plan, but will normally approve it if the forms are right. You make 60 monthly payments to the trustee, who in turn pays your creditors on a pro rata basis.

Taxes and Chapter 11 Bankruptcy

Chapter 11 bankruptcy is primarily for troubled businesses. It gives businesses protection from their creditors while attempting to make a profit and reorganize their debts. Individuals can file for Chapter 11 bankruptcy, but it's rarely done.

Chapter 11s require the help of a knowledgeable (and expensive) bank-ruptcy attorney. Fees start upwards of $10,000. Chapter 11 bankruptcies might last many years. Eventually, the business either becomes healthy or fails. If it fails, the bankruptcy may be converted to a Chapter 7.

In a Chapter 11 bankruptcy, the automatic stay stops all IRS collection efforts, but interest continues to accrue. (By contrast, in Chapter 13, interest usually stops accruing on your tax bills.)

Taxes and Chapter 12 Bankruptcy

Chapter 12 bankruptcy is for debts arising from the operation of a family farm. Its rules are similar to Chapter 13 but there are some differences not discussed here.

Protecting Your Assets From the IRS

It's illegal to transfer assets to defeat the IRS once it has started trying to collect a tax debt. However, it is possible to protect some assets through entities or family members. The key is advance planning and timing the transfers.

Before moving your property beyond the reach of the IRS, consider the following:

- Once you legally transfer ownership, it might be very difficult, if not impossible, to get it back. And, the transfers might have tax consequences.
- Asset protection strategies are not foolproof—the IRS has legal powers to challenge a transfer and recover the asset.

SEE AN EXPERT

Protect yourself. See an attorney to make sure you do a transfer legally and do not commit fraud on the IRS or any other creditors.

Listed here are a few of the most common ways tax debtors *attempt* to protect their businesses and other assets from their creditors, including the IRS.

Transfer assets to a business with a friendly owner. You can also work for a business owned by your spouse or child. If you keep the salary low, you might be able to negotiate an IRS installment agreement that you can live with. The IRS could seize corporate assets if it deems the corporation a sham, but it seldom does so.

Put assets into a family limited partnership. See an attorney if this sounds promising. Don't simply put property into joint tenancy with family members—that won't stop the IRS.

Transfer assets to a trust for a spouse or other family members. A children's trust, for example, can own assets used in your business. Again, see an attorney. Putting property into your revocable living trust won't offer any protection, because you maintain control over the asset. And the IRS considers the use of offshore trusts very suspiciously.

Put life insurance policies into an insurance trust. This generally safeguards them from IRS seizures if done in advance of tax problems.

Fully fund your IRAs, SEPs, and 401(k) retirement plans. If you're worried the IRS will grab your bank accounts, consider putting the funds—up to the legal limits—into a retirement account. While the IRS can legally seize IRAs, SEPs, and 401(k) retirement plans (with restrictions on ERISA plans), this is discouraged by IRS policy.

Transfer assets to family members outright. If you're going to leave property to your children on your death, and you fear a future IRS tax bill, this might be a way to save the property from the IRS.

File separate tax returns. Married couples who file jointly and owe the IRS have their refunds automatically grabbed by the IRS. One way to get around this might be to file separate tax returns if only one spouse owes the IRS. If you reside in a community property state, however, this might not work.

There are also ways to protect your assets by sophisticated estate planning devices. See an attorney if you want to learn more.

Tax Debtors Abroad

How far does the reach of the tax collector extend? Many countries have treaties with the IRS allowing them to collect U.S. taxes due from our taxpayers on their soil. As a practical matter, even our strongest allies don't pursue our tax deadbeats. You might be able to beat the IRS by leaving the country and taking all of your property with you. And you might have to stay away permanently, as the IRS computer is linked to the U.S. Citizenship and Immigration Services computer. And, one more thing: The 10-year statute of limitations on collections is suspended for periods of time that you're out of the country and for 180 days after your return.

Suspending Collection of Your Tax Bill

If your prospects are bleak—no job, little or no money, and pressing creditors—ask an IRS collector to "53" your case. If the collector agrees, they recommend that your tax account balance be classified as "currently not collectible" or CNC.

The collector then submits IRS Form 53 to a manager. If approved, you shouldn't hear from the IRS again for six months at least. Nevertheless, interest (and late payment penalties) still accrue. At the end of your CNC period, the computer brings your account back up and the process starts over again.

The IRS doesn't grant CNC status lightly. A collector might agree to 53 your account over the telephone, but first you might be required to submit one or more of the collection forms showing your assets, liabilities, income, and expenses. The IRS might want other documentation, too, such as doctors' statements showing you are disabled and can't work.

Being classified as currently not collectible doesn't solve your IRS problem. It only gives you more time for dealing with it. You still owe the IRS money, so interest continues to accrue on your outstanding tax debt. The IRS may still file a Notice of Federal Tax Lien to secure its interest in anything you own or acquire.

> **TIP**
> **The 53 process buys valuable time.** It can be helpful if you're hoping to beat the IRS by qualifying your tax debt for bankruptcy or waiting out the 10-year IRS collection statute. Even when your debt is in 53 status, IRS time limits for collecting are running in your favor. Moreover, the IRS won't levy on your assets or income while you have 53 status.

Suing the IRS

A taxpayer may sue the IRS for up to $1 million if an IRS collector willfully disregards the law—for example, if the collector seizes your assets after you filed for bankruptcy, or the IRS seizes your home without a court order. Be aware that taxpayers rarely win lawsuits against the IRS, and not many lawyers are willing to take IRS cases on a contingency basis.

Collection of Tax Debts by Private Debt Collectors

Starting in 2017, the IRS began assigning tax debts for collection to private debt collection agencies. The IRS has assigned over $22 billion (over 2.4 million accounts) to four collection agencies, which have collected about 1% of the amount owed.

The IRS only assigns to private collectors badly overdue tax bills it has given up collecting itself. It will assign a tax bill for private collection only if:

- it has been removed from the IRS's active inventory due to a lack of resources or inability to find the taxpayer
- at least two years have elapsed since the tax debt was assessed and the IRS has not assigned it to an employee for collection, or
- it was assigned for collection but more than 365 days elapsed without any collection interaction with the taxpayer.

In addition to individual accounts, in 2019 the IRS began assigning to collection inactive business accounts, including those of corporations, LLCs, and partnerships, as well as employment tax and excise tax delinquencies. The IRS may not assign to private debt collectors:

- accounts for taxpayers who earn less than 200% of the federal poverty rate or who receive substantially all their income from Social Security Disability Insurance (SSDI) or Supplemental Security Income (SSI) benefits (IRS computers automatically exclude taxpayers who are receiving SSDI or SSI benefits from private debt collection)
- accounts for minors under age 18
- accounts for taxpayers in designated combat zones
- accounts for victims of tax-related identity theft
- accounts that are subject to an installment agreement
- accounts subject to pending or active Offers in Compromise
- accounts currently under examination, litigation, criminal investigation, or levy
- accounts subject to a right of appeal
- accounts involved in innocent spouse cases, and
- accounts of people in presidentially declared disaster areas who request relief from collection.

If you fall into any of the above 10 categories and your account is assigned to a private collection agency, you should explain this to the collector when they call and they should return your account to the IRS. One recent U.S. Treasury Department Inspector General study found the IRS wrongly assigned over 14,000 taxpayers' overdue accounts to collection agencies.

Before your account is transferred to a collection agency, the IRS will send you written notice (IRS Notice CP-40) explaining the private collection process. The notice will contain a special 10-digit taxpayer authentication number. Before you get a call from the collection agency, they will also send you a letter stating that your account has been transferred there, also containing the authentication number. At the beginning of every phone contact with a collection agency you'll be asked for the first five digits of the authentication number, and the agency representative will provide the remaining digits. This way, you know the debt collector is legitimate. Hang up the phone immediately on any person claiming to be an IRS-assigned debt collector if they don't give you the IRS authentication number. If you can't find your taxpayer authentication number, you can ask the collection agency to resend you the letter with the number.

If a private debt collector contacts you, there's one important thing to remember: the collector is not part of the IRS and has none of the IRS's enforcement powers. For example, the collector can't file a Notice of Federal Tax Lien or issue a levy, garnish your wages, or report your tax debt to credit reporting agencies. All the collector can do is try to persuade you to pay all or part of your tax bill.

The collector will first try to get you to pay all you owe within 180 days. Failing that, they will try to convince you to enter into an installment agreement paying the amount over up to seven years. Failing that, the collector will try to at least get a one-time payment. The collector will likely be happy with anything you pay—they get to keep 25%. You should never pay anything to a private debt collector directly. All payments should be made to the U.S. Treasury and sent to the IRS.

You don't have to pay the collector anything, no matter what the collector says. If you're interested in paying off your tax debt through an installment agreement, you're better off dealing with the IRS directly. In cases of hardship, the IRS can reduce your tax bill. A private debt collector can't do this.

You don't have to talk to any private debt collector about your tax debt. The collection agency is required to stop all communication with you and return your account to the IRS if you send it a letter like the following:

Sample Letter to Private Debt Collection Agency

Yolanda Allende
1234 Any Street
Anytown, NY 12345
Social Security Number: XXX-XX-6789

ABC Collection Agency
111 Main Street
Buffalo, NY 10000

Under the Fair Debt Collection Practices Act, 15 U.S.C. § 1692c, Communication in connection with debt collection, I am requesting that you cease further communication with me with respect to all tax liabilities placed with your collection agency by the Internal Revenue Service.

Yolanda Allende
Yolanda Allende

January 15, 20xx

Only provide the last four digits of your Social Security number (or EIN) in the letter. It's best to send the letter by certified mail, and be sure to keep a copy.

Private debt collectors are not allowed to harass you—for example, threaten to sue you, or phone you very frequently or early in the morning or late at night. Such harassment is a violation of the federal Fair Debt Collection Practices Act and you can sue for damages. To make a complaint about a private collection agency, call the Treasury Inspector General for Tax Administration (TIGTA) hotline at 800-366-4484; visit: www.tigta.gov; or write to: Treasury Inspector General for Tax Administration Hotline, 901 D Street SW, Suite 600, Washington, D.C. 20024-2169.

The Taxpayer Advocate Service will help you if you experience problems with a private debt collection agency. Call 877-777-4778 or visit www.taxpayeradvocate.irs.gov. See Chapter 8 for more on the Taxpayer Advocate Service.

RESOURCE

For further information, consult the following resources:

- IRS Publication 908, *Bankruptcy Tax Guide*, and
- IRS Publication 594, *The IRS Collection Process.*

Chapter Highlights

- The IRS has far greater powers than any other bill collector. It can take your wages, bank accounts, and other property (with a few exceptions).
- The IRS collection process starts with computerized form letters. If you can't pay, request more time.
- Avoid giving bank account and employment information to the IRS. If you don't want to deal with the IRS over the phone, request that your file be sent to the local IRS office so you can meet with a tax collector.
- Treat a collector with respect, but remember—you have rights. Read IRS Publication 1. (See Chapter 15.)
- Never lie to the IRS about your assets or anything else. It is a crime. Keeping silent is okay.
- Carefully prepare your financial information before speaking with the tax collector. Don't understate your living expenses.
- If you can't pay your taxes all at once, propose a monthly payment plan. Interest and penalties keep accruing until you pay in full.
- It is possible, but never easy, to reduce your tax debts through a formal Offer in Compromise.
- Bankruptcy can wipe out tax debts or allow you to pay over time without interest and penalties mounting.
- If you're in dire financial straits, ask the IRS to temporarily suspend collection for hardship.
- The IRS can assign your overdue tax debt to a private debt collection agency, but you don't have to communicate with any debt collector.

IRS Enforced Collection: Liens and Levies

Federal Tax Liens..265

    Notice of Federal Tax Lien..265

    Effect of a Recorded Notice of Federal Tax Lien 266

    Neutralizing a Recorded Federal Tax Lien 266

    If the IRS Records a Tax Lien 268

    Avoiding or Eliminating a Tax Lien 268

    When the IRS Files a Tax Lien in Error..271

    Getting a Tax Lien Released 271

Getting a Tax Lien Withdrawn 272

Tax Levies = Seizure of Assets...273

    Significance of a Tax Levy..273

Dealing With the IRS Levy Process 274

Assets the IRS Can't or Won't Seize..274

    Exempt Assets...275

    Assets of Last Resort That the IRS Can Seize..275

    You and Your Spouse's Income 277

    Jointly Owned Assets...279

Avoiding a Levy...279

    Transfer Your Assets..279

    Convince the IRS That a Levy Would Be Uneconomical 281

    Show That the Levy Would Prevent You From Working 281

    Keep Mum About Your Assets...281

    Keep Assets Out of Sight..282

    Sell Your Assets..282

    Move Financial Accounts 282

    Rent, Don't Own 282

Deposit Money Into Retirement Accounts 283

File for Bankruptcy..283

Getting a Tax Levy Released 283

IRS Sales of Levied Assets 286

IRS Sales of Personal Property...286

IRS Sales of Homes and Other Real Estate 287

Levies of Business Assets..290

Levies of Joint Tax Refunds: Injured Spouse Claims 291

Suing the IRS for a Wrongful Levy 292

f you don't deal with the IRS using any of the options discussed in Chapter 6, "When You Owe the IRS," you're likely to face IRS enforced collection measures. These are the IRS's awesome lien and levy powers.

The average IRS levy (seizure) brings in about $1,600, mostly from bank accounts or wages. And, just because it happens to you once is no reason to believe it won't happen again—and again—until the debt is paid in full.

Federal Tax Liens

Whenever you owe taxes to the U.S. Treasury and don't pay after the IRS sends you notice and a demand to pay, a claim against you by the federal government arises by law. (I.R.C. § 6321.) This claim is called a "tax lien." The existence of the government's claim is not public information—at least initially—and so it's sometimes called a "secret" or "statutory" or an "automatic" lien.

The tax lien theoretically attaches to just about everything you own or have a right in. If you owe interest and penalties on the tax, which is often the case, the lien covers these additions too. Thankfully, there are exceptions to this general rule that are covered later in this chapter.

States might also have tax lien rights; those aren't covered in this book.

For more information, see IRS Publication 594, *The IRS Collection Process*, which describes tax lien procedures in detail.

Notice of Federal Tax Lien

If the IRS sends you a valid tax bill and you don't pay it, you might receive a written demand to pay. This paper is called a "CP-501 notice," referring to the IRS number on the right-hand corner. If you don't pay within 30 days and owe at least $10,000, the IRS may file a notice in the public records showing your tax debt. Usually the IRS takes much longer to file a lien notice, and in fact, it might never do it. This paper is officially called a "Notice of Federal Tax Lien." In a recent year, the IRS filed over 400,000 notices in the county or state public records offices where the IRS believes debtors might live, work, or own real estate. Most filed tax liens are for amounts over $25,000. In the few states without county recording systems, the IRS sends the Notice of Federal Tax Lien to the secretary of state's office. The IRS pays the state or county fee for recording the tax lien and adds it to your bill.

The IRS does not check first to see if you actually own anything before recording the lien notice. It has no reason to. Even if you don't own property now, you might later and the IRS gets first dibs on the proceeds from its sale or financing.

> EXAMPLE: Joyce owes the IRS and lives in Orange County with her Aunt Mildred. The IRS records a Notice of Federal Tax Lien at the county recorder's office, even though Joyce owns no real estate. Aunt Mildred dies and leaves her home to Joyce. The IRS's lien now attaches to the house. Joyce won't be able to sell the house with a clear title without first paying off the IRS. And Joyce won't erase the lien by transferring the title to Kayleen, her best friend. Kayleen takes the property subject to the tax lien.

During the COVID-19 pandemic, the IRS suspended filing new Notices of Federal Tax Lien. However, by the time you're reading this book, normal operations will have resumed.

Effect of a Recorded Notice of Federal Tax Lien

Just as a recorded mortgage tells anyone who searches the public records that you owe on your home, a Notice of Federal Tax Lien shows the world that you owe the IRS.

A recorded tax lien scares off buyers and potential creditors or lenders, making it difficult for you to refinance or get loans.

RESOURCE

Getting helpful credit information. For information on credit ratings and rebuilding your credit after a financial setback, including owing the IRS and many other debt and credit issues, see *Solve Your Money Troubles*, by Amy Loftsgordon and Cara O'Neill (Nolo).

Neutralizing a Recorded Federal Tax Lien

Keep in mind that the automatic, secret, or statutory tax lien and a recorded Notice of Federal Tax Lien are two distinct things.

You can't escape a valid automatic tax lien without (a) paying the tax, interest, and penalties owed; (b) eliminating it in bankruptcy; (c) reducing and paying it through an Offer in Compromise; or (d) having the time limit for collections run. An automatic tax lien won't appear in any public record, such as a county recorder's office. Hence, it's sometimes called a "silent" or "secret" tax lien.

A recorded Notice of Federal Tax Lien tells the world your secret. The best way to get rid of it is to get an IRS Certificate of Release of Federal Tax Lien. The IRS will issue a Certificate of Release if you fully pay the tax owed, discharge it in bankruptcy, or pay it through an Offer in Compromise or if the time limit for IRS collections has run out.

The IRS will *not* reduce the original amount shown on a tax lien as you make payments. So, if the lien starts out at $100,000 and you pay it down to $1,000, the lien will show as $100,000 until the last penny is paid. Only then will the IRS issue the Certificate of Release.

When the tax is paid in full, eliminated, or reduced and paid through an Offer in Compromise or bankruptcy or the time for collections has lapsed, the IRS must issue the Certificate of Release (Form 668Z) within 30 days. Once you get the Certificate of Release, you should record it (if the IRS doesn't) and pay the recording fee in the counties where the IRS filed the lien.

IRS "Fresh Start" Tax Lien Rules

In 2012, the IRS put into place a "Fresh Start" initiative that included major changes in the lien process. These now permanent changes reduced tax lien filings by tens of thousands each year. The highlights include:

- The IRS will not file tax liens if the amount owed is less than $10,000.
- The IRS will grant lien withdrawals if the balance owed is less than $25,000 and a direct debit installment payment plan is in effect.
- Small business debtors can get up to 24 months to pay installments on debts of $25,000 or less more easily than in the past.

> **TIP**
>
> **You can appeal a tax lien filing.** IRS tax lien filings can be contested in the IRS Independent Office of Appeals. For details, see the discussion in "Dealing With the IRS Levy Process," below, and Chapter 4 on appealing IRS decisions.

If the IRS Records a Tax Lien

Legally, the IRS must notify you in writing and give you a chance to pay or try to prevent the lien from being recorded before sending the notice to the public records offices. But if you've moved or the notice is lost in the mail, you might never get the warning and only learn of it when you apply for credit or a loan—and are turned down.

The IRS does not always file tax lien notices. It's hit or miss.

You can appeal an IRS tax lien notice filing to the IRS Independent Office of Appeals under the Collection Appeals Program (CAP).

First request a telephone conference with the manager of the IRS unit filing the lien. If the manager turns you down, fax or mail a completed Form 9423, *Collection Appeal Request*, to the collection office. (A copy with instructions is at the IRS website, www.irs.gov.) File your appeal within three business days after your conference with the manager or the IRS may resume collection.

The appeal request is usually decided within five business days. The appeals officer looks at whether the collectors followed correct procedures and considers the facts and circumstances of your case. You may not challenge in CAP the existence or amount of your tax liability. The officer should telephone you, so list your work, home, and cell phone numbers in your letter. Most taxpayers lose. You can't proceed to court if you don't agree with the decision in your CAP case.

For more information about the Collection Appeals Program, refer to IRS Publication 1660, *Collection Appeal Rights*.

Avoiding or Eliminating a Tax Lien

A recorded tax lien might effectively prevent you from selling or refinancing real estate. It won't, however, affect your right to sell personal property, such as a motor vehicle, boat, or furnishings.

As discussed in Chapter 6, the best way to deal with a tax lien is to avoid one in the first place.

You should respond to an IRS letter threatening a lien filing by contacting the IRS at the telephone number on the letter, or calling 800-829-1040, or if all else fails, the Taxpayer Advocate Service at 877-777-4778. Be ready to convince the IRS that you fall into the category "Will filing notice impair collection of the tax liability?" Point out that a tax lien will kill your chance of getting a mortgage loan, for example.

If you tried but failed to convince the IRS to forgo recording a tax lien, here are your options after the lien notice has been filed:

- **Appeal the lien filing.** The IRS has five business days after filing the lien to provide written notice to the taxpayer. This must include notice of the right to request a Collection Due Process (CDP) hearing with the Independent Office of Appeals within 30 days from the sixth day after the lien filing. To obtain such a CDP hearing, you must file IRS Form 12153, *Request for a Collection Due Process or Equivalent Hearing.* You must indicate on the form why the IRS should withdraw the lien (for example, you're unable to pay in full and would like to enter into an installment agreement or Offer in Compromise, the taxes were discharged in bankruptcy, you're not liable for the tax, you claim innocent spouse relief, or other reasons). Timely filing prohibits the IRS from levying on your assets until the appeal is finally determined. However, the 10-year collection period is suspended during this time. The appeals officer will conduct an informal conference by phone, letter, or in person and issue a determination letter. If you don't agree with the determination, you may appeal to the U.S. Tax Court within 30 days (see Chapter 5). If you fail to timely request your CDP hearing, you can request an Equivalent Hearing up to one year from the day of the lien filing. An Equivalent Hearing is the same as a CDP hearing, except you can't appeal to the Tax Court and it doesn't prohibit the IRS from levying on your assets or suspend the 10-year collection period. You can request an Equivalent Hearing at the same time you request a CDP hearing on the same Form 12153. If you win the CDP or Equivalent Hearing appeal, the lien will be withdrawn. (I.R.C. § 6320.) For more information about Collection Due Process appeals, refer to IRS Publication 1660, *Collection Appeal Rights.*

- **Pay in full.** If you don't have the funds, can you borrow from friends or relatives? It is better to owe just about anyone other than the IRS. The IRS must record a release within 30 days of full payment, but often the agency doesn't follow through. Call the IRS Centralized Lien Operation at 800-913-6050 to verify the release was filed, and if it wasn't, call the Taxpayer Advocate Service at 877-777-4778.

- **Request a Certificate of Discharge.** Let's say the IRS has filed a Notice of Federal Tax Lien which legally attaches to your property, usually real estate. You want to sell the property but you won't receive enough money from the sale to fully pay the tax lien. This doesn't prevent the sale. You can deliver a clear title if you get the IRS to discharge the lien in writing. If the IRS agrees, the buyers can take the property clear of the Federal Tax Lien. But, all the proceeds of the sale must go to the IRS. Your tax debt bill is reduced and the lien will remain on your record. Submit IRS Form 14135 and all required documentation.

- **Request a Subordination of Federal Tax Lien.** What if you want to refinance your mortgage but there is a Federal Tax Lien filed? Request that the IRS subordinate its lien to the refinanced loan. If approved, your refinanced loan takes a priority position over the IRS lien. You'll need to fill out IRS Form 14134 and submit all required documentation. If you receive any amount over the refinanced amount, it will be taken by the IRS to apply to your tax bill.

- **Request Withdrawal of Notice of Federal Tax Lien.** Under a (very) few circumstances, the IRS will withdraw a Notice of Federal Tax Lien. This removes the reference of the Notice of Federal Tax Lien from your records.

CAUTION

Bankruptcy doesn't wipe out a recorded tax lien. If your tax debts qualify for a discharge under any chapter of bankruptcy, the lien will remain, although your personal liability is wiped out. If you owned any real estate going into bankruptcy, it is still subject to the tax lien. The IRS could seize that property after your bankruptcy is over. Or, the more likely scenario is that the IRS would allow you to pay over the value of the property rather than seizing it. And, in some cases, the IRS never tries to enforce the lien after bankruptcy—it's hit or miss. (See a bankruptcy attorney for an analysis of your situation or call the IRS Centralized Insolvency Operation at 800-973-0424.)

When the IRS Files a Tax Lien in Error

The IRS occasionally files a tax lien notice in the public records when you don't owe anything. For example, you paid the bill but the IRS did not properly credit your account. Under the Taxpayer Bill of Rights you're entitled to a Certificate of Release stating that the lien was filed in error. Contact the IRS lien center at 800-913-6050 as soon as possible.

Getting a Tax Lien Released

The IRS must issue a formal Certificate of Release of Federal Tax Lien within 30 days after either of the following:

- The taxes are fully paid, discharged in bankruptcy, or satisfied through an Offer in Compromise.
- The lien becomes unenforceable because the statute of limitations for collections has run—usually 10 years after the tax was first assessed (I.R.C. § 6325(a)). See the prior section regarding liens filed in error. The lien eventually will become uncollectible after the 10-year statute of limitations on collection runs. However, a tax lien on real estate "secured property" never expires.

If 30 days pass and no release has yet been issued (not uncommon), file Form 12277, *Application for Withdrawal*, or write or call the IRS Centralized Lien Operation, P.O. Box 145595, Stop 8420G, Cincinnati, Ohio 45250-5595; 800-913-6050. Give the date of your request and your name, Social Security number, employer identification number, address, and telephone number with the best time to reach you, and tell why the lien should be released (such as the taxes were paid, the lien was filed in error, or the statute of limitations has run). Enclose a copy of the tax lien you want released. If you paid the tax, also enclose a copy of an IRS written acknowledgment of payment, an IRS transcript showing payment, or a canceled check.

For emergencies (such as a mortgage loan closing held up by the tax lien), call the Taxpayer Advocate Service at 877-777-4778. If there is a balance due and you need quick action, be prepared to pay with a certified check, cashier's check, or money order. Usually, the IRS will agree to accept payment out of the proceeds of the real estate escrow.

Getting a Tax Lien Withdrawn

An IRS Withdrawal of Notice of Federal Tax Lien is a little different from a Certificate of Release of Federal Tax Lien. A Withdrawal only removes the effect of the tax lien on certain property whereas the Certificate of Release extinguishes the tax lien altogether. So you might get a tax lien withdrawn by the IRS on request even though the tax liability hasn't been satisfied in full. On application, the IRS will withdraw a lien in the following circumstances:

- the lien was filed prematurely or the IRS didn't follow proper procedures
- you entered into an installment agreement to satisfy the tax liability and the agreement didn't provide for a lien to be filed
- withdrawal of the lien will facilitate the collection of the tax liability, or
- with the consent of the Taxpayer Advocate Service, the withdrawal of such notice will be in the best interest of the taxpayer and the U.S. government.

Suing the IRS for Wrongful Collection Actions

It is possible to sue the IRS in U.S. District Court for damages if it fails to release a tax lien or takes unauthorized collection actions. (I.R.C. § 7430; IRS Regulation 1.7430.) To win in court, you must prove that you suffered direct economic damages from the IRS's actions. Before suing, you must first try to solve the problem using channels within the IRS. Your litigation costs are recoverable, too, but not any costs of fighting the IRS before you filed the suit.

Don't get too excited about suing the IRS. The law makes it tough to prove your case or to recover any big money. And judges are reluctant to award attorneys' fees and costs even when you win. Very few lawyers are willing to take this kind of case on a contingency basis (in which the fee is a percentage of the amount recovered).

Tax Levies = Seizure of Assets

Recorded tax liens are just notices to the world that an individual or a business owes the IRS. No money or other assets are taken by the filing of a Notice of Federal Tax Lien. Instead, the IRS collects by seizing your real or personal property through the levy process. Typically, levies are made on financial accounts held for you by others—such as a bank, a stockbroker, or an employer. Although the IRS usually records a tax lien before levying on assets, it does not have to. The IRS ordinarily makes about 1.5 million levies per year. During the COVID-19 pandemic, the IRS's levy programs were paused. However, operations should be back to normal by the time you're reading this book.

Significance of a Tax Levy

Most levy notices the IRS issues are computer generated. Some notices are mistakes and not that hard to straighten out if you contact the IRS quickly. The vast majority of levy notices are issued to tax debtors' financial institutions and employers. The rest are usually for seizures of vehicles, business equipment, and miscellaneous property. However, such seizures are becoming increasingly rare. In one recent year, for example, the IRS conducted only 323 seizures of personal and real property, including 33 vehicles. Nevertheless, with few exceptions, anything you own—wholly, partially, or jointly with others— may be seized and sold to satisfy your tax debts.

The likelihood that the IRS will seize your assets depends on factors such as your previous history of payments—good or bad—and where you live. For some unknown reason, a delinquent taxpayer in Los Angeles is six times more likely to suffer a levy than a similar taxpayer in Chicago. About 3% of all taxes owed to the government are collected by levy. The IRS files about three million notices of levies each year.

Dealing With the IRS Levy Process

The IRS can levy on a person's assets *only* if it follows strict legal rules (I.R.C. §§ 6330 and 6331):

- Before the IRS can seize your money or personal property, it must serve a written Notice of Intent to Levy by certified mail, sent to your last known address in the IRS computer files, or the notice must be left at your home or handed to you.
- The levy notice must be accompanied by a letter explaining your appeal rights. The law provides an opportunity for review of an IRS levy process by an IRS appeals officer before the levy takes place. This is called a "Collection Due Process" (CDP) hearing. To obtain a CDP hearing, you must file Form 12153, *Request for a Collection Due Process or Equivalent Hearing*, within 30 days of the date on the notice. (See Chapter 4 for the appeals procedure.) This gives you a chance to buy some time. If the Independent Office of Appeals turns you down, you may take your case to the Tax Court or even federal district court. Few folks go the court route because of the legal fees and the small chance of success. However, going to court will delay the levy process for many months. See a tax attorney if this tactic sounds promising.
- The intent to levy notice must be given at least 30 days before any seizure is made with one rare exception, called a "jeopardy levy." (I.R.C. § 7429.) (See Chapter 3 for more on jeopardy assessments.)

If the IRS doesn't follow the rules, you are entitled to a return of any assets seized. (I.R.C. § 6343.)

Assets the IRS Can't or Won't Seize

Not everything you own can or will likely be taken by the IRS levy machine. Some items are exempt by law, and others are protected by IRS policy considerations.

Exempt Assets

It should raise your spirits to find out that the IRS can't use its levy power to seize everything you own. (I.R.C. § 6334.) Don't get carried away, however, as the list of items the IRS can't take is hardly generous. The exemption list covers tax debtors and their dependents and—subject to annual cost of living adjustment—includes:

- wearing apparel and school books (not including luxury wear, like a sable jacket, but your cloth coats should be safe)
- fuel, provisions, furniture, and personal effects to $9,690 (livestock is included if you are a farmer)
- books and tools of a trade, business, or profession up to $4,850
- 85% of unemployment benefits
- undelivered mail (no one knows quite what this means)
- Railroad Retirement Act and Congressional Medal of Honor benefits
- workers' compensation benefits
- court-ordered child support
- minimum exemption amount for wages, salary, and other income
- certain service-connected disability payments
- most public assistance payments, such as welfare and SSI, and
- assistance under federal job training partnerships.

Vehicles are generally not considered "personal effects" or "tools of the trade" and are not exempt or partially exempt from levy. However, you can often convince an IRS collector that the vehicle is necessary for your employment and it won't be levied.

Assets of Last Resort That the IRS Can Seize

The IRS can seize anything not listed above; however, IRS policies discourage collectors from taking certain items. Retirement plans and homes are generally not taken except as a last resort. A vehicle needed for work is generally not seized if you can demonstrate there is a necessity for the vehicle.

Retirement Accounts

The IRS can take your Keogh, 401(k), IRA, or SEP. With an ERISA plan, however, the IRS can only grab it if it is vested—that is, if you have the immediate right to take the benefits. In that case, you will be taxed when it's levied by the IRS but do not have to pay any penalty for early withdrawal.

In the case of hardship, the IRS can be stopped from taking retirement plans. Contact the Taxpayer Advocate Service immediately and plead that this will create "a significant and undue economic hardship" on you and your family. You might have to enter into a payment plan with the IRS to protect your retirement account from levy.

> **CAUTION**
> **Social Security and other federal payments aren't safe.** The IRS can legally seize 15% of Social Security payments. First, the IRS must serve a *Notice of Intent to Levy* (form letter IRS CP-91 or CP-298). In extreme circumstances, the IRS is allowed to levy 100% of Social Security benefits, but, thankfully, it rarely does. (I.R.C. § 6331(a).)

Primary Residences

As a last resort for dealing with an uncooperative taxpayer, the IRS can take a personal residence, mobile home, boat, or any other place you call home if you owe more than $5,000. (I.R.C. § 6334.) For married couples, if only one spouse owes the IRS, the other might be able to stop the seizure. However, today such seizures are rare. In one recent year, for example, the IRS seized only 19 personal residences of delinquent taxpayers.

> **CAUTION**
> **State homestead protection laws do not protect a primary residence from an IRS lien or levy.** The IRS must obtain a federal court order before taking a primary residence.

Seizing your primary residence requires a court order. If the IRS threatens to do so, contact the Taxpayer Advocate Service immediately. Offer to make arrangements to pay the taxes owed. A second home or vacation place, however, can be levied without a court order.

If all else fails and you're about to lose your pension plan or house, call your congressperson. A sympathetic staff person, or even the representative, might persuade the IRS to back off. Again, expect to negotiate a payment arrangement in return for keeping your house or retirement plan.

You and Your Spouse's Income

The tax code allows the IRS to take some—but not all—of your wages or other income (as determined by IRS tables). (I.R.C. § 6334(a).) These levy exemption tables are revised annually for cost-of-living increases. You can find the current numbers in IRS Form 1494, available at www.irs.gov. (It is also mailed with the IRS notice of levy.) If your income is fairly low or you have several mouths to feed, all of your earnings might be exempt from levy. In most parts of the country, you would be hard pressed to live on the paltry amount the law allows you to keep from the levy.

A portion of each paycheck or independent contractor payment you receive is exempt from IRS levy. The amount you get to keep is determined by the tax code. It is based on the number of dependents you (and your spouse) can claim on your tax return, plus your standard deduction. The amounts exempt from IRS seizures are subject to annual revisions for cost-of-living increases.

> EXAMPLE: In 2023, Ben earns $62,000 as a baker for Acme. He and his wife, Bonnie, owe the IRS $32,000 in back income taxes. If the IRS levies Ben's wages, Ben, Bonnie, and their two kids are allowed $713 per week exempt from IRS wage levy.
>
> All amounts paid to Ben over $713 per week (after income tax and payroll deductions) go to the IRS. If Bonnie also worked, the IRS could take *all* of her net income for their joint tax debt.

Claiming the Wage Exemption

If you claim only yourself—and not a spouse or dependents—you get the one exemption automatically. Otherwise, you must file a claim for additional exemptions for others that you support.

To seize part of your wages, the IRS sends a levy notice to your employer or to anyone the IRS suspects is paying you for services as an independent contractor. By law, the recipient must immediately give you a copy of the notice.

On the back of the notice is a simple form you must complete to claim the exemption amount to which you are entitled. List your spouse and dependents, date and sign the form, and immediately take it to the IRS office that issued it. After three days, your employer or the business that owed you money as an independent contractor must pay the IRS any nonexempt money owed to you. If the employer or business doesn't, it is liable to the IRS for any money paid you above the exemption.

 CAUTION

You have only three days to get the exemption claim form back to the IRS. If you don't, the IRS grants only one exemption, no matter how many you are entitled to by law.

Defending Against a Wage Levy

Once a levy on your income takes effect, it remains in force for as long as *all* of the following are true:
- Any part of the tax debt is unpaid.
- The statute of limitations on collections hasn't run out.
- You still work for the same employer.

How to stop or minimize a wage levy:
- Negotiate with the IRS to release the levy by demonstrating that the levy is creating an economic hardship, proposing an installment payment plan, or asking for time to sell an asset.
- File an Offer in Compromise. This doesn't automatically stop a wage levy, but the IRS should hold off unless it concludes your offer is just a stalling tactic.
- Change employers or temporarily quit your job. Neither you nor your employer must inform the IRS if you quit. The IRS must hunt you down at your new employment, which could take months. If you quit and are rehired after a month or two, the wage levy is no longer effective as long as your employer notified the IRS that you quit.
- File for bankruptcy. This automatically stops a wage levy, but don't do it without considering all of the ramifications.

- Contact the Taxpayer Advocate Service and ask for hardship relief. See Chapter 8.
- Reduce your income to the exemption amount. A friendly employer, especially if you work in a family business, might let you cut back your hours temporarily. But if you keep working full time while your boss holds back all wages over the exemption amount, your employer could later be forced to pay it to the IRS.

Jointly Owned Assets

The IRS can legally seize assets owned jointly by a tax debtor and a person who doesn't owe anything. But the IRS must compensate the nondebtor, meaning that the co-owner must be paid out of the proceeds of any sale.

If, however, you owe taxes and add a co-owner to an asset—without that person's paying you fair consideration—the IRS can ignore the interest of the new owner. This is called a "fraudulent transfer."

> **EXAMPLE:** Rudolph owns a vacant lot worth $50,000. He sells a one-half interest in it to his sister, Wilma, for $10. The IRS could seize the lot and sell it to pay off Rudolph's taxes, ignoring Wilma's ownership because she did not pay a fair price. Wilma might get her $10 back, though.

Avoiding a Levy

There are several ways that you might be able to avoid an IRS seizure of your assets, or at least slow an IRS collector down.

Transfer Your Assets

Under certain circumstances, you might be able to transfer ownership of property or assets—sell, give away, or a combination of the two—and avoid losing it to the IRS.

For the transfer to withstand later IRS attack, you must have conveyed your assets before the IRS issued a Notice of Intent to Levy. However, there are two "gotchas" that can defeat asset transfers, as described below.

Transferee Liability

Tax debtors sometimes try to defeat the IRS by transferring assets to family members or partnerships, trusts, or corporations for free or a bargain price. While this slows the IRS down, it might backfire. The recipient of the assets is your nominee. Nominees are not protected from IRS seizure—the tax debt attaches to the asset in their hands, and the transfer is ignored.

An IRS attorney determines if the transfer was legitimate. Bottom line: A nominee gives the IRS an additional person to pursue while you remain primarily responsible for the tax debt. Also, the IRS can charge transferors with a crime under certain circumstances. (See Chapter 10 and below.)

> EXAMPLE: Hank, who owes the IRS $75,000, gives his $80,000 rental building to his best friend Penn. The IRS can ignore the transfer and seize and sell the property.

Joint Ownership

The IRS can, but is less likely to, seize an asset when there is another owner besides the tax debtor. The IRS must compensate the other owner for that owner's share—but only if that owner can show that they paid full value for that share. Just putting someone else's name as a co-owner of the asset is not enough.

A better alternative to giving an asset away is to sell it for full value to a friend or relative, with no cash payment, taking back a promissory note. Secure the note with the property, which gives you the right to reclaim it if full payment is not made. Once the IRS is at bay, you can get the asset back.

> EXAMPLE: Hank sells one-half of his rental building to Penn in exchange for a promissory note of $40,000, the fair market value of a 50% interest. Hank owes the IRS back taxes of $75,000. The IRS doesn't like to be in the real estate business and isn't likely to seize the building, especially if Hank agrees to a payment plan or makes some other financial guarantee. Of course, the IRS can claim any cash proceeds Hank receives from the sale.

 CAUTION

Transfers made for no other reason than to deliberately evade IRS collection are fraudulent. Conveyances may be ignored by the IRS or set aside by a federal court. Before transferring assets, see a lawyer. Make sure the transfer is legally effective—use a valid deed, for example. If you make a transfer after the levy process has begun, you might be charged with attempting to evade payment of taxes by deliberately placing assets beyond the government's reach. (*U.S. v. Mal*, 942 F. 2d 682 (9th Cir. 1991).)

Convince the IRS That a Levy Would Be Uneconomical

If you can convince the IRS that the levy of a certain item would be uneconomical, the IRS might back off. Show that the expenses of the levy and sale would exceed the fair market value of the item. (I.R.C. §§ 6334(e) and 6331(f).) This is termed a "no-equity seizure" and is against IRS policy.

> EXAMPLE: Felice owes the IRS $10,000 and her primary asset is a nonrunning vehicle, which she is going to fix when she can afford the parts. Right now, the car is worth no more than $250. It would probably cost the IRS more than $250 to send a wrecker to tow the car, pay for storage, and then advertise the sale in the newspaper. The IRS backs off.

Show That the Levy Would Prevent You From Working

If the item targeted by the IRS for levy is essential for your work or to get to your job, tell the collector that it is exempt property. If the collector doesn't agree, ask for an accelerated appeals process to determine whether or not the asset is exempt. (I.R.C. § 6343(2).)

> EXAMPLE: Arnold, a farmer, owes the IRS $43,000. One of his major assets is his pickup truck, which is absolutely essential for running his farm. Arnold convinces the IRS collector not to take his truck.

Keep Mum About Your Assets

Unless the IRS issues a summons—a legal order to produce documents or appear at an IRS office—you don't have to reveal the existence or location of your assets. It's perfectly legal not to give information to the IRS or to ask to speak with a tax professional before answering any questions. Although the IRS might already know about your local real estate holdings from searching public records, it might not know about property in other states, or in the name of an entity or another person. But remember, it is a felony to lie to the IRS.

Keep Assets Out of Sight

It is illegal to actively conceal assets from an IRS collector. Rarely, however, is an ordinary citizen pursued for keeping a classic '57 Chevy in a friend's garage. Nevertheless, particularly if you're a known tax protestor or crime figure, don't try this without first getting some legal advice.

Keep movable items away from your home or business premises. The IRS won't know where to look for vehicles, boats, and similar assets if they're not located where the IRS expects them. Similarly, assets located outside the state or country can be quite difficult for the IRS to discover.

Sell Your Assets

If it's inevitable that the IRS is going to grab things, don't wait for the levy. If possible, sell your real estate, yacht, airplane, or whatever else yourself. An IRS levy followed by a so-called "forced sale" typically results in a (way) below fair market sale price. Plus the IRS will tack onto your bill various fees and costs of the forced sale.

Move Financial Accounts

There is nothing illegal about moving bank accounts whenever you owe a tax bill. In fact, it is an excellent self-protection move. The IRS is not automatically notified of taxpayers' financial accounts—except once a year on interest-bearing accounts when the institution must issue a Form 1099. Nor are IRS computers linked to financial institutions. (See Chapter 6 for more information on revealing financials to the IRS.)

Rent, Don't Own

If you lease property—real estate, vehicles, furniture, or equipment—you aren't the legal owner. The IRS can't seize items you don't own, unless you have built up equity, or an ownership interest, in a leased asset. For most items, such as a rented auto, you won't have any equity or it will be too small for the IRS to consider. But if you have a lease-purchase option for real estate or business equipment, you might be building up equity—and provide a target for IRS collectors.

Deposit Money Into Retirement Accounts

IRS policy discourages (but doesn't forbid) tax collectors from seizing retirement plan funds. Exceptionally uncooperative taxpayers are the ones at risk. So, if you owe a lot to the IRS and the levy process hasn't yet begun, consider fully funding your retirement plan with unprotected moneys.

File for Bankruptcy

Filing for any type of bankruptcy—Chapter 7, 11, 12, or 13—stops all IRS enforced collection actions. (See Chapter 6.) The relief from the tax collector is often only temporary, so use this time to work things out with the IRS while keeping your assets intact.

> CAUTION
>
> **Don't lie to the IRS.** Silence is golden but it's illegal to actively conceal assets from the IRS. If in doubt, consult a tax attorney.

Getting a Tax Levy Released

If you owe taxes, it is not easy getting anything back from the IRS once it has been seized. If the property taken is a bank account or another liquid asset, it might be nearly impossible.

Assets such as vehicles or business equipment may be returned when any of the following are true:

- The taxes for which the levy was made have been paid in full or through an Offer in Compromise or discharged in bankruptcy.
- The time limit for collections has expired—normally 10 years from the date of assessment (see Chapter 6).
- The IRS believes the release of the levy will facilitate collection of the tax debt.
- You enter into an installment payment agreement.
- The IRS is persuaded that the levy creates a financial hardship on you or your dependents.

(I.R.C. §§ 6331(e) and 6332(c).)

Argue that your situation fits into one of these categories, typically the financial hardship one. For example, you could argue that the seized item, such as an old car, has little value *and* seizing it causes a hardship in your search for employment.

Begin by calling the IRS officer who signed the levy notice. Request an immediate release based on one of the above grounds. If the officer balks, ask for an appointment with their manager—within a day or two. To get your property returned, you will probably have to:

- **Pay the IRS in full.** Borrow on credit cards, take a home equity loan, or ask Uncle Mack.

- **Request a short reprieve—some more time to pay in full.** Explain how you expect to raise the money—a bank loan, selling other assets, or whatever. If your plan sounds reasonable, the IRS might go for it. Do your utmost to follow through.

- **Propose an installment agreement.** The IRS will usually agree to one as long as you propose reasonable payments, don't have a past record of defaulting on another installment agreement with the IRS (see Chapter 6), and are current in your tax form filings.

- **Submit an Offer in Compromise.** If the officer believes you are sincere and that your offer has a shot at being accepted, the officer might release the levy.

- **Cry hardship.** The IRS must release a levy if it would cause economic hardship. But the IRS levy officer initially decides what qualifies. Be ready to show that the levy affects your health or welfare or keeps you from earning a living to keep a roof over your family's head. If your situation is dire and the officer is playing Scrooge, go straight to the manager and then to the Taxpayer Advocate Service. (See Chapter 8.)

- **Show the asset has little value to the IRS.** A valuable asset, such as a truck or business equipment, might have little equity value because chattel mortgages or other liens take priority. Show the IRS all your agreements with the secured creditors. The IRS has a policy against no-equity seizures made just to teach a lesson. If the collector persists, go straight to the manager and then to the Taxpayer Advocate Service.

- **Post a bond with the IRS.** Although this is legally an option, it is so difficult to get a bond that it is not realistic. Essentially, if you meet the qualifications to post a bond, you could pay the taxes owed in full.

How Long Does a Levy Last?

The IRS can seize your assets as long as you owe any part of a tax debt and the 10-year statute of limitations on collections has not expired.* Generally, levies are one-shot affairs; the government must prepare and send a new levy notice every time it wants to grab something (unless it's wages or independent contractor payments).

> EXAMPLE: The IRS levies Remington's account at Piker Bank on Monday. After a 21-day holding period, the bank must send to the IRS everything in Remington's account on the day of the levy notice. If the balance is $0, then the IRS gets nothing from Piker. If Remington deposits $150,000 on Tuesday, the day after the notice, the IRS can't touch it without sending a new levy notice. If Piker Bank sends the IRS anything from Tuesday's deposit without having received another levy notice, it will have to repay Remington the amount it sends the IRS.

Independent Contractors and Employees: As long as you work for the same employer, it must continuously withhold a portion of each paycheck for the IRS. This rule also now applies to independent contractors. The IRS can intercept funds owed to a self-employed person from a business.

An employer's failure to honor the IRS levy notice can mean severe penalties.

*Tax levies on wages should stop, by law, at the end of the normal 10-year statute of limitations on collections by the IRS. There is an exception to this rule if the IRS has begun a levy on a retirement fund before the end of the 10-year period; it may collect from distributions from the fund for an unlimited period. Hardly seems fair, but it's the law.

- **File for bankruptcy.** A bankruptcy court may order the IRS to return any seized property to you.
- **Appeal.** You can appeal an IRS levy or other collection action to the IRS Independent Office of Appeals. You must first request a telephone conference with the manager of the IRS unit filing the levy. If the manager turns you down, fax or mail a completed Form 9423, *Collection Appeal Request*, to the collection office. You must request the appeal within three days of your conference with the manager. The appeal request is usually decided within five business days. The appeals officer looks at whether the collectors followed correct procedures

and considers the facts and circumstances of your case. Don't get too excited, however, as the vast majority of taxpayers lose collection appeals. For more information about the Collection Appeals Program, refer to IRS Publication 1660, *Collection Appeal Rights*, or visit the IRS website at www.irs.gov.

An IRS release of levy on an item does not prevent the IRS from levying on the same item at some time in the future. (I.R.C. § 6331(e).)

IRS Sales of Levied Assets

When the IRS seizes assets other than real estate, it physically takes custody of them—cars, cash, stock, equipment, and other items. For financial assets, the IRS sends a notice to your financial institution ordering it to freeze your account and send the balance after 21 days. For other things, the IRS hires a local mover to drive a truck to your door and empty your home or office of furniture, machinery, and the like. Real estate is handled differently, as explained below.

IRS Sales of Personal Property

Once the IRS has seized your personal (not real estate) property, it can sell it at an IRS auction. (I.R.C. § 6335(e).) Before the auction, the IRS will set a minimum bid price and send you notice of it. If you believe the price is too low, you have five days to object; present documentation, such as an independent appraisal, that the bid price is unfairly low.

The IRS must determine the fair market value of an asset and then it may discount that figure by a value of 25% to 45% to determine the "forced sale" value. Generally, that amount becomes the IRS minimum bid at the auction.

The IRS must also notify you in writing of the time and place of the auction. Up until the auction takes place, you can try to negotiate to stop the sale. If you aren't successful—or don't try—the revenue officer handling the case usually acts as the auctioneer. You will then receive a letter from the IRS after the auction informing you of the outcome.

IRS auctions are usually held in federal courthouse buildings—very public. You don't have to attend, but go for it, especially if you'd like to try to get the property back from the buyer. Some people make a living out of buying property from the IRS cheap and might be open to selling it back to you or a friend after the auction.

If no one bids the IRS minimum bid figure, the IRS has two options:

- Bid the minimum amount itself and hold the property or dispose of it by private sale later.
- Give the property back to you. While this is rare, it does happen. If the IRS decides that keeping the property is not in the best interests of the government, you might get it back. The expense of the levy and attempted sale will be added to the amount you already owed. The IRS considers the cost of maintaining, repairing, transporting, or safeguarding personal property in deciding whether or not to give your property back. And if the IRS gives the property back to you, the lien remains and it could be levied again in the future.

The winning bidder must give the IRS a bank certified or cashier's check for at least 10% of the bid price and pay the balance within a few days. The IRS won't turn over the levied property until it has been paid in full.

The IRS applies the payment first to your tax bill and then to the costs of the seizure and sale, such as advertising and storage. There is no commission owed to the auctioneer, who is a government employee. If money is left over, send a letter to the revenue officer handling your case asking that it be returned to you. If you don't, the IRS will keep the excess and apply it to your future taxes.

If the proceeds from the sale of your assets don't cover your tax bill, you are still liable to the IRS for the balance.

IRS Sales of Homes and Other Real Estate

If the IRS levies on your home or other real estate, it must post a "notice of seizure" prominently on the property. If it's your residence, the paper is usually affixed to your front door. And if the IRS knows of your whereabouts, it must attempt to hand deliver a copy of the notice to you. If you can't be found or are hiding inside and don't come to the door, the IRS will most likely mail a certified letter with the notice to you. As mentioned above, the IRS must obtain a court order before it can levy your primary residence. However, there is no court order required for a levy on a vacation home, rental property, or other real estate you might own.

CAUTION

The IRS will not evict you. You do not have to move out of your home when you receive a levy notice. If IRS personnel ask to enter your home—to inspect the interior or bring in a real estate appraiser—you don't have to let them in unless they have a court order.

The IRS must publish the date, time, and location of the auction in a local newspaper. This information is also posted on a public bulletin board at the nearest federal courthouse or federal office building or in the public area of the local IRS office. The sale is usually set for a date 45 days after the seizure notice is first posted.

Any mortgages, judgment liens, real estate taxes, or other liens on your property at the time of the IRS sale remain in place after the IRS auction— as long as they were recorded *before* the IRS recorded its Notice of Federal Tax Lien. This means that the auction buyer takes the property subject to any liens, such as a mortgage. But any lien recorded *after* the IRS recorded its Notice of Federal Tax Lien is wiped out at the IRS sale—so the buyer gets it free and clear.

TIP

A well-off relative or friend can buy your home at the auction. That person can then lease or sell the house back to you. Obviously, you don't want the property back in your name until the IRS bill has been entirely satisfied, or you risk losing the house again.

Staying in Your Home After the IRS Auction

You don't have to voluntarily move out of your home after the IRS has sold it—no matter what. The high bidder at an IRS auction of real estate receives only an IRS "certificate of sale." (I.R.C. § 6335.) This certificate does not give the buyer the full rights of a deed holder. You still are the deed holder although you are now subject to the rights of the certificate holder.

If you're living in the home, the certificate holder can't enter it against your will or even ask you to leave. Instead, the person must bring an eviction lawsuit in your local state court. An eviction usually takes time and money, and so you might be able to negotiate a voluntary move-out date or ask for moving expenses in return for vacating right away. You might even be able to rent back the home. Having this right to stay also gives you time to figure out whether you can possibly redeem the property.

Getting Back Real Estate After an Auction

Even after the auction and the issuance of the certificate of sale, you might be able to get your home or other real property back. (I.R.C. § 6337.) This is called the "right of redemption." And you might be able to stop an eviction if you can convince a judge that you intend to exercise your redemption right.

You have 180 days from the date of sale to redeem your real estate from the certificate holder, who *must* let you do so. If you don't redeem within that time period, the IRS will issue a deed to the buyer. Redemption means paying the holder, not the IRS—unless the IRS was the high bidder. Payment must be by cash or by bank-certified or cashier's check for the full bid price plus interest at the rate of 20% per year, prorated to the date of your payment. You must present payment to the certificate holder on or before 180 days from the auction date. If you're a day late, the right is lost.

> **EXAMPLE:** Georgina's house sold for $100,000 at an IRS auction to Charlton, the high bidder. This satisfies Georgina's debt to the IRS in full. The home is worth about $150,000 and Georgina wants to redeem it so she and her three daughters can remain there. She finds a mortgage company willing to lend her $110,000. She will have to pay Charlton $104,932:
>
> | | |
> |---|---|
> | Bid price | $ 100,000 |
> | Interest | |
> | Prorated interest rate | |
> | (90 ÷ 365 days x 20%) = 4.932% | |
> | Interest due ($100,000 × 4.932%) | 4,932 |
> | Total needed for redemption | $ 104,932 |

It might be possible to buy the property back from the certificate holder with a promissory note and mortgage if you can't get a loan from a financial institution. It doesn't hurt to ask.

Make sure you communicate and document your intent to exercise your right of redemption. Notify the holder of the certificate of sale in writing by certified mail, and send a copy to the IRS office handling your case. Follow up with telephone calls to the buyer and the IRS employee who handled the auction. If you can't contact the certificate holder or the person states that they won't take your payment, ask that the IRS contact the holder and inform the holder of your right to redeem. If the IRS won't, contact a lawyer ASAP.

> **SEE AN EXPERT**
>
> **Get professional help when exercising your right to redeem.** Many certificate holders will be unhappy about your redemption or unaware of your right to exercise it. Even if the holder is cooperative, you will need a quitclaim deed from the purchaser. A lawyer or title or escrow company should perform this service and see that the quitclaim deed is recorded in the public record.

After the redemption is completed, write a letter with copies of the proof of payment and the quitclaim deed from the buyer to the IRS local office: Hand deliver or send it by certified or registered mail. The letter should simply state that you have exercised your right of redemption and that a deed to the certificate holder should not be issued.

If the IRS was the buyer, then you won't get a quitclaim deed, but instead will get a release of lien document. Once you record this document you will once again have title to the property—except for any mortgages or other recorded liens against the property that existed prior to the IRS lien.

Levies of Business Assets

The IRS has the power to take just about anything if you owe taxes. If you are a partner or a sole proprietor of a business, the IRS can levy on the business's bank accounts for your personal tax debts. The IRS might also intercept your accounts receivable by notifying your customers to make future payments to the IRS instead of to your business. If you're in a partnership, the IRS can go after the business's assets, even if only one partner is having IRS problems.

If your small business is incorporated, the IRS can seize your shares of stock in the corporation (but not the assets of the company) for your individual tax debts. If the IRS believes you have created the corporation simply to shield your assets from the IRS, it may levy the corporate assets. If you're faced with this, see an attorney.

Before levying on assets located inside your business, however, the IRS should ask your permission. If you refuse, the IRS can still take property from *public* areas of your business. If you own a restaurant, for example, the IRS can grab the tables and chairs, but not the kitchen equipment. To get the nonpublic area items, the IRS needs a court order, which can take days or weeks. This gives you time to negotiate or raise money to pay your bill.

As a practical matter, the IRS rarely seizes a small business's inventory, equipment, or fixtures. In one recent year, for example, it conducted only 34 such seizures. It is usually not worthwhile—auctions for used business equipment and inventory typically bring only pennies on the dollar. The IRS also realizes that if the auction proceeds don't cover the complete tax bill, the chance of collecting the balance is reduced severely if you're put out of business, with one major exception: payroll taxes.

Payroll tax exception. The IRS can seize assets and even padlock your doors if your business gets behind in payroll tax deposits. This is doubly true if you are pyramiding employment tax liabilities—you owe past payroll taxes and are not making current payroll tax deposits. The IRS will do its best to put you out of business, just to keep the problem from getting worse. For more information on a business's obligation to pay payroll taxes, see Chapter 11.

Levies of Joint Tax Refunds: Injured Spouse Claims

If the IRS takes a joint income tax refund when only one spouse owes back taxes, the other spouse can file a claim for their share of the refund money. File an amended tax return, Form 1040-X. Attach an *Injured Spouse Allocation* (Form 8379), listing the injured spouse's separate income, deductions, exemptions, and credits. The IRS computes the refund and issues a check if the spouse qualifies.

Suing the IRS for a Wrongful Levy

If the IRS erroneously seized your property—for example, you didn't owe anything—you can sue. (I.R.C. §§ 6343(b),(c).) The IRS must return the property or its value together with interest, reasonable attorneys' fees, and related legal costs. See a tax attorney to find out if you have a case. Don't wait too long. Your lawsuit must be filed within two years after the date of the levy. Be warned, however: Successfully suing the IRS won't be easy.

Chapter Highlights

- A tax lien filed in the public records can hinder your ability to get new credit, like a mortgage loan.
- The IRS has power to levy (seize) most of your worldly goods, with a few important exceptions.
- You can contest a lien or levy within the IRS or in court.

The Taxpayer Advocate: A Friend at the IRS

Who Qualifies for Help From a Taxpayer Advocate?..294

    Problems the Taxpayer Advocate Will Pursue...295

    Problems the Taxpayer Advocate Won't Pursue 297

Contacting the Taxpayer Advocate Service 297

Emergency Help: Taxpayer Assistance Orders 298

    What Constitutes a Significant Hardship to the IRS?..300

    Getting Hardship Relief—Calling the IRS's 911 Line...302

Y ou've tried to solve your problem with the IRS, but no one seems to want to help—your letters and calls have fallen on closed ears and the collectors are about to take the shirt off your back. So whom can you contact? The IRS Taxpayer Advocate Service (TAS) at 877-777-4778 (www.TaxpayerAdvocate.irs.gov).

TAS help is available only when you have tried all the other normal IRS channels and have failed. Larger cities and IRS campuses have TAS offices. Some advocates can be visited in person, but most are accessible only by phone and, in some cases, by video conferencing. (See IRS Publication 1546, *The Taxpayer Advocate Service,* available at the IRS website at www.irs.gov.) Taxpayer advocates have the power—mandated by Congress—to cut through red tape and help you. The Taxpayer Advocate Service has 2,300 employees spread across the United States. In a recent year, they received over 240,000 cases.

The IRS claims that nearly half of all requests for help from the Taxpayer Advocate Service are resolved satisfactorily to the taxpayer, in under five days. Complex problems take much longer. Sad to say, in recent years, the TAS performance has slipped considerably.

Who Qualifies for Help From a Taxpayer Advocate?

Contact the Taxpayer Advocate Service only after first attempting and failing to fix the problem within normal IRS channels. Be ready to provide the taxpayer advocate with copies of previous IRS correspondence and notes indicating dates, times, and summaries of telephone conversations.

Who initially caused the problem—you or the IRS—is immaterial, according to the *Internal Revenue Manual.* So a taxpayer advocate can't beg off by saying that you should have filed your tax return on time, paid your taxes when they were due, or whatever else you did or didn't do wrong.

The Taxpayer Advocate Service has an online TAS Qualifier Tool you can use to help determine if you qualify for assistance. You can find it at www.taxpayeradvocate.irs.gov/can-tas-help-me-with-my-tax-issue.

Problems the Taxpayer Advocate Will Pursue

The taxpayer advocate won't investigate all difficulties you're having with the IRS. Your problem must fall into one of the situations listed below, and you must have first taken the necessary steps for the given situation.

Goals of the Taxpayer Advocate Program

The IRS acknowledges that taxpayers are often ignored or shuffled among different IRS departments. The Taxpayer Advocate Service's goals are to:

- assist taxpayers facing hardships
- ensure that taxpayers have an independent, monitored system for the resolution of problems that have not been solved through regular IRS channels
- serve as a taxpayer's advocate within the IRS to make sure that the taxpayer has a say in the IRS decision-making process, and
- recommend administrative and legislative changes to Congress.

Delays of Over 30 Days

The Taxpayer Advocate Service will help you if you experience a delay of more than 30 days to resolve a tax account problem. If the IRS promises in a publication, form, or other official document to accomplish a task within a specific time, you can ask the Taxpayer Advocate Service for help if you don't hear from the IRS more than 30 days after the time promised.

> EXAMPLE: Elly filed an amended tax return on Form 1040-X claiming a refund on July 15. The IRS promises in the Form 1040-X instructions that refunds for amended returns are processed in no more than 16 weeks. If Elly doesn't hear from the IRS in 16 weeks plus 30 more days, she qualifies for taxpayer advocate assistance.

If the IRS hasn't promised to act within a specific time, the Taxpayer Advocate Service will help you if (1) you have contacted the IRS at least once, (2) at least 30 days have passed since you made your inquiry, and (3) you have not received an IRS response.

EXAMPLE: Garrett received an examination determination from a revenue agent. On January 10, he wrote to the IRS requesting an interest calculation so he could pay his account in full. On March 1, Garrett contacts the Taxpayer Advocate Service for the interest calculation because he has not received a response to his letter. Because more than 30 days have passed from January 10, Garrett qualifies for taxpayer advocate assistance.

The IRS Breaks Its Promises

The Taxpayer Advocate Service will also help if you don't receive a response or resolution to your problem or inquiry by the date promised by the IRS.

EXAMPLE: Ooma underwent a correspondence examination in which the tax examiner asked her to substantiate the basis for some stock she sold. She sent the information to the IRS and received a letter stating that a determination would be made and she would be contacted by March 5. She is not contacted by March 5, so she is entitled to taxpayer advocate assistance when she calls her local Taxpayer Advocate office on March 6.

Emergencies and Other Problems

Even if your problem doesn't fall into one of the above categories, you still might qualify for taxpayer advocate help. This is so if an IRS action or inaction has caused, or will cause, you economic hardship, or if you believe the IRS mistreated you.

EXAMPLE 1: Peter was informed by his bank that the IRS issued a Notice of Intent to Levy for his bank account. Peter never received any notice from the IRS indicating that he owed money. Peter qualifies for taxpayer advocate help.

EXAMPLE 2: A revenue officer (tax collector) showed up at Betty's job. He asked questions about her tax debt in front of her boss and customers. Her complaint to the collector's supervisor went unanswered. Betty is afraid more visits might cause her to lose her job. Betty can call the Taxpayer Advocate Service.

EXAMPLE 3: The IRS recorded a tax lien against Sam. Sam paid off the debt, but two months later the IRS still hadn't filed a Certificate of Release. Sam is trying to buy a car, but the dealer won't arrange financing because of the lien in his credit file. Sam needs immediate help and can call the Taxpayer Advocate Service.

EXAMPLE 4: The IRS recorded an erroneous tax lien against Janelle, but it was her husband, not her, who owed the debt. The collection division has exceeded the 30-day limit for filing a Certificate of Release, even after she informed them of the error. Janelle qualifies for help from the Taxpayer Advocate Service.

Problems the Taxpayer Advocate Won't Pursue

The Taxpayer Advocate Service won't help you in the following situations:

- You haven't followed an IRS-established administrative procedure, such as requesting an appeal.
- The IRS responded to you, but you don't agree with the answer. (Contacting the taxpayer advocate might be worth a try if, for example, you've requested an installment agreement and the IRS rejected your proposal and is about to seize your bank account.)
- The problem does not directly involve your taxes. For example, the Taxpayer Advocate Service won't take complaints about IRS personnel or about documents you were denied in a Freedom of Information Act request.
- The problem can't be solved by the IRS. If you don't like a particular tax law, for instance, write your congressperson, not the taxpayer advocate. Or your problem might be with another federal agency, such as the Social Security Administration.
- Your case is in the Criminal Investigation Division of the IRS.
- The IRS has classified you as a tax protestor or you have raised a similar issue, such as claiming the tax laws are unconstitutional.
- Your position is that you can't or won't pay your tax bill under any circumstances.

Contacting the Taxpayer Advocate Service

The Taxpayer Advocate Service is located at many, but not all, IRS offices. (See www.taxpayeradvocate.irs.gov/contact-us for the office nearest to you.) If it's an emergency—for example, your business vehicle is scheduled to be sold by the IRS tomorrow—call, fax, or visit the nearest IRS office and ask for the local taxpayer advocate.

Otherwise, request help by calling 877-777-4778 (toll free). If you don't get through, leave a phone number for a return call. Or if it's not an emergency, write and describe the problem. (A sample letter is below.) Mail or fax your letter to your local Taxpayer Advocate Service office.

If you call first, follow up with a letter concisely reiterating your problem. And because the IRS loves documentation, whether you write first or write as a follow-up, include in your letter:

- your full name and Social Security number, or a taxpayer identification number if it's a business issue
- copies of IRS notices and prior correspondence to and from the IRS— this is very important
- a concise explanation of your problem
- if applicable, clear, legible copies of canceled checks—both front and back—showing payments that were not credited to your account, and
- a daytime telephone number and hours when you can be reached— this is vital for quick action.

Sign and date your letter.

> ⓘ CAUTION
> **Tell the truth!** The IRS is authorized to contact third parties to verify facts about your claimed hardship.

If you qualify for taxpayer advocate help, your case will be assigned to a specific taxpayer advocate. That person will immediately begin working on your problem or assign it to a staff member.

Below is a sample letter requesting taxpayer advocate assistance.

Control yourself when working with an IRS taxpayer advocate. If you yell, you might be classified as difficult or irate, and the advocate might back off from helping you. Remember, the taxpayer advocate might be your last chance.

Emergency Help: Taxpayer Assistance Orders

Taxpayer advocates can quickly intervene on behalf of taxpayers to local IRS officers and IRS campuses. The advocates can order the IRS to cease any action that causes a significant hardship by issuing a Taxpayer Assistance

Sample Taxpayer Advocate Letter

Internal Revenue Service
Taxpayer Advocate Service
P.O. Box 1302 (Stop 1005)
Denver, CO 80201

November 18, 20xx

Re: Benedict Cooper—SSN 555-55-5555

Dear Sir or Madam:

Please help me straighten out a problem that I have been unable to resolve with the IRS.

Enclosed is a copy of a tax notice dated September 1, 20xx in the amount of $892.40. I paid this on July 15, 20xx when I sent in my tax return. Enclosed is a copy of my canceled check, front and back, which shows that the IRS received the money.

I wrote the IRS on September 5, 20xx and sent a copy of this check. On October 5, 20xx, I received another notice (copy enclosed) again requesting payment. On October 10, 20xx, I sent another letter and copy of the check. On November 15, 20xx, I received a third notice for the same amount instead of a response to my two prior letters.

I can be reached during the day at my work, 303-555-1800, from 9 a.m. to 5 p.m. My address is 47 Bear Circle, Littleton, CO 80001.

Sincerely,

Benedict Cooper
Benedict Cooper

Enclosures: Copies of IRS notices and my two responses

Order, or TAO. Or, they will try to work out a solution to your problem without actually issuing a formal TAO, especially in the following situations:

- The IRS has seized or has threatened to seize your bank account, pension plan, or car. You need to pay rent or your family will be thrown out on the street, and you need that car to get to work.
- Your paycheck was garnished by the IRS, leaving you too little on which to survive. You're willing to enter into a reasonable payment plan if the wage garnishment is stopped.

What Constitutes a Significant Hardship to the IRS?

The IRS says that a significant hardship means not being able to "provide the necessities of life" for yourself or your dependents. Whether a taxpayer advocate will give you emergency assistance depends on their view of the seriousness of your hardship. Most taxpayer advocates take their role seriously and really try to help, particularly if this is your first time in trouble with the IRS.

To get the taxpayer advocate to act, you must show more than that the IRS has harmed you or is about to do so. For example, an IRS seizure is not, in and of itself, a significant hardship. The IRS's seizure or other drastic action must jeopardize:

- your ability to obtain or keep shelter, food, and clothing for yourself and your family
- your transportation to work
- your employment
- your ability to get medical care for yourself or your family
- your education
- your credit rating, or
- your ability to meet a business payroll or stay out of bankruptcy (the IRS is less likely to help a business than an individual, however).

Taxpayer advocates consider evidence that you're overwhelmed by the enormity of the tax situation. They are instructed to be sensitive to your emotional state, whether it is tears or talk of doing yourself in. Far be it from us to suggest that you have a nervous breakdown in front of a taxpayer advocate, but ….

Request for Taxpayer Advocate Service Assistance

Form **911** (January 2022)	Department of the Treasury - Internal Revenue Service **Request for Taxpayer Advocate Service Assistance** **(And Application for Taxpayer Assistance Order)**	OMB Number 1545-1504

Section I – Taxpayer Information *(See Pages 3 and 4 for Form 911 Filing Requirements and Instructions for Completing this Form.)*

1a. Taxpayer name as shown on tax return	1b. Taxpayer Identifying Number *(SSN, ITIN, EIN)*
2a. Spouse's name as shown on tax return *(if joint return)*	2b. Spouse's Taxpayer Identifying Number *(SSN, ITIN)*

3a. Taxpayer current street address *(number, street, & apt. number)*

3b. City	3c. State *(or foreign country)*	3d. ZIP code

4. Fax number *(if applicable)*	5. Email address

6. Person to contact if no authorized representative	7a. Daytime phone number	7b. ☐ Check here if you consent to have confidential information about your tax issue left on your answering machine or voice message at this number.
8. Best time to call	☐ Check if Cell Phone	

9. Preferred language *(if applicable)*
☐ TTY/TDD Line   ☐ Interpreter needed - Specify language other than English *(including sign language)*
☐ Other *(specify)*

10. Tax form number *(1040, 941, 720, etc.)*	11. Tax year(s) or period(s)

12a. Describe the tax issue you are experiencing and any difficulties it may be creating
(If more space is needed, attach additional sheets.) (See instructions for completing Lines 12a and 12b)

12b. Describe the relief/assistance you are requesting *(if more space is needed, attach additional sheets)*

I understand that Taxpayer Advocate Service employees may contact third parties in order to respond to this request and I authorize such contacts to be made. Further, by authorizing the Taxpayer Advocate Service to contact third parties, I understand that I will not receive notice, pursuant to section 7602(c) of the Internal Revenue Code, of third parties contacted in connection with this request.

13a. Signature of taxpayer or corporate officer, and title, if applicable	13b. Date signed
14a. Signature of spouse *(if joint assistance request)*	14b. Date signed

Section II – Representative Information *(Attach Form 2848 if not already on file with the IRS.)*

1. Name of authorized representative	2. Centralized Authorization File (CAF) number
3. Current mailing address	4. Daytime phone number ☐ Check if Cell Phone
	5. Fax number
6. Signature of representative	7. Date signed

Catalog Number 16965S	www.irs.gov	Form **911** (Rev. 1-2022)

Getting Hardship Relief—Calling the IRS's 911 Line

For emergency help, request a Taxpayer Assistance Order by calling your local Taxpayer Advocate Service office (the toll-free telephone number is 877-777-4778). Don't expect to get through to a taxpayer advocate immediately. Leave your telephone number for a call back, usually within 24 to 48 hours.

For problems other than last-minute emergencies, make your request using IRS Form 911, *Request for Taxpayer Advocate Service Assistance.* Get this easy-to-remember number form at the IRS website, your local IRS office, or by calling 800-829-3676. A sample is shown above. Mail or hand deliver IRS Form 911 to the closest IRS office (see Publication 1546) or file it electronically. The website form is the best choice as it can be filled in and submitted online. It's not complicated, so there's no need to hire a professional.

Expect a telephone call from the taxpayer advocate within four days to let you know if your problem will be handled and the name of the person working on it.

Nationwide, the IRS claims that it helps about half of all taxpayers who apply with Form 911 requests. In most cases, however, the taxpayer advocate won't formally issue an order requiring the IRS to stop certain action. Typically, relief is granted informally, without an official order.

Submit a 911 form to the IRS Taxpayer Advocate Service any time you feel that the IRS is ignoring you or treating you unfairly. It is free and easy to do, and you have absolutely nothing to lose. Filing the form requires the IRS to investigate quickly. You can also request an IRS employee to complete the Form 911 in person or over the phone.

Chapter Highlights

- The Taxpayer Advocate Service helps folks with problems they are having with regular IRS channels.
- A taxpayer advocate cuts through IRS red tape and provides emergency relief in special cases.
- Contact the Taxpayer Advocate Service by calling 877-777-4778 (toll free).

Family, Friends, Heirs, and the IRS

It's a Family Affair...304

    Filing Tax Returns—Joint or Separate?...304

    Divorce and the IRS..309

    Parenting and the IRS..310

    The IRS Can Take a Tax Refund for Certain Nontax Debts...........................311

Owning Property Jointly...312

Death and Taxes...313

    Filing a Federal Estate Tax Return...314

    IRS Audits of Estate Tax Returns..315

    Joint Ownership and Death...319

The tax laws contain special rules affecting folks related by blood or marriage and people who own property together. A taxpayer's responsibilities don't end at death—the taxpayer's family might inherit tax troubles. Maybe the old saying should be changed to "Nothing is certain except death and MORE taxes."

It's a Family Affair

If you're married, divorced, or a parent, familiarize yourself with some special tax rules.

Filing Tax Returns—Joint or Separate?

Married couples always have the option of filing joint tax returns or filing separate tax returns. And, if only one spouse has income, the other doesn't have to file a return—although filing jointly will likely result in a tax savings. The only qualification for filing jointly is that the couple be legally married as of December 31 of that year. Occasionally, it pays, taxwise, for married couples to file separate returns. However, taxes are higher in most instances, especially in community property states, because each spouse is considered to have earned 50% of the other spouse's income for tax purposes. If in doubt how to file, calculate your tax liability both ways each year. Computer tax programs can do this very quickly.

Same-Sex Marriage

Same-sex marriages are licensed and recognized in all 50 states. The IRS allows married same-sex couples to file as married for tax purposes. These couples can file their tax returns separately or jointly with their spouse. Generally, joint filing means an overall tax savings, but not always. A tax preparation program such as *TurboTax* allows you to easily run the numbers both ways and then decide what is better.

(!) CAUTION

Each spouse is 100% liable for all the taxes owed on a joint return. But only the spouse in whose name a separate return is filed is liable for that spouse's income taxes. So, another reason some married couples file separate tax returns is to relieve each other of direct financial responsibility if the IRS should audit one of them, or if one can't pay a tax bill.

> EXAMPLE 1: Leon and Margaret are married and always file their tax returns jointly. Leon owns a dry cleaning business, which reported an operating loss on their tax return. The couple was audited, and the IRS discovered that the business income was understated by $50,000. Leon and Margaret didn't pay the resulting $22,000 bill and the IRS filed a lien against both of them. The IRS may collect on it from any jointly or separately owned property of either Leon or Margaret.

> EXAMPLE 2: Now assume that Leon and Margaret file separate tax returns. Leon filed the phony tax return, but Margaret's return showed only her wages as an office manager. Both returns were audited. Margaret's audit resulted in no change. Leon was slapped with a $22,000 bill. The IRS filed a lien, subjecting only his assets to collection. Margaret is in the clear.

The Innocent Spouse Rule

The innocent spouse law is the one exception to the law making both currently married or former spouses responsible for an IRS debt. (I.R.C. § 6015.) If the requirements are satisfied, a spouse, or more commonly, an ex-spouse, may be relieved of joint tax debts incurred.

There are three tax law remedies available to a spouse seeking a refund or relief of a tax debt.

1. Innocent spouse relief. An innocent spouse must meet all of the following IRS requirements:

- the innocent spouse signed a joint return with a tax understatement due solely to the other spouse's actions
- at the time the spouse signed the joint return that spouse didn't know, and had no reason to know, that there was an understatement by the other spouse, and
- it would be unfair to hold the innocent spouse liable.

Avoiding Liability for Your Spouse's Dishonesty With the IRS

The innocent spouse rule isn't the only way to avoid liability for your spouse's underreporting or overdeducting to the IRS. The rules differ, depending on what state you lived in when you filed your return. The rules for community property states, non-community property states, and those that apply to all states—including the innocent spouse rule—are briefly described below. For details, see IRS Publication 555, *Community Property*.

Community Property States
(Arizona, California, Idaho, Louisiana, Nevada, New Mexico, Texas, Washington, and Wisconsin)

Innocent Spouse Rule:
- You and your spouse did not file a joint income tax return.
- You did not know and did not have reason to know of the unreported income (this means you had no knowledge of the amount of the income, and you had no knowledge of the existence of the item of income itself).
- The income belongs solely to your spouse.
- It would be unfair to include the unreported income in your income.

Abandoned Spouse Rule:
- You and your spouse were married at some time during the calendar year.
- You lived separately and apart during the entire calendar year.
- You did not file a joint return.
- You did not receive any portion of your spouse's income.

Denying Benefit of Community Property Law Rule:
If your spouse acts as if they're solely entitled to a portion of community income and doesn't tell you about that income by the time your tax return is due, your spouse will be solely responsible for reporting the income. This is because even when spouses file separate returns, each must report one-half of the combined community income.

Avoiding Liability for Your Spouse's Dishonesty With the IRS (continued)

Non-Community Property States (the rest)

Innocent Spouse Rule:

- There is a substantial understatement of tax from income and deductions of the other spouse.
- You did not know and did not have reason to know of the dishonesty. This claim presents a problem because a spouse is required to read a joint return before signing it.
- It would be unfair to hold you liable.
- You did not receive any benefit from the unreported income.

All States

Innocent Spouse Rule:

If you had no income and believed that you were not obligated to file a return, you will not be assumed to have authorized your spouse to sign your name on a joint return. You might be able to claim that your spouse forged your name to a joint return.

On the other hand, if you have your own income and don't file separately, the IRS will assume you intended to file jointly, and you can't claim that your spouse forged your name to a joint return.

Duress Rule:

You must have been unable to resist the demands of your spouse to sign the return, and you would not have signed the return if the pressure had not been applied.

2. Separation of liability relief. A spouse must have filed a joint return and meet one of the following requirements:

- be divorced or legally separated from the other spouse
- be widowed, or
- not have been living in the same house with the other spouse in the year prior to submitting the claim for relief.

3. Equitable relief. If you don't qualify as an innocent spouse or for separation of liability relief under either (1) or (2) above, you might still get out of a tax debt by showing that it would be unfair to be held liable, under all of the following circumstances:

- you and your spouse filed a joint tax return
- no assets were transferred between you and your spouse as part of a fraudulent scheme
- you did not knowingly file a fraudulent tax return
- all or part of the understatement was due to the other spouse or some of the underpayment was due to the other spouse's income, and
- you would suffer an "economic hardship" if relief were not granted.

When you owe back taxes and later file a tax return claiming a refund, the IRS usually keeps the refund and applies it to the old debt. The IRS keeps the refund of a jointly filed return even if only one of the spouses owed back taxes. If this happens, the nonowing spouse may submit a request to the IRS as an injured spouse to get their portion of the refund returned. Request relief by filing IRS Form 8379, *Injured Spouse Allocation*. A refund isn't automatically granted, and the IRS will likely request further details of your situation.

Usually, innocent spouse claims are made by divorced taxpayers. People who are still married, however, can also use the innocent spouse rule.

> EXAMPLE: Francisco and Imelda filed a joint return, were audited, and were found to have substantially underreported Francisco's business income. Francisco had skimmed about $60,000 from his delicatessen. Imelda convinced the IRS that she was an innocent spouse—she knew nothing about the income, had no reason to know about it (she was in the hospital recovering from surgery when Francisco did their taxes), and did not benefit from it (Francisco blew the money gambling)—and so it would be unfair to hold her liable. Francisco changed his ways, and the marriage survived. Imelda went back to work and, using her good credit, bought a home and obtained a mortgage in her name alone. She and Francisco lived there, and he entered into an installment payment plan with the IRS for the taxes.

To make a claim, file IRS Form 8857, *Request for Innocent Spouse Relief*, found at the IRS website. You should file Form 8857 as soon as you become aware of a tax liability for which you believe only your spouse or former spouse should be held responsible. There is a two-year time limit to file this form (commencing when the IRS began collection), except where you claim equitable relief.

Tax Court for Innocent Spouses

Were you denied innocent spouse relief by the IRS? You can sue the IRS in Tax Court. (I.R.C. § 6015.) You must file your petition within 90 days of the IRS denial notice date. Until the court decides, the IRS may not take any collection action against you. (See Chapter 5 for details on going to Tax Court.)

Divorce and the IRS

Alimony

Several tax issues arise at divorce. Alimony, sometimes called "maintenance" or "spousal support," is one. For divorces finalized before January 1, 2019, alimony payments are tax deductible to the payer and taxable income to the recipient. The alimony must be specifically ordered by a court or in a legally binding written agreement signed by both spouses. For divorces finalized in 2019 and later, payments to a spouse aren't deductible and the other spouse does not have to report them as income.

Marital Settlement Agreements (MSAs)

Divorcing couples often agree to issues of property division, debt allocation, alimony, and child support in a writing called a "marital settlement agreement," "dissolution agreement," or "separation agreement." One item that should be covered is who pays any joint tax liability—past taxes, taxes currently owed, or any that might be assessed in the future after an audit for a period during marriage.

The IRS is not bound by marital settlement agreements with regard to tax debts. The IRS can pursue either spouse, no matter what the MSA says. If the party liable under the agreement doesn't pay the tax bill and the other one does, the person who paid can sue the other in state court for reimbursement. Good luck.

You might escape joint liability for taxes by claiming innocent spouse relief. You must be divorced, legally separated, or not living in the same household for the last 12 months. You might escape the tax completely, or at least have it reduced to your proportional share.

Parenting and the IRS

The IRS seems to pop up in all areas of our lives, including parenting. Here are the rules on child support and the dependency deduction.

Child Support—Is It Deductible?

No. Child support is neither deductible for the paying parent, nor reportable as income by the recipient.

Which Parent Gets to Claim a Child as a Dependent?

Dependent children can provide valuable tax benefits. If you have a dependent, you can qualify for the child tax credit, child and dependent care credit, earned income tax credit, student loan interest deduction, and the American Opportunity Tax Credit. Divorced, single, and married parents filing separately—including separated but not yet divorced parents—can't both claim the same children as dependents. IRS computers cross-check parents' returns for this kind of double dipping.

Without a written agreement to the contrary, the parent with the children the most days gets them as dependents. But if the other parent furnishes over 50% of the child's support, that person is entitled to claim them as dependents. However, the parent claiming a child as a dependent must file with that parent's tax return IRS Form 8332, *Release/Revocation of Claim to Exemption for Child by Custodial Parent*, signed by the other parent. If the parent claims the dependent child without filing Form 8332, the IRS might contact that parent for proof that they furnished over 50% of the support.

The IRS Can Take a Tax Refund for Certain Nontax Debts

The Treasury Offset Program (TOP) allows tax refunds to be intercepted for back child support, student loans, and delinquent state taxes.

If you owe more than $150 in child support and the other parent complains or receives welfare, your state child support agency can request that the IRS send your refund directly to the state. You should first receive an intercept notice allowing you to request a hearing. But judges will intervene only if you can show that the back support has been paid or that the tax refund is greater than you owe. Rarely will a state court judge listen to a delinquent parent's claim of a desperate need for the funds.

If you're now remarried and file jointly, your new spouse can attend the hearing and file a claim for their share of the tax refund as an injured spouse. The IRS can't take this portion to satisfy a child support debt of yours. Your current spouse should file Form 8379, *Injured Spouse Allocation*.

If all or a part of your refund is intercepted wrongly—for example, the IRS took too much, or your current spouse's share was taken—you might be able to get it back. File an amended tax return on Form 1040-X to make your claim.

States with income taxes also intercept tax refunds for child support debts. In Nebraska, for example, court clerks report all child support arrears to the state tax agency. Delinquents are mailed a notice and given a hearing. Your new spouse might have the right to file a claim to have their share withheld from what is sent to your child's other parent.

For specific info on this IRS payment plan, call the TOP office at 800-304-3107.

RESOURCE

For extensive information on divorce and taxes, including the innocent spouse rule, see *Divorce & Money: Make the Best Financial Decisions During Divorce*, by Lina Guillen (Nolo). Also see IRS Publication 504, *Divorced or Separated Individuals*.

Owning Property Jointly

Many people—friends, domestic partners, parents and children, siblings, lovers, and married people who file their taxes separately—own real estate or other assets like bank accounts together. There are three serious tax dangers inherent in co-ownership, however.

Audit risk. If the joint property is held for investment, an IRS auditor might challenge the co-owners' allocation of their tax liability—how each reported annual income or losses, or the gain or loss on the sale of the asset.

> EXAMPLE: Marcus bought a warehouse with his funds and his daughter, Anita's, separate funds. He put title to the property in his name with Anita. He wanted Anita to inherit his interest in the warehouse when he died. Marcus did substantial repairs and renovations to the building, and the rents that year did not cover the expenses. Consequently, Marcus took a rental property loss on his tax return. He was audited, and the IRS held that as co-owner, he could deduct only one-half of the loss. Anita, a college student, was entitled to deduct the other half of the loss. Anita had no income, however, and so the loss was of no tax benefit to her.

Ownership risk. If one joint owner owes the IRS, the entire property might become an IRS seizure target. For instance, the IRS can easily grab a joint bank account you hold with your mother, brother, or lover to satisfy either their tax debt or yours.

> EXAMPLE: Let's stick with Marcus and Anita and change the facts a little. Several years after Anita graduates from college, she opens a business. The business folds and she's left owing the IRS $34,000. The IRS issues a seizure notice to take the warehouse because of Anita's name on the deed. Marcus calls the IRS to object to the seizure. If Marcus presents evidence showing that he is the true owner—he paid the deposit and all the mortgage payments and Anita didn't contribute anything—the IRS might hold off from seizing the property to satisfy Anita's tax debt. (See Chapter 7 for more information on seizures, and Chapter 8 for information on contacting a taxpayer advocate.)

Death risk. At the death of a joint owner, an IRS auditor may allocate 100% ownership to the estate of the deceased to maximize taxes on the estate.

All of the IRS assumptions in the scenarios above can be overcome. Legal precedent allows joint owners to:

- allocate income, losses, and deductions unequally, according to the contributions of the co-owners toward the purchase and maintenance of the property
- keep their share of joint property away from the IRS, and
- prove that true property ownership is not necessarily what is stated on a deed or other title document.

But to convince an auditor, an appeals officer, or a Tax Court judge, you must provide testimony or other evidence showing that the way title is held does *not* reflect the property's true ownership. If this is your situation, see a tax professional—preferably a tax lawyer.

Death and Taxes

 RESOURCE
This book isn't about estate planning, but we will go over some tax basics. There is good information on the subject in *Plan Your Estate*, by Denis Clifford (Nolo). You can get free information on death-related taxes from the IRS. Visit the IRS's website at www.irs.gov.

IRS problems don't always stop at death—at least for the survivors. Past income taxes can be collected from an estate or from its heirs. For instance, a few years back a drug smuggler and his plane went down with narcotics aboard. The IRS presented a tax bill to his estate of several million dollars based upon the street value of the drugs, which were subsequently destroyed by the police.

Audits begun before death or even after must be defended by your estate's personal representative or executor. The executor is legally responsible for paying all income or estate taxes from your assets before your heirs get anything.

If you're an heir, an executor, a personal representative, or an administrator and are concerned about taxes owed by a decedent or an estate, ask a tax professional, or get IRS Publication 559, *Survivors, Executors, and Administrators*.

CAUTION
If estate taxes are due, the IRS holds an automatic tax lien on all estate assets. (I.R.C. § 6324.) The IRS can seize money or property from the heirs and executors if the tax isn't paid, for up to 10 years after the estate tax is determined. Check for updates on the estate tax.

Filing a Federal Estate Tax Return

Under the current law, 99% of us won't have to worry about the federal estate tax. Of course, if the law changes or you win the lottery, this section might be of great interest.

If the gross value of an estate—everything owned at death—exceeds the estate tax-exempt amount: $12.92 million in 2023 ($25.84 million for married couples) and indexed for inflation in future years, the estate's executor must file a federal estate tax return (Form 706). Anything over the exempt allowance for the year of death is taxed—except what is left to a spouse. (Certain other bequests are also tax free.)

If the net value of an estate is less than the exempt amount, the estate won't owe federal taxes—assuming no taxable gifts were made during the decedent's lifetime. This exception means that you can't avoid the estate tax by making large gifts to anyone other than your spouse—if the total given away and remaining in your estate exceeds the exemption allowed for the year that you die.

EXAMPLE: Doug died in 2023. He was a widower with cash worth $11.7 million and he owned two houses. House One has a market value of $800,000, with $700,000 still owing on the mortgage. The market value of House Two is $500,000; the mortgage balance is $100,000.

Gross Estate			Net Estate		
Money market		$ 11,700,000	Money market		$ 11,700,000
House 1 mkt value	+	800,000	House 1 equity	+	100,000
House 2 mkt value	+	500,000	House 2 equity	+	400,000
Gross Estate		$ 13,000,000	Net Estate		$ 12,200,000

Because Doug's gross estate exceeds the $12,920,000 exempt amount, his executor must file a federal estate tax return. Doug's estate won't owe any federal taxes, however, because the net value of $12.2 million is less than the exemption. It might owe state death taxes, however, depending on the law in the state Doug lived in.

IRS Audits of Estate Tax Returns

The larger the estate shown on the federal estate tax return, the more likely an audit. The IRS figures that there is more incentive to cheat when a lot of money is at stake. The overall estate tax return audit rate is 15%. While the estate tax audit rate has dropped in recent years, the additional tax and penalties collected has more than made up the slack.

When the IRS picks an estate tax return for audit, the estate tax auditor will automatically scrutinize the deceased taxpayer's last two income tax returns.

SEE AN EXPERT

Hire a professional if the estate is over the exempt amount. The personal representative of an estate should hire a top-flight tax professional—a CPA or tax attorney—to prepare an estate tax return whenever the estate exceeds the exempt amount. It's a deductible expense.

An estate tax audit is similar to an audit of an income tax return. Both require documentation and explanation of the data on the tax return. (See Chapter 3.) However, the legal issues are quite different from the audit of a living taxpayer—typically more complex. This is a tax professional's territory.

In contrast to an audit of a live taxpayer, an estate tax auditor does extensive investigation before the estate is notified of the audit. The auditor will likely go to the probate court and copy documents from the file and research legal issues, such as marital property rights.

The auditor begins the examination interview by requesting documentation of common items like administration expenses, such as lawyer's fees. Ordinarily, canceled checks and paid bills will adequately substantiate these deductible expenses listed on the Form 706 tax return.

After covering routine matters, the auditor moves on to thornier issues, such as the value of stock in a family corporation or whether any deathbed gifts were made to cut down the size of the estate. If so, the auditor will want to know how the stock was valued or if the proper gift tax returns were filed.

Dealing With an Estate Tax Auditor

A personal representative should not handle an estate tax audit without a top-flight tax professional. Estate return audits are usually held at the IRS offices. You or your tax professional might need to research the law or secure additional documents. If the auditor wants more records, the auditor will schedule another meeting and give you an Information Document Request at the conclusion of the day.

Estate auditors are more likely to intimidate a personal representative than an experienced tax professional. Auditors will negotiate tax issues on which the facts or law are uncertain, if you know how to play the game. Estate auditors want to close out cases without appeals. (See Chapter 3, for tips on negotiating with an auditor.)

If you aren't happy with the way the estate tax audit comes out, you can appeal (see Chapter 4) or go to Tax Court (see Chapter 5).

CAUTION

IRS estate tax auditors are the cream of the IRS crop and are usually CPAs or lawyers. They can spot things like whether the assets listed are consistent with the deceased person's lifestyle, business, or profession. They are always skeptical of the values of assets listed in estate tax returns. That's why you should always bring a tax pro.

What Estate Tax Auditors Look For

Auditors look out for certain red flags on estate tax returns. (*Internal Revenue Manual* 4350.) Some hot items include the following:

- **Unrealistically low valuations of estate assets.** This is the single most common adjustment made by auditors. Heirs and the personal representative might be tempted to undervalue an estate asset because the estate tax is so heavy. It is easy to value bank accounts and publicly traded stocks and bonds. Family businesses, real estate, art, antiques, and other items, however, all present valuation issues for the IRS to probe.

TIP

Get written appraisals. The personal representative of the estate should always get written appraisals of all large assets other than cash and listed securities. Many states mandate court-appointed appraisers for estate assets. The IRS is not bound by any appraiser's figures. The IRS may hire its own appraiser if a valuation is questionable or if the estate's value is in the millions of dollars.

- **A discount of an asset's value.** Discounts from fair market value may be legitimately taken by appraisers to value the interests in family LLCs, partnerships, or corporations. Discounts must satisfy specific tax rules. For example, the fair market value of Veronica's 40% share of a family limited partnership dry cleaning business is $1,800,000 when she dies. But because there are few buyers for a minority interest in a small business, a discount of 30% to $1,260,000 for estate tax purposes would likely pass muster.

- **Claims against the estate by heirs, for more than what they would otherwise inherit.** For example, Sam's estate tax return shows a $500,000 promissory note from Sam, the deceased parent, to Sam, Jr. Because this claim reduces the taxable estate, an auditor will want details on when and why the loan was made and to see the loan documents.
- **Property in safe deposit boxes** that might not have been shown on the tax return. The personal representative should inventory the box's contents and attach this to the estate tax return, along with an appraisal of any valuables.
- **Erroneous or incomplete estate tax returns.** Expect a problem if schedules or documentation that normally accompany an estate tax return are missing. An estate tax return (Form 706) is longer and has more attachments than does an ordinary tax return. Have it prepared by a tax pro or an attorney to reduce IRS audit issues.
- **Any gift tax returns that were filed during the deceased's lifetime.** The auditor will compare past gift tax returns with the estate tax return for consistency. For example, Malia filed a gift tax return five years prior to her death showing that she gave her daughter, Ariana, a home worth $1,500,000. The law requires all large lifetime gifts to be listed on the estate tax return. Also, the auditor will look for occasions when a gift tax return should have been filed but was not.

CAUTION

Are you the executor or personal representative of an estate with heirs other than yourself and with assets worth more than the exemption amount? See an experienced CPA or tax lawyer. (See Chapter 13 for information on finding a CPA or lawyer.) Don't take any chances—you are personally liable to the IRS, as well as to the heirs, if you understate or don't pay all estate taxes due—including those that might be assessed on an estate tax audit. The estate should pay your professional fees for this service.

EXAMPLE: Randolph, an executor, filed a federal estate return for his deceased old friend, Gregory. He listed values of various estate assets, including artwork, according to a list that Gregory prepared shortly before he died. He did not hire any professional appraisers.

Per Gregory's wishes, Randolph distributed the estate's assets to Gregory's son, Isaac, who promptly blew the money in Vegas. The IRS audited the estate tax return two years later and found the estate assets were undervalued by $2,000,000. The estate was hit with a tax bill of almost $800,000 with penalties and interest. "But all of the estate assets are gone," Randolph said. "Too bad," said the IRS. Legally, Randolph, as executor of the estate, was personally liable for the tax!

If Randolph had gotten bona fide appraisals, he could have properly prepared the tax return and paid the estate tax bill.

TIP

Reduce your chances of an IRS estate tax audit. Attach copies of appraisals and other documents supporting valuations to the federal estate tax return. This documentation is the first thing the IRS looks for in deciding whether to audit an estate tax return.

Joint Ownership and Death

Contrary to popular belief, you can't escape federal estate taxes through joint ownership of assets. The only exception is when the co-owners are legally married to each other. If a joint owner dies, an IRS auditor may reallocate all the ownership shares to the deceased person's estate if the other co-owner can't prove that they contributed equally to acquire the asset.

This issue is a concern only for nonspouse co-owners who hold their property as joint tenants with the right of survivorship—where the survivor(s) automatically inherits the deceased person's share.

EXAMPLE: Hilda (mother) and Gertie (daughter) jointly hold title to an apartment building free and clear with a market value of $5 million. Hilda bought the building many years ago with the proceeds of a life insurance policy she received when her husband died. Gertie made no contributions to the purchase price of the property or for its upkeep. When Gertie reached adulthood, Hilda added her name to the deed so that Gertie would inherit the building without going through probate.

After Hilda died, Gertie filed a federal estate tax return listing the building's value at $2.5 million, thinking that only her mother's one-half ownership portion was taxable. The IRS audited the return and properly reallocated the entire $5 million to Hilda's estate, producing a hefty tax bill. Even though Gertie avoided probate, the joint ownership didn't avoid the estate tax.

Chapter Highlights

- There are special tax rules for folks related by blood or marriage.
- Married couples filing taxes jointly should be aware of negative consequences to one spouse if there is a tax balance due.
- Owning property jointly with another might have some hidden tax traps.
- Death often brings estate tax issues requiring professional help.

Fraud and Tax Crimes: Do You Really Have to Worry?

How People Commit Tax Fraud 322

If You Are Caught Cheating 322

    The IRS Suspects You of Fraud 323

    Options When the IRS Finds Fraud 327

IRS Criminal Investigations 329

    How Special Agents Conduct Investigations 329

    IRS Considerations in Deciding Whether to Recommend Prosecution 334

    Crimes You Can Be Charged With 335

If You Are Prosecuted 336

    Should You Plead Not Guilty? 336

    What the Government Must Prove 337

    Possible Defenses 338

    If You Are Convicted 339

f you follow the news, you've seen stories about tax cheaters going to jail. In this chapter we'll take a look at exactly what gets you into criminal tax trouble, how the IRS finds out, and the worst that can happen.

According to the IRS, individuals—mostly middle- and high-income earners—do 75% of the tax cheating. Business entities do most of the rest of the cheating. Cash-intensive businesses and service providers, from laundromat businesses to doctors, are the worst offenders according to the IRS.

Second on the tax cheaters hit parade are *false claims*—for example, filing multiple tax returns claiming refunds, typically from the Earned Income Credit program, or claiming a bunch of nonexistent dependents, or falsely seeking a tax refund from an earlier year on an amended tax return.

Third on the cheating scale, and somewhat surprising, is the IRS report that exaggerating or claiming outright phony deductions comes far behind income underreporting and false claims.

How People Commit Tax Fraud

Most cheating is from deliberate—actual or willful—underreporting of income. This kind of cheating is called "tax evasion"—the most commonly charged tax crime. A government study found that a lot of underreporting of income was by self-employed restaurateurs, clothing store owners, and car dealers. Telemarketers and salespeople came in next, followed by doctors, lawyers, accountants, and hairdressers.

More recently, the IRS criminal investigators are hot on the trail of offshore tax evasion schemes. Just because your assets are out of the country doesn't mean the IRS won't find out. Just ask the people who were ratted out by their Swiss bankers.

If You Are Caught Cheating

Cheating is often first spotted during an audit. If you are caught in a tax lie, an auditor can either slap you with a heavy fraud penalty or refer your case to the IRS's Criminal Investigation Division (CI). In the vast majority of cases, the auditor won't call in the CI.

The IRS Suspects You of Fraud

Auditors are trained to look for "badges" of tax fraud. Tax fraud is defined as a willful act done with the intent to defraud the IRS—that dark area beyond honest mistakes. Badges include a false Social Security number, keeping two sets of financial books, claiming a child or spouse as a dependent when you're single, dealing in cash, and concealing your assets. While auditors look for fraud, however, they do not routinely suspect it. They know the tax law is complex and expect to find a few careless mistakes in every tax return. They will give you the benefit of the doubt most of the time.

If the auditor finds but doesn't refer suspected fraud to the CI, the auditor can impose fines, called civil penalties. This is most likely to happen if you omitted a chunk of taxable income on your tax return. Phony deductions can also be punished by the fraud civil penalty—for example, claiming deductions for nonexistent dependents. Fraud penalties can also be added for exaggerating deductions, such as adding a zero to $200 making it $2,000, or by claiming a casualty loss for a nonexistent accident.

The *Internal Revenue Manual* directs auditors suspecting serious criminal tax fraud to contact the CI. In reality, auditors make very few criminal referrals. Making a fraud referral is added paperwork. If auditors find a couple of obviously phony receipts, they usually will quietly disallow them and move on.

In recent years, CI's investigative priorities included employment taxes, virtual currency, offshore tax evasion, and return preparer fraud. The CI is currently focusing on fraud related to the coronavirus (COVID-19) pandemic. During the pandemic, millions of businesses received substantial payments from the IRS by claiming the Employee Retention Credit and got forgivable Paycheck Protection Program loans from the Small Business Administration. Billions of dollars' worth of credits and loans were likely obtained fraudulently. CI field offices are partnering with other law enforcement agencies, including state attorneys general, to prosecute such fraud.

 CAUTION

The auditor won't tell you if they've made a criminal fraud referral. One indication, however, might be an audit's stopping midstream for no apparent reason. But never assume a fraud referral was made just because months pass and you don't hear from the auditor. The person is probably just behind in their work.

Fraud or Negligence?

A negligent mistake on your tax return might get you a 20% penalty tacked on to your tax bill. While not good, this sure beats the cost of tax fraud—a 75% civil penalty. The line between negligence and fraud is not always clear, however, even to the IRS and the courts.

Field auditors, called "revenue agents," are trained to spot common types of wrongdoing. Examples include a business with two sets of books or without any records at all, freshly made documents, and canceled checks altered to increase deductions. Altered canceled checks are easy to spot by comparing written numbers with computer coding on the check or bank statements.

Indirect Methods of Proving Fraud

Direct proof of fraud by the IRS typically consists of an admission of wrongdoing or finding unsubstantiated deductions and exemptions. The IRS doesn't usually find direct proof of income underreporting. Instead, the IRS relies primarily on four indirect methods.

Specific items. If you cashed a check received by your business and pocketed the money without entering it in your books, this check is a "specific item." It can be viewed as indirect proof of fraudulent intent. If the auditor suspects fraud, they might talk to your business's customers and compare your bank account deposits and actual payments you received from customers.

The IRS wants more than just one specific item to make a fraud case—unless the item was for many thousands of dollars. While you might argue that 1 or 2 items were negligently left off the books (or your computer crashed or you lost your records), 15 or 20 omitted items shows a pattern of fraud.

Bank deposits. This is the IRS's favorite indirect method to prove unreported income, because it's so easy. The IRS simply adds up all deposits in your bank accounts. If the total exceeds your reported income, you might be suspected of fraud.

There might be a perfectly legitimate explanation, such as nontaxable sources of bank deposits—loans, gifts, inheritances, sales of assets, and tax-exempt income, such as municipal bond interest. Also, transfers from one bank account to another appear to be multiple deposits under this simplistic method. Point this out to the suspicious auditor. Or, deposits in your accounts might belong to relatives or friends who did not use their own accounts for some reason.

Expenditures. The IRS calculates your living expenses by totaling up the credit charges you paid and checks you wrote, and adding known or estimated expenses you paid by cash. If the total is greater than your tax-reported income, the IRS will suspect fraud. The IRS has statistical reference books showing average costs of various necessities, such as food and shelter, in your community.

To counter this, explain where you got the money to pay your bills. It could be savings from prior years, selling assets, or receiving loans or gifts. To figure your living expenses, the IRS often asks you to complete IRS Form 4822, *Statement of Annual Estimated Personal and Family Expenses.*

TIP

Never fill out IRS Form 4822 listing your living expenses. Just say you didn't keep track of every penny you spent for the year and don't want to guess. Or, diplomatically say you will consider it and then throw the form away. The IRS can't punish you for refusing to fill out this form. If the IRS is intent on proving fraud, it will do it with or without your cooperation.

Net worth. Under this indirect method, the IRS adds up all of your assets and deducts all of your liabilities at the start and end of the tax year. If there was an increase in your net worth—what you own minus what you owe—without an increase in income from the previous tax year, you might be suspected of fraud.

Again, there are many valid explanations as to how your net worth can increase besides unreported income. For example, you might have received nontaxable gifts or loans or inheritances. Or the IRS might have mistakenly included appreciation of assets in its calculations.

Penalties for Civil Tax Fraud

You will probably never face *criminal* fraud penalties. Up to 98% of the time, the IRS punishes fraud with *civil* penalties—fines of 75% added to the tax due. For example, if the additional tax due from fraud is $10,000, the penalty can be $7,500, for a total of $17,500. Interest is added on to both the tax and the fraud penalty, starting on the date the return was due or filed, whichever is later.

Defending Against Alleged Tax Fraud

The three defenses most often raised against tax fraud allegations are cash hoard, nontaxable income, and honest mistake. Don't expect the IRS to accept any of these defenses at face value. A skilled attorney is better able to persuade the IRS than you are. Combatting tax fraud, like brain surgery, is not a do-it-yourself project.

I lived off my cash hoard. This defense can be raised whenever the IRS uses the bank deposits, expenditures, or net worth methods of proving fraud. There is no law (not yet, anyway) against having cash of any amount buried in your backyard or kept in a safe deposit box. The IRS's only legitimate concerns with your cash holdings are whether they were from taxable income, and if you reported them and paid tax on them. The IRS understandably is suspicious of people who hold large amounts of cash rather than putting it in an interest-bearing account.

I lived off a nontaxable source. The receipt of money is not always taxable income, as discussed above. You might innocently acquire tax-free wealth by gift, loans, inheritances, and other ways. This defense can be coupled with the cash hoard defense.

I made an honest mistake. If you make an error on your tax return, it is not necessarily fraud. For example, you didn't report profit from a sale of investment real estate because you believed you had two years to reinvest the proceeds without tax consequences. In reality, the law only allows you 180 days. Because intent to cheat the IRS is required for fraud, your mistaken belief is a valid defense to a tax fraud charge—but you might have to convince a judge or jury that it really was a mistake.

> CAUTION
>
> **Don't try to lie your way out of a fraud charge.** If in doubt, keep your mouth closed. Lying to the IRS can make matters worse. The right against self-incrimination is guaranteed by the Fifth Amendment. You have the absolute right to remain silent before the IRS whenever there is a possibility you might be charged with a crime. Lying to an IRS employee can result in a felony conviction with up to three years in prison and a $100,000 fine.

Options When the IRS Finds Fraud

If an IRS auditor believes you've cheated on your taxes, the auditor has several options.

Ignore the cheating. If the amount is small, an IRS auditor will overlook it. Typically, an auditor just wants the file closed—particularly if there are other significant adjustments. The auditor will likely leave it at that and never refer your file to the CI.

Impose civil penalties. IRS auditors draw the line at outrageous cheating. Most will add civil, not criminal, penalties on to your tax bill, especially if your case is deemed too small to send to the CI.

For small mistakes, auditors can add a 20% penalty if your tax error was "accuracy related." For example, if you owe an additional $1,500 of taxes, they can add a penalty of $300, bringing the bill to $1,800. The IRS imposes civil penalties about 25 million times each year. For more serious misdeeds, auditors can add a 75% penalty, bringing your $1,500 tax bill to $2,625. And, interest will be added to both the penalty and the taxes.

Begin a criminal investigation. If the auditor suspects that you have gone too far, the CI is called in, and the audit is suspended.

The CI usually gets information that leads to an investigation from one of the following sources:

- referrals from other IRS divisions, such as the Employment Tax, Small Business, or Excise Tax departments
- tips from law enforcement agencies; the IRS isn't concerned with the nontax crime itself, often a drug-related offense, but whether the illegal income was reported.

> EXAMPLE: When Morgan was arrested for suspected drug trafficking, $150,000 in cash was in his car's trunk. After his arrest, the local police notified the IRS. The CI looked at Morgan's last few tax returns, where he reported only $35,000 of income per year. The CI immediately began a formal investigation.

- tips from citizens such as ex-spouses or disgruntled employees and business associates. These people are called "squeals" by the CI. The CI usually follows up only on well-documented tips. Many allegations are not provable and are motivated by spite, and the CI doesn't waste its time on them. It may refer the case for audit, however.

- IRS undercover or sting operations; CI agents often pose as buyers of businesses to find off-the-books income. Unwary sellers who brag about second sets of books and how much cash the business takes in get nailed. Other undercover operations investigate gross discrepancies between reported income and a taxpayer's lifestyle. This is how the U.S. government finally got Al Capone!

> EXAMPLE: Roy owned a rather seedy-looking pawn shop and was featured in a local newspaper article on successful businesspeople. Roy proudly posed for the paper in front of his waterfront home and Rolls Royce. Soon thereafter, Roy was audited. The IRS wanted to know how someone lived so well while reporting only $20,000 a year income. The audit turned into a lengthy CI investigation. Two CI agents pored over six years of Roy's financial records, business and personal. Eighteen months later, Roy was indicted for criminal tax evasion, convicted, and sentenced to five years in federal prison.

At the conclusion of a criminal tax investigation, the CI has two options—drop it forever or recommend that the Justice Department prosecute. The IRS, a part of the Treasury Department, can't directly prosecute anyone. If the Justice Department declines to prosecute, your case will likely be sent for an audit and you'll face civil fraud penalties.

The Justice Department is picky, so the CI won't waste its time referring (and, in some cases, even seriously investigating) a case unless it feels it has a sure winner, or a newsworthy defendant.

If the CI does recommend prosecuting and the Justice Department gets a conviction, you can be imprisoned, put on probation, fined, or all three. For example, if you're convicted of failing to file a tax return for three separate years, you can be sent to prison for one year and fined up to $25,000 for each year you didn't file. The total could be three years in prison and $75,000 in fines. You will also have a permanent criminal record.

That's not all. After a criminal conviction, an auditor will slap on civil fraud and other penalties for underpayment of taxes. Combining criminal and civil punishment does not constitute double jeopardy—the constitutional guarantee against being tried, convicted, or sentenced more than once for the same crime.

If you are prosecuted but not convicted, you will nonetheless probably be audited.

IRS Criminal Investigations

The IRS police force is called the "Criminal Investigation Division" (CI). This branch has 3,000 employees, 2,000 of whom are called "special agents." CI agents are spread throughout the United States and abroad. Special agents are not out to audit you or collect a dime of taxes. Their sole purpose is to put tax cheaters in prison. They are armed and have badges but no uniforms. Make no mistake—they are detectives highly trained by the IRS and FBI. If someone identifies themself as an IRS special agent, you or someone you know is under suspicion. Special agents travel in pairs for their protection and to corroborate oral evidence gathered during an investigation.

The CI is divided into general and special enforcement sections. Special enforcement targets organized crime, drugs, and unions. General enforcement watches ordinary taxpayers and everything else.

The CI also investigates nontax financial crimes like money laundering.

How Special Agents Conduct Investigations

In a recent year (pre-pandemic), 5,314 criminal investigations were started by the CI. Here are some sobering statistics: In 82% of the cases, the suspects were recommended for prosecution. Of these cases, 88% were accepted by the Department of Justice for a tax crime trial. The conviction rate at trial, or after a guilty plea, was 86%. Of those convicted, 80% went to prison. Cutting through the numbers, 2,812 folks, representing 53% of all CI investigations, went to jail. Criminal investigations and prosecutions fell off during the COVID-19 pandemic but should ramp up again, particularly for hot-button areas such as COVID-related tax fraud.

Only if the IRS has strong indications of wrongdoing does it send out its elite police. Cases involving less than $20,000 in taxes are rarely investigated. A criminal investigation starts with special agents interviewing the taxpayer's friends, business associates, professional advisers, and anyone else who might have information. Later on, the special agents usually invite the targeted individual to speak to them.

CI investigations work in the reverse order of regular detective probes. The TV series "CSI" starts with a dead body—and then figures out whodunit. Step 1 is the crime; Step 2 is finding the culprit. This is the standard solving-the-mystery approach.

In contrast, IRS investigations begin with an allegation from a source, usually an IRS auditor, a collector, or an informant, that a tax crime might have been committed. Then special agents work at building a case. Step 1 is naming the suspect; Step 2 is finding the crime. Special agents are among the best trained of all federal employees (FBI Academy). And they have the full resources of the federal government behind them. They also carry guns.

Contacting Everyone Around the Target

CI investigations are unbelievably thorough, often taking several years to complete. The IRS spends more time investigating a criminal tax case than other police departments devote to murder cases. This intensive use of federal resources explains why relatively few people are charged with tax crimes, and most are convicted. The CI recommends prosecution only when it has built a rock-solid case.

Will You Know If You're Being Investigated?

Unless and until you are formally charged, you might not know that you're being investigated by the CI. The IRS does not have to tell you, but often does. A friend, an employee, your accountant, your tax preparer, your lawyer, or anyone else contacted by the IRS during the investigation might tell you first. The IRS can't legally swear these people to secrecy.

You might be able to find out indirectly if you are under investigation. When a criminal investigation begins, IRS personnel must complete and file Form 4135, *CI Control Notice*. This data is entered into your master file in the IRS computer. Your tax account is frozen, meaning that no refunds can be made or payments credited to your account.

You might find out if Form 4135 has been filed by sending a token tax payment for a year you believe is under investigation—even if you've paid the tax already. If a freeze is in effect, you might receive notice that your payment is being held in a suspense account. Also, obtain a transcript of your account for any year in question using the IRS Get Transcript Online tool (www.irs.gov/individuals/get-transcript). The printout might indicate a Form 4135 filing or show that the payment was not credited to your account without explanation.

Alternatively, the IRS might never send your transcript if it has a criminal investigation freeze code in the computer. If you call, IRS employees are told to not answer if you ask whether a Form 4135 has been filed.

If you are under investigation, special agents may talk to your friends, family, neighbors, coworkers, employees, business associates, bankers, insurance agents, travel agents, and stores where you shop. Even your spouse may be contacted. Your mail may be monitored, in cooperation with the Postal Service. While the IRS can't open mail, it follows leads from return addresses. The CI may get copies of bills from phone and credit card companies, follow you, go through your garbage, or get a court order authorizing a phone tap.

Special agents subtly intimidate businesspeople and bankers into giving information. Don't expect even your most trusted advisers to protect you if the CI comes calling.

When IRS Special Agents Contact Your Associates and Friends

If you're contacted by IRS special agents about another person, be wary. Don't answer any questions if there is any possibility you could be connected to the individual under probe. And read "connected to" broadly. If you worked as the manager in a shop and the owner is under investigation, you might not yet be a suspect, but there's a chance you will be. Keep quiet until you speak to a lawyer.

In any event, never lie to the CI. The law does not allow you to protect others by withholding information or lying. It is legal, however, to tell someone that the IRS is asking about them.

If someone tells you that they've been contacted in an IRS criminal investigation of you and asks you what to say, don't give any suggestions. It's a separate crime to ask someone to lie to or mislead the IRS. Never call the CI and ask what's going on; you'll be grilled with questions. Instead, call a tax or criminal lawyer fast. Let them call the IRS.

If the CI Contacts You

If the CI is building a case against you, chances are you will be the last person interviewed. By the time the special agents contact you, they might have looked at thousands of records and spoken to 20 potential witnesses—your banker, ex-spouse, accountant, former employees, and others with knowledge of your financial affairs. If the CI still wants to talk to you, more than likely you are about to be recommended for prosecution. The *only* purpose for the CI questioning you is to get a confession or other damaging admission—the icing on the IRS's cake.

Once you're the target of an investigation, a special agent must read to you a version of the *Miranda* rights—the right to remain silent, the right to have an attorney, and the warning that anything you say can be used against you. Believe us, it will be. Answer only the question, "Are you [your name]?" and simply say that you want to contact an attorney. Don't call an attorney while the special agents are present, unless they threaten you with immediate arrest if you don't cooperate. Wait until they leave, you have calmed down, and you can speak freely. If you don't know a criminal-tax attorney, see Chapter 13 for tips on finding one.

How about trying to talk the special agents out of pursuing their case against you? Forget it—it's a terrible mistake. It makes no difference to them if your mother is dying, you're broke, or your marriage is falling apart. Mentioning your problems only strengthens the IRS's position; giving an excuse often shows that you knew what you did was wrong. Similarly, don't lie. Lying is as serious a crime as tax evasion.

Attorney-Client Privilege

In a criminal matter, the only person who can't be forced to speak about you to the IRS is your lawyer. This is a special relationship given protection under the law—called the "attorney-client privilege." Your lawyer can't disclose to the IRS anything you say that relates to a criminal tax matter. And, if an accountant is employed by your attorney to help render legal advice, the accountant's work also falls under the attorney-client privilege and can't be disclosed to the IRS in a criminal matter. While there is a nonattorney tax practitioner-client privilege, it doesn't extend to criminal tax matters. In short, unless your tax pro is also an attorney, they can be compelled to give evidence or testimony against you.

CAUTION

Keep your mouth shut—take this advice seriously. If you give the CI agents any opening, you're dead. They'll start with soft background questions, but before you know it, will have trapped you. And many CI questions won't be genuine—that is, the special agents already know the answers and are asking only to see if you will lie or confess.

Questions typically asked by CI agents include:

Have you reported all of your income?

Where are your bank accounts and safe deposit boxes?

Can you tell us about the cars, boats, planes, and real estate that you own?

Do you gamble?

What is the procedure for reporting sales in your business?

Do you keep a lot of cash on hand?

Who are your business associates?

Have you traveled out of the country recently?

Have you or any of your businesses been audited?

Faced with a barrage of questions from two trained CI agents who show up unannounced, most people fall apart. They blurt out a confession or a transparent lie within five minutes. This gives the Justice Department the rope to hang them with.

IRS Considerations in Deciding Whether to Recommend Prosecution

The CI's chief consideration in deciding to recommend prosecution is how strong a case it has. If you were caught red-handed or confessed, you can be sure of prosecution. But remember—for any crime, including a tax crime, the government must prove your guilt beyond a reasonable doubt. If you keep your mouth closed, a good criminal-tax lawyer might be able to mount a decent defense. As a general rule, if you have some facts in your favor, the IRS might not recommend prosecution and might impose civil penalties (fines) instead.

The IRS looks closely at the case's publicity value—locally or nationwide. A prominent local doctor or movie star is a juicy plum. The agency firmly believes that front-page headlines make would-be tax cheaters think twice.

The CI also analyzes personality traits of the individual target, including age, physical and mental health, and previous criminal record. How would a jury react to the person? Leona "Only the Little People Pay Taxes" Helmsley was no doubt selected for prosecution because the IRS guessed she'd be an unsympathetic figure. The judge and jury (and most Americans) obviously agreed. Leona went to prison.

Finally, the CI looks at the amount you cheated the government out of. The larger your indiscretion, the more likely the agents will recommend prosecution. The typical amount of taxes owed in criminal cases is over $70,000 and covers three or more years of cheating.

Crimes You Can Be Charged With

If the CI recommends prosecution, it will turn its evidence over to the Justice Department to decide the special charges. Individuals are typically charged with one or more of three crimes: tax evasion, filing a false return, or not filing a tax return.

Tax evasion or fraud. Tax evasion is defined as "intentional conduct to defeat the income tax laws." Any sort of tax scheme to cheat the government can fall into this broad category. Tax evasion is a felony, the most serious type of crime. For each tax year, the maximum prison sentence is five years; the maximum fine is $100,000. (I.R.C. § 7201.)

Filing a false return. Filing a false return is what it sounds like. Your tax return contained a material misstatement, such as describing your line of work as bricklaying when you are a bookie. More people are charged with filing a false return than with tax evasion because in a filing-a-false-return case, the government does not have to prove an intent to evade the income tax laws—only an intent to file a false return. Filing a false return is a less serious felony than tax evasion and for each tax year it carries a maximum prison term of three years and a maximum fine of $100,000. (I.R.C. § 7206(1).)

Failure to file a tax return. Not filing a return is the least serious tax crime. It's defined as intentionally failing to file a return when you were obligated to do so. Not everyone must file tax returns. For example, only those people earning above a specified amount must file. The minimum changes from year to year. Not filing a tax return is a misdemeanor. The maximum prison sentence is one year in jail and/or a fine of $25,000 for each year not filed. The vast majority of nonfilers are never prosecuted criminally and are only hit with civil fines.

Money laundering. Although technically not tax crimes, the CI also investigates and can recommend prosecution for money laundering and filing false claims against the IRS. Typically, these crimes are charged in the same case along with tax crimes against the same individual or entity.

If You Are Prosecuted

Once the Justice Department receives a file recommended for criminal prosecution, an assistant U.S. attorney reviews it. If the prosecutor feels that the IRS has a strong felony case, they will seek an indictment from a federal grand jury, which almost always goes along with the government. You can be directly charged for a tax misdemeanor—such as not filing a tax return—without a grand jury indictment.

Once charged, you will either be arrested or, if you are not deemed a flight risk, ordered to report before a federal judge to enter a plea. You might be required to post bail or be released on your own recognizance.

If you ever find yourself in this position, find a criminal or tax lawyer immediately. Don't delay, as the government has already completed its investigation. Your lawyer will need time to catch up and learn the government's case. Keep heart; the government's case might be legally defective, or your attorney might recognize defenses to the charges. In any case, don't be your own lawyer.

Should You Plead Not Guilty?

Unless you have made a plea bargain with the government before your first court appearance, your lawyer will have you plead not guilty. Remember: The IRS recommends for prosecution only those cases in which conviction seems a near certainty. The Justice Department weeds these cases out even further. Therefore, it's not surprising that over two-thirds of all defendants eventually change their pleas to guilty without going to trial.

This is called "plea bargaining," meaning you will plead guilty if the Justice Department agrees to reduce or drop some charges, or both. For example, if you are charged with three years of tax evasion, the government might drop two years for a guilty plea to one year. Sometimes the government will also agree to a favorable sentencing recommendation. However, the final sentence will depend on a presentence investigation report, federal laws governing minimum sentences, and the judge's discretion.

What the Government Must Prove

If you don't plead guilty, your case will be set for trial. At the trial, the Justice Department and the IRS, working together, must prove you are guilty of the crimes charged. Essentially, the government must show you acted intentionally and that you are guilty beyond a reasonable doubt. You are entitled to a trial by a jury, or you can choose to be tried by the judge alone. A jury is the best choice for most people.

Intent. The primary element of any tax crime is intent. In legalese, this intent is called "willfulness." If the government can't prove you acted intentionally, you can't be convicted. Put another way, you can't be convicted of a tax crime if you only made a mistake, even if it was a big mistake. For example, if you didn't file a tax return because you honestly believed that 65-year-olds didn't have to file any longer, you did not act intentionally.

Before you senior citizens get carried away with this example, bear in mind that to succeed, you will have to convince a jury that your mistaken belief was honest. Given that most people remember watching their parents or grandparents fill out returns—and many people, in fact, completed those returns for their elderly relatives—you will have a hard time convincing your 12 peers that your omission was an honest mistake. More believable is a recent immigrant who did not report their income from investments made back home, which they wrongly thought were tax exempt.

Beyond a reasonable doubt. All crimes must be proven beyond a reasonable doubt. If a judge or jury has any degree of doubt that you did what you were accused of or acted intentionally, the government's case will fail. For instance, without additional evidence showing an intent to cheat the IRS, a juror might not believe beyond a reasonable doubt that an immigrant who omitted his foreign investment income was filing a false tax return. The reasonable doubt standard is why the Justice Department prosecutes only airtight cases.

Possible Defenses

Not everyone charged with a tax crime is found guilty. For example, keep in mind the story of Dr. Rudy Mays, a former client whose name has been changed.

> EXAMPLE: Dr. Mays worked at an inner-city clinic. Over 80% of his income was from Medicare, with the rest paid mostly in cash. He was indicted for income tax evasion when the IRS found that he had reported $240,000 in total income in a year in which his Medicare income alone was $280,000.
>
> Dr. Mays was offered a plea bargain—if he'd plead guilty, the charge would be reduced and he'd receive probation, not a prison term. But this plea bargain meant that Dr. Mays's medical license would be revoked, ending his career. He rejected the offer and went to trial.
>
> Dr. Mays testified that he was a man of medicine, not a businessman. He relied on his bookkeeper and accountant; he signed whatever they put in front of him. The prosecuting attorney scoffed at this defense by telling the jury that everyone bears the responsibility for the accuracy of their tax returns. The jury sympathized with the good doctor and found him not guilty.
>
> P.S. Immediately after the trial, the IRS began an audit. Dr. Mays had to pay thousands of dollars in taxes, interest, and fraud penalties, but at least he stayed out of jail and kept his medical license.

In another case, Mr. Cheek, an airline pilot, was found guilty of tax evasion. The U.S. Supreme Court reversed his conviction. (*United States v. Cheek*, 498 U.S. 192 (1991).) Mr. Cheek claimed that he had formed a belief, based on materials provided by a tax protester group, that certain income tax laws did not apply to him. The trial judge told the jury not to consider this as a defense to tax evasion. The Supreme Court, however, held that his mistaken belief was a valid defense, and ordered Mr. Cheek to be retried. The question in the new trial was whether Mr. Cheek's belief was a good-faith misunderstanding of the tax laws or was a criminal intent to evade paying taxes.

Mr. Cheek wasn't as lucky his second time around in court as he was his first. At his new trial, Mr. Cheek raised the Supreme Court-approved defense, but was convicted by a new jury of several tax crimes anyway. The judge sentenced him to one year and one day in prison and fined him $62,000. (*Wall Street Journal*, March 25, 1992.)

If You Are Convicted

If you are convicted of a tax crime after putting the government to the trouble of a trial, chances are 8 in 10 that you'll be sent to federal prison. The Federal Sentencing Guidelines and the judge determine how long the sentence will be.

If, however, you reach a plea bargain without a trial, chances are better that you'll be fined and/or placed on probation, given home confinement, or sent to a halfway house, rather than sent to jail. Added to the fine may be the costs incurred by the government in prosecuting you.

In general, public figures are most likely to go to jail. Back in the 1930s, President Hoover ordered that our income tax evasion law be used to put away the notorious Al Capone. This is the only charge ever made to stick on Scarface, who found his way to Alcatraz.

Today, instead of landing on the Rock, tax convicts are usually sent to a Club Fed minimum security facility filled with bankers, lawyers, politicians, and Wall Street sharpies. The average length of time served for a tax crime is a little less than two years. If this sounds like a breeze, think twice. Tax alumni of the federal prison system all agree that it was a humiliating and crushing experience. And licensed professionals—lawyers, doctors, stockbrokers, and CPAs—lose their professional licenses after conviction.

Phillip S. Fry, author of *Pay No Income Taxes Without Going to Jail*, was apparently unclear on the concept. In 1986, he pleaded guilty to tax fraud and, you guessed it, went to jail. Other tax criminals with whom you're probably familiar and their prison terms include:

- Pete Rose—five months
- Chuck Berry—four months
- Aldo Gucci—one year
- Wesley Snipes—three years, and
- Leona Helmsley—four years.

Richard Hatch failed to pay taxes on the $1,000,000 he won on the show *Survivor*, but he didn't survive the IRS police; he was sentenced to 51 months in federal prison.

A star of yesteryear, Sophia Loren, served 17 days in jail in her native Italy for tax evasion. It appears that big stars get off lighter in Italy than in the United States. So if you're thinking of evading taxes, maybe you want to brush up on your Italian and find a job in Venice, Florence, or Rome.

Chapter Highlights

- Tax fraud is more than carelessness or honest mistakes and can be punished by the IRS either civilly or criminally or both.
- The IRS seldom puts tax cheaters in jail but often imposes heavy fines.
- See a criminal or tax attorney if the IRS is investigating you for a tax crime.

Small Business/Self-Employed: When IRS Trouble Comes

Self-Employed—You're a Prime Audit Target 342

Employees or Independent Contractors? 343

How to Classify a Worker 344

People Who Are Automatically Employees by Law 345

Exempt Employees and Small Business Owners 345

How Independent Contractor Rules Are Applied 346

How Business Owners Can Protect Themselves 347

Payroll Taxes—IRS Dynamite 348

The Dreaded Trust Fund Recovery Penalty 350

How the IRS Determines the Responsible People 351

Appealing a Trust Fund Recovery Penalty 353

If You Lose Your Trust Fund Recovery Penalty Appeal 357

Cash Transactions Over $10,000 359

I f you are in business for yourself, or you work for someone who is, know that the IRS is watching. The three major concerns of the IRS here are:

- Are workers wrongly classified as independent contractors when they are legally employees?
- Is the business making payroll tax deposits?
- Are all transactions—especially large cash transactions—made to the business being reported to the IRS?

 RESOURCE
This chapter provides an overview of the most common small business tax issues. For details, see *Tax Savvy for Small Business*, by Frederick W. Daily and Stephen Fishman (Nolo). In addition, *Consultant & Independent Contractor Agreements*, by Stephen Fishman (Nolo), contains the forms and information needed by employers who do, or plan to, hire independent workers. Finally, there is *Legal Guide for Starting & Running a Small Business*, by Stephen Fishman (Nolo), for general information (including some tax advice) for any small business owner.

Self-Employed—You're a Prime Audit Target

Because the IRS claims that most tax cheats are self-employed, it isn't surprising that this group is more closely scrutinized than are wage earners. With about half of all employees, the IRS's Small Business/Self-Employed Division is the biggest of its four divisions. If the IRS chooses to come after you and your business by way of an audit—or worse, a criminal investigation—be aware that it can easily get to your bank and other financial records. So, if you've been foolish enough to deposit unreported income in your bank accounts, the IRS can find it.

If your small business is audited, the IRS will want to know:

- Did you report all of your business's sales or receipts?
- Did you write off any personal living expenses as business expenses?
- Does your lifestyle apparently exceed the amount of self-employment income reported?
- Did you write off automobile expenses for travel that was not business related?

If you are self-employed and audited, be sure to read Chapter 3 and concentrate on "Living Beyond Your Means" and "Bank Deposit Method."

Employees or Independent Contractors?

If your business is improperly treating workers as self-employed individuals— that is, as independent contractors—expect trouble if the IRS calls. The IRS has the power to change the classification of any worker, with expensive consequences for the business owner.

By calling workers "independent contractors," business owners avoid burdensome tax reporting, bookkeeping, and withholding taxes from their workers' paychecks. Moreover, entrepreneurs dodge the tax expense of matching employees' FICA contributions and paying the unemployment tax. The tax savings and reduced paperwork of improperly calling employees independent contractors can be significant—unless you get caught. Violators can be penalized up to 35% of the payments made to the wrongly classified worker, plus interest.

In any event, a business must annually report to the IRS amounts paid to true independent contractors as well as employees. By January 31 of each year, owners must file Form 1099-NEC for each independent contractor paid more than $600 by cash, check, or direct deposit (you don't have to report electronic payments through third-party payment providers, such as those made by PayPal). Owners must also send a copy of Form 1099-NEC to the contractor.

If the IRS finds that you failed to issue a Form 1099-NEC, you might be hit with a separate penalty. (I.R.C. § 3509.) Plus, it bolsters the IRS's case that you misclassified the worker.

Misclassification of independent contractors is an IRS priority. The IRS has targeted for audit businesses suspected of wrongly classifying workers, such as building contractors, medical professionals, graphic designers, and neighborhood beauty shops, to name a few.

IRS and state auditors can assess an employer not only the payroll taxes that should have been collected and paid, but also the reclassified employee's unpaid income taxes. And as the penalties and interest mount, businesses can receive audit bills of 50% or more of wages paid. For example, if you paid Millie Ways, an employee, $20,000 as an independent contractor, the IRS might hit you with $10,000 in taxes, penalties, and interest for the misclassification. The total would be lower if you can show that Millie reported the $20,000 on her tax return.

How to Classify a Worker

To determine worker classification from the IRS point of view, see Form SS-8, *Determination of Worker Status for Purposes of Federal Employment Taxes and Income Tax Withholding.* (Available at the IRS's website at www.irs.gov.) Here is a summary of the SS-8 factors, gleaned mostly from court decisions.

Factors Tending to Show the Worker Is an Employee

- You require—or can require—the worker to comply with your instructions about when, where, and how to work.
- You train the worker to perform services in a particular manner.
- You integrate the worker's services into your business operations.
- You require the worker to render services personally; the worker can't hire others to do some of the work.
- You hire, supervise, and pay assistants for the worker.
- Your business has a continuing relationship with the worker or work is performed at frequently recurring intervals.
- You establish set hours of work.
- You require the worker to devote the majority of the work week to your business.
- You have the worker do the work on your premises.
- You require the worker to do the work in a sequence that you set.
- You require the worker to submit regular oral or written reports.
- You pay the worker by the hour, week, or month, unless these are installment payments of a lump sum agreed to for a job.
- You pay the worker's business or traveling expenses.
- You furnish significant tools, equipment, and materials.
- You have the right to discharge the worker at will and the worker has the right to quit at will.

Factors Tending to Show the Worker Is an Independent Contractor (IC)

- The worker hires, supervises, and pays the worker's assistants.
- The worker is free to work when and for whom the worker chooses.
- The worker does the work at their own office or shop.
- The worker is paid by the job or receives a straight commission.
- The worker invests in facilities used in performing services, such as renting an office.
- The worker can realize a profit or suffer a loss from their services, such as a worker who is responsible for paying salaries to their own employees.
- The worker performs services for several businesses at one time— although sometimes a worker can be an employee of several businesses.
- The worker makes their services available to the general public.
- The worker can't be fired so long as the worker meets the contract specifications.

People Who Are Automatically Employees by Law

In most situations, the status of a worker is determined by the above-listed factors. Certain workers fall into special tax code categories, and the usual IRS criteria don't apply. Workers who are automatically employees include:

- officers of corporations who provide service to the corporations
- food and laundry drivers
- full-time salespeople who sell goods for resale
- full-time life insurance agents working mainly for one company, and
- at-home workers who are supplied with material and given specifications for work to be performed.

Exempt Employees and Small Business Owners

The tax code states that licensed real estate agents and door-to-door salespeople are tax classified as nonemployees or exempt employees. They may be treated as regular employees for nontax purposes, however, such as liability insurance and workers' compensation.

Sole proprietors or partners in their own business are neither employees nor independent contractors. They pay their own income tax and Social Security/Medicare self-employment tax by making quarterly estimated tax deposits. But a shareholder in an incorporated business is legally an employee of the corporation in most cases.

How Independent Contractor Rules Are Applied

Let's look at two workers—one an employee and the other an independent contractor—who provide similar services but fall into different tax classification categories.

State Rules Might Be Different

IRS classification rules are similar to those of most states for state taxes and unemployment rules, but there are differences. For example, California has adopted an ABC test to determine if most workers are employees or independent contractors for state law purposes. Under this test, a worker is an independent contractor only if that person: (A) is free from the control and direction of the hiring entity, (B) performs work outside the usual course of the hiring entity's business, and (C) is customarily engaged in an independently established trade, occupation, or business. If you plan to hire independent contractors, check the law in your state to see if special rules are in effect.

EXAMPLE 1—EMPLOYEE: Wendy Wordsmith teaches marketing at a community college. Wendy also works for ABC Enterprises writing ads, catalogs, and consumer information blog posts. Wendy works every Wednesday at ABC's offices, receiving a $500 salary each week. Wendy receives direct supervision and instructions from the owner. Wendy occasionally does some work at home when required to by ABC and is not allowed to do this kind of writing for anyone else. Wendy is an employee of both ABC Enterprises and the college. She is not an independent contractor under the law.

EXAMPLE 2—INDEPENDENT CONTRACTOR: XYZ Distributors has similar needs for writing on an occasional basis. But when XYZ needs an online ad or catalog produced, it calls upon Frank Freelance. Frank always works out of his home and frequently hires assistants whom he pays directly. Frank pays all his own expenses. Each time he completes a job for XYZ, he sends the company an invoice. Frank is not prohibited from writing ads for other businesses. He clearly is an independent contractor and not an employee of XYZ.

Part-Time Help

John operates a desktop publishing shop specializing in writing and designing brochures, flyers, and other promotional materials for small businesses. At the start, John does most of the work himself, turning any overload over to others, including Sue, Ted, and Ellen, all working out of their homes. John collects from the customer and pays these people as independent contractors. So far, so good.

But as John's business grows, he brings Sue, Ted, and Ellen into his office to work part time under his broad supervision, an average of about one or two days per week each. The rest of the time they work for themselves. John continues to treat them as independent contractors. By law, he shouldn't. John is tempting fate by exercising significant control over these workers and using their services in-house on a regular basis. Under the IRS guidelines, they are now employees, even if they are regularly employed or working as independent contractors elsewhere.

How Business Owners Can Protect Themselves

To be able to prove a worker was an independent contractor if you are audited:

- Enter into a written contract with the independent contractor. Spell out the responsibilities of each party and how payment is to be determined for each job. The contract should allow the independent contractor to hire their own assistants.

- Require the independent contractor to furnish the tools, equipment, and material needed for the job.
- Have the independent contractor do all or most of the work at their own place—not at yours.
- Make it clear that the independent contractor is free to offer services to other businesses besides yours.
- Pay for work by the job rather than by the hour, week, or month.
- Require the independent contractor to submit invoices for each job before you make payment.
- Require the contractor to show proof of a business license and insurance.
- Require the contractor to prove they are reporting what you pay on their tax return.

The IRS invites businesses or their workers to submit Form SS-8 for an IRS analysis of whether a particular worker qualifies as an independent contractor. I don't suggest using this form because it will alert the IRS to the issue. Instead, consult a tax professional, or use your own judgment based on what you read here and in other Nolo books.

Payroll Taxes—IRS Dynamite

If you own a business with employees, each payroll period you must hold back from each employee's paycheck:
- federal (and usually state) income tax, and
- FICA contributions (Social Security and Medicare).

How much money you withhold from each employee's earnings depends on the number of exemptions claimed by the employee on Form W-4 when they started working for you. The FICA contribution is a percentage of the employee's gross earnings, which you must fully or partially match.

An employer must deposit payroll taxes semiweekly, monthly, quarterly, or annually depending on the size of the payroll. With few exceptions, payroll taxes must be deposited through the Electronic Federal Tax Payment System, known as EFTPS.

A small business employer must deposit payroll taxes weekly, monthly, or quarterly, depending on the size of the payroll.

All employers must also send the IRS:

- Form 941, *Employer's Quarterly Federal Tax Return*. This form is filed every three months as long as your business has employees. Form 941 reports the amount of your employees' federal income tax and FICA withheld for the previous quarter.
- Form 940, *Employer's Annual Federal Unemployment Tax Return*, or FUTA. Form 940 is filed once a year. On it, you report your total quarterly payroll tax deposit. On this amount, a federal unemployment tax is calculated. The FUTA tax is paid by your business and is not withheld from your employees' paychecks.
- Form 944, *Employer's Annual Federal Tax Return*. This form is filed annually if your total liability for payroll taxes is $1,000 or less. If you qualify to file Form 944, you do not file Form 941.

How Businesses Can Minimize Payroll Tax Trouble

Give top priority to making payroll tax deposits when they are due. Never borrow from your employees' tax funds. Even if you eventually make the payment to the IRS, the penalties and interest can be substantial. Pay Uncle Sam first, not last. If you can't pay, then maybe you shouldn't be in business.

Stay out of trouble by using a bonded payroll tax service to both file and make all payroll tax deposits. Banks and companies like ADP and Safeguard offer this service at reasonable prices. If they goof up and don't get a form or payment in on time, they will pay the late payment penalty.

If your business is able to make only a partial payment of payroll taxes, write on the lower left-hand portion of the check that the payment is designated to the trust fund portion of the tax. Also, enclose a letter stating that you designate the payment to the trust fund portion.

The trust fund portion is the employee's income tax and FICA contributions. The smaller part—the employer's share of the FICA contribution—is not subject to the Trust Fund Recovery Penalty. This reduces the amount that the IRS can assess against responsible persons by around 8% (every little bit helps).

According to the IRS, most businesses are delinquent in filing or paying employment taxes at one time or another. The IRS considers payroll taxes the most serious of all tax debts. The theory of the payroll tax law is that the employer acts as a collector for the government, holding its workers' taxes in trust until paid over to the IRS. Consequently, the IRS views operating a business while owing payroll taxes as illegally borrowing money from the U.S. Treasury.

> **CAUTION**
>
> **IRS collectors are extremely tough if you owe payroll taxes.** Review Chapter 6 for how to deal with IRS collections. Keep in mind that revenue officers can seize assets and force you out of business if you owe back payroll taxes.

The Dreaded Trust Fund Recovery Penalty

Here's a familiar scenario: Your small business is struggling. You pay the rent and your employees' wages, but not the payroll taxes. You know things will turn around next month, however, when the big order comes in. And Christmas is just around the corner; you are sure you'll pull out of the slump and be able to pay Uncle Sam in full.

Six months go by. Your sales have gone down. Orders stopped coming in and holiday sales were terrible. Your suppliers have sued you and your landlord is threatening to evict. You haven't filed payroll tax forms or deposited payroll taxes for the last four quarters. You shut down and sell your assets to pay off the creditors—although you don't pay the IRS the payroll taxes you owe. You manage to avoid bankruptcy by the skin of your nose.

If you did it this way, woe unto you. You should have paid the IRS first and then, if need be, filed for bankruptcy to handle private creditors. This is because the IRS is the creditor to be most feared.

When payroll taxes haven't been paid, the IRS can review a company's books, speak to employees, and then hold its owners, managers, and bookkeepers personally responsible for the payroll taxes due. The IRS transfers the business payroll tax obligation to individuals—penalizing them for the business's failure to make the payroll tax deposits. This is known as the "Trust Fund Recovery Penalty" (TFRP). It applies primarily to incorporated businesses. If your small business was an LLC, a partnership, or a sole proprietorship, you can be found directly responsible for payroll taxes without the TFRP provision.

Because the penalty equals the taxes owed, it's also called the "100% Payroll Penalty." (I.R.C. § 6672.) And although in most instances the TFRP is transferred to employees of a defunct business, the IRS can—and will—impose the liability on people working for an ongoing business as well.

The relevant section of Internal Revenue Code Section 6672 states:

> *Any person required to collect, truthfully account for, and pay over any tax imposed by this title who willfully fails to collect such tax, or truthfully account for and pay over such tax, or willfully attempts in any manner to evade or defeat any such tax or the payment thereof, shall, in addition to other penalties provided by law, be liable for a penalty equal to the total amount of the tax evaded, or not collected, or not accounted for and paid over.*

 CAUTION
The IRS makes over 50,000 TFRP assessments each year, averaging $21,000 per responsible person.

The IRS has three years to assess the TFRP against responsible people after the tax was originally assessed against the business. Once the TFRP is assessed against the responsible people, the IRS has 10 years to collect it from them.

How the IRS Determines the Responsible People

On average, the IRS finds 1.6 responsible persons for each defunct business owing payroll taxes. There is no limit, however, and it's not uncommon for six or more people to be declared equally responsible. And all are jointly and severally liable for the entire amount; the penalty is not divided among the group—each person owes *all* of it to Uncle Sam until the penalty is paid in full.

EXAMPLE: Skyrocket Corporation went out of business owing $60,000 in federal payroll taxes. The IRS finds Zoe, Emily, and Robb responsible for the money owed. Each is liable for the whole $60,000, and the IRS will go after the easiest target. The IRS can't collect more than $60,000 total, however. If Zoe pays, Emily and Robb are off the hook. If this happens, Zoe might be able to sue Emily and Robb in state court and get back $40,000.

The TFRP is one of the scariest parts of the tax code. It is directed at business owners, but it can also be assessed against low-level employees with no financial stake in the business. IRS investigations of businesses owing payroll taxes are conducted by revenue officers. They begin by putting together a list of people with any authority over business finances:

- Who made the financial decisions in the business?
- Who signed or had authorization to sign on the checking account?
- Who had the power to pay or direct payment of bills?
- Who had the duty of tax reporting?

To get this information, the officer may interview everyone whose name comes up when asking the above four questions. The officer looks at bank and corporate records for the names on bank signature cards and to find out who actually signed checks and who were corporate officers.

IRS Interviews of Potentially Responsible People

In interviewing each potentially responsible person, revenue officers ask the questions on IRS Form 4180, *Report of Interview With Individual Relative to Trust Fund Recovery Penalty or Personal Liability for Excise Tax*. If you are ever called for IRS questioning about a business with which you were associated, study the form ahead of time so that you won't be caught off guard. The IRS does not make this form available to the public, but you can find copies online through a Google search or get a copy from your attorney or tax pro. Depending on how much tax is owed, you might also review the form with a tax attorney before meeting the IRS.

At the interview, you can bring a representative with you—a tax lawyer, a CPA, or an enrolled agent. (See Chapter 13.) And you should, especially if you were the bookkeeper or check writer or had financial dealings in the business and don't believe that you should be held responsible.

Anyone whom the revenue officer believes acted willfully in preventing the IRS from receiving the payroll taxes is found liable. Unfortunately, "willful" does not mean that you intentionally tried to beat the government out of payroll taxes. It means only that you knew about the payroll taxes and knew they weren't being paid. Under this test, the IRS has found $100-per-week bookkeepers liable for enormous sums of money. The reasoning is that if the bookkeeper paid other bills, they could have paid the IRS.

Revenue officers often ignore business realities to find responsible persons. Most vulnerable are people with check-signing power and with corporate titles, but without any real authority.

Check-signing power. Revenue officers often assume that anyone who had the power to sign checks is guilty. They often ignore IRS rules stating that the TFRP should not be imposed based on check-signing authority alone. (*Internal Revenue Manual* 5.7.3.3.1.2(2).) This is in line with court decisions that an employee with no financial interest in a business, but who signed checks under the explicit directions of a boss, is not a responsible person under the TFRP.

Corporate titles. Running a close second to check-signing power is the IRS assumption that anyone with a corporate title—president, secretary, or treasurer—is a responsible person. IRS policy, however, states that this presumption should be made only if the corporate officers don't cooperate in the IRS's investigation. (*Internal Revenue Manual* 1.2.1.6.3(7), IRS Policy Statement 5-14.) In many small corporations, titles bear little relationship to who really runs the business.

An individual might be responsible for the TFRP but not for all the tax periods. You aren't liable for the TFRP for payroll taxes owed before you came onto the scene or after you departed.

Appealing a Trust Fund Recovery Penalty

If you are found to be a responsible person by a revenue officer, you'll be sent a preliminary notice and a tax bill. Revenue officers tend to find as many people responsible as is remotely possible. But their decisions can be protested to the appeals division, where many TFRP responsible-person findings are reversed. If you don't think you really were responsible, then you should appeal.

Sample Letter to Appeal Trust Fund Recovery Penalty

September 20, 20xx

Internal Revenue Service
P.O. Box 408
Church Street Station
New York, NY 10008

Protest of Trust Fund Recovery Penalty
Sandy Swinger
SSN: 555-55-5555

VIA CERTIFIED MAIL–RETURN RECEIPT REQUESTED

Dear Sir or Madam:

This is a protest of the proposed assessment of a Trust Fund Recovery Penalty. I request a hearing. I have enclosed copies of IRS Letter 1153 (DO) and Form 2751 dated September 10, 20xx.

I deny that I was a responsible person and/or was willful in not paying over employment taxes for Crazy Calhoun's Incorporated under Internal Revenue Code Section 6672.

I never had any authority to make any tax payments to the IRS or to order another person to do so while I was employed by Crazy Calhoun's. I never had a financial stake in the business, other than as a salaried employee. I was never an officer or director of the corporation. I was only the manager of the bar operation and subject to the direction of the president, Tom Ranoff.

Under penalties of perjury, I declare that I have examined the statement of facts presented in this protest and to the best of my knowledge and belief, they are true, correct, and complete.

Sincerely,

Sandy Swinger
Sandy Swinger

Copy to Manuel Indiana, Revenue Officer

Enclosed: IRS Letter 1153 (DO) and Form 2751

The preliminary notice you are mailed or handed informs you of the amount of the penalty and that you have 60 days to file an appeal. The procedure is similar to the appeal of an audit—you must file a written protest with the appeals office. (See Chapter 4.) If you don't appeal, after 60 days, the preliminary notice becomes final and you will receive a formal demand for payment. (I.R.C. § 6672.) If you don't pay, the IRS can go through its normal lien and levy process to enforce collection. (See Chapter 6.)

A sample protest letter is shown above, followed by the case history that led up to this letter.

Sandy and Crazy Calhoun's—A Case History

Crazy Calhoun's was a popular singles spot owned by three partners. At the height of its glory, the least competent of the partners, Tom, bought out the other two partners. Tom lived in the fast lane and preferred play to work. He let his employees run the business. His neglect and expensive tastes caused the business to fall behind in its bills—including federal payroll taxes.

Sandy was a longtime employee of Crazy Calhoun's. She worked her way up from cocktail waitress to bar manager. Because C.O.D. liquor deliveries during Tom's frequent absences needed to be paid, Sandy was authorized to sign checks. She was uneasy about it, but went along because she knew if the bar didn't have any booze, she'd be out of a job.

One day, a revenue officer showed up asking for Tom, who was out. The officer said he was padlocking the doors if he didn't get immediate payment of at least $2,000 for back payroll taxes. Sandy replied that she had authority to write checks for liquor deliveries only, unless Tom specified more. Several times in the past, Tom had phoned the bookkeeper saying that Sandy could sign payroll checks. Sandy asked her fellow workers what to do. They all agreed Tom would want her to write the check to the IRS, so she did.

Several months later Crazy Calhoun's was padlocked by the same revenue officer. By then, Tom had disappeared. Suppliers had stopped making deliveries for nonpayment; most employees had quit. Sandy got a new job. Eventually, Tom showed up in jail in Hawaii.

Sandy and Crazy Calhoun's—A Case History (continued)

Sandy is found responsible

About two years later, a new IRS revenue officer paid a surprise visit to Sandy at home. Unlike the first guy, this man was very nice. He said he was investigating Crazy Calhoun's and needed to ask a few questions. He went through an interview and asked Sandy to sign a statement, thanked her, and left.

Two months later Sandy found in her mailbox an IRS notice of Proposed Assessment of Trust Fund Recovery Penalty. The nice man had found Sandy liable for $128,000 in payroll taxes of Crazy Calhoun's. She was hysterical. At 28 years old, Sandy owned a five-year-old Chevy, some old furniture, and a cat. She earned $350 a week as a waitress and was supposed to pay an IRS bill on which interest and penalties were running at over $1,500 per month.

Sandy appeals

Sandy hired an attorney for her appeals hearing. The attorney felt that Sandy had a fair chance of winning an appeal. The most difficult thing to overcome would be the statement—Form 4180—that she had signed. The form is designed to virtually guarantee anyone interviewed will be found liable.

Her attorney sought out other former Crazy Calhoun's employees, who backed Sandy's story that she never had authority to pay business taxes. The former manager, Jack, was living 2,500 miles away. Jack was sympathetic and said Sandy was telling the truth. He was afraid to put this in writing for fear the IRS would come after him.

Lois, the former bookkeeper, had prepared checks for the business but never signed them. She was not being pursued by the IRS. She gave a statement that Sandy could sign checks only to pay for liquor C.O.D.s and that Tom had sole authority to pay all other bills. Sandy's lawyer submitted a statement from Lois.

At the hearing, Sandy's lawyer presented a statement from Lois and her own statement summarizing the attorney's conversation with Jack. Also, Sandy stated she had paid the IRS only once, under the duress of the revenue officer. At the end of the hearing, the appeals officer stated that the case was closed. About 60 days later, Sandy received his report—she was not held to be responsible for the taxes.

> **TIP**
>
> **Appealing a proposed TFRP assessment will buy time—even if you're clearly responsible.** An IRS collector can't come knocking at your door while you are appealing. And interest does not run during the time an appeal is being considered. This is an unexplainable quirk in the law. For example, if you are eventually found responsible for $50,000 in unpaid payroll taxes and your appeal process takes a year, you'll avoid about $3,500 in interest. Of course, if you lose the appeal, interest starts to run again.

If You Lose Your Trust Fund Recovery Penalty Appeal

Many TFRP cases don't have endings as happy as Sandy's in the example above. If you really were a responsible person—that is, you knew about, had the authority to pay, and should have paid the payroll taxes—there might be no way to avoid the penalty. Nevertheless, if you find yourself in this awful predicament, keep reading to find your options.

Go to court. If you really believe you aren't liable, you can challenge a TFRP in court. You can sue in Tax Court (the easiest route), in the U.S. District Court nearest to you, or in the U.S. Court of Claims. (See Chapter 5.)

Tax Court doesn't require you to pay the IRS any tax before filing your suit. However, to sue in a District Court or the Court of Claims, you must first pay at least some of the taxes claimed due and then file a lawsuit seeking a refund. The minimum amount you must pay is equal to the unpaid payroll taxes due for one employee for one quarter of any pay period. This means that if you are found liable for a large amount—say $50,000—under the TFRP, you only need to pay the taxes for a minor employee—perhaps only $100—to contest the whole $50,000.

While you can go to Tax Court without a lawyer, as a practical matter, you will need an attorney to sue in either a District Court or the Court of Claims. (See Chapter 5, "Other Federal Courts—Paying First Is Required.") Expect to pay a minimum of $10,000 in legal costs.

File for Chapter 13 bankruptcy. A TFRP can't be discharged, or wiped out, in a Chapter 7 bankruptcy. However, you can include a TFRP in a Chapter 13 repayment plan. See Chapter 6 for a description of bankruptcy. To try to get the TFRP partially wiped out in Chapter 13, consult a good bankruptcy lawyer.

Pay or compromise. If you throw in the towel, just deal with the TFRP as with any other kind of tax bill. See Chapter 6 to find out your options. Your best bets might be either an installment agreement or an Offer in Compromise.

Request a nonassessment or nonassertion. A little-known tax code provision allows people found responsible for TFRPs to request a "nonassessment" or "nonassertion." (I.R.C. § 6672; *Internal Revenue Manual* 5.7.5.1 et seq.) We have had this request granted when a client showed she was broke and the IRS concluded it wasn't worth the effort to try to collect the penalty—even though she was clearly responsible for the payroll tax.

Are Other People Responsible?

If you or your tax professional submits a written request to the IRS, the agency must disclose the names of other people found responsible for the TFRP. Furthermore, the IRS must describe in writing its efforts to find and collect from each of them. It's clearly in your best interest to give the IRS any information you have regarding the location of assets of other responsible persons—unless you're feeling charitable.

Also, if you end up paying more than your proportional share of the TFRP, you can sue the others for the difference. For example, you and two other people are found responsible for a TFRP of $33,000. The IRS grabs your $15,000 IRA. Since your share is only $11,000, you may sue the other two people for the $4,000 difference. But don't look to the IRS for help in collecting from the two others; it's not their job. (I.R.C. § 6672.)

Cash Transactions Over $10,000

As part of a government campaign against the underground economy and money laundering, all cash and cash equivalent *business* transactions over $10,000 must be reported to the IRS, using Currency Transaction Reports, or CTRs. Some state tax agencies have similar reporting laws and forms.

Cash equivalents include traveler's checks, money orders, and bank drafts. Personal checks of any amount are exempt from CTR reporting, presumably because banks keep copies of personal checks, thereby creating a paper or electronic trail the IRS can follow.

All businesses that receive cash or cash equivalents must report each customer's name and Social Security number for each transaction over $10,000 on IRS Form 8300. Financial institutions must report these transactions on Form FinCEN 104, *Currency Transaction Report*. (For details, see IRS Publication 1544.)

CTRs are used by the IRS to identify people who unload nontaxed money by purchasing luxury goods—such as cars, yachts, and jewels—or by taking lavish trips.

Within 15 days of receiving over $10,000 in cash or cash equivalents in a business transaction, you must send Form 8300 to the IRS. And when you deposit that money into your bank—or if your total cash deposits for one day exceed $10,000—your bank will report it to the IRS unless you are specifically exempt from this law. Large grocery stores and a few other types of businesses are exempt from CTR reporting.

> CAUTION
> **There is a law against "structured transactions."** This entails separating one $10,000 transaction into several smaller ones to avoid currency transaction reports. If multiple small transactions from the same source exceed $10,000 in total, you still must file a CTR. Similarly, if you make three cash deposits of $4,000 over a short period of time, your bank is obligated to report the total on a CTR.

Failing to file a Form 8300 can get you fined, audited, or both. And CTR violations may be sent to the IRS Criminal Investigation Division. (See Chapter 10.) In short, not filing a CTR can cause you more problems than if you had reported the cash in the first place.

Chapter Highlights

- Self-employed people have the highest audit risk so they should keep very good records.
- If you hire others for your small business, be aware of the tax rules for independent contractors and employees.
- Hiring employees means you have to withhold taxes from their pay and follow all federal and state payroll tax requirements.
- Cash transactions in your business must be reported to the IRS if they are over $10,000.

Penalties and Interest

Penalties Added to Tax Bills...362

    Accuracy Penalties 363

    Fraud Penalties 363

    Failure to Withhold, Deposit, or Pay Taxes for Employees.............................363

    Failure to File Information Returns 364

    Failure to Pay Penalties 364

    Late-Filing Penalties—Late Filing and Late Paying..364

    Combined Penalties..366

Interest on Tax Bills...367

Understanding Penalty and Interest Notices...367

Reducing or Eliminating Penalties and Interest..368

    Reasonable Cause for a Penalty Abatement 368

    How to Request a Reasonable Cause Penalty Abatement 370

    Penalty Relief Due to Statutory Exception...372

    If Your Abatement Request Is Rejected 372

    First-Time Penalty Abatement..373

    Abating Interest...376

    How to Request an Interest Abatement 377

Designating Late Tax Payments...377

    Advantages of Designating Your Payments..377

    How to Designate a Payment...378

RS-imposed penalties and interest charges are discussed throughout the book. These fines can be very expensive. A $7,000 tax bill can turn into $15,000 with interest and penalties. Tax penalties, from the IRS's perspective, are explained in Notice 433, *Interest and Penalty Information*. (A copy is available on the IRS's website at www.irs.gov.)

Some questions we frequently get:

Is it possible to get the IRS to drop a penalty?

What can I do about the interest on my audit bill?

How many different ways can the IRS penalize me?

Can I negotiate a penalty down?

Does the IRS ever have to pay me interest?

Penalties Added to Tax Bills

When the IRS hits you with an additional tax bill (from an audit, for example), it usually adds penalties and interest. Penalties are added automatically by IRS computers or by IRS personnel at their discretion. Interest charges are required by law (and are discussed below).

Penalties are authorized whenever you file or pay your taxes late, have been found to owe additional taxes, or have failed to file all required tax forms.

Although penalties were originally meant to punish errant taxpayers—that's why they are called penalties—they are now considered a regular and dependable source of revenue in our national budget. Reflecting this, in the past decade, the total dollar amount of penalties imposed on taxpayers increased by 1,000%. In a recent year, over 39 million penalties were assessed for over $73 billion. In short, penalties have become a tax—on a tax.

IRS penalties fall into five basic categories—accuracy, fraud, failure to pay taxes, late filings, and a combined late-filing and -paying penalty.

TIP
Take heart—you might be able to beat the IRS at the penalty game.
The IRS can remove a penalty if you can show that your failure to comply with
the tax law was due to "reasonable cause" or if you qualify for first-time penalty
abatement.

Accuracy Penalties

The IRS can add a 20% accuracy-related penalty to your tax bill if IRS
auditors find your tax return understated your tax liability. This is a
commonly imposed penalty by the IRS "due to negligence or intentional
disregard of the tax law." This means you didn't pay heed to the tax law
or you were just plain careless when filing your tax return.

Fraud Penalties

If the IRS concludes that you fraudulently omitted or underreported income,
it can add a heavy fraud penalty. This penalty is up to 75% of the amount
you underreported. For example, if you fraudulently underreported $10,000,
the maximum fraud penalty is $7,500.

Or, if the IRS finds that you fraudulently failed to file a return, it can
penalize you—15% for every month you didn't file for up to five months—
a total of 75% based on the taxes owed. This fraudulent late-filing penalty is
rarely, if ever, imposed. Instead, the IRS usually just hits you with a late-filing
penalty of 5% per month for a maximum of five months, a total of 25%.

Failure to Withhold, Deposit, or Pay Taxes for Employees

This is a stiff penalty on employers who do not withhold or pay over their
employees' Social Security, Medicare, and income taxes. This happens when
employers aren't timely filing IRS Form 941 and making the deposits. The
penalty varies by how late the payments are made. (For details see *Tax Savvy
for Small Business*, by Frederick W. Daily and Stephen Fishman (Nolo).)

Failure to File Information Returns

This penalty is on business owners who don't file reports with the IRS, most often Form 1099 showing payments to service providers like independent contractors. The penalty varies depending on the type of form and the number of nonfiled forms.

Failure to Pay Penalties

The IRS can add to your bill a penalty of ¼% to 1% per month of the amount you failed to pay on time. The penalty starts off at ½% per month. If you enter into an installment agreement to pay the taxes, the IRS drops the penalty to ¼% per month. If you don't pay and the IRS later issues a Notice of Intent to Levy (see Chapter 7), it can raise the penalty to 1% per month on the balance due.

This penalty starts on the day after the original due date, April 16 for individual tax returns. It is imposed on the unpaid balance and added to your bill on the 16th day of each month thereafter. This penalty is imposed monthly and is not prorated daily.

Late-Filing Penalties—Late Filing and Late Paying

Did you file your individual tax return late and didn't request an extension? The IRS can impose a penalty of 5% per month on any tax balance due, up to 25% of the bill. You max out on this penalty if, on September 16—five months and one day after April 15—you still haven't filed your individual tax return. If you file late but don't owe any taxes, you must pay a $485 penalty for 2024 ($450 for 2023). For some information-type forms (such as 1099s) filed late, the IRS can impose a penalty in varying amounts according to specific tax code provisions.

To help struggling taxpayers affected by the COVID-19 pandemic, the IRS waived late filing penalties for most individuals and businesses who filed their 2019 or 2020 tax returns late. To qualify, tax returns for these years had to be filed by September 30, 2022. Such penalty relief is automatic; taxpayers don't have to apply for it. The 1.6 million taxpayers who already paid a late penalty for these years will receive refunds from the IRS. (IR 2022-155.)

IRS Penalties

Reason for Penalty	Penalty Amount	IRC Section
Failure to file a tax return	• 5% of the unpaid balance per month; maximum of 25% • If more than 60 days late, the lesser of $485 or 100% of the tax due • No penalty if due a refund • A failure to file penalty is reduced by the failure to pay penalty if both apply	6651(a)(1) 6651(c)(1)
Failure to pay tax due	0.5% of the unpaid balance per month; maximum of 25%	6651(a)(2)
Fraudulent failure to file a tax return	15% of the unpaid balance per month; maximum of 75%	6651(f)
Failure to deposit employment taxes	• 2% of underpayment if the amount is properly deposited not more than five days after the due date • 5% of underpayment if the amount is properly deposited more than 5 days but not more than 15 days after the due date • 10% of underpayment if the amount is properly deposited more than 15 days after the due date	6656(b)(1)(A)
Failure to file information returns	Penalty assessed per information return: • $50 if correctly filed within 30 days after the required filing date; maximum $500,000 per year ($175,000 for small businesses with gross receipts of $5,000,000 or less) • $100 if correctly filed more than 30 days after the due date but before August 1; maximum $1,500,000 per year ($500,000 for small businesses with gross receipts of $5,000,000 or less) • $290 if correctly filed after August 1 or not filed at all; maximum $3,532,500 ($1,177,500 for small businesses with gross receipts of $5,000,000 or less) • Minimum $500 if failure to file or furnish due to intentional disregard of the requirements	6721, 6722

IRS Penalties (continued)		
Reason for Penalty	**Penalty Amount**	**IRC Section**
Accuracy related penalty	20% of underpayment due to: • negligence, including the failure to make a reasonable attempt to comply or intentional disregard • substantial understatement of tax, more than the greater of 10% (5% if claiming IRC Section 199A deduction) of the actual amount or $5,000	6662
Fraud	75% of understatement due to fraud	6663
Tax evasion	Willful attempt to evade tax is a felony with a maximum fine of $100,000 ($500,000 for a corporation) and/or up to five years in prison	7201
Failure to collect or pay over tax	Willful failure to collect, account for, and pay over tax is a felony with a maximum fine of $10,000 and/or five years in prison	7202

Combined Penalties

Did you both file late and pay late? The IRS can impose a combined penalty of 5% per month (0.5% per month less than the separate penalties for each). The combined penalty is based on the unpaid tax balance for each month your return is late. When you reach 25%—five months—for filing late, the penalty for late filing stops. The failure-to-pay portion of the combined penalty continues at 0.5% per month until it reaches a total of 22.5%. Thus, the maximum combined penalty is 47.5%. Note that tax penalties *do not* include charges for interest, which never stops running.

Late-filing penalties, late-payment penalties, or the combined penalty can be stacked—imposed in addition to other penalties, such as accuracy or fraud penalties resulting from an audit of your tax return.

Interest on Tax Bills

The second unwelcome addition to every overdue tax bill is IRS-charged interest. By not paying your taxes on time, you are considered to be borrowing from Uncle Sam. Congress does not like to lend money interest-free (except to various dictators and deadbeat foreign countries), so it requires the IRS to charge interest.

The interest rate is also set by Congress and is adjusted by formula four times a year and compounded daily. Compounding means interest is charged on interest. For older tax bills, interest calculations can't be easily verified without a computer that emulates the IRS's program. In recent years, the interest rate has ranged between 4% and 7% per year. Interest is computed on *both* the tax and penalties due.

Understanding Penalty and Interest Notices

When you receive a tax bill from the IRS, it usually states penalty and interest charges separately. If you don't understand the IRS computation—it's unlikely you will—obtain an account transcript from the IRS for the year or years involved. Use the IRS Get Transcript Online tool (www.irs.gov/individuals/get-transcript), postal mail IRS Form 4506-T, *Request for Transcript of Tax Return*, or call the IRS at 800-908-9946.

The account transcript is a multipage computer printout showing:

- your tax account (by Social Security number or employer identification number) showing all tax penalty and interest computations
- dates, interest rates, penalties assessed, and any credits—payments or refunds
- principal tax amounts on which interest and penalties were charged
- explanations of which penalties were applied, and
- a summary of your account with balance due, including up-to-date penalty and interest amounts.

Check the figures on the transcript to see that you agree with the amount of the taxes shown, and that you have been credited for all payments you made.

Reducing or Eliminating Penalties and Interest

The IRS can eliminate or reduce a penalty upon your request. The term the IRS uses for wiping out a penalty is "abatement." The main ways to get the IRS to abate a penalty are:

- you can get the IRS to abate any penalty for a *reasonable cause*
- you fall within a statutory exception for penalty relief, or
- you qualify for first-time penalty abatement.

About one-third of IRS-imposed penalties are later canceled (abated). Interest, however, is rarely abated. By law, interest can be canceled only if it was erroneously applied or if it was due to lengthy IRS delays. Additionally, if you qualify for an Offer in Compromise, the IRS may reduce an interest charge or a penalty along with the tax due. (See Chapter 6.)

Abatement requests can be granted at any IRS level—IRS campus, Automated Collection System, or personnel at local IRS offices.

For more detailed guidance on abating IRS penalties, see the *IRS Penalty Handbook*. This handbook is part of the *Internal Revenue Manual* and is available online at www.irs.gov/irm/part20/irm_20-001-001r.

Reasonable Cause for a Penalty Abatement

You can get any IRS penalty removed if you can show the IRS some *reasonable cause* for your failure to follow the tax law resulting in the penalty. Reasonable cause is any excuse that an IRS officer will buy. The *Internal Revenue Manual* (1.2.1.4.2, IRS Policy Statement 3-2) says:

> *Any sound reason advanced by a taxpayer as the cause for delay in filing a return, making deposits … or paying tax when due will be carefully analyzed …. Examples of … reasonable cause:*
>
> 1. *Death or serious illness of the taxpayer or … immediate family. In the case of a corporation, estate, [or] trust … death or serious illness must have been of an individual having sole authority to execute the return or make the deposit or payment.*
> 2. *Unavoidable absence of the taxpayer ….*
> 3. *Destruction by fire or other casualty of the taxpayer's place of business or records.*

4. Taxpayer was unable to determine amount of deposit or tax due for reasons beyond taxpayer's control ….

5. Taxpayer's ability to make deposits or payments has been materially impaired by civil disturbances.

6. Lack of funds is an acceptable reasonable cause for failure to pay any tax or make a deposit … only when a taxpayer can demonstrate the lack of funds occurred despite the exercise of ordinary business care and prudence.

7. Other explanations may be acceptable …. Acceptable explanations of delinquency are not limited …. Any reason … established that the taxpayer exercised ordinary business care and prudence but was nevertheless unable to comply within the prescribed time will be accepted as reasonable cause.

Practical suggestions. If possible, choose one or more of the first six items when requesting a penalty abatement. Also mention Number 7, that you acted with "ordinary business care and prudence" but still couldn't file or pay your taxes on time.

Here are some explanations the IRS has accepted:

- You relied on a tax professional who steered you wrong. For example, if your accountant or bookkeeper caused the tax problem by giving you bad advice or filing the wrong form, say so. Bear in mind that the IRS might counter that because you picked the tax professional, you are responsible for that person's action.

- The IRS wouldn't help you earlier. If you called, wrote, or visited the IRS and got the wrong information or no response when you tried to clear things up, make the point. Be sure to provide copies of letters you sent, the names and IRS identification numbers of all IRS personnel you spoke with, and the dates and summaries of your conversations.

- Someone else caused your problem. For example, if your employer submitted an incorrect 1099 or W-2 form, be sure to tell that to the IRS.

- If your penalty is from a late payment, plead that you would have suffered an undue hardship if you had paid on time. Be warned that this approach is a tough sell to the IRS. You will need to show that had you paid your taxes on time, you wouldn't have been able to put food on the table. The IRS is often sympathetic if the hardship is medically related, including alcohol or drug abuse. Again, supply documentation, such as letters from doctors explaining your condition.

If it's true, stress your clean past IRS record: You've never before requested an abatement, had a penalty, or been behind in paying your taxes.

How to Request a Reasonable Cause Penalty Abatement

You can get relief from the failure to file, failure to pay, and/or failure to deposit penalties over the phone. Call the IRS at the toll-free number at the top right corner of your notice or letter. Have the following information when you call:

- the notice or letter you received
- the penalty you want relieved, and
- the reasons you think it should be removed.

During the call, the IRS agent will tell you if your penalty relief is approved.

If you can't get penalty relief over the phone, or other types of penalties are involved, you should request relief in writing. Use IRS Form 843, *Claim for Refund and Request for Abatement*. (A copy is available on the IRS's website.) Attach a copy of the IRS notice showing the penalty.

Also attach copies of substantiating documents—such as a doctor's statement, fire department report, insurance claim, or death certificate of a family member. Without supporting papers, your abatement request might not get serious consideration.

If possible, enclose payment for the underlying tax, and write on your check that the payment is for the tax portion only. Paying the tax stops the accrual of interest on that balance. Send the form with enclosures to the IRS address in the notice, and use the IRS enclosed bar-coded envelope.

Keep copies of any letters or documents sent to the IRS. The IRS is notorious for ignoring or losing taxpayer correspondence. Send the additional copies if you get another IRS billing before getting a reply to your initial abatement request.

For penalties imposed in an audit, ask the auditor or a manager to drop them before you sign the report. If that doesn't work, you can protest the penalty to the Independent Office of Appeals. (See Chapter 4.)

Form 843, Claim for Refund and Request for Abatement

Form **843** (Rev. August 2011) Department of the Treasury Internal Revenue Service	**Claim for Refund and Request for Abatement** ▶ See separate instructions.	OMB No. 1545-0024

Use Form 843 if your claim or request involves:

   (a) a refund of one of the taxes (other than income taxes or an employer's claim for FICA tax, RRTA tax, or income tax withholding) or a fee, shown on line 3,

   (b) an abatement of FUTA tax or certain excise taxes, or

   (c) a refund or abatement of interest, penalties, or additions to tax for one of the reasons shown on line 5a.

Do not use Form 843 if your claim or request involves:

   (a) an overpayment of income taxes or an employer's claim for FICA tax, RRTA tax, or income tax withholding (use the appropriate amended tax return),

   (b) a refund of excise taxes based on the nontaxable use or sale of fuels, or

   (c) an overpayment of excise taxes reported on Form(s) 11-C, 720, 730, or 2290.

Name(s)	Your social security number
Address (number, street, and room or suite no.)	Spouse's social security number
City or town, state, and ZIP code	Employer identification number (EIN)
Name and address shown on return if different from above	Daytime telephone number

1 **Period.** Prepare a separate Form 843 for each tax period or fee year.
    From   to

2 **Amount** to be refunded or abated:
    $

3 **Type of tax or fee.** Indicate the type of tax or fee to be refunded or abated or to which the interest, penalty, or addition to tax is related.

   ☐ Employment   ☐ Estate   ☐ Gift   ☐ Excise   ☐ Income   ☐ Fee

4 **Type of penalty.** If the claim or request involves a penalty, enter the Internal Revenue Code section on which the penalty is based (see instructions). IRC section:

5a **Interest, penalties, and additions to tax.** Check the box that indicates your reason for the request for refund or abatement. (If none apply, go to line 6.)

    ☐ Interest was assessed as a result of IRS errors or delays.

    ☐ A penalty or addition to tax was the result of erroneous written advice from the IRS.

    ☐ Reasonable cause or other reason allowed under the law (other than erroneous written advice) can be shown for not assessing a penalty or addition to tax.

  b Date(s) of payment(s) ▶

6 **Original return.** Indicate the type of fee or return, if any, filed to which the tax, interest, penalty, or addition to tax relates.

    ☐ 706   ☐ 709   ☐ 940   ☐ 941   ☐ 943   ☐ 945

    ☐ 990-PF   ☐ 1040   ☐ 1120   ☐ 4720   ☐ Other (specify) ▶

7 **Explanation.** Explain why you believe this claim or request should be allowed and show the computation of the amount shown on line 2. If you need more space, attach additional sheets.

Signature. If you are filing Form 843 to request a refund or abatement relating to a joint return, both you and your spouse must sign the claim. Claims filed by corporations must be signed by a corporate officer authorized to sign, and the officer's title must be shown.

Under penalties of perjury, I declare that I have examined this claim, including accompanying schedules and statements, and, to the best of my knowledge and belief, it is true, correct, and complete. Declaration of preparer (other than taxpayer) is based on all information of which preparer has any knowledge.

Signature (Title, if applicable. Claims by corporations must be signed by an officer.)   Date

Signature (spouse, if joint return)   Date

Paid Preparer Use Only	Print/Type preparer's name	Preparer's signature	Date	Check ☐ if self-employed	PTIN
	Firm's name ▶			Firm's EIN ▶	
	Firm's address ▶			Phone no.	

For Privacy Act and Paperwork Reduction Act Notice, see separate instructions.   Cat. No. 10180R   Form **843** (Rev. 8-2011)

Penalty Relief Due to Statutory Exception

You can also get relief if your penalty falls within a specific exception in the Internal Revenue Code. You can request relief the same way as for reasonable cause relief—call the IRS or file Form 843.

You can get this relief only for one of the following reasons:

You relied on bad written advice from the IRS. You can qualify for relief if you ended up owing a penalty because you received incorrect written advice from the IRS to your written request for information, *and* you relied on the incorrect advice. You'll need to show the IRS a copy of the written advice and explain how you relied on it.

You mailed your return on time. You mailed your tax return on time but received a late filing penalty. A paper return or payment is considered filed on time if you:

- mailed it in the United States on or before the deadline to file or pay
- addressed it correctly
- included proper postage, and
- mailed it with the U.S. Postal Service or an IRS-approved private delivery service.

An e-filed return is considered on time if it:

- was sent via an authorized electronic return transmitter
- has a timely electronic postmark, and
- was sent in processable form.

If your e-filed return was rejected for any reason that would have made a paper return not processable, it isn't considered filed on time.

You were in a federal disaster area or combat zone. If you were affected by a federal disaster or serving in a combat zone, you might be eligible for penalty relief.

If Your Abatement Request Is Rejected

If the IRS officially rejects your abatement request, you'll get a written notice. You then have four options besides accepting your fate.

Appeal. File a protest—a letter requesting an appeal. See the sample letter below. You have 30 days from the date of the rejection letter to file your appeal.

Send your appeal letter to the IRS address on the letter that explains your appeal rights. Unlike an appeal of an audit, the IRS doesn't grant you an in-person appeal hearing after an abatement request is rejected. The appeal is handled by mail or telephone.

Request a transfer of your file. Write the IRS requesting that your file be transferred to your local IRS office. Then request a meeting with a revenue officer to try and convince the officer that your penalty should be removed.

Pay and claim a refund. Pay the penalty and then file for a refund. Despite what you might think, paying first does not hurt your chance of getting a refund granted. Your refund request should be submitted to your IRS campus on Form 843, *Claim for Refund and Request for Abatement*. Give your explanation in the space provided on Form 843.

If your Form 843 claim is refused, you can sue in a U.S. District Court or the Court of Claims. (See Chapter 5.) Rarely, however, are tax penalties large enough to justify the costs of going to court.

Make an Offer in Compromise. An Offer in Compromise is a formal procedure for contesting or negotiating any IRS bill, including a penalty. (See Chapter 6.)

First-Time Penalty Abatement

If you haven't been assessed an IRS penalty for the prior three years, you could qualify for first-time penalty abatement (FTA). This allows you to remove failure-to-file and/or failure-to-pay penalties for a single year. It has been estimated that as many as 4.5 million taxpayers qualify for FTA each year, but only 200,000 took advantage of it in one recent year. The IRS does not go out of its way to inform the public about FTA, though it does have a section about it at its website. You must ask for it.

The great advantage of first-time abatement is that you don't have to show the IRS that you had a reasonable cause for failing to follow the tax law or fall within one of the narrow statutory exceptions. Instead, the IRS waives the penalty as a reward because you've been mostly in compliance over the past few years. The IRS is supposed to remove the penalty automatically if you satisfy the FTA requirements.

If you request reasonable cause relief, but IRS records show you qualify for FTA, the IRS will apply FTA. It will notify you that it granted you FTA due to your good compliance history.

Sample Letter Appealing Denial of Abatement of Penalties

January 15, 20xx

IRS Campus
P.O. Box 9941
Ogden, UT 84409

Re: Appeal of Penalty Abatement Denial
    SSN: 555-55-5555

To Whom It May Concern:

I wish to appeal the denial of my penalty abatement request, which I received on January 10, 20xx. A copy of the denial is attached.

The grounds for my appeal are that I had a reasonable cause for [*state type of penalty*] filing late, paying late, not reporting some income because [*state reasons*]:

- I was in a coma
- my tax preparer had just died, or
- [*any other excuse.*]

I can prove my condition with [*state type of proof*]:

- letter from Dr. Stein proving my condition
- death certificate confirming my tax preparer's death, or
- [*any other documentation.*]

Thank you,

Sanford Majors

Sanford Majors
43 Valley Road
Salt Lake City, UT 84000
Telephone: 801-555-1212

Enclosed: IRS Tax Notice; [*Dr. Stein's letter; death certificate or whatever*]

Penalties that qualify for FTA. The FTA erases failure-to-file and failure-to-pay penalties for a *single year*—ordinarily, the previous year. It can also be used to abate failure-to-deposit penalties for business payroll taxes for one year. It can't be used for any other penalties.

Three requirements to qualify for FTA. To qualify for FTA, you must satisfy three requirements.

- *Clean penalty history:* First, you must have incurred no IRS penalties or penalty abatements for the three tax years prior to the year in which you received the penalty you want abated. Check your tax transcript to make sure you have no such penalties on your IRS record. Estimated tax penalties don't count for FTA purposes. You also don't need to count any penalties that were removed by the IRS.
- *Filing compliance:* You have filed all currently required returns, or filed an extension of time to file.
- *Payment compliance:* You have paid, or arranged to pay, any tax due the IRS. You can have an open installment agreement so long as all your payments are current.

How to apply for FTA. Call or write the IRS to apply for FTA. If the IRS wrongly denies your FTA, you can appeal. See "If Your Abatement Request Is Rejected," above.

Call the toll-free number on your IRS notice. Tell the agent you wish to request a first-time penalty abatement for the tax year involved. The agent will run a computer check to see whether you've been assessed any penalties over the past three years or had any other tax issues. If not, the agent should grant the penalty abatement. However, some-times you can't get an FTA approved on the phone because IRS records are inaccurate or the amount is too large. If the FTA is approved, the penalty amount will be applied to other years for which you owe tax, if any. If there are no tax debts, the amount will be paid to you as a refund. Send the IRS a confirming letter if the FTA is approved over the phone.

Alternatively, you may request an FTA by filing IRS Form 843, *Claim for Refund and Request for Abatement.* Send it to the IRS at the address shown on your IRS notice. Attach a copy of the IRS notice showing the penalty. If you don't qualify for FTA, the IRS will consider reasonable cause relief and notify you of its decision.

Abating Interest

Congress makes the IRS charge interest on a tax bill. Of course, if a tax or penalty is canceled for any reason, interest on it is wiped out as well. Usually the IRS computer does this automatically, but check your bill to make sure.

The tax code authorizes the abatement of interest only in the following circumstances:

- The IRS was wrong in charging interest—meaning that either you paid the tax when it was due or didn't owe any taxes on which interest could be charged.
- The IRS incorrectly sent you a refund, wants its money back, and is charging you interest all the way back to the time the check was issued. This is not so unusual. Computer-generated tax refunds sometimes come out of the blue. You are entitled to an interest abatement as long as your actions did not cause the refund. Once the IRS asks for its money back, it can, however, charge you interest, but only from the date of the request, until you repay it. (I.R.C. § 6404.)
- The interest resulted from delays of the IRS in performing ministerial acts. For example, the IRS delays sending a tax bill after you agree to an audit report. You are entitled to an interest abatement of all but the first 30 days of the delay. (Revenue Procedure 87-42; IRS Regulation 301.6404-2.) So if, following an audit, a bill with interest arrives 90 days after you agree to the result, you can have the last 60 days of interest abated.
- The exception for ministerial acts does not cover interest while you challenge a bill or while the IRS audits you, or while you appeal or go to Tax Court. This interest can't be abated, unless you win your case.
- The interest accrued more than 18 months after the original due date of a tax return or the date the return was filed, and the IRS didn't notify you that additional tax was due during that period. (I.R.C. § 6404.)
- The interest accrued on a return you filed late because you were living in a federally declared disaster area when the return was due.

As with taxes and penalties, interest also may be reduced or eliminated by an Offer in Compromise or through bankruptcy. (See Chapter 6.)

How to Request an Interest Abatement

Although interest is seldom abated except when the IRS has made a mistake, it never hurts to ask. To request an interest abatement, file Form 843, *Claim for Refund and Request for Abatement*. In the explanation space, make clear why the interest should be abated. For example: "The IRS wrongfully sent me a refund and is charging interest. I should not have to pay interest because my actions did not cause the refund to be sent."

Once the IRS receives your Form 843, the IRS Interest Abatement Coordinator will make a determination. If your claim is denied, call the Taxpayer Advocate Service at your local IRS office. (See Chapter 8.) You also can sue in U.S. District Court or the federal Court of Claims to recover interest already paid, but this option is too costly to be a practical alternative. If you are in a disaster area, call the IRS for instructions at 800-829-1040.

Designating Late Tax Payments

If you can't pay in full, be sure to tell the IRS how a late payment should be applied to your tax account. If you don't, the IRS allocates it first to taxes, then to penalties, and last to interest. Payments are automatically applied to the oldest tax period for which you owe. For example, you owe $10,000 in taxes, penalties, and interest for several of the past eight years. You make a $1,500 payment. Tell the IRS in writing that it is to be applied to the most recent year.

Advantages of Designating Your Payments

On the date income taxes are assessed, the IRS has 10 years to collect these taxes, penalties, and interest. If part of your tax bill is for a year for which the 10-year limit is about to expire, then be sure to designate in writing that your payments are to be applied to your most recent tax debts. For example, suppose in 2024 you want to make a payment to a tax debt for years 2015 and 2016. Designate the payment to 2016, because the 2015 tax debt expires on April 16, 2026, assuming you filed your 2015 tax return by April 15, 2016. (See Chapter 6.)

Another reason to designate payments to the most recent years is your right to reduce some tax bills in bankruptcy. Generally, older tax bills are more easily reduced or eliminated in bankruptcy than newer ones. (See Chapter 6.)

How to Designate a Payment

When making an income tax payment by check or money order, write in the lower left-hand corner your Social Security number and the tax period or year you are paying. For a business tax, use your taxpayer identification number instead of your Social Security number.

Unless the payment is for the current tax bill, enclose a letter with the payment clearly stating that payment is to be applied to the tax period or year noted on your check or money order. Otherwise, the IRS will apply the payment to the oldest tax period. If you're concerned that the IRS has misapplied the funds, you can request an account statement, called a "Record of Account" for individuals with Social Security numbers or businesses with separate identification numbers. (See Chapter 1.)

If the account statement shows that the IRS ignored your designation request, send photocopies of your letter and the checks to show that payments were misapplied. With proof of your designation of payment, the IRS will correct its records.

If the IRS refuses or ignores your request, complain to the taxpayer advocate. (See Chapter 8.)

 CAUTION
Only voluntary payments can be designated to particular tax periods.
If the IRS levies your wages or bank account or withholds a refund, you have no right to designate how it's applied.

Chapter Highlights

- The IRS can add penalties to your bill for a variety of tax misdeeds.
- Interest is always added to a tax bill if the bill isn't paid on time.
- You might get the IRS to remove a penalty for "reasonable cause."

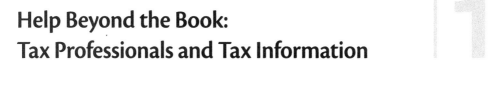
Help Beyond the Book:
Tax Professionals and Tax Information

Finding and Using a Tax Professional..380

How Tax Professionals Can Help 381

Types of Tax Professionals 382

Choosing the Right Tax Pro..383

What to Look for in a Tax Professional 384

Tax Professionals' Fees...385

Tax Pros for Serious Problems..386

The Right Type of Tax Professional..387

Tax Professional Analysis After an Audit 388

Hiring a Tax Return Preparer 388

Researching Tax Questions...389

Free IRS Information 390

Private Tax Guides..392

Other Research Materials—Using the Library or Internet 393

This book gives you strategies for coping with most tax problems—audits, bills, and Tax Court. If you need more help, try any of these:

- **A tax professional.** An enrolled agent, a certified public accountant, or a tax attorney can prepare tax returns or provide tax information, guidance, or representation before the IRS.
- **The IRS.** The IRS has free tax publications, telephone prerecorded and live information, internet access, and taxpayer service representatives at many offices.
- **A library.** You can research tax questions in larger public libraries and law libraries in your community.
- **The internet.** You can do much research on tax issues at the IRS's and others' websites.

Finding and Using a Tax Professional

You can successfully take on the IRS alone most of the time. But if you feel over your head or want professional reassurance, consider consulting or hiring a tax professional.

Under the Taxpayer Bill of Rights (Chapter 15), you may have a representative handle any IRS matter for you. You never have to face the IRS alone if you hire a tax professional. You also have the right to call "time out" to consult a tax professional during the process whenever you are taking on the IRS by yourself. But you don't have the right to free help. You'll have to pay whomever you hire.

You can safely go it alone in the two most common, but serious, IRS situations:

- You are being audited and your records are in order, you can substantiate almost everything on your return, and you have nothing to hide.
- The IRS is seeking to collect an overdue tax bill of $10,000 or less and you can pay it off over time.

But before making any decision on proceeding alone or working with a tax professional, weigh the pros and cons of each.

Going it alone

Pro: You save professional fees.

Con: It takes a lot of time.

You might find it very stressful.

You might say or do the wrong thing.

Consulting a tax professional before facing the IRS on your own

Pro: You gain knowledge, strategy, advice, and confidence.

Con: Most tax professionals charge for a consultation, but it will be less than if you hire the tax professional to represent you.

Hiring a tax professional to represent you before the IRS

Pro: The IRS respects knowledgeable tax professionals.

You don't have to face the IRS in most cases.

Tax professionals know tax issues.

Con: Tax professionals are expensive if they are good.

You understand your tax records best.

You risk hiring someone who is inexperienced or incompetent.

How Tax Professionals Can Help

Myth: The IRS will think I am guilty of something if I hire a tax professional or will get mad at me for not facing them myself.

Fact: IRS auditors and collectors prefer dealing with experienced tax professionals. It makes their job easier. Good tax professionals know what the IRS wants and don't get overly emotional.

If you face an audit, collection of a tax bill, or a Tax Court hearing—and you've decided to find a tax professional—you should get the services listed here.

Consultation and advice. A tax professional can analyze your situation and suggest a strategy. Rarely is there only one way to handle an IRS matter. Once you know the alternatives, you can make an informed choice. Of course, a tax professional might pitch their services. Weigh the professional's advice against what you have learned by reading this book and your own judgment. If the tax professional suggests a course of action you believe is excessively expensive, is dishonest, or doesn't make sense, find someone else. There are good ones and bad ones, as in any profession.

Negotiation. An experienced tax professional should know what kinds of deals can and can't be made with the IRS.

Representation. Tax professionals know IRS procedures and how to maneuver around the IRS bureaucracy. They can neutralize the intimidation factor the IRS knows it holds over you. And, if you have something to hide, a tax professional usually can keep the lid on it better than you can.

Free or Low Cost Tax Help

- *Low-Income Taxpayer Clinics* (LITCs) provide free or low cost legal representation for eligible individuals with IRS tax disputes. You must meet financial eligibility requirements. This is a great service if you qualify.
- *Taxpayer Advocate Service* (TAS) is an independent department of the IRS which can help resolve problems with the IRS, for instance, if you're facing financial hardship due to an IRS action or you have tried repeatedly to resolve an issue but the IRS has not responded. There is no charge for this help, but don't expect miracles. (See Chapter 8 for contact information.)

Types of Tax Professionals

For an audit, a collection, or an appeals problem, you can choose among enrolled agents, tax attorneys, and certified public accountants. A fourth category—tax return preparers with no professional certifications—can help you around April 15, but might not have the right to represent you before the IRS.

Enrolled agent (EA). An EA is a full-time tax adviser and tax preparer who is licensed to practice before the IRS. Most EAs can't represent you in Tax Court, however. They became enrolled agents by either passing a difficult IRS exam or having at least five years of IRS work experience. They also must participate in continuing education programs to retain their EA designations.

There are approximately 24,000 EAs in the United States. EAs are the least expensive of all tax professionals. For a cost-effective approach to handling a tax problem, consider an EA.

Tax attorney. Tax attorneys are lawyers who specialize in complex tax and estate planning; others focus on IRS dispute resolution and some do complex tax return preparation. Look for a tax attorney with either a special tax law degree (LL.M.-Tax) or a certification as a tax law specialist from a state bar association. If a great deal of money is at stake, the IRS is accusing you of fraud, or you're headed to court, call a tax attorney.

Certified public accountant (CPA). Like attorneys, CPAs are licensed and regulated in all states. They do sophisticated accounting and internal audit work and prepare tax returns. To become a CPA, an accountant must have a college degree and experience with a CPA firm and must pass a rigorous examination. Some CPAs have a great deal of IRS experience, but many never deal with the IRS. CPAs charge about the same as attorneys. As a rule, CPAs are not as aggressive as tax lawyers when facing IRS personnel.

CAUTION

Is your preparer legit? All paid tax return preparers must have an IRS-issued Preparer Tax Identification Number (PTIN) and list it on all returns they prepare. The IRS maintains a searchable online directory of all registered tax professionals at http://irs.treasury.gov/rpo/rpo.jsf.

Choosing the Right Tax Pro

There are several ways to find a good tax professional for help beyond tax return preparation.

Personal referrals. Referrals are frequently the best source. Ask friends, relatives, and acquaintances whose judgment you trust for the names of tax professionals who helped them. If their tax professionals can't help, ask for a referral.

Your tax preparer or accountant. Your tax return preparer or accountant should know a good tax professional who can help you deal with an IRS problem, or that person might be qualified.

Prepaid legal plans. Prepaid legal plans offer basic services for a low monthly fee and discounted fees for additional work. Few lawyers in prepaid legal plans have tax or IRS experience, however. Tax attorneys rarely participate because of relatively low fees paid by the plans.

Chain tax services. Some national outfits offer audit assistance free with their tax return preparation service. One chain says they will go with you to the IRS to explain how a return was prepared. This service might fall short of actual representation. And there is no guarantee the person going with you prepared your return or is a tax expert. Not all tax preparers are created equal—not by a long shot. These folks might know how to prepare simple tax returns, but we wouldn't rely on them to help with an IRS problem.

Advertising. Various directories, online or in print, carry lists of tax professionals. Look under Accountants, Tax Return Preparers, Tax Consultants, and Attorneys-Tax. Some tax professionals offer a first consultation by phone or in their office at no charge. Bear in mind, however, that professionals heavily advertising or giving away their time might be new to the game.

Professional associations and referral panels. Search online. Most local bar associations will give out the names of tax attorneys who practice in your area. But bar associations don't meaningfully screen the attorneys listed; those who are listed might not be experienced or competent. To find an EA in your area, check the National Association of Enrolled Agents online directory at https://taxexperts.naea.org/expertdirectory. To find a CPA, try calling a local or state CPA society.

Direct solicitation. If the IRS has filed a Notice of Federal Tax Lien against you, you might receive a call, letter, or email from a tax service. Be wary. In general, good tax professionals are too busy to do this.

What to Look for in a Tax Professional

Once you have the name of a tax professional, call and ask to speak with the person directly. If that person is too busy to talk to you—and your call isn't transferred to another tax specialist—assume the office is too busy to handle your case. Call the next person on your list.

When you speak to a tax professional, try to develop a rapport. Mention how you got their name, especially if it was a personal referral. Then get to the point—talk about your tax problem. If they don't handle your type of case, ask for the names of professionals who do.

Here are some other suggestions for making a good match:

- Don't rush to hire the first tax professional you speak to. Your decision is important, and rarely is there only one person for the job. Talk to a few. Choose the one you communicate with best—do you understand the advice and answers to your questions?

- Question the tax professional carefully about their IRS experience. No matter how well someone knows the tax code, prior IRS dealings are key. Previous IRS employment is not always a plus; it might have forever impressed the IRS point of view on the person. Also, be skeptical if the person hasn't been in practice at least five years.

- Does the tax professional seem to be aggressive or timid in discussing your case? If they seem awed by the IRS, find someone else.

- Does the tax professional give you a feeling of confidence? Ask about the likely outcome of your case. While no one can predict the future, this answer should create trust. Look for an honest response, not necessarily a rosy picture.

If you lose faith in your tax professional, find another one fast. But don't dismiss the first one until you get a second opinion on their work. And don't fire a tax professional simply because nothing is happening. Frequently, inaction is because the IRS is dragging its feet. Be patient—delay often works to your advantage in dealing with the IRS.

Tax Professionals' Fees

Get an understanding about the tax professional's fees at your first meeting. Will you be charged by the hour or a flat fee? Professionals can charge anything from $50 (for an enrolled agent) to $700 (for a top tax attorney) per hour, depending on where you live, the type of case, and the tax professional. To some extent, you can control costs. Tax professionals can be hired either as consultants, meaning you handle your own case and ask for advice as needed, or hired to represent you from start to finish. In other words, hiring a tax professional doesn't have to be an all or nothing affair.

Tips on Controlling a Tax Professional's Fees

- If you like the tax professional but not the fee, ask if it can be done for less. If the person isn't very busy, they might be flexible on fee and payment arrangements. Small tax firms or solo practitioners are more likely than professionals in large offices to negotiate their fees.
- Ask for a written fee agreement and monthly billings with itemized statements of time and services rendered. This will keep the tax professional honest and keep the large-bill shock down. In many states, attorneys are required to give you a written fee agreement before starting work.
- If you disagree with a bill, call your tax professional. If the firm is interested in retaining your business, it should listen to your concerns, adjust the bill, or work toward satisfying you. If the tax professional won't budge, call your state or local CPA society or your state's bar association. Many groups have panels that help professionals and clients mediate fee disputes.

Although uncertainty about open-ended fee arrangements leaves most folks uncomfortable, many good tax professionals won't quote a flat fee. But they should be able to ballpark a range of hours necessary for your case.

Most tax professionals require a fee and cost retainer paid in advance, often equal to the minimum time estimated to be needed on the case.

Tax Pros for Serious Problems

If you're being pursued by a tax collector or you're headed to Tax Court, the information in this chapter, and in Chapters 5 and 6, should guide you in your decision about using a tax professional. Audits, however, require special attention: Spending a small percentage of your potential IRS exposure for professional help can be a wise investment for the peace of mind and confidence that good advice brings. Before reading this information, however, read the information above and Chapter 3.

If you consult a tax professional, bring your IRS audit notice, tax return, and documents on which the return was prepared to the first meeting. If you face an *office*—as opposed to a field—audit, go over the audit letter checklist with the tax professional—explain why you reported your income as you did or took the deductions that the IRS is now questioning. Ask the tax professional what documentation will help you prove your position.

If you face a *field* audit, your audit will likely go beyond any prepared list of items to be examined. This makes a field audit more difficult to prepare for than an office audit. Show an audit-experienced tax pro your IRS audit letter and tax return and ask which items they would expect the IRS to question. Next, ask if they see any legal problem areas and how to deal with them. You might ask the person to provide some supporting tax law authority or prepare a memorandum of law pertaining to your case to show the auditor.

Finally, ask the tax professional for suggestions on how best to explain and present your documents to the auditor. You might want assistance in making summaries or spreadsheets showing your business or investment transactions. The more clearly you present information, the less time you'll spend with the auditor. Auditors appreciate and, more importantly, reward well-prepared taxpayers.

If your tax professional was the preparer of the tax return, ask them to explain all figures and schedules to you. If workpapers or notes were used to prepare your return, ask for copies and interpretations, if needed. You won't necessarily show them to the auditor; they might be just for your reference.

The Right Type of Tax Professional

Using an enrolled agent is a cost-effective choice when you need representation in an audit. But if you face complex legal or accounting issues or if the IRS accuses you of fraud, hire a tax attorney or CPA. In some cases, you might need both.

Your tax return preparer may legally represent you at an audit. Or an immediate family member, a business partner, or an employee can with written permission on IRS Form 2848. (Call 800-829-3676 or go to the IRS website for this form.) Bringing any of these people along for support is okay, but we don't recommend having any of them represent you at an audit.

Tax Professional Analysis After an Audit

If you handled your own audit and it did not turn out well, you might want to ask a tax professional why. The tax pro can analyze the examination report, tax return, and documents you produced at the audit. Tell the tax pro what you said and what the auditor said about items that are disputed. The tax professional can then evaluate the strengths and weaknesses of your legal position.

If the person believes you are at least in a legal gray area, they might examine the quality of the documents and consider the credibility of your explanations. In an hour or so, the tax pro should be able to decide whether you should contest the IRS's report. They might advise you to try again with the auditor or the auditor's manager, or to make a formal appeal or go to Tax Court. (See Chapter 4.) You should do this soon after the audit because there are strict deadlines for appealing and going to Tax Court.

Hiring a Tax Return Preparer

IRS problems often stem from the accuracy of your tax return and who prepares it. Over half of all tax returns are professionally prepared. The commissioner of the IRS has said that the "tax system has become so complex … something must be done to make it less burdensome." Until this happens, consider having a tax professional prepare your returns, especially if you are self-employed.

You might also lessen your chance of being audited by having a professional preparation. Insiders say that IRS personnel (see Chapter 3) are more likely to pick self-prepared returns for audit than those signed by a reputable tax professional.

Enrolled agents, tax attorneys, and CPAs are the cream of the crop. Others might call themselves tax preparers, too. But unless they are admitted to practice before the IRS, they can't represent you there. Fees for preparing individual income tax returns range from $80 to $2,500 and up, depending on the complexity of your return and the professional qualifications of the tax preparer.

Whether you hire a tax preparer or do it yourself, you alone are responsible for the accuracy of the tax forms. So check out the qualifications of the preparer you hire. The IRS and most states don't license tax preparers, but states do license attorneys and CPAs. Almost anyone can call themself a tax return preparer.

Internet and chain tax preparers' fees are the lowest, but their work product is inconsistent. These McTax outfits depend on inexperienced seasonal employees earning minimum wage. Emphasis is on quantity, not quality, and workers earn bonuses for turning out a lot of returns. You might never meet the actual preparer of your return. And even if you do, chances are they won't be around after April 15 if you—or the IRS—have questions about your return.

For most people, enrolled agents are the best bet to prepare tax returns. They are licensed by the IRS. Their prices are higher than chains, but lower than CPAs and tax attorneys. If you want a tax preparer for many years down the road, start looking long before the tax season starts. Don't switch tax preparers unless you have a good reason.

CAUTION
Avoid certain tax preparers. Never hire a tax preparer who bases their fee on a percentage of the refund you will receive, guarantees refunds in all cases, or won't sign your tax return as the preparer. If the IRS designates someone as a problem preparer, it casts out its audit net to bring in the preparer's clients.

Researching Tax Questions

Although most tax matters require no research, some do. Your auditor might go beyond looking at your records. For instance, the question might be whether or not the deductions are legally allowable. Your home office expenses might be disallowed not because you didn't prove them, but because the auditor says that you don't qualify for a home office deduction. To find out if the IRS is correct, you must know what the legal requirements are to qualify for a home office.

There are many good sources to augment the information in this book.

Free IRS Information

The IRS offers free publications and telephone and face-to-face help. To meet with someone from the IRS in person, call your nearest local IRS office. At larger IRS offices, there are Taxpayer Assistance Centers where you can sit down and talk to a taxpayer service representative—you need to make an appointment to do this. Check the IRS website at www.irs.gov or call 800-829-1040 for the closest Taxpayer Assistance Center. Just don't expect any tax savings tips or sophisticated advice from the IRS.

IRS Publications

The IRS distributes free taxpayer pamphlets, nicknamed pubs, numbered from 1 to over 1000. Pubs contain tax information on all kinds of issues— from the IRS's point of view, of course. For example, Publication 334, *Tax Guide for Small Business*, has rules from how to claim depreciation of a business vehicle to reporting losses on the sale of assets.

These pubs are free and are all available for download at the IRS's website at www.irs.gov. You can get paper copies at IRS offices or by calling 800-829-3676.

IRS Telephone Information

The IRS toll-free number is 800-829-1040 for individuals and 800-829-4933 for small businesses. Live people answer questions on tax preparation and tax notices. You'll be asked to give your Social Security or employer identification number if you need information about your account. However, due to high call volumes and low IRS staffing, it can be hard to get through on these numbers. Be prepared to wait.

The best thing we can say about talking to the IRS on the telephone is that it's free. You will only get the official IRS position, which is conservative and not necessarily beneficial. And many times the answers are misleading or outright wrong (although the IRS claims IRS answers are accurate over 80% of the time). Start, but don't stop here, with your tax law research.

IRS Website

A vast amount of information is available on the IRS website at www.irs.gov.
The IRS has devoted enormous resources into making its website the go-to
destination for tax information. In addition to tax publications, it contains:

- An online tool called the Interactive Tax Assistant that provides
  answers to many tax questions—it's at www.irs.gov/help/ita.
- Hundreds of usually brief written discussions on various tax issues
  called "Tax Topics" (www.irs.gov/taxtopics).
- Extensive frequently asked questions (FAQs) on recent tax legislation
  and basic tax issues and procedures. Many are updated often. Do
  a keyword search at www.irs.gov to find relevant FAQs. IRS FAQs
  are intended to provide general information to taxpayers and do
  not have the force of law. They may not be relied on or used by the
  IRS to resolve a case. However, the IRS will not impose penalties
  on taxpayers who reasonably rely on FAQs that are later found to be
  wrong by the IRS. Keep a copy of any FAQ you rely on.

You can also access the *Internal Revenue Manual*, which is the IRS rule
book. It contains a wealth of useful information on IRS procedures.

Free IRS Programs

The IRS video portal (www.irsvideos.gov) contains video and audio presentations on topics of interest to taxpayers. The IRS also offers seminars
on various topics for small businesses, such as payroll tax reporting. You
can ask questions at these programs, which are given at schools and federal
buildings. Use the links at www.irs.gov/businesses/small-businesses-self-
employed/small-business-tax-workshops-meetings-and-seminars to see if any
programs are offered near you.

If you are age 60 or older or qualify as low income, with or without a
small business, you might be eligible for free tax assistance under the VITA
(Volunteer Income Tax Assistance) or TCE (Tax Counseling for the Elderly)
programs. For details, call the IRS at 800-906-9887 or check the IRS website.

Tax Information on the Internet

Many legal and tax resources intended both for lawyers and the general public are available online. Visit any of the following websites, each of which provides links to other tax and legal information resources:

- **www.nolo.com.** The Nolo site includes tax and legal information. There are FAQs (frequently asked questions) on a wide variety of legal topics and articles on legal issues. The website has a section devoted exclusively to personal and business tax issues.
- **www.law.cornell.edu.** This site, another law pointer, is maintained by Cornell Law School.
- **www.legalbitstream.com.** This invaluable site contains a free online library of tax cases from all courts; IRS materials, notices, and rulings; and the tax code and IRS regulations.

Tax information is available at many other sites on the internet. But an internet search engine like Google is likely to offer the least reliable tax information.

Private Tax Guides

For hard-copy research, there are numerous privately published tax guides that are widely available.

Popular Guidebooks

The most widely used guidebook to taxes is *J.K. Lasser's Your Income Tax* (Wiley), which is updated each year. It is sold just about everywhere during tax season. It covers the most current tax rules for income reporting and deduction taking. It is also easier to read than IRS publications and has better examples of how the tax law works. J.K. Lasser also has more specialized guides such as *Small Business Taxes* and *Guide to Self-Employment*.

Tax Professional Deskbooks and Guides

Accountants, IRS agents, and attorneys use more sophisticated tax deskbooks. The three top professional guides are the *Master Tax Guide* (Commerce Clearing House/Wolters Kluwer), *RIA Federal Tax Handbook* (Thomson

Reuters), and *Pearson's Federal Taxation*. They are all over 1,000 pages of fine print. Don't let this scare you, as you might need to read only a few pages. These deskbooks summarize the law on the most common tax law problems. They are available online at www.amazon.com and in libraries, especially law libraries, and they are sold in larger bookstores.

IRS personnel seem to prefer the *Master Tax Guide*. If you have a choice of which of the three to consult, choose that one.

Other Research Materials—Using the Library or Internet

The original source materials for the tax law are the Internal Revenue Code and Congressional committee reports. IRS regulations and federal court decisions interpret the law and show how it is applied to a set of facts. The Internal Revenue Code and reports are available online at www.irs.gov and found in federal building libraries, large public libraries, and law libraries. Tax Court decisions are available online at www.ustaxcourt.gov and www.legalbitstream.com. Most are technical in the extreme and are only recommended as a cure for insomnia. The guidebooks listed above are an attempt to make sense out of this mass of legalese and are your better bets.

Nevertheless, if you want to look at law court decisions or legal treatises, find a law library or go online. To find a library, call your local courthouse or college or a lawyer and ask where the nearest law library open to the public is located. Many private law libraries only allow use by lawyers, judges, and law students.

Search the library computer databases for:
- tax deductions, credits, audits, and so on
- Internal Revenue Code (with section number)
- IRS regulations
- U.S. Tax Court and other federal court opinions, and
- books by research companies and legal scholars explaining the tax law, such as this book and the tax guides mentioned earlier.

Use the IRS website at www.irs.gov to get this material. Or, use a search engine like www.google.com.

Start your research with the number of an Internal Revenue Code section, an IRS regulation, or a name of a case you have run across.

If you go the library route, once armed with the call numbers and the citation or topic, head for the material or throw yourself on the mercy of the library staff. A librarian might even show you how to use the books. But, few law librarians have great familiarity with tax law, so don't expect too much.

Further Reading for Dealing With IRS Problems

- *Representing the Audited Taxpayer Before the IRS, Representation Before the Collection Division of the IRS,* and *Representation Before the Appeals Division of the IRS* (Thomson Reuters). All three are loose-leaf and supplemented annually. They are written clearly by experienced people in the field although they are too expensive for anyone but a serious tax professional. We especially recommend the collection book.
- *Tax Management Tax Practice Series* (Bloomberg BNA, www.bloomberglaw.com. This is a top-of-the-line pricey research resource tool online. Most likely access to it will be found at a law library or a tax professional's office.

Chapter Highlights

- Usually you can file tax returns and deal successfully with the IRS on your own, but sometimes you should hire a tax professional.
- The best tax professionals are enrolled agents, certified public accountants, and tax attorneys.
- There are free and low-cost sources of good tax information, including books, the IRS, and some websites.

When You Owe State Income Taxes

The IRS and State Taxing Authorities..396

Does Your State Have a Taxpayer Bill of Rights? 397

State Time Limits to Assess and Collect Income Taxes....................................397

State Tax Collection Departments 398

State Tax Bills..398

Getting a State Payment Plan 399

Enforced Collection—Seizing Assets..400

Bankruptcy...400

Compromising a State Tax Assessment..400

Suspending Collection 401

When All Else Fails, Try Your Political Connections..402

All states except Alaska, Florida, Nevada, New Hampshire, Tennessee, South Dakota, Texas, Washington, and Wyoming impose an income tax. Usually the filing requirements, penalties, and collection techniques mirror those of the federal IRS. For more specific information, write or call your state taxing authority. Even if you live in a state without an income tax, there might be helpful information in this chapter—for example, your state may tax business entities or estates.

The IRS and State Taxing Authorities

States' agencies have computer links with the IRS. Only Nevada does not share residents' data with the IRS.

Most state taxing authorities act quickly when they receive IRS information if it means the taxpayer will owe the state more, too. In fact, many states act on IRS-supplied information before the IRS does. By the time the IRS comes to collect, you might have set up a state installment plan or lost your property to a state tax collector, leaving little for the IRS. Why the IRS gives this information to the states before it acts on it is a mystery.

Audit adjustments. Because of the computer linkage, if you are audited by the IRS, your state automatically finds out. Based on IRS adjustments, the state can change your state tax bill without conducting a separate audit.

TIP

If you contest an IRS audit in Tax Court, notify your state's income tax department to prevent a premature state tax assessment. Send the state agency a copy of your Tax Court petition. (See Chapter 5.) Request that no further action be taken until your case has been decided.

States seldom audit individual taxpayers. They prefer to let the IRS audit you and then tag on a bill. States are more likely to audit businesses for sales or employment taxes. If you are audited by your state taxing authority, most of the general principles of this book will apply.

Most state tax assessments can be appealed, as with IRS audits. If your appeal of a proposed state assessment is rejected—even an assessment following a state audit—you can't contest the tax bill in most state courts unless you pay the bill first.

Collections. If the IRS pursues you as a nonfiler, so probably will your state. Most states automatically dun taxpayers based on IRS bills. So, if the IRS makes a mistake in the bill, the state will, too.

Does Your State Have a Taxpayer Bill of Rights?

Some states have enacted their versions of the federal Taxpayer Bill of Rights. To find out if your state has one, and to obtain a copy, call or write your state taxing authority. Many of the state bills include grievance procedures. The California bill, for example, provides an administrative hearing to protest an improper seizure of property.

Also, ask if your state has a taxpayer advocate who acts much the same as an IRS taxpayer advocate. (See Chapter 8.) For example, taxpayer advocates might get state wage levies released or property returned, if they are convinced that the seizures threaten the taxpayers' health or welfare.

If your state has a taxpayer advocate whom you want to contact, first try by phone. If that fails, show up at the advocate's office or write and tell them your phone number and the best times to reach you.

If your state doesn't have a taxpayer advocate, contact your state representative or assemblyperson.

State Time Limits to Assess and Collect Income Taxes

As you've learned, once you file a federal return, the IRS generally has three years to assess additional taxes by way of an audit. In some situations, the IRS has six years. (See Chapters 3 and 6.) Similarly, state time limitations vary from one to five years.

Once additional taxes are assessed, the IRS has 10 years to collect them. Again, state limitations differ tremendously.

Beware—in many states, the period to collect the tax is renewable; that is, it is not limited. In California, for example, the 10-year period can be renewed twice, for a total of 30 years.

State Tax Collection Departments

Like the IRS, most states have computerized collection systems that spit out a series of notices. If you don't respond, involuntary collection starts. Just like the IRS, your state files liens and seizes your property. (See Chapter 7.) States act quickly at grabbing property, often much faster than the IRS. And some states hire private collection agencies, usually to go after debtors who have moved beyond state lines.

If you disagree with the state's assessment notice, there is likely an appeals process similar to the IRS's. If your state doesn't have a specific form to appeal, follow the sample protest letter in Chapter 4.

The state may have an informal conference or appeal hearing. If you are unsuccessful, you must pay the tax and then file a claim for a refund or sue in state court. Some states let taxpayers go to court without first paying a tax bill, similar to Tax Court.

Many state tax agencies don't run as smoothly as the IRS. That's pretty scary, huh? Letters are lost and calls not returned. Most state taxing authorities must respond to your inquiries within a certain number of days. If the agency denies receiving your letter or won't return calls, however, what can you do?

Avoid lost mail and unreturned phone calls by dealing with the state taxing authority in person. Always get the name and direct telephone number of any employee you talk to. This fixes some responsibility and might keep them from vanishing when you call back. If you reach any agreement over the phone or in person, immediately send a confirming letter. Later, if anyone disputes the agreement, speak to a supervisor or the state taxpayer advocate. Consider asking for political help.

State Tax Bills

Most state tax collectors operate similarly to the IRS—they might accept installments, seize assets, or settle tax bills for less than the full amount owed. States can also suspend collection for hardship. Some states, such as California and New York, are especially tough to deal with.

Getting a State Payment Plan

Most tax collectors will grant installment agreements if they don't believe you can make a full payment. As with the IRS, you might be able to get a time payment agreement over the phone or by writing. You might have to visit the state tax office in person. Call to make an appointment or go to the office and wait in line.

You might be required to complete financial disclosure forms showing your assets, bank accounts, and sources of income.

Many states use an abbreviated version of the IRS financial disclosure Form 433. (See Chapter 6.) State forms usually don't have enough room for listing all expenses. Therefore, before meeting with a state tax collector, thoroughly review the material in Chapter 6 on Form 433-A (and Form 433-B if you own a business). Gather together your proof of expenses, such as credit card bills and rent receipts. Expect an argument if you list expenses the collector does not think are absolutely necessary. Charitable contributions, cigarette expenses, and entertainment are usually in this category.

Provide a copy of your most recent pay stub. If your pay varies due to bonuses or overtime, take the lowest recent stub. If self-employed, take in your last tax return—unless your income has dropped lately. In that event, write up a projection of your income and expenses for the next three months to a year.

States don't usually verify the information in a financial statement as stringently as the IRS. State tax offices tend to accept any documentation that appears to be genuine. This doesn't mean, however, that you should be less than truthful. Let your conscience be your guide.

State tax collectors often display a take it or leave it attitude. They demand payment plan commitments on the spot, without much negotiating. They might reject requests for agreements to last more than 12 months. If you need longer, you might have to agree for now and ask for more time later. Most can give you more time to pay, regardless of how tough they talk. And even if you get an installment agreement, the state may record a tax lien, just like the IRS.

Enforced Collection—Seizing Assets

States often act quicker than the IRS in seizing the property of tax delin-quents. State laws vary as to the amount of wages that the state can take. In California, for example, the state can grab 25% of your net pay.

Keeping your bank account from tax collectors—state or federal—is always a concern. (See Chapter 6 about protecting your bank accounts from collectors.)

If you have made financial disclosures, the state will have a list of your assets, such as your bank accounts, car, and home. Most states have the power to seize houses, but you might be entitled to full or partial protection under the state homestead exemption.

Homestead exemptions never protect you from the IRS, however. In some states, if tax collectors take a house, they must pay the homeowner the amount of their statutory homestead exemption. Every state is different, so check with an attorney or do some legal research. (See Chapter 13.)

Bankruptcy

State tax bills, like IRS debts, can be handled under federal bankruptcy law. If the state is about to take your property, filing for bankruptcy could give you a reprieve. Collection activities must stop. State tax debts might or might not qualify for discharge in a Chapter 7 bankruptcy. See a bankruptcy lawyer in your area for details. But, if the state taxes don't qualify for Chapter 7, you can force a payment plan on the state in a Chapter 13 bankruptcy. (See Chapter 6.)

Compromising a State Tax Assessment

You must settle an IRS tax bill through the Offer in Compromise procedure. (See Chapter 6.) Many states, too, will consider settling a tax bill you can't afford to pay. Contact your state tax agency and ask if it can be done and, if so, how. There is probably a form for making the request. If you're told it can't be done, speak to the clerk's supervisor. Keep going up the ladder until you're satisfied you have received the final word.

Coordinating Installment Plans With the IRS and Your State Tax Department

If you owe both federal and state income taxes, coordinate your payment plans. Let each taxing agency know you owe the other. Make your federal and state financial disclosure forms match. Propose installment plans simultaneously with payments in proportion to your total tax debt.

> EXAMPLE: Hamlet owes Minnesota $3,000 for state income taxes and the IRS $12,000. Although it's a strain, he can scrape together $500 a month for back taxes. He offers $100 to the state and $400 to the IRS. When questioned about his allocation, Hamlet says, "What could be more fair? I owe the IRS four times as much as I owe Minnesota. I should pay in that proportion."

Assuming the usual case—you owe the state far less than you owe the IRS—consider stalling the IRS and paying off the state first. Negotiating is simpler when your monster has one head, not two. Typically, states seize wages and property more quickly than the IRS. Finally, if you borrow money to pay off the state, this is another debt and expense to list on your IRS financial disclosure form.

Suspending Collection

If you can convince the state that paying would be a hardship, you might get a collection reprieve. You will likely have to tell a sob story and make a financial disclosure, in person, in writing, or perhaps on the phone. Expect the state to balk, so be persistent with your request. If you are unemployed or have health problems or other serious difficulties, you should prevail.

When All Else Fails, Try Your Political Connections

If the state tax agency is treating you unfairly, use whatever political connections you can muster. Someone in your broad circle of friends, relatives, acquaintances, or business associations might know a state legislator. Contact the elected official's office even if you don't have a connection. State tax agencies tend to be more sensitive to political pressures than the IRS. It's certainly worth a call to your state representative's office.

Chapter Highlights
• IRS computers automatically exchange your tax data with all states except Nevada.
• Most state tax agency procedures are modeled after the IRS.
• State tax agencies generally have the same powers of audit and tax collection as the IRS.

The Taxpayer Bill of Rights

Taxpayer Bill of Rights I 404

    The Good 404

    The So-So..405

    The Window Dressing 405

Taxpayer Bill of Rights II 406

    The Good 406

    The So-So..407

    The Window Dressing 408

Taxpayer Bill of Rights III 408

    The Good 408

    The So-So..411

    The Window Dressing 411

n 1988, Congress passed the first of three Taxpayer Bills of Rights. Senator Pryor announced that:

> [This law will] *stem the abuse of taxpayers by the IRS and provide redress when abuse does occur. It marks a victory for the little taxpayer. It levels the playing field.*

Well, you know how politicians get carried away with the sound of their own voices. TBOR I, as it is known, was a step in the right direction. TBOR II added a few more taxpayer protections, and TBOR III, passed in 1998, finally made real progress in giving taxpayers rights.

The IRS now must let taxpayers know that they have certain rights when facing the agency. Congress required the IRS to publish a plain-English pamphlet summarizing these rights, which is Publication 1, *Your Rights as a Taxpayer*. Take time to read this pamphlet if you are being audited or dealing with an IRS collector. It is reprinted at the end of this chapter.

Taxpayer Bill of Rights I

The following summarizes some of the key features of TBOR I.

The Good

- The IRS created the position of ombudsman, now called "taxpayer advocate." This IRS official is empowered to issue Taxpayer Assistance Orders (TAOs) stopping the IRS from taking certain actions against taxpayers. For instance, the taxpayer advocate can stop a seizure of your property if you can show that it will cause a significant hardship. This advocate works through the Taxpayer Advocate Service (see Chapter 8).
- The IRS developed Publication 1, *Your Rights as a Taxpayer*. The IRS must enclose it with your first notice concerning delinquent taxes. Oddly, it doesn't have to be sent with an audit notice. This pamphlet summarizes your rights during any IRS noncriminal interview, such as an audit, an appeal, or a collections matter.
- You can propose an installment plan to the IRS if you can't pay a bill in full. This doesn't mean you can force the IRS to accept your deal, but the IRS must fairly consider your request.

- You generally don't have to meet with the IRS personally if you send a qualified representative—a lawyer, a CPA, or an enrolled agent. (See Chapter 13.)
- You can stop an audit or other IRS meeting to contact a tax professional for advice. (See Chapter 3.) This is the IRS equivalent of your right to an attorney before talking to the police. The IRS won't furnish you a free tax professional, however.
- You generally can't be forced to meet with an IRS auditor at an inconvenient time or place. Congress was concerned about a small business being forced to close during an audit. In this situation, the IRS must hold the audit at its office or elsewhere. The IRS can, however, visit your business to verify items on your tax return, such as inventory or equipment. (See Chapter 3.)

The So-So

- Dollar amounts of property and wages exempt from IRS seizure were increased a bit. (See Chapter 7.)
- The district director—your IRS local chief—or the director's assistant must personally approve seizures of your principal residence. Revenue Officer Rambo can't decide on their own to take the roof over your head.
- You must be sent a Notice of Intent to Levy before the IRS seizes your property. You have 30 days to contest the seizure. In practice, if you owe the IRS, you'll have no legal grounds to contest. This freeze period, however, gives you time to negotiate further with the IRS.

The Window Dressing

- Penalties can be removed from your tax bill if they resulted from your relying on incorrect IRS *written* advice. The IRS rarely provides written advice.
- You can *audio record* most meetings with the IRS. Taping a meeting would probably make the IRS agent apprehensive and hard to deal with. You can't legally videotape or record telephone conversations with the IRS.
- You can sue any IRS employee who intentionally disregards the law, up to $100,000, plus legal costs. In the decade that it was law, 20 taxpayers (at most) won such cases. And, if you sue and lose, the IRS can get its costs awarded against you.

Taxpayer Bill of Rights II

TBOR II is a supplement to TBOR I, not a replacement. Here is a summary of some of TBOR II's provisions, which we have also put into the categories of the Good, the So-So, and the Window Dressing.

The Good

- Taxpayers can formally appeal liens, levies, and seizures to the IRS Independent Office of Appeals, which is totally independent of the collection division. The appeals office can either stop a lien, levy, or seizure if collectors did not follow correct procedures, or it can consider less drastic actions. Collectors are now more respectful of taxpayers, knowing there is another department looking over their shoulders.
- The IRS can withdraw a Notice of Federal Tax Lien or return seized property in any of the following cases:
  - The IRS action was premature.
  - The IRS action was not in accord with established procedures.
  - The taxpayer enters into an installment agreement.
  - It would facilitate collection of the tax debt.
  - It is in the best interests of the taxpayer.
- The IRS can forgive penalties for failing to timely deposit payroll taxes for first-time offenders. Also, the IRS can abate penalties for sending the payment to the IRS instead of depositing it with a proper financial institution. These should ease the burden somewhat for the small business person just starting off.
- If you personally owe payroll taxes under the Trust Fund Recovery Penalty, the IRS must now inform you of the efforts it makes to collect taxes from any other people who might be liable for the same taxes. (See Chapter 11.) Before, the IRS often made little effort to collect from all but the easiest target. Now, collectors must conscientiously pursue others as well and tell you of the efforts being made. TBOR II also establishes a federal basis for a lawsuit by one codebtor against the others.

- For married or divorced couples with joint tax bills, the IRS must tell both spouses what collection efforts have been made to get payment from the other spouse. The IRS typically pursues whichever divorced spouse is easier to find. The IRS might now more seriously pursue the other ex-spouse than in the past.

The So-So

- Interest or penalties on tax bills won't begin for 21 days after an assessment. If the added tax is $100,000 or more, the interest-free period is dropped to 10 business days. This is an incentive to encourage payment by audit victims as soon as the audit ends. It could save you a few bucks, but not many.
- Courts can more easily award attorneys' fees and legal costs to taxpayers who run up against the IRS. The IRS must prove it was substantially justified in bringing a case. While this sounds good, it is still within the discretion of the judge, not a jury, to allow recovery of your legal costs in fighting the IRS. In the past, few people have ever been awarded fees against the IRS, even when they won their cases.
- If you dispute the validity of income attributed to you on a Form 1099 or W-2—for example, a business incorrectly reports money paid to you as an independent contractor—now the IRS, not you, must hash it out with the third party.
- The IRS must notify a taxpayer within 60 days if it has a credit it can't match up with a tax bill. The IRS sometimes misapplies payments to accounts. At least now the agency must try to straighten it out in a reasonable period of time. We'll see.
- Married taxpayers who previously filed separately and owe taxes can amend their returns to file jointly, without paying the taxes due. Paying first was required to file this type of amendment.

The Window Dressing

- The term "ombudsman" from TBOR I was replaced with "taxpayer advocate." The "problems resolution office" is now also known as the Taxpayer Advocate Service. Proponents failed, however, in making this job independent of the IRS.
- Taxpayers can sue anyone who files a false Form 1099 or W-2 with fraudulent intent—that is, someone who falsely and deliberately reports to the IRS that you were paid money. Some militia groups have filed reports on IRS officials and other perceived enemies; this provision is the IRS's version of revenge.
- The amount you can sue an IRS collector for illegal acts is $1 million. This sounds good, but just try to get it.
- The Tax Court can decide whether the IRS's failure to abate interest was in error. It's hard to imagine an ordinary taxpayer taking this issue to court, but for multimillion-dollar cases, this could be significant.
- You can file your tax return by certain private delivery services, such as UPS, FedEx, or Airborne, as well as by the U.S. mail.
- Annual notices must be sent to anyone owing the IRS, showing a current balance due. Most people are probably not especially eager to get this information, if they need it.

Taxpayer Bill of Rights III

In 1998, the most significant IRS reform ever became law. While the outcome for the taxpayer was not perfect, it was far better than expected.

The Good

- Innocent spouse help became easier to get for joint return filers. And, a "separate liability election" is now possible for an ex or a legally separated spouse or one living apart for at least 12 months. The election limits the tax just to items relating to the innocent spouse (typically a wife). But there's no help if assets were transferred fraudulently or if the spouses both knew of the tax cheating. This is one of the real highlights of the reform act.

- The Tax Court can now hear disputes about innocent spouse relief.
- The monthly penalty for paying a tax bill under an installment agreement was cut from 0.5% to 0.25%. Anything helps.
- The IRS can't charge interest or certain penalties unless it contacts the tax debtor at least once a year. Usually, this just means a computer-generated notice. This rule doesn't apply to the failure to pay a penalty or tax fraud.
- A tax notice showing a penalty must indicate its source (the tax law section) and how it was computed. But, this doesn't apply to failure to file, failure to pay, or a few other types of penalties.
- Every IRS notice that includes interest must show how it was computed. This has helped cut down on the number of famous IRS "mystery" bills of the past.
- The IRS must notify individuals when a Notice of Federal Tax Lien is filed. And, more importantly, for the 30-day period after the mailing of the notice, the taxpayer can go before an appeals officer. Could be of significance in a few cases.
- All Notices of Intent to Levy must be sent by registered or certified mail, return receipt requested. No levy can take place within 30 days of the mailing. The taxpayer can contest it before an appeals officer. Great added taxpayer protection.
- There can be no seizure of a principal residence without a court order and prior notice of the hearing. At the hearing, the IRS must show that there is no reasonable alternative for the collection of the tax. This provision has virtually eliminated residence seizures by the IRS. Hooray!
- The attorney-client confidentiality of communications privilege is extended to anyone authorized under federal law to practice before the IRS. Theoretically, this puts CPAs and enrolled agents on the same footing as attorneys. Sounds good, but not really very important in practice.
- IRS auditors can't use financial status or economic reality probes to find unreported income without a reasonable indication that there is a likelihood of it. What the heck is a "reasonable indication"?
- The IRS may not contact anyone other than the taxpayer during an audit or a collection investigation without providing reasonable notice to the taxpayer those contacts are being made. Not much change in IRS procedures, just extra paperwork.

- IRS supervisory approval is required for any lien, levy, or seizure to affirm that the collector's action is appropriate under the circumstances. Circumstances include the amount due and the value of the asset. Restricts gunslinger collectors from acting on their own. Since levies and seizures decreased dramatically after the IRS reform act, this provision might deserve part of the credit.

- Levy exemption amounts for property are indexed for inflation and adjusted annually. These amounts are still pretty minimal.

- The IRS must provide a written accounting of sales of seized property, whether real or personal, to the tax debtor. The IRS has always done this anyway as a matter of policy, and now it's law.

- The IRS can't seize a residence for a tax debt of $5,000 or less. No big deal as the IRS isn't seizing residences anymore anyway.

- The IRS must exhaust all other payment options before seizing the taxpayer's business assets, which might slow down a few rogue IRS collectors.

- The IRS can't force a debtor to agree to extend the 10-year statute of limitations on collections. However, extensions may be required as part of an installment agreement. So, the double-talk here is that IRS really can force you to extend the collection period after all.

- For folks undergoing an audit, the IRS may request an extension of the normal (three-year) audit period. If it does so, the IRS must also tell the audited person that they have the right to refuse to sign or to limit the extension to particular audit issues. Well, if you don't sign, it usually means the IRS will disallow deductions or find you didn't report all your income and hit you with a bill.

- The IRS must allow folks making Offers in Compromise enough money for basic living expenses. The IRS can't reject an offer just because it is low. This is so vague, it's a source of amusement at IRS offices.

- IRS levies are prohibited during an Offer in Compromise, 30 days following the rejection of an offer, during an appeal, or while an installment agreement is in force.

- The IRS must have internal review procedures when rejecting requests for installment agreements. Good protection in theory as it requires supervisors to approve actions of their underlings.

The So-So

- The IRS now has the burden of proof in any *court proceeding* on a factual issue once a taxpayer presents credible evidence to the contrary. Four conditions must be met. The taxpayer must (1) substantiate the item; (2) maintain records; (3) cooperate with reasonable IRS requests for meetings, information, and documents; and (4) for entities (not individuals), meet certain net worth limitations. Congress considered, but unfortunately rejected, the original part of this law, which placed the burden of proof on the IRS in audits.
- A federal court can award up to $100,000 to a taxpayer if an IRS employee negligently breaks the law in collecting a tax bill and up to $1 million if the employee willfully violates the bankruptcy code automatic stays or discharge provisions. In reality, we've seen very few cases where taxpayers got a dime. However, IRS collectors seem to have become more timid since the law passed.

The Window Dressing

- The IRS will adopt a liberal acceptance policy for Offers in Compromise. From what we've seen, the IRS has completely ignored this "suggestion" from Congress.
- Tax audit losers must be told of the deadline dates for taking their bills to Tax Court. This date wasn't always easy to figure out for someone not in the tax world and is more important than it might appear to be.
- Certain fair debt collection practices were made applicable to the IRS (for example, a prohibition against harassing or abusive communications).
- An installment agreement must be granted if (1) the tax bill is under $10,000 (excluding penalties and interest); (2) in the previous five years, the debtor has had another installment agreement and didn't default on it; (3) the debtor submits financial statements, if requested, showing the debtor can't pay in full; and (4) the installment agreement provides for full payment within three years.
- Joint and several liability rules must be explained to married tax debtors. The spouses must be told about electing separate liability and how to get out of the debt altogether.

- Taxpayers' rights must be set forth in Publication 1 clearly, including the right to be represented.
- Explanations to taxpayers of the audit, appeals, and collection processes are required. And folks must be informed about the taxpayer advocate whenever the IRS proposes a new tax bill.
- Annual statements must be sent to debtors on IRS installment agreements showing the past year's payments and the remaining balance.
- IRS correspondence (other than routine notices) must include the name, telephone number, and ID number of an IRS employee the taxpayer may contact. IRS employees calling on the phone must give their telephone number and IRS badge number.
- IRS employees may use pseudonyms only if there is adequate justification, such as protecting personal safety, and IRS management has approved. This stops overzealous employees from abusing taxpayers while hiding behind phony names.
- Illegal tax protester designations are prohibited. These permanent character stains can't be listed anywhere in the IRS files or in its computer. The IRS only can designate folks as "nonfilers," but must remove this designation after the taxpayer has filed tax returns and paid all taxes.
- Any person (whistleblower) providing confidential information to Congress can't be punished if they believe such information relates to misconduct or taxpayer abuse.
- Local IRS telephone numbers and local IRS offices must be listed in directories. Believe it or not, the IRS did not do this before Congress ordered them to by law.

Chapter Highlights

- A federal law known as the Taxpayer Bill of Rights establishes certain rights for individuals and entities in dealing with the IRS.
- Your primary rights are to be treated fairly and in a prompt manner and to have a representative deal with the IRS for you.
- Read the two-page IRS Publication 1, *Your Rights as a Taxpayer*, whenever you have a problem with the IRS.

Publication 1, *Your Rights as a Taxpayer*

This publication explains your rights as a taxpayer and the processes for examination, appeal, collection, and refunds. Also available in Spanish.

The Taxpayer Bill of Rights

1. The Right to Be Informed

Taxpayers have the right to know what they need to do to comply with the tax laws. They are entitled to clear explanations of the laws and IRS procedures in all tax forms, instructions, publications, notices, and correspondence. They have the right to be informed of IRS decisions about their tax accounts and to receive clear explanations of the outcomes.

2. The Right to Quality Service

Taxpayers have the right to receive prompt, courteous, and professional assistance in their dealings with the IRS, to be spoken to in a way they can easily understand, to receive clear and easily understandable communications from the IRS, and to speak to a supervisor about inadequate service.

3. The Right to Pay No More than the Correct Amount of Tax

Taxpayers have the right to pay only the amount of tax legally due, including interest and penalties, and to have the IRS apply all tax payments properly.

4. The Right to Challenge the IRS's Position and Be Heard

Taxpayers have the right to raise objections and provide additional documentation in response to formal IRS actions or proposed actions, to expect that the IRS will consider their timely objections and documentation promptly and fairly, and to receive a response if the IRS does not agree with their position.

5. The Right to Appeal an IRS Decision in an Independent Forum

Taxpayers are entitled to a fair and impartial administrative appeal of most IRS decisions, including many penalties, and have the right to receive a written response regarding the Office of Appeals' decision. Taxpayers generally have the right to take their cases to court.

6. The Right to Finality

Taxpayers have the right to know the maximum amount of time they have to challenge the IRS's position as well as the maximum amount of time the IRS has to audit a particular tax year or collect a tax debt. Taxpayers have the right to know when the IRS has finished an audit.

7. The Right to Privacy

Taxpayers have the right to expect that any IRS inquiry, examination, or enforcement action will comply with the law and be no more intrusive than necessary, and will respect all due process rights, including search and seizure protections, and will provide, where applicable, a collection due process hearing.

8. The Right to Confidentiality

Taxpayers have the right to expect that any information they provide to the IRS will not be disclosed unless authorized by the taxpayer or by law. Taxpayers have the right to expect appropriate action will be taken against employees, return preparers, and others who wrongfully use or disclose taxpayer return information.

9. The Right to Retain Representation

Taxpayers have the right to retain an authorized representative of their choice to represent them in their dealings with the IRS. Taxpayers have the right to seek assistance from a Low Income Taxpayer Clinic if they cannot afford representation.

10. The Right to a Fair and Just Tax System

Taxpayers have the right to expect the tax system to consider facts and circumstances that might affect their underlying liabilities, ability to pay, or ability to provide information timely. Taxpayers have the right to receive assistance from the Taxpayer Advocate Service if they are experiencing financial difficulty or if the IRS has not resolved their tax issues properly and timely through its normal channels.

The IRS Mission Provide America's taxpayers top-quality service by helping them understand and meet their tax responsibilities and enforce the law with integrity and fairness to all.

Publication 1 (Rev. 9-2017) Catalog Number 64731W Department of the Treasury **Internal Revenue Service** www.irs.gov

Publication 1, *Your Rights as a Taxpayer* (continued)

Examinations, Appeals, Collections, and Refunds

Examinations (Audits)

We accept most taxpayers' returns as filed. If we inquire about your return or select it for examination, it does not suggest that you are dishonest. The inquiry or examination may or may not result in more tax. We may close your case without change; or, you may receive a refund.

The process of selecting a return for examination usually begins in one of two ways. First, we use computer programs to identify returns that may have incorrect amounts. These programs may be based on information returns, such as Forms 1099 and W-2, on studies of past examinations, or on certain issues identified by compliance projects. Second, we use information from outside sources that indicates that a return may have incorrect amounts. These sources may include newspapers, public records, and individuals. If we determine that the information is accurate and reliable, we may use it to select a return for examination.

Publication 556, Examination of Returns, Appeal Rights, and Claims for Refund, explains the rules and procedures that we follow in examinations. The following sections give an overview of how we conduct examinations.

By Mail

We handle many examinations and inquiries by mail. We will send you a letter with either a request for more information or a reason why we believe a change to your return may be needed. You can respond by mail or you can request a personal interview with an examiner. If you mail us the requested information or provide an explanation, we may or may not agree with you, and we will explain the reasons for any changes. Please do not hesitate to write to us about anything you do not understand.

By Interview

If we notify you that we will conduct your examination through a personal interview, or you request such an interview, you have the right to ask that the examination take place at a reasonable time and place that is convenient for both you and the IRS. If our examiner proposes any changes to your return, he or she will explain the reasons for the changes. If you do not agree with these changes, you can meet with the examiner's supervisor.

Repeat Examinations

If we examined your return for the same items in either of the 2 previous years and proposed no change to your tax liability, please contact us as soon as possible so we can see if we should discontinue the examination.

Appeals

If you do not agree with the examiner's proposed changes, you can appeal them to the Appeals Office of the IRS. Most differences can be settled without expensive and time-consuming court trials. Your appeal rights are explained in detail in both Publication 5, Your Appeal Rights and How To Prepare a Protest If You Don't Agree, and Publication 556, Examination of Returns, Appeal Rights, and Claims for Refund.

If you do not wish to use the Appeals Office or disagree with its findings, you may be able to take your case to the U.S. Tax Court, U.S. Court of Federal Claims, or the U.S. District Court where you live. If you take your case to court, the IRS will have the burden of proving certain facts if you kept adequate records to show your tax liability, cooperated with the IRS, and meet certain other conditions. If the court agrees with you on most issues in your case and finds that our position was largely unjustified, you may be able to recover some of your administrative and litigation costs. You will not be eligible to recover these costs unless you tried to resolve your case administratively, including going through the appeals system, and you gave us the information necessary to resolve the case.

Collections

Publication 594, The IRS Collection Process, explains your rights and responsibilities regarding payment of federal taxes. It describes:

- What to do when you owe taxes. It describes what to do if you get a tax bill and what to do if you think your bill is wrong. It also covers making installment payments, delaying collection action, and submitting an offer in compromise.

- IRS collection actions. It covers liens, releasing a lien, levies, releasing a levy, seizures and sales, and release of property.

- IRS certification to the State Department of a seriously delinquent tax debt, which will generally result in denial of a passport application and may lead to revocation of a passport.

Your collection appeal rights are explained in detail in Publication 1660, Collection Appeal Rights.

Innocent Spouse Relief

Generally, both you and your spouse are each responsible for paying the full amount of tax, interest, and penalties due on your joint return. However, if you qualify for innocent spouse relief, you may be relieved of part or all of the joint liability. To request relief, you must file Form 8857, Request for Innocent Spouse Relief. For more information on innocent spouse relief, see Publication 971, Innocent Spouse Relief, and Form 8857.

Potential Third Party Contacts

Generally, the IRS will deal directly with you or your duly authorized representative.

However, we sometimes talk with other persons if we need information that you have been unable to provide, or to verify information we have received. If we do contact other persons, such as a neighbor, bank, employer, or employees, we will generally need to tell them limited information, such as your name. The law prohibits us from disclosing any more information than is necessary to obtain or verify the information we are seeking. Our need to contact other persons may continue as long as there is activity in your case. If we do contact other persons, you have a right to request a list of those contacted. Your request can be made by telephone, in writing, or during a personal interview.

Refunds

You may file a claim for refund if you think you paid too much tax. You must generally file the claim within 3 years from the date you filed your original return or 2 years from the date you paid the tax, whichever is later. The law generally provides for interest on your refund if it is not paid within 45 days of the date you filed your return or claim for refund. Publication 556, Examination of Returns, Appeal Rights, and Claims for Refund, has more information on refunds.

If you were due a refund but you did not file a return, you generally must file your return within 3 years from the date the return was due (including extensions) to get that refund.

Taxpayer Advocate Service

TAS is an *independent* organization within the IRS that can help protect your taxpayer rights. We can offer you help if your tax problem is causing a hardship, or you've tried but haven't been able to resolve your problem with the IRS. If you qualify for our assistance, which is always free, we will do everything possible to help you. Visit www.taxpayeradvocate.irs.gov or call 1-877-777-4778.

Tax Information

The IRS provides the following sources for forms, publications, and additional information.

- *Tax Questions:* 1-800-829-1040 (1-800-829-4059 for TTY/TDD)
- *Forms and Publications:* 1-800-829-3676 (1-800-829-4059 for TTY/TDD)
- *Internet: www.irs.gov*
- *Small Business Ombudsman:* A small business entity can participate in the regulatory process and comment on enforcement actions of the IRS by calling 1-888-REG-FAIR.
- *Treasury Inspector General for Tax Administration:* You can confidentially report misconduct, waste, fraud, or abuse by an IRS employee by calling 1-800-366-4484 (1-800-877-8339 for TTY/TDD). You can remain anonymous.

The 25 Most Frequently Asked Questions

1. How long should I keep my tax papers?... 417

2. How long should I worry if I haven't filed tax returns that I should
   have filed?... 417

3. Do many people cheat on their taxes?.. 417

4. If I can't pay my taxes, should I file my return anyway? 418

5. Can I get an extension to pay a tax without penalties and interest? 418

6. My state had an amnesty period for nonfilers. Can I ever hope the
   IRS will have one?.. 418

7. Who has access to my IRS file? 418

8. Is it true that the IRS pays rewards for turning in tax cheaters?.................. 419

9. Should I notify the IRS when I move? 419

10. What should I do if I don't get my refund?... 419

11. What should I do if I encounter a dishonest IRS employee? 420

12. Can the IRS charge me interest if I was incorrectly sent a refund
    and the IRS now wants it back?.. 420

13. How legitimate are the claims by "tax experts" that you don't have
    to pay income taxes?.. 420

14. Do auditors use computers? If so, does it make it harder to beat
    an audit?.. 421

15. What are my chances of getting through an audit without owing
    additional taxes?... 421

16. I am being audited and the deadline for filing this year's return is fast
    approaching. Should I file? 421

17. I am being audited and haven't heard from the auditor for months.
    What can I do to get the audit over with?.. 421

18. The auditor or collector is impossible to get along with. What can I do?..... 422

19. I have always deducted a certain expense. During a recent audit, the deduction was denied and now I know I was wrong all those other years. What should I do? 422

20. Do I have to let the IRS into my home? 423

21. Can the IRS take my house? 423

22. I recently got married. Am I responsible for my spouse's past taxes? 423

23. How likely am I to get in trouble for tax fraud? 424

24. Can I make a deal with the IRS to pay less than my tax bill? 424

25. Can I recover my accountant's and lawyer's fees for fighting the IRS? 425

1. How long should I keep my tax papers?

At least three years, but six years is preferable. The IRS has at least three years after you file a tax return to complete an audit. For example, if you filed on April 15, 2023, for 2022, keep those records until at least April 16, 2026.

The IRS can audit you for up to six years if it suspects that you underreported your taxable income by 25% or more. If the IRS suspects fraud, there is no time limit for an audit, although audits beyond six years are extremely rare.

Keep records of purchases of real estate, stocks, and other investments for at least three years after the tax return reporting their sale was filed. (See Chapter 3.)

2. How long should I worry if I haven't filed tax returns that I should have filed?

At least six years. The government has six years from the date the nonfiled return was due to *criminally* charge you with failing to file. There is no time limit, however, for assessing *civil* penalties for not filing. If you didn't file for 1998, you still have an obligation if you owed taxes for that year. Not until you actually file a return does the normal audit time limit—3 years—and collection time limit—10 years—start to run.

Don't overworry about a nonfiled return due more than six years ago if you haven't heard from the IRS. The IRS usually doesn't go after nonfilers after six years—unless the IRS began its investigation before the six years elapsed. After six years, the IRS transfers its computer files to tape for storage. (See Chapter 2.)

3. Do many people cheat on their taxes?

According to the IRS Oversight Board, 13% of Americans admit to believing that tax cheating is okay. Presumably, these folks—as well as the ones who don't admit it—are practicing their beliefs, keeping the IRS audit mills churning. Small business owners and self-employed people have the most opportunities to play fast and loose—and they get audited the most. Arguably, cheating by self-employed people approaches 100%. It might just be a question of degree—did you ever mail a personal letter with a business-bought stamp?

4. If I can't pay my taxes, should I file my return anyway?

Yes. Filing saves you from the possibility of being criminally charged or, more likely, from being hit with a fine for failing to file or for filing late. Interest continues to build up until you pay. Of course, filing without paying will bring an IRS collector into your life—who might be friendlier if they don't have to hunt you down. The sooner you start filing, the better. (See Chapter 6 for an explanation of the benefits of filing even when you can't pay.)

5. Can I get an extension to pay a tax without penalties and interest?

Probably not. Although you can get an extension to file your tax return until October 15, you still must pay by April 15 or the IRS can impose a penalty and charge interest. Try pleading hardship on IRS Form 1127 to get up to six months extra to pay. Few payment extensions are granted. Even then, only penalties, not interest, stop accruing. Form 1127 works best in requesting an extension to pay estate taxes. (See Chapter 6.)

6. My state had an amnesty period for nonfilers. Can I ever hope the IRS will have one?

Maybe—it is frequently kicked around in Congress. The IRS has always opposed tax amnesty legislation—which lets nonfilers come forward without being criminally prosecuted or civilly fined. The IRS's reasoning is that after the amnesty period expires, significant numbers of people won't file, expecting another amnesty. Based on the success of various states' amnesty programs, we think the IRS is wrong.

7. Who has access to my IRS file?

Federal law makes IRS files private, not public records. The law has many exceptions, however. IRS files can be legally shared with other federal and state agencies. Most leakage comes as a result of sloppy state agencies that are granted access to IRS files. Furthermore, IRS employees have been caught snooping, and computer hackers have broken into government databases. While violation of the privacy act is a crime, rarely is anyone prosecuted for it, though IRS personnel can be fired if caught.

8. Is it true that the IRS pays rewards for turning in tax cheaters?

Yes. The IRS rewards snitches (aka whistleblowers). The catch is that payments are made only if and when the IRS collects the taxes due from the miscreant. More often than not, this means little or no reward at all. If it comes, it will likely be years after the report is made. The good news for squealers is that the IRS can pay 15% of the amount collected, with a maximum of $10,000,000 (you can get up to 30% with no limit if the case involves over $2 million in taxes). (I.R.C. § 7623.) Good luck. It takes about eight years to receive an award. Any reward you recover is taxable income. Identities of informers are kept secret, but tax cheats usually know who reported them—mostly ex-spouses or disgruntled business associates.

The IRS places low priority on investigating tips and paying rewards. Typically, you'll never know what action, if any, is taken on your tip. If you want to try it, submit IRS Form 211, *Application for Award for Original Information*, or call 800-829-0433, the IRS tip line.

P.S. Rumor has it that turning someone in to the IRS can result in the informant's being investigated as well. (See Chapter 10.)

9. Should I notify the IRS when I move?

Report your new address on IRS Form 8822. A post office change of address form might *not* work. Notifying the IRS ensures that you will get audit letters and other vital notices, which often have strict time limits for replies. (See Chapter 3.)

10. What should I do if I don't get my refund?

If you filed your tax return electronically and it's been over 21 days (6 weeks if you file by mail), check on your refund's status using the IRS online Where's My Refund tool at www.irs.gov/refunds, or call the IRS automated tax refund hotline at 800-829-1954. Or, call the 24-hour assistance number at 800-829-1040 and request assistance from the taxpayer advocate. If you filed your return on or before April 15 and don't receive your refund until after May 31, the IRS must pay you interest.

If you never get a refund, it might have been intercepted to pay other state or federal taxes you owe; a defaulted student, SBA, or other federal government loan; delinquent child support; or overpayment of a public benefit, such as HUD, VA, or Social Security. In these situations, you are supposed to be notified in writing, but don't count on it. (See Chapter 8.)

11. What should I do if I encounter a dishonest IRS employee?

Report any employee who lies or suggests you give them any favors. Dishonest employees are a rarity at the IRS. If you find one, however, call the chief inspector at 800-366-4484 or make an online report of the misconduct at www.tigta.gov/reportcrime-misconduct. You can make your complaint anonymously or give your name. Either way, don't expect to hear the results of the investigation.

12. Can the IRS charge me interest if I was incorrectly sent a refund and the IRS now wants it back?

It depends on who was at fault. The *Internal Revenue Manual* states that "taxpayers should not be held liable for interest on … erroneous refunds if the IRS was clearly at fault … and the taxpayer is cooperative in repaying." But if you caused the erroneous refund by your actions and now can't repay it, the IRS can and will charge interest. (See Chapter 12.)

13. How legitimate are the claims by "tax experts" that you don't have to pay income taxes?

Not at all. These con artists are very convincing, but if they were legit, we'd be first in line to stop paying taxes. Constitutional arguments against the tax laws are routinely dismissed by courts, and their proponents are fined or jailed. More sophisticated scams involve multiple family trusts, limited partnerships, and credit cards issued by offshore banks. While these schemes can confuse and slow down the IRS, they are bogus, period. Would a federal judge—whom you will appear before if you are prosecuted for tax evasion and whose salary comes from the federal government—ever uphold one of these schemes? Get serious. (See Chapter 2.)

14. Do auditors use computers? If so, does it make it harder to beat an audit?

Yes—computers are used by all auditors to prepare their final reports. No—it doesn't make it harder to beat an audit. Computers are just machines; it's the person operating the computer who counts. Computers can't make the judgments that are at the heart of the tax audit process. (See Chapter 3.)

15. What are my chances of getting through an audit without owing additional taxes?

A minority of audit victims make a clean getaway. The IRS, thanks to its sophisticated computer selection process, only audits returns in which adjustments are almost a certainty. Realize the odds are against you and focus on limiting the damage from an audit. (See Chapter 3.)

16. I am being audited and the deadline for filing this year's return is fast approaching. Should I file?

Not if you can help it. The danger in filing is that the auditor might expand the audit to include that return. Instead of filing, submit IRS Form 4868 by April 15 to obtain an automatic extension to delay filing until October 15. If the audit is still alive on October 15, don't file until it is completed. As long as you have paid all the taxes due, you won't incur any penalties or interest for not meeting the deadline. If you owe additional taxes, send in your payment with your extension form. Auditors can't make you file a return. If requested, simply say, "I am not yet ready to file." (See Chapter 3.)

17. I am being audited and haven't heard from the auditor for months. What can I do to get the audit over with?

Don't be overanxious. IRS auditors are instructed to close examinations within 28 months of the date you filed your tax return. For example, if you filed your 2022 return on April 15, 2023, the IRS wants the audit completed by August 15, 2025. Legally the IRS has until April 14, 2026 (or longer in the case of fraud), but auditors are instructed to allow at least eight months for processing any audit appeals. If you haven't heard from the auditor, it could mean any number of things. Maybe the auditor was ill, transferred, or terminated. Or your file might be lost in the system. When your case resurfaces, a new auditor is under a deadline to close it, which can work in your favor. In the best of all worlds, the three-year time limit for completing the audit might expire while your file is in IRS never-never land. So why not leave the sleeping dog alone? (See Chapter 3.)

18. The auditor or collector is impossible to get along with. What can I do?

Calm down and use some basic psychology. Put yourself in the auditor's shoes. Most IRS employees are 9-to-5 types just trying to do a job. Their pay is often too low to support a family in many urban areas. They deal with hostile and untruthful citizens all day long. Understandably, IRS morale is low. Would you like this kind of job?

And even if an agent hates you, they don't get paid bonuses for giving you a hard time. So, if you've exchanged harsh words through an audit or collection interview, instead of escalating the war, offer an olive branch. For instance, say, "I'm sorry we can't get along. But let's work it out, okay?"

If conciliation fails, speak to the auditor's manager, whose job is to close cases and smooth things over with taxpayers.

19. I have always deducted a certain expense. During a recent audit, the deduction was denied and now I know I was wrong all those other years. What should I do?

Let your conscience be your guide. If your audit is still open, the auditor can make adjustments in other open years—periods for which the three- or six-year time limit from the date you filed your return hasn't yet expired. The auditor may ask you for copies of your tax returns for those years. You're not legally obligated to provide them. If you don't, the auditor may request them from IRS record centers. But if the auditor is facing a deadline, they might just let it pass. Don't worry about being audited on returns filed more than 3 years ago—unless you understated your tax liability by 25% or more or committed outright fraud.

If you feel guilty, give the auditor copies of your tax returns for the open years and accept the disallowances. Or file amended tax returns and pay the additional taxes after the audit is completed. (See Chapter 3.)

20. Do I have to let the IRS into my home?

No. IRS employees can't enter your home without an express invitation from a rightful occupant. The only exception is if the IRS has a court order, which is very rare. A field auditor may ask to come in to verify your home office deduction. You don't have to let the person in, but they might disallow the deduction. Your choice.

21. Can the IRS take my house?

Yes, but the Taxpayer Bill of Rights discourages the IRS from seizing primary residences (your vacation home or rental property is fair game). The IRS must obtain a court order to take your house, which you can contest. And you can request help to stop the seizure from the Taxpayer Advocate Service.

The IRS doesn't like publicity about taxpayers losing their homes, so a call to the press might help. Typically, the IRS will seize your home only if you are a druglord or tax protestor or just totally failed to communicate or cooperate with the IRS collectors. Your state homestead law, which might entitle you to keep all or some of the equity in your house if you were sued or filed for bankruptcy, won't protect you from the IRS. (See Chapter 7.)

22. I recently got married. Am I responsible for my spouse's past taxes?

Maybe. Your wages and property might be at risk of IRS seizure for your spouse's tax bill, depending on the laws of the state where you live. In most states, property owned by one spouse before marriage remains that spouse's separate property during marriage. Assets acquired during marriage, however, are generally considered joint property. When couples own property together, IRS problems can arise. The IRS can legally go after jointly owned assets to cover the tax debt of just one spouse. The IRS can't, however, take the share of the nondebtor spouse. See a local attorney for help.

Be particularly aware of these specific problem areas:
- **Gifts.** If a spouse without an IRS tax debt gives a spouse who has a tax debt an interest in property, the IRS can grab it. For example, Tiffany deeds her separate property boat to her husband, Bobbo, and herself as joint tenants. The IRS can seize the boat for Bobbo's debt, although the IRS would have to pay Tiffany for her half interest in the boat once it was sold.
- **Commingled property.** If spouses deposit funds into a joint account and use that account to pay joint expenses, the funds are commingled. The IRS can take the *entire* account to satisfy the tax debt of one spouse.

    However, if the couple uses commingled funds to purchase property, and the IRS seizes it for only one spouse's tax debt, the IRS must give the nondebtor spouse one-half of the sales proceeds.
- **Wages.** The IRS, quite unfairly, can take the wages of one spouse to pay for the sole tax debt of the other spouse. Some couples have divorced just to stop the IRS from taking spouse 1's wages for taxes owed by spouse 2 prior to marriage. They might continue to live together after the divorce, but spouse 1's earnings are no longer within the IRS's grasp. (See Chapter 9.)

23. How likely am I to get in trouble for tax fraud?

Not very. Fewer than 1% of us are ever investigated for tax fraud. The unofficial minimum amount of taxes owed before the IRS will file criminal fraud charges is over $70,000 and involves at least three years of fraud. To some extent, whether you are charged depends on your line of work or visibility in the community. Most of those prosecuted for tax fraud work in organized crime or are public figures. (See Chapter 10.)

24. Can I make a deal with the IRS to pay less than my tax bill?

Maybe. Consider filing Form 656, *Offer in Compromise*. The IRS will thoroughly investigate your finances before deciding if settling for less than what you owe is in the best interests of the government. Recently, over 40% of all offers were accepted by the IRS. A filing fee and a down payment are required. You can greatly increase your chances of success by carefully following the IRS rules for offers and submitting all of the paperwork correctly. (See Chapter 6.)

25. Can I recover my accountant's and lawyer's fees for fighting the IRS?

It's possible, but unlikely. Legally, if you win, you may get reimbursed for your costs. But the IRS seldom pays attorneys' fees, and when it does, it's at a rate lower than what most tax lawyers charge. Absent special circumstances, the maximum attorneys' fee allowed is $230 per hour. The judge makes the final determination of the reasonableness of the entire bill. And, to win, you must "substantially prevail" in court, the IRS must have taken an unreasonable position, and you must have exhausted all procedural remedies within the IRS before going to court.

Fees paid for representation in an IRS administrative proceeding, such as an appeals hearing, can be recovered only if the IRS brought an unreasonable claim. So far, few taxpayers have gotten the IRS to admit it was wrong. No surprise.

Glossary of Tax Terms

Note: These terms are defined as they are used in this book. They might have different meanings in other contexts.

Abatement. The IRS's partial or complete cancellation of taxes, penalties, or interest owed by a taxpayer.

ACS. *See* Automated Collection System.

Adjustment. Change to your income tax liability as you reported in your tax return by an IRS auditor or service center. Typically adjustments result from disallowed deductions.

Amended Tax Return. A tax return filed within three years to make one or more changes to a previously filed tax return. Taxpayers usually file amended tax returns to claim refunds. Amended individual income tax returns must be filed on IRS Form 1040-X.

Appeal. The IRS formal administrative process for taxpayers to contest decisions, such as an audit, within the IRS. Most, but not all, administrative decisions can be taken to the IRS Independent Office of Appeals. If the appeal is lost, a taxpayer might be able to contest the IRS decision in a court of law.

Assess. The IRS process of recording a tax liability in the account of a taxpayer.

Asset. Any property, real or personal, that you own and that has a monetary value.

Audit. An IRS review of the correctness of a tax return. The IRS official term for an audit is "examination." *See also* Field Audit, Office Audit.

Auditor. An IRS Examination Division employee who reviews the correctness of a tax return. *See also* Revenue Agent, Tax Auditor.

Automated Collection System (ACS). A computerized collection process in which IRS collectors contact delinquent taxpayers by telephone and mail.

Bankruptcy. A federal law—separate from the Internal Revenue Code—which, in limited circumstances, can be used by taxpayers to eliminate their tax debts (Chapter 7 bankruptcy). In other instances, taxpayers can use bankruptcy to pay off their tax debts over three to five years (Chapters 12 and 13 bankruptcy).

Basis (Tax Basis). For tax purposes, this is the cost of an asset, which may be adjusted for tax reporting purposes downward by depreciation or upward by improvements.

Certified Public Accountant (CPA). CPAs are the most highly skilled of those in the accounting profession. They do sophisticated accounting and business audit work, and prepare tax returns and financial statements for clients. To earn the professional designation of CPA, an accountant must have a college degree and work experience with a CPA firm and must pass a series of rigorous examinations. CPAs are regulated by state law and are allowed to practice before the IRS.

Claim for Refund. Taxpayers who feel that they have overpaid their taxes may file a claim to the IRS for refund consideration. The IRS provides Form 843 for claims. An amended tax return (Form 1040-X) may also be treated as a claim for a refund. If the claim is denied, the taxpayer can bring a "refund suit" in a federal District Court or the U.S. Court of Claims. *See also* Amended Tax Return.

Code. *See* Internal Revenue Code.

Collection Division. The branch of the IRS that is staffed by tax collectors at the IRS service center, Automated Collection System, or local IRS office.

Commissioner of Internal Revenue. The head of the entire IRS organization.

Correspondence Audit. An IRS examination conducted by mail.

Criminal Investigation Division (CI). The branch of the IRS that investigates individual and business entities to determine whether or not they have committed tax crimes. *See also* Fraud.

Death. The other certainty.

Deduction. An expense which the Internal Revenue Code allows taxpayers to subtract from their annual gross income to reduce the amount of their tax liability.

Delinquent Return. A tax return not filed by the legal due date or by the dates allowed through the IRS extension periods.

Dependent. A child or other relative who relies on a taxpayer for over half their support and for whom the taxpayer may claim a tax deduction.

Depreciation. A tax deduction allowed for the wear and tear on an income-producing asset, such as a business automobile or rental real estate.

Disallowance. An IRS finding that you weren't entitled to a tax benefit claimed on your tax return, usually a deduction or loss. *See also* Adjustment.

Discriminant Function (DIF) Scoring. An IRS computer program that measures tax returns for audit potential. The Discriminant Function assigns each tax return a DIF score; the higher the DIF score, the higher the audit possibility.

Documentation. Any tangible proof that substantiates an item on your tax return, usually an expense claimed as a deduction. Documentation is ordinarily something in writing. *See also* Records.

Enrolled Agent (EA). An EA is a tax adviser and tax preparer permitted to practice before the IRS. An EA earns the designation either by passing a difficult IRS exam testing tax knowledge or by having at least five years of employment by the IRS. EAs also must participate in annual continuing education programs to retain their designations.

Examination. Official IRS terminology for an audit. *See also* Audit.

Exemption. The limited list of property that the IRS can't legally take if it levies on your property to satisfy your tax debt. *See also* Levy.

Extension to File. Income tax returns are normally due to the IRS by April 15. An extension to file gives a taxpayer extra time to file a return but not to pay the taxes owed. A taxpayer can obtain an automatic extension until October 15 by filing a form with the IRS.

Failure to File Tax Return. The most frequently charged tax crime. Defined as intentionally failing to file a return when you were obligated to do so. A misdemeanor punishable by up to one year in jail and/or a fine of $25,000 for each year not filed.

Fair Market Value. The price a buyer and seller of real or personal property would agree upon as fair, when neither is under any compulsion to buy or sell.

Field Audit. An examination that takes place outside the IRS offices—at your business, home, or tax representative's office. *See also* Audit, Revenue Agent.

Fifth Amendment Right. A well-known right guaranteed by the U.S. Constitution that protects people from being forced by the government to incriminate themselves. You can assert your Fifth Amendment right against the IRS by refusing to answer questions or provide certain documents.

Filing. The act of giving in person or otherwise delivering to the IRS a tax return or another IRS document.

Fraud. Conduct meant to deceive the IRS in the determination of any tax liability. Fraud can be either (a) civil (resulting in a penalty of 75% of the taxes owed), or (b) criminal (tax evasion, a felony with a maximum prison sentence of five years and a maximum monetary fine of $100,000; or filing a false return, a felony with a maximum prison sentence of three years and a maximum monetary fine of $100,000), or (c) both civil and criminal.

Fraud Referral. A transfer to the IRS Criminal Investigation Division from another department when IRS personnel suspect a taxpayer of tax fraud. *See also* Criminal Investigation Division.

Freedom of Information Act. A federal law giving people the right to see U.S. government documents, including their IRS files.

Gift. Transfer of property without any financial payment in return. A true gift is not taxable to the recipient but might cause tax consequences for the giver, depending on the size of the gift.

Gross Income. Income from all sources, which taxpayers must report on their income tax returns. Not all money received is income for tax purposes, however. *See also* Taxable Income.

Group Manager. The immediate superior of an auditor or a tax collector at an IRS office.

Income. All monies and other things of value you receive, except items specifically exempted by the tax code. For example, a gift or an inheritance is not considered income. *See also* Gross Income, Taxable Income.

Independent Contractor. A self-employed worker. Income taxes and Social Security contributions are not withheld or made by the business for which the services are performed. Each year, businesses that hire independent contractors must file a Form 1099 with the IRS for each independent contractor paid more than $600 for the preceding year.

Information Return. A report filed with the IRS showing monies paid by or to a taxpayer. The most common information returns are Form W-2 (wages) and Form 1099 (independent contractors and other income, such as interest paid by a bank, stock dividends, or royalties).

Installment Agreement (IA). An IRS monthly payment plan for past taxes.

Internal Revenue Code (IRC). The tax laws of the United States as enacted by Congress. Also called the "tax code."

Internal Revenue Manual **(IRM).** A collection of handbooks that set forth the internal operating guidelines for IRS personnel. Most, but not all, of the manual is now public information and can be found at the IRS website.

Internal Revenue Regulations. *See* Regulations.

Internal Revenue Service (IRS). The tax law administration branch of the U.S. Treasury Department.

Jeopardy Assessment. An expedited procedure by which the IRS determines your tax liability without first notifying you. A jeopardy assessment is rare and usually limited to when the IRS believes you are about to flee the country or hide assets.

Joint Tax Return. An income tax return filed by a married couple.

Levy. An IRS seizure of your assets or wages to satisfy a delinquent tax debt.

Lien. *See* Tax Lien.

Limitation on Assessment and Collection. *See* Statutes of Limitations.

Market Value. *See* Fair Market Value.

Negligence. Whenever you have carelessly disregarded the tax law in preparing a tax return, the IRS can deem your conduct negligent and impose a penalty (fine) against you. Also called an "accuracy-related penalty."

Nonfiler. A person or an entity who does not file a timely tax return even though required by law to do so.

Notice of Deficiency. *See* 90-Day Letter.

Notice of Federal Tax Lien. *See* Tax Lien.

Offer in Compromise. A formal written proposal to the IRS to settle your tax account balance for less than the amount the IRS says you owe. An Offer in Compromise must be submitted on IRS Form 656.

Office Audit. An IRS examination of your tax return by a tax auditor at a local IRS office. *See also* Audit, Field Audit, Tax Auditor.

Payroll Taxes. Federal income tax and FICA contributions—which include both Social Security and Medicare—that a business owner must deposit regularly and report quarterly to the IRS for each employee. These are also called "trust fund taxes." *See also* Trust Fund Recovery Penalty.

Penalties. Civil fines imposed by the IRS on a taxpayer who disobeys tax laws, such as by filing a form beyond the time limit set by law.

Personal Property. Any item of property that is not real estate—such as cash, stocks, cars, and the shirt on your back. *See also* Asset, Real Property.

Petition. A written form filed with the U.S. Tax Court to contest a proposed IRS tax assessment. *See also* Tax Court.

Power of Attorney. A form you sign appointing a tax representative to deal with the IRS on your behalf.

Problems Resolution Officer (PRO). Former title of the taxpayer advocate.

Property. *See* Personal Property, Real Property.

Protest. A written or an oral request to appeal a decision within the IRS. *See also* Appeal.

Real Property. Real estate, consisting of land and structures attached to it.

Reconsideration. A discretionary IRS procedure that lets you reopen a closed audit or another tax assessment previously made.

Records. A collection of tangible proof, usually in writing, which shows income, expenses, and financial transactions. Records are one form of documentation.

Refund Suit. *See* Claim for Refund.

Regular Tax Case. A Tax Court case in which a taxpayer contests $50,000 or more per tax year. This is a complex proceeding, in which formal rules of procedure and evidence apply. *See also* Petition, Small Tax Case, Tax Court.

Regulations. IRS written interpretations of selected Internal Revenue Code provisions. *See also* Internal Revenue Code, Revenue Procedures, Revenue Rulings.

Representative. *See* Tax Professional, Tax Representative.

Return. *See* Tax Return.

Revenue Agent. An IRS employee who conducts a field, as opposed to an office, audit. *See also* Audit, Field Audit, Office Audit.

Revenue Officer. A tax collector who works out of a local IRS office.

Revenue Procedures. IRS interpretations of selected Internal Revenue Code provisions which specify the procedures taxpayers must follow to comply with certain sections of the code. *See also* Internal Revenue Code, Regulations, Revenue Rulings.

Revenue Rulings. IRS interpretations of selected Internal Revenue Code provisions as applied to specific factual circumstances. *See also* Internal Revenue Code, Regulations, Revenue Procedures.

Seizure. *See* Levy.

Self-Employed. Anyone who works for themself, not receiving wages from an employer; synonymous with small business owner. *See also* Independent Contractor.

Service Centers. Regional IRS facilities where tax returns are filed and processed. Most IRS bills and notices come from service centers.

Small Business Owner. *See* Self-Employed.

Small Tax Case. A Tax Court case in which a taxpayer contests less than $50,000 per tax year. This is a simple, small claims court type proceeding, in which formal rules of procedure and evidence don't apply. *See also* Petition, Regular Tax Case, Tax Court.

Special Agent. An IRS officer who investigates suspected tax crimes. *See also* Criminal Investigation Division (CI).

Statutes of Limitations. Differing time limits imposed by Congress on the IRS for assessing and collecting taxes, on the Justice Department for charging taxpayers with tax crimes, and on taxpayers who claim refunds.

Summons. A legal order issued by the IRS compelling a taxpayer or another person or entity (such as a taxpayer's employer or bank) to appear or provide financial information to the IRS.

Tax Attorney. A lawyer who does various types of tax-related work, including tax and estate planning, IRS dispute resolution, and tax return preparation. Usually, only an attorney may represent a taxpayer in a court proceeding against the IRS. A tax attorney should have either a special tax law degree (LL.M.) or a certification as a tax law specialist from a state bar association.

Tax Auditor. An IRS employee who conducts an office, as opposed to a field, audit. *See also* Audit, Field Audit, Office Audit.

Tax Code. *See* Internal Revenue Code.

Tax Court. The only U.S. federal court where a taxpayer can contest an IRS tax assessment without first paying the taxes claimed due by the IRS. *See also* Petition, Regular Tax Case, Small Tax Case.

Tax Fraud. *See* Fraud.

Tax Law. The Internal Revenue Code, written by Congress, and the decisions of all federal courts that interpret it. *See also* Internal Revenue Code.

Tax Levy. *See* Levy.

Tax Lien. Whenever you owe money to the IRS and don't pay after the IRS has demanded payment, the IRS has a claim against your property. This is called a "tax lien," which arises automatically by "operation of law." The IRS has the right to inform the public that you are subject to a tax lien by recording a Notice of Federal Tax Lien at the county recorder's office or with your Secretary of State's office. A tax lien allows the IRS to seize (levy on) your property to satisfy your tax debt. Also most state tax agencies are given lien powers for state taxes due. *See also* Levy.

Tax Preparer. A person who fills in your tax return forms for a fee.

Tax Professional. Anyone working privately in the tax field, such as an accountant or a tax lawyer. *See also* Certified Public Accountant, Enrolled Agent, Tax Attorney, Tax Preparer, Tax Representative.

Tax Representative. A tax professional who is legally qualified to represent you before the IRS and whom you have authorized to deal with the IRS on your behalf. *See also* Certified Public Accountant, Enrolled Agent, Tax Attorney.

Tax Return. A form that individuals, partnerships, limited liability companies (LLCs), and corporations are required to file each year with the IRS stating income, exemptions, credits, and deductions. Tax liability, if any, is based on this form for individuals and corporations.

Taxable Income. The amount of money on which you must pay taxes each year. It's determined on your tax return by subtracting deductions and exemptions from your gross income. *See also* Deduction, Exemption, Gross Income.

Taxpayer Account. An IRS computer record containing your taxpaying history. Your tax account includes all tax assessments, penalties and interest, and credits for payments for each tax year.

Taxpayer Advocate. An IRS troubleshooter who acts for taxpayers whose problems were not solved through normal IRS channels. The taxpayer advocate works out of IRS local offices and service centers.

Taxpayer Assistance Order (TAO). An order that a taxpayer advocate can issue to override an action against a taxpayer by the IRS. *See also* Taxpayer Advocate.

Taxpayer Bill of Rights (TBOR). Federal laws imposing standards and limits on the IRS, and establishing your rights in dealing with the agency.

Taxpayer Identification Number (TIN). An IRS-assigned number used for computer tracking of tax accounts. For individuals, it is their Social Security number (SSN). For other entities, such as corporations and trusts, it is a separate 13-digit number called the "employer identification number" (EIN).

Third Party. Any person or entity other than you who has knowledge of your finances, such as your bank, stockbroker, or employer.

Trust Fund Recovery Penalty (TFRP). A tax law giving the IRS the power to assess unpaid payroll taxes against "responsible" individuals involved in a business owing the taxes. *See also* Payroll Taxes.

Trust Fund Taxes. *See* Payroll Taxes.

Unreported Income. Any income you were required to report on your income tax return, but didn't.

Waiver. An agreement where you voluntarily give up a legal right, such as the right to have the IRS collection period on a delinquent tax debt expire. Often, the IRS requires waivers in exchange for granting installment agreements.

Willful. Intentional conduct that violates the tax laws and can subject the wrongdoer to criminal prosecution.

Workpapers. Notes made by accountants and IRS auditors that explain items or adjustments made on a tax return. *See also* Adjustment, Disallowance.

100% Payroll Penalty. *See* Trust Fund Recovery Penalty.

30-Day Letter. IRS written notice following an audit giving you 30 days to protest the audit by requesting an IRS appeals hearing.

90-Day Letter. The letter the IRS must send if it seeks to impose additional taxes—usually after an audit—which you don't agree to. The letter gives you 90 days to file a petition in U.S. Tax Court to protest the proposed assessment of taxes. If you don't file a petition, the tax assessment becomes final. Also called a "Notice of Deficiency." *See also* Petition, Tax Court.

Index

A

Abatement
  defined, 77, 427
  of interest, 368, 372–373, 376–377
  See also Penalty abatement
Abusive tax shelters, 47
Accounts receivables, tax levy on, 290
ACS. *See* Automated Collection System
Address changes, 129–130, 166, 419
Adjustments, 427
  as preferred term instead of "dollars" discussion, 115–116, 154
  See also Audits; Automated adjustment notices from IRS; Tax bills
Aggressive tax filing
  defined, 45
  small businesses and, 46–47
  as tax professional litmus test, 46
Alimony/spousal support, 213, 309
Amended tax returns
  overview, 44–45, 427
  audit risk of, 45, 65–66
  audit statute of limitations and, 66
  checking status of (online), 44
  to convert joint filing to separate, 407
  to correct errors in assessed tax bill, 193
  correspondence audit as common form for, 79
  IRS Form 1040X, *Amended U.S. Individual Income Tax Return,* 44–45
  IRS not required to accept, 45, 65–66
  and refunds, time requirements for, 44, 65–66
  for states, 45, 251
  for wrong interception of refund for child support arrears, 311
Appeals
  defined, 427
  of FOIA requests, failure of IRS to comply with, 16
  of installment agreement denials, 223, 228

of installment agreement revocation, 229
of levies by IRS, 198, 274, 281, 285–286, 406, 409
of Offer in Compromise denials, 248
of penalty abatement rejection, 372–373
Tax Court—regular cases, 183–184
Tax Court—small tax cases have no right to, 167
of tax liens, 268, 269, 406, 409
in Taxpayer Bill of Rights, 406
of Trust Fund Recovery Penalty, 353–357
See also Audit appeals
Assessment of tax by IRS
  for audit conducted without taxpayer or representative, 101
  average, by type of audit, 79
  defined, 53, 427
  delay of notice by IRS, interest abatement due to, 376
  "economic reality" as basis for, suggested response to, 63
  extension for time requested by auditor, negotiation of, 117–118
  jeopardy assessments, 131, 274, 431
  nonfilers and, 25
  for phantom audit, 130–131
  questioning auditor about, and negotiation of, 118
  right of taxpayer to explanation of, 81
  statute of limitations on collection begins with ("23C" date), 192
  See also Tax bills; Tax debts
Assets
  defined, 427
  financial status/economic reality audits and, 60–63
  fraudulent transfer of, 279, 280–281
  liquid, prepaying future expenses with, 211
  listed on collection forms, 210–212
  and net worth, field audits and, 91–92

Offer in Compromise and net value of, 241–242
out-of-state, difficulty of finding, 281, 282
protection via transfers of, and collections, 255–256, 279–281
public records of ownership, IRS access to, 99–100
revenue officer verifying, 220
sale of, as IRS demand, 220
sale of, as question in financial status audit, 62
sale of, as uneconomical, 281
sale of, field audits and, 93
sale of, prior to tax levy, 282
sale of, tax levies and, 281
silence is golden, and don't lie, 281–282
storing away from your home or business premises, 282
tax basis of, 94, 428
tools of the trade, exemption for, 275, 281
transferee liability, 280
valuation of, for collection forms, 210–212
valuation of, for estate tax returns, 317–319
valuation of, tax levy sales and, 286
See also Bank accounts; Fair market value; Financial accounts; Joint ownership of assets; Levies; Personal property; Real estate; Residence
Asset seizure. *See* Levies
Attorneys
  overview, 383
  attorney-client privilege, 36, 98, 333, 409
  audits and request for recess to consult with, 106–107, 117, 405
  audits and taxpayer right to representation, 81
  consultation and advice services, 381–382
  definition of tax attorney, 434
  federal courts requiring, 185, 186
  finding and hiring, 383–385
  IRS preference for dealing with, 381

Low Income Taxpayer Clinic
  (TITC) program, 33, 245, 382
negotiation services, 382
pros and cons of hiring, 380–382
representation services, 382
right to representation by, 380, 405
right to "time out" to consult
  with, 380, 405
See also Attorneys' fees; Attorneys,
  specific services from; Lawsuits;
  Tax professionals
Attorneys' fees
  overview, 385–386
  for appeals of audits, 160
  for Chapter 11 bankruptcy, 255
  for court challenge of Trust Fund
    Recovery Penalty, 357
  paid by IRS, 185, 186, 272, 407,
    425
  for tax return preparation, 388
Attorneys, specific services from
  assets auctioned, right of
    redemption of real estate, 290
  assets, storing away from home or
    business premises, 282
  asset transfers, 255–256, 280–281
  audits. *See* Audit(s), attorney/tax
    professional services
  bankruptcy, 187, 251, 253, 254,
    255, 270, 358
  cash transactions, questioning
    on, 63
  criminal charges, avoidance of,
    35–36
  criminal charges for nonfiling, 30
  employees misclassified as
    independent contractors, 348
  estate taxes, 315, 316–317, 318
  federal court tax disputes, 185, 186
  Fifth Amendment tax returns,
    65, 81
  fraud, associates of, 332
  fraud charges, 326, 332–333,
    334, 336
  Information Document Request,
    96
  jeopardy assessments, 131
  for jointly owned assets, 423
  jointly owned assets by separate
    filers, tax liabilities, 313
  suing IRS for willfully
    disregarding the law, 257

suing IRS for wrongful levies, 292
suing IRS for wrongful liens, 272
Tax Court regular cases, 184
Tax Court small cases, 172, 179
Tax Court small cases, advising,
  172, 173, 174, 178, 179, 182
tax levies on business assets, 291
tax levy appeals, 274
tax liens, 270
tax return preparation, 388–389
Trust Fund Recovery Penalty,
  352, 357
Auctions
  for business asset tax levies, 291
  for tax levies, 286–287, 288–290
Audio recording of meetings with
  IRS, as right of taxpayer but not
  recommended, 81, 152, 405
Audit(s)
  overview, 51–52, 54–55
  adjustments in your favor, 113
  audio recording, right of taxpayer
    to (not recommended), 81, 405
  auditor's findings. *See* Examina-
    tion report
  automated adjustments as no
    protection from, 67
  burden of proof for, 52, 53, 111,
    125
  caution against filing current tax
    returns during, 421
  correspondence audits, 79–80,
    83, 428
  death of taxpayer and
    continuation of, 54, 314
  defined, 427
  do not be too eager to help the
    auditor, 87
  of estate tax returns, 315–319
  extension of time limit requested
    by auditor, negotiation of,
    117–118, 410
  failure of, analysis by tax
    professional, 388
  fraud revealed by. *See under* Fraud
  interest-free period following, 407
  internal IRS time limits on, 53
  of IRS-filed returns (SFR), 29, 64
  lost audit file, 119
  "no-repeat" audit policy, 81, 82
  original documents: do not give
    or mail to IRS (copies only), 111

"phantom": audit you didn't
  know about, 129–131
prior, 81, 82, 87
rates of, 51
reason for audit, figuring out, 60
reexamination procedure, 131
refunds resulting from, 51, 102
representation for, right to, 81, 405
resources on, 56, 63, 80, 101–102
states alerted by IRS of, 396
states conducting, 396
stopping or slowing, 54
tax bill resulting from, 51
tax code knowledge and, 55
taxpayer as focus of examination,
  vs. the return, 85, 90, 104
Taxpayer Bill of Rights and, 81,
  82, 90, 94–95, 405
timeframes expected for, 52–54,
  422–423
transfer of location of, 54
types of. *See* Correspondence
  audits; Field audits; Office audits
See also Audit(s), attorney/tax
  professional services; Audit
  appeals; Audit notices; Auditors
  and auditor training; Auditor/
  taxpayer interactions; Audit
  reconsideration (reopening an
  audit); Audit risk; Audit risk
  reduction; Audit selection;
  Audits, statute of limitations for;
  Examination report; Financial
  status/economic reality audits
Audit(s), attorney/tax professional
  services
  analysis of audit failure, 388
  appeal fees, 160
  appeal of audit, 140, 145,
    160–161
  detection of reason for selection
    to audit, 60
  field audit location at office of,
    91, 95
  field audit preparation, 100, 101,
    114, 386–387
  field audit strategy of
    noncooperation, 101, 104
  "informal" appeal, 128
  office audits, 82, 87, 386–387
  request for recess to consult with,
    106–107, 117, 405

right to representation, 81

right to representation without attending, 87, 405

risk of audit selection decreased for returns prepared by, 34, 388

summons to field audit, 98, 101

Audit appeals

overview, 140

admitting weaknesses in your case, 152, 154

for amounts over $25,000 (regular case), 143, 145, 146

for amounts under $25,000 (small case), 143, 144

appeals officer/taxpayer relations, 148–149, 152, 153, 154, 158, 161

attorneys rarely needed for, 140

attorneys/tax professionals for, 145, 160–161

audio recording, right of taxpayer to (not recommended), 152, 405

audit agreement as barring option of, 125

auditor contacted by appeals officer, 153

auditor's workpapers, and access to by law. See Workpapers

case history of an appeal, 155–158

challenged items, focus on, 151

as discretionary to IRS, 141

documents, organizing and presenting, 150

estate tax audits, 316

extension of time, appeals officer or taxpayer asking for, 153

extension of time to file, applying for, 142

hearings conducted by phone or video conference, rarely in-person, 152

"informal" appeal to auditor's manager, 126–127, 128, 142

interest continues to accrue during, 141, 376

IRS Form 12203, 142, 143, 144

IRS Form 12203, sample, 144

IRS policy on mission of, 140

IRS Publication 5, *Your Appeal Rights and How to Prepare a Protest if You Disagree,* 127, 140

language: "dollars" as term to be avoided, 154

motivation of Appeals Office to negotiate with you, 148–149, 154

negotiating with the appeals officer, 154, 157–158

negotiation disallowed for some situations, 159

number of, 140

penalties, request for IRS to drop, 154, 370

postponement for lack of access to auditor's workpapers, 148

preappeal consultation with tax professional, 161

preparation for, 152, 161

preparation for the hearing, 149–151

presentation of your case, 152–153

pros and cons of, 141

"protest" as the official IRS term for, 142

protest letter, 142, 143, 145, 146

protest letter, sample, 146

records, finding and organization of, 150, 151, 161

of state audits, 396

statistics are good for success in, 140

statistics of success in, 149

tax bill following, 161

Tax Court automatically sending case to, 141

tax resisters/protestors won't be heard in, 160

30-day letter following examination report rejection, 142, 436

timeframes expected for, 53, 149, 153

time limit for, 142

time limit for, signing waiver for extension of, 153

used as subtle threat by taxpayer, 63, 127

witness statements, 151

See also Audit appeals, settlement of

Audit appeals, settlement of

checking final form before signing, 159

as goal of IRS, 148–149, 154

lack of settlement, and Tax Court as next option, 161

motivation of IRS to stay out of court, 149

negotiation of, 154, 157–158

signing the settlement forecloses Tax Court option, 159

Tax Court encouragement of, 172

written form of, 159

Audit notices

delivery is only by U.S. postal service, 52

law only requires to be sent to last known address, 129–130, 419

missing, and "phantom" audits, 129–131

summons, 98

of third-party contact, 100, 409

timeframe for, generally, 52

See also Notice of Deficiency

Auditors and auditor training

overview, 7, 434

appeals officer contacting, 153

Audit Technique Guides, 63, 101–102

computers used by, 421

definition of auditor, 427

estate tax auditors, 317

for field audits, 89, 324

overly conscientious, 117

performance rating based on closing ratio, 115

senior agents, and examination report, 127

time pressures on, 53, 116–117

See also Auditor/taxpayer interactions; Examination report; Workpapers

Auditor/taxpayer interactions

adjustments in your favor, 109

asking questions as the audit progresses, 110, 118

auditor tests the taxpayer for lying, 105

defiant aggressive attitude of taxpayer, 106

do not be too eager to help the auditor, 87

do not offer any favors, 105

dressing for the audit, 104

ending the audit, strategies for, 116–117

for estate tax audits, 316–317

examination focus is on taxpayer, not just the tax return, 85, 90, 104

examination report dispute negotiation, 126–127

First Commandment: establish and maintain credibility, 112

getting along: chattiness vs. polite interest, 105–106

negotiating with an auditor, 107, 110, 115–116, 118

new auditor, IRS sending, 107–108, 119, 422

new auditor requesting additional copies of same documents, 108

new auditor, taxpayer request for, 107

recess of audit, taxpayer demanding, 106–107, 117

same auditor from previous recent audit, 107

silence is golden, and don't lie, 87, 104–105

standing up to the auditor, 110–115, 117

tax professional, request for recess to consult with, 106–107, 117

unreasonable treatment from auditor, 106–107, 422

See also Questioning by IRS agent or auditor, suggested responses to

Audit reconsideration (reopening an audit)

defined, 432

as discretionary with the IRS to grant, 131

IRS-filed returns (SFR) and, 28

IRS initiating, 129

legal research on, 129

phantom audits and taxpayer initiating, 130–131

Audit risk

overview, 58–59

aggressive filing, 45–47

amended tax returns, 45, 65–66

businesses with net losses for the year, 43, 47, 59, 155–156

cash-oriented businesses, 91

COVID-19 pandemic tax credits, 59

criminal source of income and Fifth Amendment returns, 65

and deductions, national averages for income bracket, 57

and deductions, ratio to income, 56, 57

and deductions, round numbers vs. precise amounts, 42, 59

digital assets (e.g. Bitcoin), 59

estate tax returns and, 315

expenses, item size compared to overall income, 58

extensions to file not increasing risk, 40

foreign accounts, 59

frivolous returns (claiming income not subject to tax), 67

higher income amount (over $100K), 43, 51, 57, 58

high expense/low-income ratio. See Financial status/economic reality audits

informant tips, 66, 328

jointly owned property by separate filers, 312

location of residence and, 43, 66

messy returns, 42, 59

nonfiling and, 52, 64

out-of-character items, 58

previous audits as, 65

refunds and, 55

of returns sent in lieu of SFR, 28

self-employment as, 51, 59, 342–343, 417

self-prepared returns, 388

"significant items" standard and, 58–59

tax preparer designated a problem by IRS, 46, 389

tax return form errors, 58

valuation of, 212

See also Audit risk reduction; Audit selection

Audit risk reduction

actions to take, 42–43

auditor training materials for specific professions and businesses as source of information on, 63, 101–102

computer-prepared returns, 34, 43

extensions to file and, 40

tax-professional-prepared returns, 34, 388

Audit selection

classifier (human being) scrutiny, 10, 42, 45, 57–58, 80, 155

compliance initiative projects, 64–65

computer scoring (DIF score), 10, 56–57, 145, 429

computer scoring (random selection study), 66–67

computer scoring (UIDIF score), 57, 60

local IRS office makes final selections, 58, 89

local IRS office special projects, 64

Market Segment Specialization Program (MSSP), 63, 101–102

percentage of returns selected, 10, 57, 58

political requests for, as crime, 67

random selection (National Research Program), 66–67

"significant items" standard, 58–59, 80

See also Audit risk; Audit risk reduction

Audits, statute of limitations for

overview, 52

amended tax returns and, 45

appeal of audit and extension of, 153

expiration of, 118

extension requested by auditor, negotiation of, 117–118, 410

fraudulent returns not protected by, 52

lost audit files and expiration of, 119

and nonfiled tax years, 52

retention of records and, 417

starts only on filing return, 52

if understatement of income 25% or more, 52, 117

Audit Technique Guides, 63, 101–102

Automated adjustment notices from IRS

overview, 67

correction notices, 67

disputing, 76–79, 164

disputing, as delay of collections, 79

errors in, 67, 77

interest assessment notices, 68

Notice of Deficiency sent by IRS, 78

penalty assessment notices, 67

timeframe for IRS response to disputes of, 78–79

time to respond to, 78

underreporter program notices, 68

See also IRS CP-2000 Notice

Automated Collection System (ACS)
overview, 6, 198–199
accuracy of tax bill, questioning
of, 201, 205
computer data inaccuracies in, 199
defined, 427
delaying, 199–201
freeze codes, 199–200
long-term holds, 200–201
offer in compromise as delay of, 201
short-term holds (up to 45 days),
200
timeframe for case staying with,
199
transfers from, to local IRS office/
revenue officer, 205
transfers from, written requests
for, 205
See also Currently not collectible
(CNC) status; Installment
agreements (IA)
Automatic stay, 249–250

B
Back taxes. *See* Tax bills; Tax debts
Bank accounts
business, levy/seizure of, 290
canceled checks, as proof in audit,
109
check-signing power, 352, 353
commingled funds, 424
financial status audit questions
about, 62
foreign, mandatory reporting for,
37, 59
installment agreement payments,
caution to avoid revealing
account numbers when making,
226
installment agreements, direct
debit payments for, 221, 223,
224, 226
interest reported each January, 219
jointly owned by separately filing
taxpayers, 312
levies/seizure of, 41, 198, 209,
285, 286, 290, 312
no automatic reporting of
existence of, 219
out-of-state, difficulty for IRS to
find, 209, 219
partial tax payments, caution to
avoid revealing account numbers
when making, 41
personal checks as traceable
record, 359
protection of, by fully funding
retirement accounts, 256, 283
protection of, by moving to new
accounts, 219, 282
reduction of balances to a
minimum, 219
seizure of, for noncooperation
with financial investigation, 209
separate, for direct debit
payments on installment
agreements, 223
taxpayer analysis prior to audit, 92
unreported income revealed
through deposits in, 92–93,
324–325, 326
Bankruptcy
overview, 249–250
asset protection strategies, 255–256
attorneys for, 187, 251, 253, 254,
255–256, 270, 358
automatic stay, 249–250
Chapter 7 (straight bankruptcy),
250–253, 400
Chapter 11 bankruptcy, 254–255
Chapter 12 bankruptcy, 255
Chapter 13 bankruptcy, 251,
253–254, 358, 400
computerized billing by IRS and,
197
counseling requirement, 250
credit rating and, 250
currently not collectible status
and, 257
current on tax filings,
requirement of being, 250
dates, checking with account
transcript, 252
defined, 428
delay of collections and, 201, 283
and designating late payments to
most recent year, 378
downsides of, 250
fraud charges and, 251
installment agreements compared
to, 254
interest and penalties stop
accruing (Chapter 13), 254
interest continues to accrue
(Chapter 11), 255
interest, reduction of, 376
IRS-filed tax returns and, 29
Offer in Compromise and, 252
penalties, reduction of, 254
as preferable to payroll tax debt,
350
prior bankruptcies, 252
as public record, 250
resources for, 187, 249, 253, 261
secured taxes and, 253, 254
state tax collection and, 400
statute of limitation for collection
and, 250
tax disputes settled in court of, 187
tax levies and, 278, 283, 285
tax liens and, 252–253, 267, 270,
271
three-year rule, 251, 252
and Trust Fund Recovery Penalty,
251, 358
240-day rule, 252
two-year rule, 252
types of, 249, 250–255
Basis (tax basis), 94, 428
Bench decisions, Tax Court, 184
Bitcoin, as audit risk, 59
Bond
in lieu of tax levy, 284
as stopping interest accrual in Tax
Court, 166
Burden of proof
for audits, 52, 53, 111, 125
for federal courts, 52, 175, 182,
411
for fraud, 52
Bureau of Labor Statistics, 28, 64,
213
Businesses
aggressive filing and audit risk,
45–47
appointment books or diaries, 109
assets of, tax levies and, 282,
290–291, 410
asset transfers to, 255–256
audit appeal time period, 143
bankruptcy (Chapter 11), 254–255
EIN (employer identification
number), 11, 143, 435
estate taxes and valuation of
interests of, 317
expenses under $75 each, no
receipts for, 113
family limited partnerships, LLCs,
and corporations, 256, 317

field audit held on premises of, 94–95

financial status audit investigations and, 61

and income levies on independent contractors, 277–278, 285

installment agreements and, 222, 224

interest on tax-debts is deductible, 37

IRS estimate of income from, 64

and IRS Form 433-B, 202, 208, 219, 232

location of field audits, 91

Market Segment Specialization Program (MSSP), 63, 101–102

Offers in Compromise (OIC), 232

prior and related audits, 65

and profit motive, 155–158

record keeping for, adequate, 109

record keeping lacking, and auditor guesstimate of income, 109

resources for, 342

and revenue officers, 208

Schedule C and audit risk, 43

"specific items" as indirect proof of fraud, 324

tax return errors, as audit risk, 58

travel and entertainment expenses, 113

undercover operations (CI) to reveal fraud in, 328

vs. hobby, defined, 156–157

and wage levies on employees, 277–278, 279, 285

See also Business with net losses for the year; Cash; Corporations; Employees; Expenses and audits; Field audits; Independent contractors, misclassification of employees as; LLCs; Partnerships; Payroll taxes; Self-employment; Sole proprietorships

Business identification code, 65

Business with net losses for the year auditor, mentioning recent losses to, 100

as audit risk, 43, 47, 59, 155–156

case history of audit appeal for, 155–158

C

Carrybacks
audits and, 87
late filing and refund due, 38

Cash
business dealing in, and audit risk, 91

business dealing in, and criminal charges for nonfiling, 30

businesses dealing in, and fraud risk, 322

on hand, suggested answer to questions on, 62

hoarding of, as not illegal, 326

hoard of, as defense of fraud charges, 326

installment agreement payments via retail partners, 226

as liquid asset, prepayment of future expenses with, 211

possession of, and jeopardy assessments, 131

structured transactions, 359

transactions over $10,000, reporting, 63, 359–360

transactions, suggested answer to questions on, 63

See also Bank accounts

Cash equivalents, reporting transactions over $10,000, 63, 359–360

Certified public accountants (CPAs), 160, 179, 383, 384, 388–389, 428

See also Tax professionals

Chain tax services, 384, 389

Changes to tax returns. *See* Amended tax returns

Chapter 7 bankruptcy, 250–253, 400

Chapter 11 bankruptcy, 254–255

Chapter 12 bankruptcy, 255

Chapter 13 bankruptcy, 251, 253–254, 358, 400

Charitable deductions, 57, 86, 100

Checks. *See under* Bank accounts

Children, dependency deduction, 310–311

Children. *See* Family

Child support
as exempt asset (tax levies), 275

on installment agreement financial forms, 213

as neither deductible nor reportable income, 310

tax refunds intercepted to pay arrears in support, 311

CI. *See* Criminal Investigation Division (CI)

Citizenship, renouncing U.S., 42

CNC. *See* Currently not collectible (CNC) status

Code. *See* Internal Revenue Code

Cohan Rule, reconstruction of records, 114–115

Collection Appeals Program (CAP), 268

Collection by IRS
asset protection against, 255–256

computerized notices, 196–198

"enforced collection" rapid action, 207, 209

fair debt practices required in, 411

goal of IRS as maximum collection for minimum effort, 192, 196

immediate payment, demand for, 220

installment agreement application as suspending activity of, 223

IRS organizational structure and, 7

and Letter 1058, failure to respond in 30 days, 198

loans to pay taxes, request for, 204, 220

and payroll taxes owed, 350

private debt collection agencies, 258–261

refunds used to pay other taxes owed, 198, 419

resource for understanding (Publication 594), 197

states alerted by IRS of, 397

tax gap (amounts uncollected by IRS nationally), 194

for Trust Fund Recovery Penalty, 355

See also Automated Collection System (ACS); Bankruptcy; Currently not collectible (CNC) status; Enforced collection; Financial information forms (433 series forms); Installment agreements (IA); Offers in Compromise (OICs); Questioning and requests by IRS agent or auditor, suggested responses to; Revenue officers; Statutes of limitation

Collection statute expiration date.
See Statutes of limitation

Commissioner of Internal Revenue,
428

Compliance initiative projects, 64–65

Compliance Research Exams, 66–67

Computer-prepared tax returns
audit selection less likely for, 34, 43
as preferred by IRS, 33

Computer scoring for audits. *See
under* Audit selection

Computer tax preparation programs
comparing married filing jointly
vs. filing separately, 304
computer-prepared returns as
lowering audit risk, 34, 43
for extension to file, 40
forms for past years obtained
via, 32

Conditional expenses (not
"necessary" expenses), 218, 228

Congressional Medal of Honor
benefits, tax levies and, 275

Congress, U.S.
and help with asset seizures, 277
whistleblower protections, 412

Constitution, U. S., income tax and,
17

Cornell Law School website, 392

Corporations
check-signing power, 352, 353
corporate titles of individuals, 353
family cooperations, 317
and levies of business assets, 291
personal liability for payroll
tax debts of. *See* Trust Fund
Recovery Penalty (TFRP)
prior and related audits and, 65
shareholders in, as employees, 346
See also Businesses

Correspondence audits, 79–80, 83,
428

Court orders
inside business asset seizure
requiring, 291
primary residence seizure
requiring, 276, 287–288, 409,
423

Courts. *See* Federal courts

COVID-19 pandemic and the IRS
overview, 2
criminal investigations less
pursued during, 330

as hardship consideration, 244
late-filing penalties waived
during, 364
mail backlog, 2, 13
paperless operation as goal of
IRS, 2
paper tax return backlog, 2, 10
pause of collection notices
during, 196
pause of levy programs during, 273
pause of tax lien notices during,
266
Paycheck Protection Program,
fraud investigations, 323
People First Initiative (temporary
measures), 2
tax credits, audit risk and, 59
tax credits, fraud investigations
and, 323
video conferencing with taxpayers
initiated, 2

Credit counseling, bankruptcy and,
250

Credit rating
effect of bankruptcy on, 250
effect of tax lien on, 266, 269
Offer in Compromise improving,
245
resource on, and rebuilding
credit, 266

Criminal activities
death and taxes and, 313
Fifth Amendment tax return and,
65, 81
IRS tipped off by law
enforcement about, 65
jeopardy assessment and, 131
keeping assets out of sight and, 282
noncooperation with audit as
strategy to conceal, 101, 104
Offer in Compromise rejection
for, 247
political audit selection, 67

Criminal charges
appeals officer cannot negotiate in
cases of potential, 159
arrest or order to appear, 336
attorney for, 30, 35–36, 326,
332–333, 334, 336
auditor referrals for, 323, 327
for cash transactions not
reported, 359–360
defending against, 326, 338–339

for favors offered to auditor, 105
for filing a false return, 335
for fraudulent asset transfers, 281
grand jury indictment, 336
intent and, 335, 337–338
licenses for professionals lost in
convictions for, 339
for lying to the IRS, 27, 281, 327
mandatory reporting of foreign
financial accounts and, 37
for misstating source of income, 65
for money laundering, 329, 336,
359–360
for nonfiling of tax return, 24,
25–27, 29–30, 35–36, 38, 336,
429
plea bargaining, 336–337, 339
pleading not guilty, 336, 338–339
policy of not criminally charging
voluntary late-filers, 30–31, 35
prison sentences and, 339–340
as public information, 15
punishment allowed by law, 26,
29, 335–336, 339–340
reasonable doubt standard and,
338
for summons noncompliance, 98
Tax Court petitions deemed
frivolous, 165
for telling third party not to
comply with summons, 98
for telling third party to lie to the
IRS, 332
trial for, 337–338
voluntary filing to minimize
chances of, 35–36
See also Criminal Investigation
Division (CI); Fraud

Criminal Investigation Division (CI)
overview, 7, 329–330
attempts to talk your way out of,
not recommended, 30
attorney-client privilege and, 333
attorney needed by target of
investigation, 332–333, 334, 336
attorney obtaining agreement of
protection for voluntary filing,
35–36
auditor referring to, 323, 327
blurting out inappropriately to
auditor causing referral to, 101
defined, 428
Form 4135 filing, 331

how you might know if you're being investigated, 323, 330, 332
interviewees alerting the target of investigation, 331, 332
interviewees, attorney needed by, 332
interviewees, caution against lying by, 332
interviewees, caution against target making suggestions to associates, 332
interviews with friends and associates, 330–332
interview with target, 332–334
Justice Department as prosecuting cases, 328, 329–330, 336–338
Miranda rights read to target of, 332–333
money laundering investigations, 329, 336
nonfiler contact by agent of, 27
nonfiler investigation, 29–30
and prosecution, decision to recommend, 328, 329, 330, 334–335
silence is golden, and don't lie, 30, 332–334
special agents, 433
statistics on successful prosecutions, 329–330, 331, 334, 337
tips and referrals to, 327–328, 330, 419
undercover or sting operations, 328
See also Criminal charges; Fraud
Cryptocurrency
as audit risk, 59
valuation of, 212
CTRs (Currency Transaction Reports), 63, 359–360
Currency Transaction Reports (CTRs), 63, 359–360
Currently not collectible (CNC) status
overview, 257
computerized billing by IRS and, 197
conditional expenses usually disallowed in, 218
as delay of collections, 257
denial of request for, 201
federal tax liens may be filed during, 200, 257
financial information forms and, 257
interest and penalties continue to accrue, 257
IRS Form 53, 257
qualifying for, 200, 257
review of status, 201
state version of, 401
statute of limitation on collections continues to run during, 200, 257

D

Death
audits as continuing after, 54, 314
computerized billing by IRS and, 197
income taxes due after, 313–314
of joint owner of asset, 313, 319–320
See also Estate planning; Estate taxes
Debts, bad debt losses, 44
See also Tax debts
Debts, late filing and bad debt losses, 38
Deductions
aggressive filing and, 45–47
alimony/spousal support rules, 309
amendment of tax return and, 423
amendment of tax return to claim, 44
audit risk and, 42–43, 56, 57, 58
audits and proving of, 109, 111
charitable donations, 57, 86, 100
child support not deductible, 310
defined, 428
dependent children, 310–311
disallowed, and handling of prior years not in audit, 422–423
field audit and, 100, 101, 111–115
foreign housing deduction, 42–43
fraudulent claiming of, 322, 323
home office deduction, 62, 95, 101, 152–153, 389, 423
improper placement on return form, 58
interest on tax debts for businesses, 37
interest on tax debts not deductible for individuals, 37
itemized, at audit, 86
legal research to ensure correct usage of, 101
national averages for your income bracket, 56
negotiation with auditor, if questionable legal ground for, 116
penalties never deductible, 37
precise amounts vs. round numbers, 42, 59
ratio of deductions to income, 56, 57
records of unusual items attached to paper return, 42
rental property, 47, 93, 109
resource for, 46
See also Expenses and audits; Losses; Records; Records, missing
Delinquent return, defined, 429
See also Late-filing of tax returns; Nonfiling of tax returns
Dependency deduction for children, 310–311
Dependency exemption for children, 429
Depreciation, 87, 109, 429
Digital assets
as audit risk, 59
valuation of, 212
Direct debit payments
avoidance of, to protect bank account numbers, 41, 226
installation agreements and requirement for, 221, 223, 224, 226
IRS Direct Pay, 41
Direct payroll deduction for installment agreements, 226
Disabilities, taxpayers with
late filing and refund due, 39
low-income, may not be assigned private collection agency, 258
right to request auditor come to your home or business, 83
See also Medical issues
Disallowance, defined, 429
Disaster zones, taxpayers living in
interest abatement for, 376, 377
penalty abatement for, 372
Discriminant Function (DIF) score, 10, 56–57, 145, 429
Divorce
alimony/spousal support, 213, 309
collection efforts made from both spouses for joint tax bills, 407
dependency deduction for children, 310–311

innocent spouse claims, 227, 305–309, 310, 408–409
marital settlement agreements (MSAs), 309–310
resources for, 311
and spite tips to CI, 328, 419
wage seizure prevented by, 424
See also Child support
Documentation, defined, 429
See also Records

E

Economic reality. *See* Financial status/economic reality audits
EIN (employer identification number), 11, 143, 435
Electronic Federal Tax Payment System (EFTPS), 348
Electronic filing
accessibility to IRS of, vs. paper returns, 88
audit selection and avoidance of, 43
audit selection less likely for on-time, 34
for extension to file, 40
of installment agreement application, 195
of late returns, 34
paperless filing as goal of the IRS, 2, 10, 11
penalty relief for erroneous late filing penalty, 372
refunds arriving faster via, 43
of Tax Court petition, 170, 171
tax professionals required to use, unless taxpayer directs otherwise, 43
on time, conditions for, 372
Email communication with the IRS, 13
Email scams, 68
Employee Retention Credit (ERC), 59, 323
Employees
as attendees at audit, 103
exempt employees, 345
part-time, 347
as representative at audit, 387
shareholders of corporations as, 346
and spite tips to CI, 328
unreimbursed business expenses of, 86

workers who are automatically employees by law, 345
See also Businesses; Independent contractors, misclassification of employees as; IRS employees; Wage seizure/tax levies; Wage withholding
Enforced collection
overview, 265
appeal of denied installment agreement as delaying, 223
installment agreement denied and beginning of, 228
installment agreements as preventing, 223
revenue officers and risk of, 207
revenue officers and risk of rapid action, 209
See also Tax levies; Tax liens
Enrolled agents (EAs), 160, 179, 382–383, 384, 388–389, 429
See also Tax professionals
ERISA plans, 256, 276
See also Retirement plans and pensions
Estate planning
asset protection via, 256
joint tenancy with the right of survivorship, 319–320
See also Death; Estate taxes
Estate taxes
overview, 314–315
appraisals of estate, 317, 319
attorney or tax professional representation, 315, 316–317, 318
audits of estate tax returns, 315–319
automatic tax lien to get paid, 314
claims against the estate by heirs, 318
errors on return, 318
estate tax returns, 314–315
executor held liable for mistakes in, 318–319
extension of time to pay, 418
of foreign countries, 42
gifts and, 314, 318
jointly owned assets by separate filers and, 313
only 1% of taxpayers must pay, 314
resource for, 314
state, 315
tax-exempt estate amount, 314–315

valuation of assets in, 317–319
Estimated tax payments
foreign residents and, 41
must be current on, for installment agreement, 39, 223, 228
must be current on, for Offer in Compromise, 246, 247, 248
overpayment of, 39
Eviction lawsuits, required to remove owner after levy sale, 289
Examination report
overview, 119
agreement with/signing of ("agreed case"), 125–126
amended, 126
appeals settlement on, 159
approval by auditor's manager required, 125
contesting. *See* Audit appeals; Refund suits (claim for refund); Tax Court
disagreement with/refusal to sign, and negotiation of disputes, 126–127
extension of time requested by auditor, negotiation of, 117–118
final, 127
ignoring/doing nothing ("unagreed case"), 127, 129
"informal appeal" to manager, 126–127, 128, 142
IRS Form 1902-B, *Report of Individual Income Tax Examination Changes,* 119, 122–124
IRS Form 4549, *Income Tax Examination Change,* 119, 125, 159
issued despite noncooperation by taxpayer, 99, 101
and new auditor sent by IRS, 107
Notice of Deficiency, 127
Notice of Tax Due, 129
payment of balance, options for, 125–126
sample report, 120–125
statute of limitation expires, 118
Tax Court deadline dates must be conveyed to taxpayer, 411
timeframes to receive, 119, 421–422
win/lose/mixed elements of, 119

Examinations. *See* Audits

Exemption for dependents, 310–311

Exemption of property from tax levy, 275, 277–279, 281, 410, 429

Expenditures method of determining unreported income, 92

Expenses and audits
    business expenses under $75 each, no receipts for, 113
    community norms, 57
    employee business expenses, unreimbursed, 86
    field audits and verification of, 93
    out-of-character expenses, 58
    ratio of high-expense/low-income. *See* Financial status/economic reality audits
    ratio of item expense to income, 58
    record keeping and, 109
    travel and entertainment expenses, 113, 115
    unusually large or extravagant, 111
    See also Audit risk; Deductions; Records

Expenses and collection
    checklist (detailed), 214–215
    conditional expenses (not "necessary"), 218, 228
    defending expenses, 210
    denial of installment agreement and, 227–228
    flexibility in allowing greater expenses, 218
    listing of expenses on forms, 212–213, 218
    local standards, 213
    national standards, 212–213
    prepayment of future expenses with liquid assets, 211
    underestimation of expenses on 433 forms, 208–210
    See also Financial information forms (433 series forms)

Extension of time to pay, and avoidance of late-filing penalty, 40, 418

Extensions to file
    overview, 36, 429
    amended returns and refunds due, 44
    audit risk not increased by, 40
    audit risk possibly decreased by, 40
    during audit, for current year, 421
    filing for, 40
    for foreign residents (not vacationers), 40
    late-filing penalty avoided by, 40
    number of requests for, 24, 40
    penalties and interest accrue during, 36, 418
    penalties and interest for late payments accrue during, 40
    tax payment due at original due date, 40, 418

F

Failure to file tax return, 429
    See also Nonfiling of tax returns: criminal charges possible

Fair Debt Collection Practices Act, 260

Fair market value
    defined, 430
    discount on, and IRS sale of personal property, 286
    estate tax returns and discounts on, 317
    of real estate, 242
    uneconomical sale of assets for tax levies, 281

Family
    as attendees at audit, 104, 387
    buying real estate at levy sale, 288
    Offer in Compromise hardship exception and, 244
    and political influence on state tax collections, 402
    referrals for tax professionals from, 383
    size of family, standards for living expenses and, 213
    transfer of assets to, as protection against collections, 255–256
    See also Child support; Divorce; Spouses

Family limited partnerships, LLCs, and corporations, 256, 317

Farms and farming
    audit risk and, 56
    Chapter 12 bankruptcy for, 255
    exempt assets (tax levies), 275, 281

FATCA rules, 37

Favors offered to auditor, 105

FBAR (Form 90-221), 37

Federal courts
    overview, 185
    appeals officers as motivated to avoid cases going to, 149
    attorneys' fees and court costs paid by IRS, 185, 186, 272, 407, 425
    attorneys required for, 185, 186
    awards for IRS employees negligently breaking the law, 411
    burden of proof in, 52, 411
    interpretation of tax code by, 18
    jury trial possible in, 187
    Offer in Compromise application and loss of right to, 245
    for passport denial/revocation for tax debts, 227
    payment of tax bill in advance required for, 185
    payment of taxes ahead of time for, 357
    prior identical cases limiting appeals officer negotiations, 159
    reasons to choose a particular court, 187
    refund suits (claim for refund), 129, 185–186, 357, 373, 377, 428
    timeframes in, 186
    See also Tax Court; U.S. Court of Federal Claims; U.S. District Court

Federal tax liens. *See* Tax liens

Fees
    copy of tax return, 15
    installment agreement reinstatement, 226
    installment agreement set-up, 226
    Offers in Compromise application, 232, 245, 246
    Tax Court filing, 78, 167, 170, 171
    Tax Court witnesses, 177, 178
    tax lien recording, 265
    tax lien recording of release, 267
    See also Attorneys' fees; Tax professionals' fees

FICA contributions
    employer contribution, 348
    forms for filing, 349
    and misclassification of employees as independent contractors, 343
    withholding of employee's contribution, 348
    See also Payroll taxes

Field audits
overview, 89
auditor change during, 107–108
auditor training for, 89, 324
average assessments resulting
from, 79
blurting out inappropriate
remarks, 101
common audit issues (from the
office audit section), 85–88
common issues specific to, and
defenses, 91–94
conducted without taxpayer or
representative, 101
defined, 430
do not bring records not related
to tax year under audit, 102, 103
do not show other tax returns, 103
ending, strategies for, 116–117
expansion of, and how to prevent,
102–103
goals of taxpayer in, 102
Information Document Request
(IDR), 96–97
initial taxpayer interview (from
the office audit section), 84–85,
104
local IRS office making final
selections for, 89
location of, 90–91, 94–95
location, right to refuse on
business premises if it would
shut down business, 94
loss in business, mentioning to
auditor, 100
minimization of financial damage
of, 102
noncooperation with/failure to
appear, as strategy, 101, 104
open tax years, expansion into,
101, 102
people who should attend, 103–104
pointing out an error to the
auditor, 116–117
public and private records,
auditor access to, 99–100
recess of, taxpayer demand for,
106–107, 118, 405
request for additional records
during, response to, 95
requests for information,
noncompliance with, 96, 99, 103

revenue agents as auditor for, 7, 433
scheduling of, 90, 405
silence is golden in, 104–105
summons, 98, 101
summons to third parties, 98
taxpayer account information, 99
taxpayer as focus of examination,
vs. the return, 85, 90, 104
telephone call prior to notice by
mail, suggested response to, 89
third-party contacts by auditor,
100, 409
tools used by auditor, 96–100
unreported income, probe for,
91–93
See also Audit(s), attorney/
tax professional services;
Auditor/taxpayer interactions;
Examination report; Field
audits, preparation for
Field audits, preparation for
attorney/tax professional help
during, 100, 101, 114, 386–387
Audit Technique Guides (ATGs),
101–102
internal IRS checklist forms, 96
records, finding and organizing,
100
review tax return under audit, 100
tax law research to ensure correct
deductions, 101
Fifth Amendment (right to avoid
self-incrimination)
audit summons and, 98
defined, 430
fraud charges, 327
tax returns, 65, 81
"53" process. See Currently not
collectible (CNC) status
Filing, defined, 430
See also Tax returns
Financial accounts
financial status audit questions
about, 62
foreign, mandatory reporting of,
37, 59
levy notices and freezes on, 41,
198, 209, 285, 286, 290
moving, as protection following
tax levy, 282
See also Bank accounts; Retirement accounts and pensions

Financial information forms
(433 series forms)
overview, 208–210
assets listed on, 210–212
expenses checklist (detailed),
214–215
expenses, defending, 210
expenses listed on, 212–213, 218
information must be true on the
date you give it, 219
for installment agreements, 207,
225, 228, 229
Offer in Compromise and, 232,
233–240, 241–243, 246
options available to IRS after
review of, generally, 220
preparation for interview with,
207, 208
request 433 series form prior to
interview, 207
reviewing after meeting, 209, 218
revision of forms, 209–210
sample Form 433-A (OIC),
233–240
sample Form 433-F, 216–217
signing, cautions about, 208–209,
218
state taxes and use of, 399
updates of information on, IRS
requests for, 219
See also Collection by IRS;
Revenue officers
Financial status/economic reality
audits
overview, 60
computer scoring for (UIDIF),
57, 60
investigation of lifestyle, 60–63, 86
questions on lifestyle, and
suggested responses, 61–63
"reasonable indication" of
unreported income as standard
for, 60, 409
undercover operations (CI) to
reveal fraud, 328
FinCEN Form 114, 37
First-time offenders, penalty abatements for (FTA), 368, 373, 375, 406
Flat tax, 17
Foreign companies or foreigners
operating businesses, jeopardy
assessments of, 131

Foreign earned income exclusion, 41–42
Foreign financial accounts
  mandatory reporting of, 37, 59
  tax evasion schemes, 322, 420
Foreign governments
  cooperation agreements with IRS, 42, 256
  taxes paid to, by U.S. residents of, 42
Foreign housing deduction, 41–42
Foreign housing exclusion, 41–42
Foreign residents
  extension to file, 40
  filing tax returns, 41–42
  foreign government cooperation agreements with IRS, 42, 256
  renouncing U.S. citizenship, 42
  and statute of limitations on collections, 256
  tax debts, escaping, 256
  taxes owed to foreign government, 42
  time to respond to Notice of Deficiency, 166
Foreign tax credit, 38
401(k), 244, 256, 276
Fraud
  overview, 322
  aggressive filing vs., 45–47
  arrest or order to appear, 336
  attorney for charges of, 326, 332–333, 334, 336
  audit as revealing, 322–325, 326
  audit as revealing, and non-cooperation as strategy, 101, 104
  auditor ignoring the cheating, 327
  auditor imposing civil penalties vs. reporting to CI, 323, 327
  auditor referring to CI, 323, 327
  audit to follow investigation and/or criminal conviction for, 328–329
  "badges" of, 323
  bankruptcy not discharging taxes or penalties for, 251
  burden of proof for, 52
  cash hoard as defense against, 326
  civil fraud charges in addition to criminal charges, 329
  civil penalties, 323, 326, 327, 363
  criminal investigation into. See Criminal Investigation Division (CI)

  criminal penalties, 329, 335–336
  criminal record resulting from, 329
  deductions exaggerated or phony, 322, 323
  defending against, 326, 338–339
  defined, 52, 323, 430
  false claims, 322, 335
  filing Form 1099 or W-2 with intent of, 408
  grand jury indictment, 335
  honest mistake as defense against, 326
  indirect methods of proving, 324–325
  intent to cheat as necessary for charges of, 326, 335, 337–338
  IRS Form 4822, ignoring request to fill out, 325
  and joint filing, caution against, 48
  Justice Department as prosecuting, 328, 329–330, 335–337
  late-filing penalty, 363
  lying to get out of, criminal penalties for, 327
  negligence vs., 324
  nontaxable income as defense against, 326
  numbers of taxpayers charged with, 424
  offshore tax evasion schemes, 322, 420
  plea bargaining, 336–337, 339
  pleading not guilty, 336, 338–339
  prison sentences, 339–340
  public figures, and likelihood of criminal prosecution/jail time, 335, 339–340, 424
  reasonable doubt standard and, 338
  self-incrimination, Fifth Amendment right against, 327
  silence is golden, 327
  transfer of assets to avoid collections, 279, 280–281
  trial for, 337–338
  unreported income and investigation of, 322, 324–325, 326, 363
  See also Criminal charges; Tax evasion
Fraud referral, defined, 430
  See also Criminal Investigation Division (CI)

Freedom of Information Act (FOIA)
  and auditor's workpapers, access to, 126, 147–148, 150
  defined, 430
  internal IRS operations and, 16
  IRS file data and, 16
  sample letter for request, 147
Friends
  as attendees at audit, 104, 387
  buying real estate at levy sale, 288
  interviewed by CI, 330–332
  and political influence on state tax collections, 402
  referrals for tax professionals from, 383
  See also Family
Frivolous Tax Court petitions, 165
Frivolous tax returns, as audit risk, 67
FUTA tax, 349
  See also Payroll taxes

G
Garage sale/thrift shop prices, 212
Gifts
  defined, 430
  seizure of, 424
  taxes on, 314, 318
Glossary of tax terms, 427–436
Gross income, defined, 430
Group managers, 430

H
Hardship exceptions
  COVID-19 as hardship, 244
  definition of significant hardship, 300
  extension of time to pay without incurring penalty, 40, 418
  levies and, 275, 276, 278, 279, 281, 283, 284, 300
  Offer in Compromise, 231, 244–245
  penalty abatement for late payment, 369–370
  private debt collection agencies cannot offer, 59
  state tax collection suspended for, 401
  Taxpayer Advocate Service assistance with, 228, 298, 300, 404, 435
  See also Currently not collectible (CNC) status
Health insurance, as expense, 212
Health. See Medical issues

Hobby losses, vs. business losses, 155–158
Homeland Security TECS system database, auditor access to, 99
Home office deduction, 62, 95, 101, 152–153, 389, 423
Home. *See* Residence
Homestead exemption, 276, 400, 423
Housing and utility expenses, allowed, 213

IA. *See* Installment agreements (IA)
Income
    amendment of tax returns for failure to report, 44
    criminal activities as source of, 65, 81
    defined, 430
    executive compensation as audit issue, 102
    field audits and examination of, 91–93
    gross income, 430
    higher (over $100K), audit risk and, 43, 51, 57, 58
    higher (over $100K), field audit assessments and, 79
    higher (over $100K), revenue officers visiting nonfilers at home, 27
    from interest, 26, 219
    from investments, 26, 105
    IRS estimate of, 28, 64, 109
    nontaxable, as defense against fraud charges, 326
    ratio of high-expense/low-income. *See* Financial status/economic reality audits
    reduction of, as defense of tax levy, 279
    from side-jobs, 43, 86
    source of, statement on return, 65
    taxable income, 435
    tax levies and seizure of, 277–279
    total positive income, 57
    understatement of, and audit statute of limitations, 52
    understatement of, as primary IRS concern, 85–86, 91
    See also Alimony; Child support; Financial information forms; Income data; Unreported income; Wage seizure/tax levies

Income data
    audit risk of reporting less income than shown on forms, 43
    correspondence audits for missing data on return, 79
    disputed filings of, 407
    fraudulent filings of, 408
    Information Returns Program (IRP), 26
    IRS-filed returns using, 28, 64
    levy notices based on, 198
    lost, obtaining, 31–32
    mismatched with Form 433, and denial of installment agreement, 228
    mismatched with return, 68
    transcript of, obtaining, 14–15, 31–32
    See also Income, non-W-2 and 1099; 1099 income reports; Unreported income; W-2 wage statements
Income, non W-2 and 1099
    foreign financial accounts, mandatory reporting of, 37, 59
    late filing of returns and reconstruction of, 32
    side-job, reporting to avoid audit risk, 43
    Tax Return Transcript showing minimum amount that must be reported, 32
    See also Unreported income
Income tax
    death of taxpayer and payment of, 313–314
    establishment of, 17
    rates, current maximum, 17
    rates, early, 17
    as self-assessment system, 19
    See also State income taxes; Tax returns; Wage withholding
Independent contractors, misclassification of employees as
    attorney/tax professional for, 348
    defined, 431
    Form 1099-NEC filing and, 343
    IRS Form SS-8, caution against filing, 348
    as IRS priority, 343
    motives for, 343
    penalties for, 343–344
    proper classification, examples of, 346–347

proper classification, factors of, 344–345
    protection of business from, 347–348
    state classification rules, 346
    unpaid income taxes as liability in, 343
    See also Self-employment
Information Document Request (IDR), 96–97
    sample, 97
Information returns, 364, 431
    See also Income data; 1099 income reports; W-2 wage statements
Information Returns Program (IRP), 26
Installment agreements (IAs)
    amount of debt and other qualifications, 201–202, 220–221, 222, 224–225
    annual statements sent by IRS, 412
    appeal of rejection of, 223, 228
    appeal of revocation of, 229
    approval/denial by supervisor required, 225, 410
    approval of, 195, 225, 411
    audit agreement and, 125
    cash payment option via retail partners, 226
    change in financial circumstances, 229
    collection suspended while application pending, 223
    conditional expenses, allowable vs. elimination of, 218, 228
    contact by IRS collection prior to preparation, response to, 202
    contacting IRS to apply by telephone, directions for handling the interaction, 202–204
    coordination with state agreements, 230, 401
    credit card payments (and surcharge), 195
    current on tax filings, requirement of being, 39, 223, 228
    for debts over $50,000, 224–225
    default on previous, 228
    defined, 431
    denial of, and negotiation to reconsider, 228
    denial of, reasons for, 227–228
    direct debit payments on, 221, 223, 224, 226

direct payroll deduction for
payment of, 226
extension(s) of tax bill due date
and, 196
extension of 10-year limit on
collections as condition of, 224,
410
extension of time to make
monthly payment, 229
fee for reinstatement after
revocation, 226
fee for set-up, 226
filing by mail with your tax
return, 195
filing by Online Payment
Agreement application, 195
financial information forms and,
225, 228, 229
first payment with proposed
agreement, 225
full pay agreements, 221, 222
guaranteed IA, 222
interest and penalties on, 195,
222, 254
IRS Form 433-F or Form 433-B
in preparation for, 202
IRS Form 9465, *Installment
Agreement Request,* 195, 196,
221, 222
making payments before IA is
approved, 225
making payments by mail, 226
making payments by postdated
check, 225
missed payments, 226, 229–230
negotiation of monthly payment,
204, 225
number of taxpayers using, 193
partial pay agreement (PPIA), 221
for payroll taxes, 223, 224
preparation by organizing
financial information, 202, 203
reinstatement after revocation of,
226, 230
resubmitting application if no
response, 196
resubmitting application if you
receive a tax bill, 195
revision of, 229
revocation of, 226, 228–230
right to propose IA to IRS, 404

start payments on time even if
paperwork not received, 204
state agreements, 230, 399, 401
and statute of limitation on
collection, 221, 224, 410
streamlined IA, 222
tax levies and, 278, 283, 284
tax liens and, 221, 223, 272
in Taxpayer Bill of Rights, 404
timeframes for approval, 195
for Trust Fund Recovery Penalty,
224
Insurance. *See* Health insurance; Life
insurance
Interest
overview, 362, 367
abatement (reduction of), 368,
372–373, 376–377
for abusive tax shelters, 47
account transcript as explanation
of, 367
annual notice of tax debts and, 409
and audit appeals, 141, 376
audit closure and interest-free
period, 407
automated assessment notices
for, 68
bankruptcy and cessation of
(Chapter 13), 254
bankruptcy and continuation of
(Chapter 11), 255
bankruptcy and reduction of, 376
on both tax and penalties due, 367
compounded, 367
computation method shown on
notices, 409
currently not collectible status
and, 257
deductible for businesses, 37
delays in IRS administration and,
376
delays of more than 18 months
and, 376
errors in computation of, 376, 408
extension for late filing and, 36, 40
extension of time to pay tax, 40,
418
installment agreements and, 195,
222, 254
IRS Notice 433, *Interest and
Penalty Information,* 362
no amnesty for, 28

no statute of limitations for, 24
not deductible for individuals, 37
Offer in Compromise and
reduction of, 368, 376
partial payments as lowering, 41
rates of, 36, 367
on refunds sent in error, 376, 377,
420
Tax Court petitions, interest
continues to accrue during, 166,
183, 376
Tax Court petitions, partial
payment deposit/cash bond to
stop, 166
Trust Fund Recovery Penalty
appeals as stopping, 357
See also Penalties
Interest as deduction, audit risk and,
58
Interest income, 26, 219
Internal Revenue Code (IRC, "tax
code")
appeals officers as more
knowledgeable about, 153
burden of proof in Tax Court, 182
complexity of, 12, 17–18, 55
delay of notice, interest abatement
and, 376
exemptions from tax levies, 275
intention to make a profit and,
156
interpretation of, 18
lawsuits against IRS for willfully
disregarding, 257
legal research of, 392–394
online resource for, 393–394
payroll tax debts, personal
liability for, 351
and preparation for an audit, 101
refunds sent in error, interest on,
376
right to make an offer on tax
debts, 230
social, economic, and political
goals of, 18
"substantial compliance" with, as
legal standard, 112
Trust Fund Recovery Penalty, 358
and wage seizure, exemptions
from, 277
See also Legal research

Internal Revenue Manual (IRM)
  overview, 431
  accuracy of tax bill, requests to
    check, 201
  appeals agent negotiations, 154
  assets of last resort for seizure,
    275–277
  audit appeals, 140
  auditors to report fraud to CI, 323
  conditional expenses, 218
  corporate-officer responsibility for
    unpaid payroll taxes, 353
  flexibility in necessary expense
    amounts, 218
  importance of initial audit
    interview, 104
  importance of initial collection
    interview, 207
  IRS-filed returns (SFR), 64
  IRS Penalty Handbook, 368
  local standards for living
    expenses, 213
  national standards for living
    expenses, 212–213
  no criminal prosecutions on
    voluntary filers, 30, 35
  no-equity seizures, 281, 284
  nonfiling, 24–25
  no-repeat audits, 81, 82
  reasonable cause for penalty
    abatement, 368–369
  retirement benefits as last resort
    for seizure, 256, 276, 283
  same auditor from previous three
    years, 107
  tax bill accuracy, taxpayer
    questioning, 201
  time limits for audit completion,
    53, 118
  Trust Fund Recovery Penalty, 358
  types of cases audit appeals
    officers won't hear, 160
Internet searches, auditors making, 99
Investment income, 26, 105
Investment losses, as audit risk, 44,
  47, 59
IRAs, 68, 253, 256, 276, 358
IRC. *See* Internal Revenue Code
  (IRC, "tax code")
IRM. *See Internal Revenue Manual*
IRS (Internal Revenue Service)
  overview of structure of, 6–7,
    9–10, 12

Annual Report on organization
  and performance, 21
  approach to winning against,
    generally, 19–20
  bad written advice from, penalty
    relief due to, 369, 372, 405
  Business and Specialty Tax
    assistance line, 224
  Centralized Insolvency
    Operation, 249, 270
  Centralized Lien Operation, 270,
    271
  Collection Division, 428
  Commissioner of, 428
  communication with, preferred
    and nonpreferred methods of, 13
  compliance initiative projects,
    64–65
  computers and, 11
  defined, 431
  email communication with, 13
  foreign government cooperation
    agreements with, 42, 256
  free information and services
    from, generally, 390–391
  funding increases for next decade,
    8, 51
  inefficiencies and, 11–12
  Information Returns Program
    (IRP), 26
  Large and International Business
    Division, 51
  law enforcement sharing infor-
    mation with, 15, 65, 327–328
  letter communications, problems
    with, 13
  Market Segment Specialization
    Program (MSSP), 63, 101–102
  operational status (link), 2
  organizational chart, 12
  scam emails and phone calls, 68
  service centers, 433
  significant hardship, defined, 300
  Small Business/Self-Employed
    Division, 342
  states sharing information with,
    15, 25, 99, 396–397, 418
  Tax-Exempt and Government
    Entities Division, 51
  Taxpayer Assistance Centers, 390
  tax refund hotline, 419
  telephone services of, generally,
    390

Treasury Offset Program (TOP),
  311
  U.S. Citizenship and
    Immigration Services, computer
    link with, 256
  video conferencing, 2, 94–95, 152
  website resources, generally, 391
  See also Appeals; Audit(s);
    Automated adjustment notices
    from IRS; Collection by IRS;
    Internal Revenue Code (IRC,
    "tax code"); *Internal Revenue
    Manual* (IRM); IRS campuses;
    IRS employees; IRS forms; IRS
    Independent Office of Appeals;
    Local IRS offices; Taxpayer
    Advocate Service (TAS)
IRS account. *See* Taxpayer account
IRS campuses (service centers)
  overview, 6
  as handling voluntary filing of old
    returns, 30
  processing of tax returns,
    generally, 10
IRS CP-14, *You Have Unpaid Taxes,*
  196–197
IRS CP-40, 259
IRS CP-49, *Overpaid Tax Applied to
  Other Taxes You Owe,* 198
IRS CP-90, *Final Notice—Intent to
  Levy and Notice of Your Right to a
  Hearing,* 197, 198
IRS CP-500 series, 197
IRS CP-501, *You Have a Balance
  Due,* 197, 265
IRS CP-503, *Immediate Action Is
  Required,* 197
IRS CP-504, *You Have an Amount
  Due—Intent to Levy,* 197
IRS CP-508C, 227
IRS CP-523, *Notice of Intent to
  Levy—Intent to Terminate Your
  Installment Agreement,* 229
IRS CP-2000 Notice
  as automatic adjustment notice,
    68
  disputing, 76–79
  sample letter disputing, 76–77
  sample of, 69–75
IRS CP-2501, 68
IRS CP-2566, 28, 29
IRS CP-4624C, 200

IRS employees
appeals officers, 148–149
bonuses and, 90
brevity and conciseness in letters preferred by, 78
communication with, preferred forms of, 13
correspondence with taxpayer must contain name, ID number, and contact information of, 412
dishonest, reporting of, 420
favors offered to, 105
inefficiency and, 11
Interest Abatement Coordinator, 377
mandatory reporting of political audit requests, 67
number of, 7
as overworked, 90
privacy of tax returns violated by, 100, 418
pseudonym use as limited for, 412
quotas and, 90
seasonal, mistakes in processing by, 10
special agents (CI), 329, 330
taxpayer right to be treated fairly by, 81
See also Auditors and auditor training; Auditor/taxpayer interactions; Criminal Investigation Division (CI); Lawsuits; Lying to the IRS; Questioning and requests by IRS agent or auditor, suggested responses to; Revenue officers
IRS forms
assistance with identifying, 13
contact phone number for obtaining, 32
correct year's form must be used, 32
past year forms, ways to obtain, 32
as preferred communication method, 13
See also Specific forms
IRS Form 53, 257
IRS Form 211, *Application for Award of Original Information,* 419
IRS Form 433 series. *See* Financial information forms (433 series forms)

IRS Form 433-A (OIC), *Collection Information Statement for Wage Earners and Self-Employed Individuals,* 232, 241–243, 246
sample, 233–240
IRS Form 433-A, *Collection Information Statement for Wage Earners and Self-Employed Individuals,* 202, 208, 219, 221
IRS Form 433-B, *Collection Information Statement for Businesses,* 202, 208, 219, 232
IRS Form 433-D, *Installment Agreement* (for direct debits), 221
IRS Form 433-F, *Collection Information Statement,* 200, 208, 225
sample, 216–217
IRS Form 433-H, *Installment Agreement Request and Collection Information Statement,* 208
IRS Form 656 Booklet, *Offer in Compromise,* 231, 244, 246
IRS Form 656-L, 231
IRS Form 668Z, *Certificate of Release of Federal Tax Lien,* 245, 267
IRS Form 843, *Claim for Refund and Request for Abatement,* 186, 428
for abatement of interest request, 377
for abatement of penalty request, 370, 371, 373, 375
See also Refund suits
IRS Form 870 series, 159
IRS Form 872, *Consent to Extend the Time to Assess Tax,* 118
IRS Form 900, 224
IRS Form 911, *Request for Taxpayer Advocate Service Assistance,* 302
sample, 301
IRS Form 940, *Employer's Annual Federal Unemployment Tax Return,* 349
IRS Form 941, *Employer's Quarterly Federal Tax Return,* 349, 363
IRS Form 944, *Employer's Annual Federal Tax Return,* 349
IRS Form 1040X, *Amended U.S. Individual Income Tax Return,* 44–45
IRS Form 1098, 68, 86
IRS Form 1099-R, 32, 68
IRS Form 1099. *See* 1099 income reports

IRS Form 1127, *Application for Extension of Time for Payment of Tax,* 418
IRS Form 1127, *Application for Extension of Time for Payment of Tax Due to Undue Hardship,* 40, 418
IRS Form 1494, 277
IRS Form 1902-B, *Report of Individual Income Tax Examination Changes,* 119, 122–124
IRS Form 2039, *Summons,* 98
IRS Form 2159, *Payroll Deduction Agreement,* 226
IRS Form 2555, *Foreign Earned Income,* 42
IRS Form 2848, *Power of Attorney and Declaration of Representative,* 95, 387
IRS Form 4135, *CI Control Notice,* 331
IRS Form 4180, *Report of Interview With Individual Relative to Trust Fund Recovery Penalty or Personal Liability for Excise Tax,* 352
IRS Form 4506, *Request for Copy of Tax Return,* 15
IRS Form 4506-T, *Request for Transcript of Tax Return,* 14–15, 31, 252, 367
IRS Form 4549, *Income Tax Examination Change,* 119, 125, 159
IRS Form 4700, *Examination Workpapers,* 84, 96, 132–136
See also Workpapers
IRS Form 4700-A *Supplement,* 84, 133–134
IRS Form 4700-B *Business Supplement,* 84, 96, 135–136
IRS Form 4822, *Statement of Annual Estimated Personal and Family Expenses,* 325
IRS Form 4852, *Substitute for Form W-2,* 32
IRS Form 4868, *Application for Extension of Time to File Individual U.S. Income Tax Return,* 36, 40
IRS Form 8300, 359–360
IRS Form 8332, *Release/Revocation of Claim to Exemption for Child by Custodial Parent,* 310–311
IRS Form 8379, *Injured Spouse Allocation,* 291, 308, 311

IRS Form 8822, *Change of Address,* 130, 166

IRS Form 8857, *Request for Innocent Spouse Relief,* 309

IRS Form 8938, 59

IRS Form 9423, *Collection Appeal Request,* 229, 268, 285

IRS Form 9465, *Installment Agreement Request,* 195, 196, 221, 222

IRS Form 12153, *Request for a Collection Due Process or Equivalent Hearing,* 269, 274

IRS Form 12203, *Request for Appeals Review,* 142, 143, 144
    sample of, 144

IRS Form 12277, *Application for Withdrawal,* 271

IRS Form 13711, *Request for Appeal of Offer in Compromise,* 248

IRS Form 13844, 226

IRS Form 14134, 270

IRS Form 14135, 270

IRS Form FinCEN 104, *Currency Transaction Report,* 359

IRS Form K-1, 68

IRS Form SS-8, *Determination of Worker Status for Purposes of Federal Employment Taxes and Income Tax Withholding,* 344, 348

IRS Form W-2. *See* W-2 wage statements

IRS Form W-4, 348

IRS Independent Office of Appeals
    overview, 148
    appeals officers, about, 148–149
    Collection Appeals Program (CAP), 268
    Collection Due Process (CDP) hearing, 269, 274
    Equivalent Hearing (appeal of tax lien), 269
    See also Audit appeals

IRS Letter 1058, *Final Notice, Notice of Intent to Levy and Notice of Your Right to a Hearing,* 198

IRS Letter Number 3219. *See* Notice of Deficiency

IRS Notice 433, *Interest and Penalty Information,* 362

IRS Notice 1219-B, *Notice of Potential Third Party Contact,* 100

IRS Publications, overview, 390

IRS Publication 1, *Your Rights as a Taxpayer* (summary of Taxpayer Bill of Rights), 81, 404, 413–414

IRS Publication 5, *Your Appeal Rights and How to Prepare a Protest if You Disagree,* 127, 140

IRS Publication 17, *Your Federal Income Tax,* 54

IRS Publication 54, *Tax Guide for U.S. Citizens and Resident Aliens Abroad,* 42

IRS Publication 559, *Survivors, Executors, and Administrators,* 314

IRS Publication 583, *Starting a Business and Keeping Records,* 109

IRS Publication 594, *The IRS Collection Process,* 197, 242, 265

IRS Publication 1544, 359

IRS Publication 1546, *The Taxpayer Advocate Service,* 294

IRS Publication 1660, *Collection Appeal Rights,* 268, 269

IRS Publication 3498-A, *The Examination Process (Audits by Mail),* 80

IRS Publication 3598, 28, 130

IRS regulations, 18, 433

IRS revenue procedures, 433

IRS revenue rulings, 18, 433

IRS Schedule A, *Itemized Deductions,* 56

IRS Schedule B, 59

IRS Schedule C, *Profit or Loss From Business,* audit risk and, 43, 56

IRS Schedule F, *Profit and Loss From Farming,* 56

J

Jeopardy assessments, 131, 274, 431

J.K. Lasser's Your Income Tax, 392

Job training partnerships, tax levies and, 275

Joint ownership of assets
    overview, 423–424
    audit risk and, 312
    commingled funds, 424
    estate taxes and, 313, 319–320
    gifts creating, 424
    joint tenancy, and bankruptcy, 256
    joint tenancy with the right of survivorship, estate taxes and, 319–320

by separate filers, tax dangers of, 312–313

and tax levies, 279, 280–281, 312

Joint tax returns
    amendment to convert filing from separate to, 407
    caution not to sign if you suspect fraud by spouse, 48
    collection efforts made from both spouses, 407
    defined, 431
    innocent spouse protections, 227, 305–309, 310, 408–409
    separate filing vs., factors influencing, 304–305
    separate liability option, 308, 408, 411
    Tax Court petition, and names of both spouses as they appear on, 170
    tax refunds and, injured spouse claims for, 291, 308, 311

Justice Department, as prosecuting criminal charges, 328, 329–330, 335–337

K

Kelley Blue Book, 211

Keogh plans, 276

L

Late filing of information returns, 364

Late filing of tax returns
    assistance for low-income taxpayers, 33, 245, 382
    assistance from attorney, 35–36
    assistance from local IRS office, 33
    assistance from tax professionals, 33, 34
    assistance via computer tax preparation software, 33
    better to file before the IRS contacts you, 30–31
    deadline set by IRS for prior year filing, 27
    in disaster areas, 376, 377
    filing current year without filing previous years, 39
    filing even if you can't pay balance owed, 25–26, 39
    filing without first contacting the IRS, 35

forms, obtaining correct year, 32
fraudulent late filing, 363
lost W-2 and 1099 forms,
    obtaining, 31–32
partial payment with, 41
penalties for. *See under* Penalties
"quiet disclosure," 35
refunds denied due to (and
    exceptions), 38–39
screened by IRS, 34
state return filed with, 25
submission of return, methods
    for, 34
See also Criminal charges;
    Extensions to file; Interest;
    Nonfiling of tax returns; Partial
    payments; Penalties
Law enforcement, data sharing with
    IRS, 15, 65, 327–328
Law libraries, 393–394
Lawsuits
    against IRS for wrongful levies,
        292
    against IRS for wrongful liens, 272
    against the IRS for willfully
        disregarding the law, 257, 405,
        408, 411
    awards from, audits and, 102
    eviction, of homeowner after IRS
        auction, 289
    for fraudulent Form 1099 or W-2
        filings, 408
    to obtain FOIA compliance by
        IRS, 16
    refund suits, 129, 185–186, 357,
        373, 377, 428
    for Trust Fund Recovery Penalty
        payment responsibility, 358, 406
    See also Federal courts
Legal aid
    Low Income Taxpayer Clinics,
        33, 245, 382
    for Tax Court, 184
    See also Taxpayer Advocate
        Service (TAS)
Legalbitstream.com, 392, 393
Legal plans, prepaid, 383
Legal research
    overview, 380, 389
    on audit reconsideration, 129
    to ensure deductions are proper,
        101
    free IRS programs, 391

guidebooks and deskbooks,
    392–393, 394
internet sites, 391, 392, 393
IRS publications, generally, 390
law libraries, 393–394
tax code, 392–394
Tax Court decisions, 393
telephone services of IRS, 390
See also Attorneys; Tax
    professionals; *Specific IRS Forms
    and Publications*
Letter rulings, 18
Letter to Dispute an IRS Tax
    Adjustment, 76–77
Levies
    overview, 198, 273
    appeals of, 198, 274, 281,
        285–286, 406, 409
    approval by supervisor required
        for, 405, 410
    assets of last resort for, 275–277
    assets, return of, 283–284, 406
    asset transfers and protection
        from, 279–281
    automatic seizures, 198
    avoidance of, 279–283
    of bank/financial accounts, 41,
        198, 209, 285, 286, 290
    bankruptcy and, 278, 283, 285
    bond posted in lieu of, 284
    computerized notices for, 198, 273
    court orders required for, 276,
        287–288, 291, 409, 423
    currently not collectible status
        and, 200
    defending against, 278–279
    defined, 431
    delays of process, 274, 283, 284
    designation of payments not
        allowed for, 378
    as economic hardship, 275, 276,
        278, 279, 281, 283, 284, 300
    employment jeopardized by, 275,
        281
    errors in, 273
    exempt assets, 275, 277–279, 281,
        410, 429
    foreign residents and out-of-
        country assets or wages, 42
    fraudulent asset transfers and,
        279, 280–281
    installment agreements and, 278,
        283, 284, 410

jeopardy assessments allowing
    immediate seizure, 131, 274, 431
jointly owned assets and, 279,
    280–281, 312
joint tax refunds and injured
    spouse claims, 291, 308, 311
likelihood of, 273
no-equity seizures, 281, 284
and noncooperation/refusing to
    give financial information, 207,
    209
notice of auctions, 286, 288
Notice of Intent to Levy, 198,
    274, 276, 405, 409
"notice of seizure" for real estate,
    287
notice sent to last known address,
    274
numbers of, 273
Offer in Compromise and, 278,
    283, 284, 410
out-of-state, difficulty of, 209
passport denial/revocation and,
    227
payment in full of, 283, 284
political contacts to help with,
    277
release of, 283–286
removal of personal property, 286
repeat, on same property, 286, 287
right of redemption on real estate
    sales, 289–290
sale of assets by IRS, 286–291
self-employment income seizure,
    198, 277–278, 285
silence is golden, and don't lie,
    281–282, 283
state taxes and, 400
statute of limitations on
    collections and, 285
suing IRS for wrongful levy, 292
Taxpayer Advocate Service for
    help with, 276, 279, 296, 300
tools of the trade as exempt from,
    275, 281
as uneconomical, as defense, 281,
    284
and value of assets for collection
    procedures, 210
written accounting for sales of
    assets, 410
See also Wage seizure/tax levies

Licensed professionals, criminal convictions and loss of license, 339

Liens. *See* Tax liens

Life insurance
bankruptcy protection of trust for, 256
Offer in Compromise and value of, 247

Lifestyle. *See* Financial status/economic reality audits

Limitation on assessment and collection. *See* Statutes of limitation

Living Expense Checklist, 214–215

Living expenses. *See* Expenses and collection

LLCs, 65, 317, 351

Loans to pay tax bill
IRS cannot demand, 204
IRS request for, 220
for state taxes, 401
tax liens and, 270

Local IRS offices
overview of structure of, 6–7, 9–10
contact information required to be listed in directories, 412
file-stamped copies from, 34
final selection of audits made by, 58, 89
FOIA request for auditor's workpapers from, 147–148, 150
group managers, 430
hand filing amended returns with, as preferred, 44
hand filing late returns with, as preferred, 34
help in preparing late-filed returns, 33
nonfiler accounts handled by, 30
as source for forms, 32
special audit projects by, 64, 128
Taxpayer Assistance Centers, 390
transfer of correspondence audit to, request for, 80
transfer to, to contest penalty abatement rejection, 373
See also Revenue officers; Taxpayer Advocate Service (TAS)

Local standard expense allowances, 213

Losses
bad debts, 38, 44

and lifestyle questions in financial status audit, 62
theft and casualty deductions, 86
worthless securities, 44
See also Business with net losses for the year

Low Income Taxpayer Clinic (TITC) program, 33, 245, 382
See also Taxpayer Advocate Service (TAS)

Low-income taxpayers
exceptions for Offers in Compromise, 232, 241, 245, 246
fees for installment agreements, 226
free tax assistance programs, 391
private debt collection agencies may not be assigned to, 258
Tax Court representation, 184
See also Low Income Taxpayer Clinic (TITC) program

Lying to the IRS
ACS collectors and avoidance of, 202–203
aggressive filing vs., 46
auditor questions to test taxpayer for, 105
criminal charges for, 27, 281, 327
as felony, 281
and fraud charges, attempts to evade, 327
by interviewees of CI, 332
revenue officers and avoidance of, 206–207, 208
silence is golden, and don't lie, 87, 104–105, 281–282, 283, 327, 332–334
suggestions to interviewees given by target of investigation, 332
as violation of First Commandment of winning your audit, 112
See also Auditor/taxpayer interactions; Criminal Investigation Division (CI); Questioning and requests by IRS agent or auditor, suggested responses to

M

Mail correspondence. *See* U.S. Postal Service

Market Segment Specialization Program (MSSP), 63, 101–102

Mark-up method of determining unreported income, 93

Married couples. *See* Divorce; Joint tax returns; Spouses

Master Tax Guide, 392–393

Math errors
automated adjustment notice to correct, 67
computer-generated returns as free from, 33, 43

Medical issues
audit and proof of bills, 86
as exception to refunds denied on late-filings, 38–39
as expense, 212
late-payment penalty abatement due to, 369–370
as Offer in Compromise hardship exception, 244–245
as reasonable cause for failure to follow tax law, 368
See also COVID-19 pandemic; Disabilities, taxpayers with

Medicare. *See* FICA contributions; Payroll taxes

Military
disability payments, as exempt from levy, 275
penalty relief for those in combat zones, 372
retired, late filing and refund due, 39

Miranda rights, 332

Money laundering, 329, 336, 359–360

Mortgage interest, 68, 86

N

National Research Program (NRP), 66–67

National standard expense allowances, 212–213

Negligence, 431
penalty for, vs. fraud penalty, 324

Net worth method of determining unreported income, 91–92, 325

90-Day Letters. *See* Notice of Deficiency

Nonfiling of tax returns
amnesty for, discussion of, 418
audit risk and, 52, 64
computerized billing cycle and, 197
criminal charges possible, 24, 25–27, 29–30, 38, 336, 429

criminal charges possible, voluntary filing to avoid, 35–36
criminal investigation of, 27
defined, 431
detection by IRS, 26, 417
IRS filing your return (SFR) due to, 27, 28–29, 64
notices requesting to file, 27
number of people nonfiling, 24
questioning by IRS, suggested responses to, 25, 27, 30
requests for tax returns older than six years, handling of, 25
revenue officer visit at home, 27
state income taxes and, 25, 397
statute of limitations and, 24–25, 52, 417
Taxpayer Delinquency Investigation into, 26–27
Tax Return Transcript showing, 32
See also Interest; Late filing of tax returns; Penalties
Notice
annual, of tax debts, 409
of auctions for levied assets, 286–287, 288–290
computerized collection notices, 196–198
delays by IRS, interest abatement and, 376
errors in, 68, 78, 82, 164
Intent to Levy, 198, 274, 276, 405, 409
IRS-filed tax returns (SFR), 28–29, 64
for lost or misapplied payments, 407
to nonfilers requesting to file, 27
of seizure, for real estate, 287
Tax Court notices, 174
for Taxpayer Delinquency Investigation, 26–27
of Trust Fund Recovery Penalty, 355
See also Audit notices; Automated adjustment notices from IRS; IRS CP-2000 Notice; Notice of Deficiency; Notice of Federal Tax Lien
Notice of Deficiency (90-Day Letter)
attached to Tax Court petition, 171

for automated adjustments, 78
defined, 436
failure to receive, and phantom audits, 130
following appeal that doesn't settle, 161
information on Tax Court petition form, 170
for IRS-filed returns (SFR), 28, 64
law does not require that you actually receive the notice, 166
and nonfiled returns, 64
timeframes for receiving, 127
time to respond to (90 days) with Tax Court petition, 78, 127, 166
Notice of Federal Tax Lien, 227, 243, 257, 265–268, 384, 409, 434
withdrawal of, 267, 269, 270, 272, 406

O

Occupation
criminal, and Fifth Amendment tax return, 65, 81
of particular audit risk, 63–65, 101–102
self-employed business identification code, 65
statement on tax return, 65
Offers in Compromise (OICs)
overview, 230–231, 424
appeal of IRS rejection, 248
approvals, liberal policy specified by law, 411
assets, exclusions allowed, 241, 242
assets, hardship-related exception, 231, 244–245
assets, net value of, 241–242
bankruptcy and, 252
basic living expenses, IRS must allow enough money for, 410
businesses and, 232
common errors in forms for, 246
conditional expenses usually disallowed in, 218
contact with IRS offer specialist, 246–247, 248
court adjudication of tax debt, OIC application and loss of right to, 245
current on tax filings, requirement of being, 246, 247, 248

defined, 432
as delay of collection, 201, 245, 248
as discretionary with the IRS, 230
disposable monthly income, 243
"doubt as to collectibility" grounds, 231
"doubt as to liability" grounds, 131, 231
"effective tax administration" (ETA) grounds, 231, 244–245
fee for application, 232, 245, 246
financial information forms, Form 433-A (OIC), 232, 241–243, 246
financial information forms, sample Form 433-A (OIC), 233–240
grounds for, 231
interest abatement in, 368, 376
IRS Form 656 Booklet, *Offer in Compromise,* 231, 244, 246
low-income exception for fee and partial payment, 232, 241, 245, 246
Low Income Taxpayer Clinic for help with, 245
lump sum payment option, 241, 243
mailing address for, 246
minimum offer, 232
missing payments, 241
offering more than minimum not recommended, 232
partial payment required with application, 232, 241, 245, 246
payment and payment periods, 241, 243
penalty abatement in, 368
penalty abatement rejection, contesting via, 373
periodic payment option, 241, 243
prequalifier online test for, 231
pros and cons of making, 245
reasonable collection potential (RCP), 232, 247
recent tax debts and, 242
reconsideration of rejection, 247, 248
and records, providing copies of, 232, 246–247
rejection of, 247–248

requests for further documentation, 246–247

revocation of, 245

state version of, 400

statute of limitation on collections and, 242, 243, 245

submission of another OIC, 247

successful percentage of applications, 230

tax levies and, 278, 410

tax liens and, 243, 245, 267, 271

tax professional for, 244

timeframe for decision on, 247

for Trust Fund Recovery Penalty, 358

voided/revocation of, 241

written letter stating IRS error in rejecting OIC, 247

Office audits

overview, 80

asking to transfer to correspondence audit, 83

auditor, meeting and communicating with, 84

average assessments resulting from, 79

common audit issues, 85–88

defined, 432

delaying of, 83

do not be too eager to help the auditor, 87

do not bring other returns to the audit, 87, 88

expansion of scope of, 102

follow-up to record requests, 88–89

initial taxpayer interview, 84–85, 104

length of appointment, 88

"no-repeat" audit rule and, 82

original documents: do not give or mail to IRS (copies only), 111

preparation: internal IRS workpapers, 84, 96, 132–136

preparation: tax professional consultation, 114, 386–387

questioning by auditor over the phone, delay response, 83

questions about background/ identifying the taxpayer, 84

questions about prior audits, 87

questions not on the original list, 80, 88–89

request for additional years' returns, 87–88

requests for records you didn't bring to the audit, 83, 88–89

request to photocopy your records, 87

reviewing the audit notice for errors, 82

scheduling of, 82–83, 405

statute of limitations and, 82

taxpayer as focus of examination, vs. the return, 85, 104

See also Audit(s), attorney/ tax professional services; Auditor/taxpayer interactions; Examination report

Offshore tax evasion schemes, 322

Offshore trusts, 256

Online resources

advertising by tax professionals, 384

amended returns, status of, 44

Audit Technique Guides, 63, 101–102

bankruptcy, 249

change of address form, 130

Collection Information Statement, 207

CPAs, finding, 384

enrolled agents, finding, 384

fair debt collection violations by private agency, 260

FOIA guidelines, 16

form resources, 13

forms for past years, obtaining, 32

installment agreement revision, 229

Interest and Penalty Information, 362

Internal Revenue Service Inflation Reduction Act Strategic Operating Plan FY2023-2031, 8

IRS *Annual Report,* 21

IRS Direct Pay, 41

IRS Get Transcript Online tool, 14

IRS information, generally, 390–391

IRS payments, 195

IRS publications, generally, 390

Kelley Blue Book, 211

legal research sites, 391, 392, 393

local standards for living expenses, 213

national standards for living expenses, 213

Nolo.com, 391

Offer in Compromise booklet, 231

Offer in Compromise prequalifier test, 231

real estate valuation, 211

Section 8A Master File Codes, 194

tax account registration, 15

Tax Court, 188

Tax Court filing requirement updates, 171

Tax Court forms, 166, 167, 177

Tax Court petition filing, 170

Tax Court video conferencing motion, 174

Taxpayer Advocate Qualifier Tool, 294

Taxpayer Advocate Service near you, 297

Taxpayer Roadmap, 8

See also Legal research

P

Partial payments

delaying the computerized billing notice cycle and inclusion of, 198

designating payments to most recent year, 377–378

filing on time and sending what you can, 41

form of payment for, and caution against using personal check or electronic debit, 41

and "no refund" rule for late payments, 38–39

Offers in Compromise applications accompanied by, 232, 241, 245, 246

of payroll taxes, designation to the trust fund portion, 349

penalties and interest decreased by, 41

record keeping of, 41

Partnerships

and levies of business assets, 290–291

as neither employees nor independent contractors, 346

partner as audit representative, 387

payroll tax debt liability and, 351

prior and related audits and, 65

Passports
  denial/revocation for tax debts, 227
  records of, IRS access to, 99
Paycheck Protection Program, fraud investigations, 323
Payments
  attorney's trust fund checks, 41
  cash payment option via retail partners, 226
  by credit card, 195, 226
  direct debits for installment agreements, 221, 223, 224, 226
  direct payroll deductions for installment agreements, 226
  immediate, IRS collector demanding, 220
  IRS contact information for, 195
  IRS Direct Pay, 41
  misapplied or lost by IRS, 407
  money orders and cashier's checks, 41, 226
  protection of bank account numbers when making, 41, 226
  and protection of new accounts, 219
  See also Collection by IRS; Loans to pay tax bill; Partial payments
Payroll taxes
  overview, 348–350
  acceleration of collection process for, 197
  bankruptcy as preferable to debts for, 350
  bankruptcy cannot eliminate, 251
  bonded payroll tax service for, 349
  defined, 432
  deposit of, frequency required for, 348
  deposit of, through EFTPS, 348
  employee/employer's contribution to, 348, 349
  first-time offenders and penalty abatement, 406
  forms for filing, 349
  installment agreements for, 223, 224
  liability for unpaid. *See* Trust Fund Recovery Penalty
  minimizing problems with, 349, 350
  as most serious of tax debts, 350

  partial payment of, designation to the trust fund portion, 349
  penalty for failure to comply with, 363, 406
  resource for, 363
  seizure of business assets for failure to pay, 291, 350
Pearson's Federal Taxation, 392–393
Penalties
  overview, 362–363
  abatement (reduction or elimination of). *See* Penalty abatement
  for abusive tax shelters, 47
  account transcript as explanation of, 367
  accuracy penalties, 363
  annual notice of tax debts and, 409
  audit closure and delay period for, 407
  automated assessment notices for, 67
  bankruptcy and cessation of (Chapter 13), 254
  bankruptcy and lowering of, 254
  chart summarizing, 365–366
  combined penalties, 366
  currently not collectible status and accrual of, 257
  defined, 432
  for failure to file information returns, 364
  for failure to pay penalties, 364
  for fraud. *See under* Fraud
  fraudulent underreported income, 363
  installment agreements and, 195, 222, 254
  IRS Notice 433, *Interest and Penalty Information,* 362
  late-filing and late-payment, combined, 366
  late-filing, fraudulent, 363
  late-filing penalty, 36–37, 195, 364
  late-filing penalty (even if you don't owe tax), 37, 364
  late-filing penalty, abatement. *See* Penalty abatement
  late-filing penalty, COVID-19 waivers of, 364

  late-filing penalty, extension to file and avoidance of, 36, 40
  late-payment penalty, 36–37, 40, 195, 364, 366
  late-payment penalty, abatement of, 369–370, 375
  late-payment penalty, extension of time and avoidance of, 40, 418
  for misclassification of employees as independent contractors, 343–344
  no amnesty for, 28
  no statute of limitations for, 24
  number and dollar amounts assessed, 362
  partial payments as lowering, 41
  stacked, 366
  tax code section to be quoted on notices for, 409
  See also Criminal charges; Interest; Penalty abatement (reduction or cancellation); Trust Fund Recovery Penalty
Penalty abatement (reduction or cancellation)
  overview, 368
  appeal of denial of, 372–373, 374
  audit appeals and request for, 154, 370
  bankruptcy and, 254
  combat zone, taxpayer in, 372
  contesting the rejection of request for, 372–373
  for delay of IRS, 369
  disaster zone, taxpayer affected by, 372
  erroneous late filing penalty, 372
  first-time offenders (FTA), 368, 373, 375, 406
  for incorrect written advice from IRS, 369, 372, 405
  IRS Form 843, *Claim for Refund and Request for Abatement,* 370, 371, 373, 375
  late-payment due to hardship, 369–370
  late-payment, first-time offender, 375
  Offer in Compromise to contest rejection of, 373
  Offers in Compromise and, 368
  payment enclosed with request, 370

of payroll tax penalties, 406

pay the penalty and claim a refund, 373

percentage of penalties abated, 368

for reasonable cause for failure to comply with tax law, 368–370

refund lawsuits, 373

request for, 370–371

request transfer to local IRS office to contest denial of, 373

resource on, 368

for statutory exceptions, 372

Personal property

defined, 432

as exempt from tax levies, 275

IRS retention of, due to lack of bids at auction, 287

Offer in Compromise and net value of, 241

proceeds left over after debt satisfied, 287

return of property due to lack of bids at auction, 287

sale by IRS, buying back from the purchaser, 286–287

sale by IRS for tax levy, 286–287

seizure via tax levy, 286

valuation of (garage sale/thrift shop prices), 212

Petition, defined, 432

Phone call scams, 68

Policy of IRS. See Internal Revenue Manual

Potentially dangerous taxpayers (PDTs), 165

See also Tax protestors/resisters

Power of attorney, 95, 387

defined, 432

Prepaid legal plans, 383

Preparer Tax Identification Number (PTIN), 383

Prisons

and IRS collection, 197

sentences for tax evasion, 339–340

Privacy Act and tax information, 15, 16, 100, 418

See also Public records

Problems Resolution Officer (PRO). See Taxpayer Advocate Service (TAS)

Proof. See Burden of proof

Property. See Personal property; Real estate

Protests. See Tax protestors/resisters

Public assistance payments, and tax levies, 275

Public figures, and likelihood of criminal prosecution/jail time, 335, 339–340, 424

Public records

of assets, IRS access to, 99–100

auditors accessing, 99

bankruptcy, 250

financial disclosures of Congress members, 15

tax crimes, 15

tax debts, 265

and tax levies, 282

tax liens, 15, 265, 266, 434

Q

Questioning and requests by IRS agent or auditor, suggested responses to

overview of 6 best responses, 104–105

asset identification, 281, 281–282

background and identity of taxpayer, 84

economic reality questions for financial status audit, 61–63

field audits and requests for records, 95, 96, 99

field audits, telephone call prior to notice by mail, 89

on filing current year during audit, 421

for installation agreement application, 203–204

noncooperation with audit (as strategy), 101

nonfiling of returns, 30, 87

office audits and requests for records, 80, 87–88

office audits, telephone call from auditor, 83

on prior audits, 87

requests for information not on original audit list, 80, 88–89

requests for new copies of same documents, 108

requests for unfiled tax returns, 25, 27

request to photocopy your records, 87

revenue officer interactions and questions, 206–210, 296

silence is golden, and don't lie, 87, 104–105, 281–282, 283, 327, 332–334

by Taxpayer Delinquency Investigation (TDI), 27

on whether you filed tax returns for all years, 27, 87

See also Auditor/taxpayer interactions; Criminal Investigation Division (CI); Specific topics

Quitclaim deed, for right of redemption, 290

R

Railroad Retirement Act benefits, tax levies and, 275

Real estate

acquired after tax lien recorded, 266

bankruptcy and, 253

buying property back from auction winner, 290

denial of installment agreement for unreported, 228

escrow papers, 109

eviction lawsuit required to remove owner after IRS auction, 290

fair market value of, 242

and lifestyle questions in financial status audit, 62

Offer in Compromise and net value of, 242

out-of-state, difficulty for IRS to find, 209

prior liens remain after tax levy, 288, 290

refinancing, and subordination of tax lien, 270

rental property deductions, 47, 93, 109

revenue officer checking assets, 220, 282

right of redemption of, 289–290

"secured property," 253, 254, 271

seizure of, for noncooperation with financial investigation, 209

valuation of, 211

See also Joint ownership of assets; Levies; Real estate sales; Residence; Tax liens

Real estate sales
 Certificate of Discharge (of
  federal tax lien) and, 270
 escrow papers, 109
 gains and losses, documentation
  of, 93
 tax levy sale by IRS, 287–290
 tax lien release not timely, 271
 unreported income from, as
  matter of time before IRS
  discovers, 26
Reasonable cause for failure to
 comply with tax law, penalty
 abatement for, 363, 368–370
Reasonable collection potential
 (RCP), 232
Reconsideration. *See* Audit
 reconsideration (reopening an
 audit)
Record of Account Transcript, 14, 378
Records
 for appeal of audit, 150, 161
 being asked to produce records
  twice, 108
 copies ordered from companies
  and banks, 112
 defined, 432
 faulty, as biggest reason for
  adjustments, 53
 original documents: do not give
  or mail to IRS (copies only), 111
 record keeping, 109
 retention of, time limits for, 417
 See also Auditor/taxpayer
  interactions; Questioning and
  requests by IRS agent or auditor,
  suggested responses to; Records,
  collection and; Records, missing
Records, collection and
 cancelled checks, alteration of,
  324
 and fraud, badges of, 323
 for interview, 209–210
 Offer in Compromise proofs,
  232, 246–247
Records, missing
 overview, 111
 approximation of records, 112
 business expenses under $75 each,
  no receipts for, 113
 the *Cohan* Rule and, 114–115
 documents to explain, 109

 negotiation of compromise with
  auditor, 115
 oral explanations of, 112
 reconstruction of, 109, 113–115,
  126
 substantial compliance with tax
  laws, 112
 time to produce, 110, 112, 126
Refunds
 amended tax returns and, 44
 applied to other taxes you owe,
  198, 311, 420
 audit contestation via claim for,
  129
 audit risk following, 55
 audits resulting in, 51, 102
 child support arrears and
  interception of, 311
 denied for late filing (and
  exceptions), 38–39
 electronic filing as speeding
  arrival of, 43
 injured spouse claims for joint tax
  refunds, 291, 308, 311
 large, reasons for, 39
 late, checking on, 419
 late, interest owed to taxpayer
  on, 419
 as "savings plan," 39
 sent by IRS in error, interest
  charged on, 376, 377, 420
 spouses filing separately to
  protect, 256
 Taxpayer Advocate Service for
  problems with receiving, 295
 timeframes for, 43
 See also IRS Form 843, *Claim
  for Refund and Request for
  Abatement*; Refund suits (claim
  for refund)
Refund suits (claim for refund), 129,
 185–186, 357, 373, 377, 428
Remarriage, 311
Rental property expenses and
 depreciation, 47, 93, 109
Rentals vs. ownership, and tax levies,
 282
Representative, defined, 435
 See also Attorneys; Tax
  professionals
Request for Place of Trial form, 167,
 170, 171

Research. *See* Legal research
Residence
 changing state to avoid high audit
  risk, 43
 eviction lawsuit required to
  remove owner after levy sale, 289
 home office deduction, 62, 95,
  101, 152–153, 389, 423
 homestead exemption, 276, 400,
  423
 IRS entering or not, 95, 212, 423
 location of, audit risk and, 43, 66
 location of, levy risk and, 273
 primary, as last resort for seizure/
  levy, 276–277, 409, 423
 primary, court order required for
  seizure of, 276, 287–288, 409,
  423
 primary, seizure and sale of (rare),
  287–290, 405, 409, 410
 primary, supervisor approval
  required for liens, levies, or
  seizures, 405, 410
 right of redemption of, 289–290
 state seizure, 400
 See also Real estate; Real estate
  sales
Residents, foreign. *See* Foreign
 residents
Resisters. *See* Tax protestors/resisters
Retirement plans and pensions
 bankruptcy and, 253
 fully funding, as protection of
  liquid assets, 256, 283
 income recapture as exception in
  late-filing refund denials, 39
 late filing and refund due, 39
 Offer in Compromise and net
  value of, 242
 Offer in Compromise hardship
  exception and, 244
 protection of, 256
 tax levy on, unlimited period for,
  285
 tax levy seizure of, as discouraged
  by IRS policy, 256, 276, 283
 See also Social Security
Revenue officers
 overview, 7
 "ambush" first visit by, 206–207,
  296
 business entities and, 208

defined, 433
delaying meeting with, 207
four-step process of, 206
initial interview, 207–210
letter requesting leftover proceeds from tax levy auction, 287
lying to, and possible criminal charges, 208
lying to, avoidance of, 206–207, 208
noncooperation with/refusing to divulge financial information, 113, 207
nonfilers visited at home by, 27
options for resolution available to, generally, 220
questioning by, responses to, 206–210, 296
risk of "enforced collection" action, 207, 209
Taxpayer Advocate Service for problems with, 296
verifying your assets and tax returns, 220
See also Collection by IRS; Field audits; Financial information forms (433 series forms); Questioning and requests by IRS agent or auditor, suggested responses to
Revenue procedures, 18
Revocable living trusts, 256
RIA Federal Tax Handbook, 392–393

S
Safe deposit box, 326
Safe deposit boxes, 318
Sales tax, 251, 396
Same-sex married couples, 304
Sample Information Document Request, 97
Sample Letter to Private Debt Collection Agency, 260
Sample Protest (Appeal) Letter, 146
Scam phone calls and emails, 68
Section 8A Master File Codes, 194
Securities, worthless
amending returns for, 44
late filing and refund due, 38
See also Stocks
Seizure of assets. *See* Levies

Self-employment
audit risk for, 51, 59, 342–343, 417
business identification code, 65
defined, 433
as exception for late-filing refund denials on self-employment tax, 39
expenses, field audit and, 93
home office deduction, field audit and, 95
income seizure (tax levy) and, 198, 277–278, 285
length of office audits for, 88
location of field audits, 91
nonfiling return, as matter of time before IRS discovers, 26
no-repeat audit policy not applicable to, 81, 82
resources for, 342
revenue officer negotiation requirements for, 208
See also Businesses; Estimated tax payments; Field audits; Independent contractors, misclassification of employees as
Self-incrimination. *See* Fifth Amendment (right to avoid self-incrimination)
SEPs, 256, 276
Settlement, Tax Court and, 164, 173–174, 179, 184
See also under Audit appeals, settlement of
SFR (Substitute For Return), 27, 28–29, 64
Side-job income, 43, 86
Significant hardship cases. *See* Currently not collectible (CNC) status
Silence is golden, and don't lie, 87, 104–105, 281–282, 283, 327, 332–334
Sixteenth Amendment, 17
Small business owners. *See* Businesses; Self-employment
Social Security
auditor access to information, 99
payments, seizure of, 276
See also FICA contributions; Payroll taxes
Social Security number (SSN), 11, 143, 359, 435

Sole proprietorships
and levies of business assets, 290
liability for unpaid payroll tax debts, 351
as neither employees nor independent contractors, 346
Special agent, 433
See also Criminal Investigation Division (CI)
"Specific items" as indirect proof of fraud, 324
Spouses
abandoned spouse rule, 306
as attendees at audit, 103
in audit appeal letter, 143
avoiding liability for spouse's dishonesty with IRS, 305–309
common-law states, 307
community property states, 306
denying benefit of community property rule, 306
duress rule, 307
equitable relief, 308, 309
estate tax and gifts to, 314
filing jointly vs. separately, factors influencing, 304–305
filing separately to protect refund, 256
gifts, seizure of, 424
innocent spouse rule, 227, 305–309, 310, 408–409
and Offer in Compromise, 246
and prevention of primary residence seizure, 276
same-sex, 304
separation of liability relief, 308
Tax Court attendance by, 180
Tax Court for innocent spouses, 309, 409
on Tax Court petition, 170
tax refunds, injured spouse claims for joint, 291, 308, 311
See also Divorce; Family; Joint ownership of assets; Joint tax returns
SSDI income, 358
SSI income, 258
Standard of living
and financial status audits, 60
and IRS estimate of income, 64
State Department, passports and, 227

State income taxes
  overview, 396
  amending returns for, 45
  audit adjustments and, 396
  bankruptcy and, 251
  child support arrears and
    interception of tax refunds, 311
  employer withholding of, 348
  forms for past years, obtaining,
    32
  information sharing with IRS, 15,
    25, 99, 396–397, 418
  installment agreement
    negotiation, 230
  late filing, 25, 37
  list of states without, 396
  nonfilers and, 25, 397
  notifying the state of your federal
    audit contest, 396
  statutes of limitation on, 397
  See also Payroll taxes; State tax
    collection
State laws
  cash transaction reporting, 359
  classification as employees vs.
    independent contractors, 346
  homestead exemption, 276, 400,
    423
  Taxpayer Bill of Rights, 397
*Statement of Taxpayer Identification
Number* form, 167, 170, 171
State of residence, audit risk and,
  43, 66
State tax collection
  overview, 398
  appeals of, 398
  asset seizure, 398, 400
  bankruptcy, 400
  compromises of assessments, 400
  contact with, in-person
    recommended, 398
  dealing with before federal, 401
  inefficiency and, 398
  information sharing with IRS, 15,
    25, 99, 396–397, 418
  installment agreements, 230, 399,
    401
  levies, 400
  political connections and, 402
  statute of limitations for, 397
  suspending collection for
    hardship, 401

tax bills, overview, 398
tax liens, 399, 434
and Taxpayer Bill of Rights, 397
State taxes
  appeal of, 396
  audits for, 396
  death taxes, 315
  sales tax, audits of, 396
  sales tax, bankruptcy and, 251
  See also State income taxes; State
    tax collection
Statutes of limitation
  for bankruptcy and tax debts, 250
  for collection of tax debt (10-year),
    generally, 410
  for collection of tax debt (10-year),
    generally ("23C" date), 192
  currently not collectible status
    and, 200, 257
  defined, 433
  and designating late payments to
    most recent year, 377
  for Employee Retention Credit
    (ERC), 59
  installment agreements for
    income taxes and, 221, 224,
    410
  installment agreements for payroll
    taxes and, 224
  IRS-filed returns (SFR) not
    protected by, 29
  IRS policy on nonfiling, 24–25
  nonfiling and, 24–25, 52, 417
  Offer in Compromise and, 242,
    243, 245
  for payroll tax debt liability
    assessment, 351
  "secured property" never expires,
    271
  for state tax collections, 397
  tax levies and, 285
  tax liens and, 267, 269, 271
  See also Audits, statute of
    limitation for
Statutory Notice of Deficiency. *See*
  Notice of Deficiency
Stocks
  estate tax return audits and, 317
  gains and losses from sales,
    documentation of, 93
  as liquid asset, prepayment of
    future expenses with, 211

nonfiling of income from, as
  matter of time before IRS
  discovers, 26
tax levies and seizure of, 291
See also Securities, worthless
Student loans
  interception of tax refunds to
    pay, 311
  interest deduction, 310
Subpoenas for witnesses, 178
Substitute For Return (SFR, IRS-filed
  returns), 27, 28–29, 64
Summons
  attorney for, 98, 101, 209
  defined, 434
  for taxpayer, 98
  for taxpayer noncooperation with
    audit, 101
  for taxpayer noncooperation
    with collection information
    gathering, 209
  for third parties, 98, 99

T

Taxable income, 435
Tax account. *See* Taxpayer account
Tax Account Transcript, 14, 252,
  367
Tax Act. See Computer tax
  preparation programs
Tax amnesty
  discussion of, 418
  as not available, 28
Tax attorneys. *See* Attorneys
Tax bills
  overview of process, 196–198
  accuracy of, methods for
    checking, 193–194
  accuracy questioned, as delaying
    tactic, 201
  audit agreement signed and
    decision of how to pay, 125–126
  computerized notice cycle,
    196–198
  computerized notices, delaying
    the cycle of, 197–198
  delay after audit agreement,
    interest abatement during, 376
  extension(s) on due date, 196
  filing in Tax Court as delay of,
    164
  following appeal that doesn't
    settle, 161

notices stopped by IRS, 197, 198
payment in advance for refund
 suits, 185
payments and credits not properly
 credited, 193–194
received after sending in an
 installment agreement request,
 195
responding to each notice with
 45-day delay requests, 197–198
special circumstances, 197
timeframe of cycle of, 197
transcript of account to examine
 for accuracy, 194
See also Collection by IRS;
 Interest; Penalties; Tax debts
Tax code. *See* Internal Revenue Code
Tax Counseling for the Elderly
 (TCE), 391
Tax Court
 overview, 164, 165–166
 address changes and, 166
 appeals of tax levies, 269, 274
 audit agreement as barring option
  of, 125
 audit appeal not necessary but
  recommended prior to, 164
 audit appeal review automatically
  filed by, 141, 172
 audit appeal settlement as barring
  option of, 159
 audit strategy of noncooperation
  and choosing, 104
 for automated adjustment notice
  errors, 78, 164
 bankruptcy and, 252
 binder of records from audit
  appeal, use of, 151
 burden of proof in, 52, 175, 182,
  411
 contact information, 188
 deadline for petitioning, IRS
  must inform the taxpayer of, 411
 defined, 434
 delaying tax bill with petition
  for, 164
 docket number (case number),
  171–172
 electronic filing and case
  management system
  ("DAWSON"), 170, 171
 for estate tax audits, 316

fees for, 78, 167, 170, 171, 177, 178
forms, obtaining, 166, 167
frivolous petitions, criminal
 penalties for, 165
as independent from the IRS, 165
for innocent spouses, 309, 409
interest accrual, deposit/cash
 bond to stop, 166
for interest computation errors,
 408
interest continues to accrue
 during, 166, 183, 376
for IRS-filed returns (SFR), 28, 64
judges for, 165
location and sessions of, 165
numbers of petitions filed, 164
Offer in Compromise application
 and loss of right to, 245
other federal courts as choice vs.,
 186–187
for passport denial/revocation for
 tax debts, 227
for phantom audits, 131
reduction of tax liability in, 164
Request for Place of Trial form,
 167, 170, 171
settlement prior to trial, 164,
 173–174, 179, 184
*Statement of Taxpayer
 Identification Number* form, 167,
 170, 171
statistics of success in, 149, 164
timeframes expected for
 resolution of, 166, 172, 174
time to file petition, 78, 127, 166,
 170, 171
for Trust Fund Recovery Penalty,
 357
*Unsworn Declaration Under
 Penalty of Perjury* (Form 18), 177
updates on filing requirements, 171
website, 166, 188
See also Notice of Deficiency;
 Tax Court—regular tax cases;
 Tax Court—small tax cases
 (S case)
Tax Court—regular tax cases
 overview, 183–184
 appeals available for, 183–184
 attorney representation in, 184
 bench decisions and self-
  representation in, 184

defined, 183–184, 432
dropping down to small case
 category, and self-representation
 in, 184, 185
filing deadline, 170, 171
filing the petition, 170–172
legal briefs required for, 184
petition and forms, completion
 of, 167, 170
petition and forms, obtaining,
 167
settlement prior to trial, 184
Tax Court—small tax cases (S case)
 overview, 167, 179–183
 answer from IRS (written
  response), 172
 appeal of audit, Tax Court
  encouraging last chance to
  settle, 172
 appeals not available for, 167
 attend another trial to alleviate
  anxiety, 180
 attorney/tax professional advising
  for, 172, 173, 174, 178, 179, 182
 attorney/tax professional
  representation in, 172, 179
 behavior tips for the courtroom,
  180–181
 burden of proof in, 175, 182
 calendar call, 179–180
 calendar call, permission not to
  appear for, 179
 closing statement, 178, 183
 clothing advice, 180
 continuance of (postponement),
  174, 180
 defined, 167, 433
 documents (exhibits), 172, 181
 documents, copies for judge and
  IRS attorney, 176, 181
 documents, originals, 181
 dropping a regular case dispute
  down to the small case category,
  184, 185
 election for, 170
 evidence, 176
 filing deadline, 170, 171
 filing fee, 167, 170, 171
 filing requirements, updates on,
  171
 filing the petition by mail, 171,
  172

filing the petition electronically, 170, 171

IRS attorney/taxpayer interactions, 179

joint returns, spouse name and signature, 170

judge's decision, 183

judges for, 180, 181

legal authorities, citing, 178, 181

location for, 180

notice setting case for trial, 174

notices from the court before trial, 174

opening statement, 175, 181

petition and forms, completion of, 167–170

petition and forms, obtaining, 167

place of trial, 174

preparation of your case, 175–179

pretrial meeting with IRS attorney, 172–173, 179

rehearsal of your case, 175

remote trials (video conferencing with Zoomgov), 174, 180

sample Tax Court petition, 168–169

settlement before trial, 173–174, 179

spectators and supporters, 181

spouse attendance, 180

standing pretrial order, 174

stipulated Tax Court decision, 174

stipulations of facts and, 173

tax bill following, 183

telephone notice, 179

testimony, 176, 181–182

time the trial will require, 174, 183

trial date, asking for change to, 179

trial memorandum, 174

trial notebook, 175–179

witnesses, 172, 173, 176–178

witnesses, expert, 177

witnesses, questioning, 182–183

witnesses, sitting in courtroom, 180

witnesses, subpoenas for, 178

witnesses, trial date impossible for, 179

witnesses, written statements vs. testifying in person, 177

witness fees and mileage rates, 177, 178

Tax credits

child dependency deduction and, 310

COVID-19 pandemic, 59

Tax debts

overview, 191–194

amount of, and computerized billing cycle, 197

amount of, and installation agreements, 201–202, 220–221

amount of, and transfers from ACS to local revenue officer, 205

extension(s) on date due for tax bill, 196

filing on time even if you can't pay the balance owed, 195

of foreign residents, 256

interest deductible for businesses, 37

interest not deductible for individuals, 37

IRS-filed returns (SFR) and discharge ability in bankruptcy, 29

options for dealing with, generally, 193

passport denial/revocation and, 227

payment in full, 193

payoff amount, obtaining total, 15

payroll taxes as most serious of, 350

penalties never deductible, 37

as public record, 265

reasons for, generally, 191

See also Collection by IRS; Fraud; Interest; Payroll taxes; Penalties; Statutes of limitation; Tax bills

Tax evasion

bankruptcy will not discharge tax debt in case of, 251

and criminal charges for nonfiling, 29

defined, 335

as felony, 335

fraudulent asset transfers and, 281

offshore schemes, 322, 420

scams and schemes, 420

sentences for, 335

tax protestors/resisters and charges for, 340, 420

unreported income in investigations of, 322, 324–325, 326

See also Criminal charges; Fraud; Unreported income

Tax law, defined, 434

Tax levies. *See* Levies

Tax liens

overview, 265–266

appeal of, 268, 269, 406, 409

approval by supervisor required for, 405, 410

automatic, as "silent" or "secret" tax lien, 265, 266–267

automatic, if estate taxes due, 314

bankruptcy and, 252–253, 267, 270, 271

Certificate of Discharge, 270

Certificate of Release of Federal Tax Lien, 245, 267, 271

contact IRS to forgo recording of, 269

contact IRS to verify release of lien, 270

credit rating, effect on, 266, 269

currently not collectible status and, 200

defined, 434

errors in, and release of, 271

fee for recording of, 265

fee for recording of release, 267

"Fresh Start" rules, 267

installment agreements and, 221, 223, 272

Notice of Federal Tax Lien, 227, 243, 265–268, 384, 409, 434

Notice of Federal Tax Lien, withdrawal of, 267, 269, 270, 272, 406

notice sent to last known address, 268

Offer in Compromise and, 243, 245, 267, 271

passport denial/revocation and, 227

payment in full of, 270

property acquired after lien recorded, 266

as public information, 15, 265, 266, 434

real estate sales and, 271

release of lien, 245, 267, 270, 271, 290

resources, 266, 268
"secured property" and, 271
state taxes and, 399, 434
and statute of limitation for collections, 267, 271
subordination of, to refinance mortgage, 270
suing IRS for wrongful liens, 272
Taxpayer Advocate Service and, 269, 270, 271, 272
Taxpayer Advocate Service help with, 296–297
and tax services, direct solicitation by, 384
Taxpayer account
access to, by auditor, 99
annual notice of tax debts sent by IRS, 408, 409
computer accessed by SSN or EIN (not by name), 11
copy of tax return, obtaining, 15
defined, 435
fraud investigation, indirect methods to check for, 331
Freedom of Information Act (FOIA) and access to data, 16
frozen, and criminal investigation, 331
online access, registration for, 15
privacy of, 15, 16, 418
privacy violations, 100, 418
private debt collections, 261
total payoff amount, obtaining, 15
See also Automated adjustment notices from IRS; Taxpayer account transcripts
Taxpayer account transcripts
accuracy of tax bill, analyzing, 193–194
bankruptcy and tax dates, 252
criminal investigation may be indicated on, 331
designated payments, checking, 378
free of charge to obtain, 14
obtaining by phone, 14, 31–32
obtaining by postal mail (IRS Form 4506-T), 14, 31–32
obtaining online (IRS Get Transcript Online tool), 14
penalties, checking for first-time offender status, 375

penalty and interest computation, checking, 367
as proof of tax lien payment, 271
Record of Account Transcript, 14, 378
Tax Account Transcript, 14, 252, 367
Tax Return Transcript, 14, 32
transaction codes, deciphering, 194
Wage and Income Transcript, 14–15, 31–32
Taxpayer Advocate Service (TAS)
overview, 7, 294, 302, 382
caution to tell the truth to, 298
contact information for, 297–298
contact letter asking for help from, 298
contact letter sample, 299
defined, 435
documentation to provide with contact letter, 298
emotional state of taxpayer and, 300
established by Taxpayer Bill of Rights, 404, 408
goals of the program, 295
interactions with the advocate, 298, 300
IRS Form 911, *Request for Taxpayer Advocate Service Assistance,* 301–302
IRS Publication 1546, *The Taxpayer Advocate Service,* 294
problems TAS will not pursue, 297
problems TAS will pursue, 295–297
qualifying for help from, 294
state equivalent of, 397
Taxpayer Assistance Order, request for, 301–302
Taxpayer Assistance Orders (TAO) for hardship problems, 298, 300, 404, 435
Taxpayer Roadmap, 8
See also Taxpayer Advocate Service (TAS), specific situations
Taxpayer Advocate Service (TAS), specific situations
complaints for denial of field audit location preference, 95

delays of over 30 days, 295–296
emergencies and other problems, 296–297
enforced collection as serious hardship, 228
installment agreement revocation, prevention of, 229
interest abatement request denied, 377
late refund, 419
no response by IRS to your inquiries, 295–296
no response by the date IRS promised, 296
notice errors and problems, 78
Offer in Compromise help, 245
phantom audits, 130
refunds not received, 295
seizure of primary residence, 423
tax bill, accuracy check of, 201
tax levies, 276, 279, 284, 296, 300
tax liens, 269, 270, 272, 296–297
Taxpayer Assistance Centers, 390
Taxpayer Bill of Rights (TBOR)
overview, 404
audit appointments, scheduling of, 82, 90, 405
audit location, 90, 94–95
auditors may not be evaluated based on dollar amounts produced, 90
audit rights, summary of, 81
defined, 435
IRS Publication 1, *Your Rights as a Taxpayer* (summary of TBOR), 81, 404, 413–414
right to call "time out" to consult a tax professional, 380, 405
right to representation for any IRS matter, 380, 405
state versions of, 397
tax lien errors and releases, 271
TBOR I, 404–405
TBOR II, 406–408
TBOR III, 408–412
Taxpayer Delinquency Investigation (TDI), 26–27
Taxpayer First Act (2019), access to audit file, 145, 147–148
Taxpayer Identification Number (TIN), 435

Tax preparers
aggressiveness vs. dishonesty and, 46
caution to avoid certain "problem preparers," 46, 389
chain tax services, 384, 389
defined, 434
explanation of return by, as audit preparation, 387
hiring, 46, 388–389
Preparer Tax Identification Number (PTIN) required of, 383
referral to tax professional from, 383
See also Computer tax preparation programs; Tax professionals
Tax professionals
overview of role of, 18
advertising by, 384
aggressiveness vs. dishonesty in, 46
audits (field) and request for recess to consult with, 106–107, 117
audits and right to representation, 81
audit selection risk decreased for returns prepared by, 34, 388
certified public accountants (CPAs), 160, 179, 383, 384, 388–389, 428
consultation and advice services, 381–382
defined, 380, 434
deskbooks and guides used by, 392–393, 394
direct solicitation by, 384
electronic filing required by, unless taxpayer directs otherwise, 43
enrolled agents (EAs), 160, 179, 382–383, 384, 388–389, 429
erroneous advice or actions of, and penalty abatement, 369
finding and hiring, 46, 383–385
IRS preference for dealing with, 381
negotiation services, 382
professional associations and referral panels, 384
pros and cons of hiring, 380–382
representation services, 382

right to call "time out" to consult with, 380, 405
right to representation by, 380, 405
right type for the job, 387
safely going it alone, 380
as source for forms, 32
tax practitioner-client privilege, 36, 333, 409
See also Attorneys; Tax preparers; Tax professionals' fees; Tax professionals, specific services from
Tax professionals' fees
overview, 385–386
for appeals, 160
reimbursement of, 425
for tax return preparation, 388, 389
tips for controlling, 386
Tax professionals, specific services from
accuracy of tax bill, checking, 193
amending returns, 44, 45
audits. *See* Audit(s), attorney/tax professional services
automated adjustment notice errors, 79
changing state of residence to avoid high audit risk, 43
employees misclassified as independent contractors, 348
estate taxes, 315, 316–317, 318
extension to file, 40
foreign financial accounts reporting (FinCEN), 37
internal IRS forms, preparation of, 84
Offer in Compromise, 244
statute of limitations rules on collection, 192
Tax Court adviser, 172, 173, 174, 178, 179, 182
tax resistance/protests, 160
tax return preparation, 388–389
tax shelter advice, 47
Trust Fund Recovery Penalty, 352, 357
Tax protestors/resisters
appeals of audits won't be heard for, 160
categorized in IRS computer as "potentially dangerous taxpayers" (PDTs), 165

fraudulent Form 1099 or W-2 filings, 408
frivolous Tax Court petitions, with criminal penalties, 165
frivolous tax returns, audits for, 67
identification in files allowed only as "nonfilers", and removal requirement, 412
and keeping assets out of sight, 282
scam artists, 420
taxes as mandatory despite claims of, 13, 19, 420
and tax evasion charges, 340, 420
Taxpayer Advocate as limiting assistance to, 297
Tax records. *See* Records
Tax refunds. *See* Refunds
Tax returns
overview of processing, 10
copy of complete, obtaining, 15
current filing of, as required for installment agreements, 39, 223, 228
current filing of, as required for Offer in Compromise, 246, 247, 248
current year, don't file while being audited, 421
deductions reported in wrong place on, 58
defined, 435
errors in. *See* Automated adjustment notices from IRS
evidence of intent to mislead on, 58
Fifth Amendment tax returns, 65, 81
filed by mail. *See* U.S. Postal Service
filed by private delivery service (IRS-approved), 34, 372, 408
filed in person at local IRS office, 34, 44
filed online. *See* Electronic filing
filing on time even if you can't pay what you owe, 41, 195, 418
frivolous tax returns, 67
IRS-filed returns (SFR—Substitute For Return), 27, 28–29, 64
as mandatory, 13, 19, 420
messy, as audit risk, 42, 59

paper returns are stored in warehouses, 88, 99
processing of, 10, 34, 40
profit shown, preparation to ensure, 157
question on whether all prior years filed, 27, 87
revenue officer requesting, 220
storage of, time limits for, 417
timeframe most people file, 24
transcripts. *See* Taxpayer account transcripts
See also Amended tax returns; Audits; Deductions; Installment agreements; Late filing of tax returns; Nonfiling of tax returns; Records; Taxpayer account
Tax Return Transcript, 14, 32
Tax shelter investments
abusive, 47
appeals officer cannot negotiate in situations of, 159
defined, 47
Tax transcripts. *See* Taxpayer account transcripts
TBOR. *See* Taxpayer Bill of Rights (TBOR)
TCE (Tax Counseling for the Elderly), 391
TCMP (Taxpayer Compliance Measurement Program), 66
1099 income reports
audit risk of reporting less income than is shown on, 43
correspondence audits for missing data on return, 79
disputed filings of, 407
errors in, and penalty abatement, 369
failure to file, penalty for, 364
failure to issue, penalty for, 343
fraudulent filings of, 408
guesstimate of tax liability based on, by IRS, 28, 64
late filing, penalty for, 364
levy notices based on, 198
lost, obtaining data needed, 14–15, 31–32
and misclassification of employees as independent contractors, 343
mismatched on Form 433, and denial of installment agreement, 228

mismatched on return, 68
nonfilers with record of, computer as detecting, 25, 26
occupation stated on, 65
requirement of business to submit, 343
transcript of previous years, obtaining, 14–15, 31–32
Third party, defined, 435
TIN (Taxpayer Identification Number), 435
Tips and referrals to IRS, 66, 327–328, 330, 419
rewards for, 419
Tools of the trade, as exempt from tax levies, 275
Total positive income, 57
Transcripts. *See* Taxpayer account transcripts
Transportation, expense standards for, 213
Travel and entertainment expenses, 113, 115
Treasury Inspector General for Tax Administration (TIGTA), complaint for fair debt collection violations, 260
Treasury Offset Program (TOP), 311
Trust Fund Installment Agreement, 224
Trust Fund Recovery Penalty (TFRP)
overview, 350–351
appeals of, 353–357
attorneys for, 352, 357
case history of, 355–356
Chapter 7 bankruptcy cannot eliminate, 251, 358
Chapter 13 bankruptcy and reduction of, 358
check-signing power and, 352, 353
corporate titles and, 353
court challenges of, 357
defined as personal liability for payroll tax debts of corporation, 350–351, 435
definition of trust fund, 349
delay of tax bill, 357
installment agreements for, 358
interviews by IRS, 352
nonassessment/nonassertion of (not collectible), 358

notice of assessment of, 355
number of assessments annually, 351
number of liable persons per business, 351–352
Offers in Compromise for, 358
ongoing vs. defunct businesses, 351
partial payment of payroll taxes and, 349
people found responsible, disclosure of, 358, 406
people found responsible, factors determining, 351–353
people found responsible, sharing cost of assessment, 351–352, 358, 406
preparation by using IRS Form 4180, 352
representation at interview, 352
sample letter of appeal, 354
statute of limitation for, 351
Taxpayer Bill of Rights on, 406
See also Payroll taxes
Trust fund taxes. *See* Payroll taxes
Trusts, as asset protection, 256
TurboTax. See Computer tax preparation programs

U

Unemployment benefits
Offer in Compromise and, 242
and tax levies, 275
Unemployment tax (FUTA), 349
Unreported income
audit computer scoring (UIDIF) for, 57, 60
auditors probing for, 85–86, 91–93
audits for suspected. *See* Financial status/economic reality audits
bank deposit method of determining, 92–93, 324–325, 326
cryptocurrency, 59
defined, 436
expenditures method of determining, 92, 325, 326
fraud investigations and, 322, 324–325, 326
mark-up method of determining, 93

as matter of time before discovery
  by IRS, 26
net worth method of determining,
  91–92, 325, 326
penalty for, 363
as primary concern of IRS,
  85–86, 91
"reasonable indication" of, as
  standard for financial status
  audits, 60
types of professions and businesses
  likely to underreport, 26, 322
Unreported Income Discriminate
  Information Function (UIDIF)
  score, 57
U.S. Court of Federal Claims,
  refund suits, 129, 185–186, 357,
  373, 377, 428
U.S. District Court
  appeals of tax levies, 274
  for passport denial/revocation for
    tax debts, 227
  refund suits (claims for refund),
    129, 185–186, 357, 373, 377, 428
U.S. Postal Service
  filing amended returns via, 44
  filing late returns via, 34
  filing response to correspondence
    audits via, 80
  IRS access to personal records of
    use (auditors), 99
  IRS and monitoring of your mail
    (CI), 331
  on-time filing, conditions for, 372
  original documents: do not mail
    to IRS (copies only), 111
  penalty relief for erroneous late
    filing penalty, 372
  retain photocopies of everything
    sent, 80
  sending audit appeal, 145
  sending CP-2000 notice dispute
    letter, 78
  sending FOIA letter, 148
  sending right of redemption
    letter, 290
  Tax Court petition filed via, 171,
    172
  See also Correspondence audits
U.S. Tax Court. See Tax Court

V
Vacationers, extensions to file as
  foreign resident not available to, 40
Vehicles
  auditor questions about, 105
  denial of installment agreement
    for unreported, 228
  exemption for equity in, 211
  and financial status audits, 62
  keeping assets out of sight, 282
  log books for, audits and, 109
  rentals/leases, and tax levies, 282
  revenue officer checking assets, 220
  tax levies and, 275, 281, 284
  tax levies and return of, 283
  tax levy accelerated appeals, 281
  transportation expenses, allowed,
    213
  valuation of, 211
Video conferencing
  audit appeals officer interview, 152
  COVID-19 pandemic initiating
    use of, 2
  for field audits, 94–95
  Tax Court trial via (Zoomgov),
    174, 180
VITA (Volunteer Income Tax
  Assistance), 391
Volunteer Income Tax Assistance
  (VITA), 391

W
W-2 wage statements
  audit risk of reporting less income
    than is shown on, 43
  correspondence audits for missing
    data on return, 79
  disputed filings of, 407
  errors in, and penalty abatement,
    369
  fraudulent filings of, 408
  guesstimate of tax liability based
    on, by IRS, 28, 64
  levy notices based on, 198
  lost, obtaining data needed,
    14–15, 31–32
  mismatched on Form 433, and
    denial of installment agreement,
    228
  mismatched on return, 68

nonfilers with record of, computer
  as detecting, 25, 26
occupation stated on, 65
reconstruction using Form 4852,
  32
transcript of past years, obtaining,
  14–15, 31–32
Wage garnishment. See Wage
  seizure/tax levies
Wage seizure/tax levies
  overview, 198, 277
  cost of living increases, 277
  defending against, 278–279
  divorce for prevention for, 424
  employer, changing, 278
  exemptions from, 277–278
  foreign residents and out-of-
    country wages, 42
  length of time levy is active, 285
  notices for, 198, 277–278
  reduction of income and, 279
  self-employed persons, 198,
    277–278, 285
  spouse and dependents and, 277
  of spouse, taken for tax debts of
    the other, 424
Wage withholding
  foreign residents and, 41
  misclassification of independent
    contractors and, 343
  not matching return, 68
  overwithholding, 39
  See also Payroll taxes
Waiver, defined, 436
Whistleblower protections, 412
Willful, defined, 436
Witnesses
  audit appeal statements by, 151
  subpoenas for, 178
  See also under Tax Court—small
    tax cases (S case)
Workers' compensation benefits
  Offer in Compromise and, 242
  tax levies and, 275
Workpapers
  defined, 436
  IRS Form 4700, *Examination
    Workpapers,* 96, 132–136
  right of taxpayer to access, 126,
    145, 147–148, 150

Save 15% *off your next order*

Register your Nolo purchase, and we'll send you a **coupon for 15% off** your next Nolo.com order!

Nolo.com/customer-support/productregistration

On Nolo.com you'll also find:

Books & Software

Nolo publishes hundreds of great books and software programs for consumers and business owners. Order a copy, or download an ebook version instantly, at Nolo.com.

Online Forms

You can quickly and easily make a will or living trust, form an LLC or corporation, or make hundreds of other forms—online.

Free Legal Information

Thousands of articles answer common questions about everyday legal issues, including wills, bankruptcy, small business formation, divorce, patents, employment, and much more.

Plain-English Legal Dictionary

Stumped by jargon? Look it up in America's most up-to-date source for definitions of legal terms, free at Nolo.com.

Lawyer Directory

Nolo's consumer-friendly lawyer directory provides in-depth profiles of lawyers all over America. You'll find information you need to choose the right lawyer.